Donald Thomas has worked in publishing, adult education, and is now a lecturer in the University of Wales. He received the Eric Gregory Award for his first volume of poetry, *Points of Contact* (Routledge, 1963), and is the author of *Prince Charlie's Bluff* (Macmillan, 1974), *A Long Time Burning: The History of Literary Censorship in England* (Routledge, 1969) and *Treason and Libel: State Trials Volume I* and *The Public Conscience: State Trials Volume II* (Routledge, 1972)

Donald Thomas

Charge! Hurrah! Hurrah!

A Life of Cardigan of Balaclava

Futura Publications Limited
An Omega Book

An Omega Book

First published in Great Britain in 1974
by Routledge & Kegan Paul Ltd

First Omega edition published in 1976
by Futura Publications Limited

ISBN 0 8600 7737 3

Printed in Great Britain by
Hazell Watson & Viney Ltd
Aylesbury, Bucks

Futura Publications Limited
110 Warner Road
Camberwell, London SE5

For George and Isabel

CONTENTS

Contents

PREFACE

The life of the 7th Earl of Cardigan has been long overshadowed by his leadership of the charge of the Light Brigade at Balaclava. Indeed, the whole of his career has, perhaps inevitably, been coloured by historical judgments passed on that incident. He was, according to some interpretations of that event, an aristocratic and self-important fool, who contributed in great measure to the destruction of the British cavalry. In another view, he seemed a man of the most redoubtable physical and moral courage, who was in no way responsible for the error but whose example and self-discipline saved the greater part of his men.

Yet the Balaclava incident was merely one of several peaks in Cardigan's career, which included the most remarkable proceedings for divorce, criminal conversation, and criminal libel; one of the greatest court-martial scandals of the century; a very public and un-Victorian love affair with a woman hardly more than half his own age; a number of 'matters of honour', one of which brought a charge of intent to murder and earned him the distinction of being the only Victorian peer to be tried by the House of Lords.

In the panorama of Cardigan's life, for all the popular appeal of the Light Brigade story, the fashions of regimental life in the 1840s or 1850s may seem as sensational in their own way as the Balaclava charge. In a still wider perspective, Cardigan was as much a figure in the clubs of St James's or the life of the Shires as he was in the 11th Hussars. In recent years there has developed a fashion for unearthing the 'Other Victorian' way of life, which furtively repudiated the social and sexual morality of the court and of middle-class convention. This furtive rebellion was dependent on the exploitation of an urban working class, whose squalor and hunger proved an infertile soil for the seeds of evangelical morality. Yet there was a quite different 'Other Victorian' fashion, which Cardigan typified in many respects. It was military and sporting, patrician and gallant. Its principal chronicles were not the *Morning Post* or the Radical press, but such papers as

ix

the *Age* or *Bell's Life in London*, the sketches of 'Nimrod', and the memoirs of society beauties. Lacking the inhibitions of the middle class, it was usually self-contained even in its sexual indiscretions.

In the earlier Victorian period the adherents of this fashion were deprived of the royal favour which was ungrudgingly shown them by George IV and William IV. However, they remained at their ease in the clubs of St James's, in the mess of many a cavalry regiment, in the Royal Yacht Squadron, or at the meetings of the Pytchley and the Quorn. On the whole, they held their place by right of birth, yet theirs was a society which, as in the case of Catherine Walters, 'Skittles', was open to an accomplished courtesan, however humble her origin. By the 1840s, it seemed that such a way of life must be no more than the last, dying spasm of Regency indecorum, yet even Cardigan lived long enough to see it reborn in the 1860s as the alternative style of high life preferred by the Prince of Wales and his followers.

In their misbehaviour, Cardigan and his contemporaries were rarely furtive, neither did they repudiate traditional social morality. With an eighteenth-century flair for compromise, they did not insist or expect that a man's physical or emotional requirements should necessarily match his moral aspirations. The Christian duty of forgiving enemies, for instance, did not overrule the satisfaction of calling them out on the duelling ground. In general terms, the negative respectability which consisted of not doing wrong seemed infinitely less attractive than an allowance for breaches of the moral code which was repaid by benevolence and generosity in another sphere.

Cardigan's reputation has by no means received uniform treatment in those books which have described his career. He has been dealt with critically by Cecil Woodham-Smith in *The Reason Why*, more sympathetically by Joan Wake in *The Brudenells of Deene*, and Piers Compton in *Cardigan of Balaclava*. His faults were under posthumous examination at least as long ago as Kinglake's *Invasion of the Crimea*: his virtues were less often and less loudly proclaimed. Yet, on the evidence, it hardly seems that his flagrant misconduct and his undoubted courage or benevolence mitigate one another. However inconvenient it may be in terms of twentieth-century psychiatry, the best and the worst that was said of him appeared equally true.

To deal with Cardigan purely in modern terms, to doubt the motives of his benevolence and recoil from his belligerence, makes for a tedious predictability of judgment. I have chosen, so far as possible, to present him in the context of his own time and in the light of those values to which he and his contemporaries owed their allegiance.

Among the many debts of gratitude incurred during the period of writing this book, I must first acknowledge the great kindness of Mr Edmund Brudenell of Deene Park. I owe it to his generosity in giving me access to the Brudenell family papers, and in allowing me to quote from them, that this book was written at all.

I am greatly indebted to Lord Raglan for his permission to use the Crimean Papers of Field Marshal Lord Raglan, and to the late Duke of Wellington for the use of the papers of the 1st Duke of Wellington. For the military aspect of Cardigan's career, I have also been assisted by the kindness of those whose regiments have close associations with him: Lieutenant Colonel P. K. Upton, 10th/11th Royal Hussars; Major T. V. Leckie, Queen's Royal Irish Hussars; Major B. O. Simmonds, 15th/19th King's Royal Hussars.

My work has been made immeasurably easier by the facilities and guidance given me by Mr B. Mollo and the staff of the National Army Museum Library, and by Mr P. I. King and the staff of the Northamptonshire Record Office.

I should also like to record my thanks for the help given me by the London Library; the British Museum Newspaper Library, and Manuscripts Room; the Public Record Office; the Historical Manuscripts Commission; the Ministry of Defence Library; the University Library, Cambridge; Brighton Public Library; Cardiff Central Library; and the Library of the University of Wales Institute of Science and Technology.

Finally, I must acknowledge a great debt of gratitude to Mr Gordon Grimley, Mr Andrew Wheatcroft and Mr Tony Orme for their encouragement in the various stages of the work, and to my wife for her enthusiasm throughout the writing of the book.

CHAPTER 1

PRELUDE

By the middle of the morning, almost a quarter of a million men were in position, either upon the line of rising ground before Mont St Jean, or upon the plain below, where fields and hedgerows rolled southward towards Charleroi. The ground was wet with the summer rain of the previous night, so that the wheels of gun-carriages slithered and stuck on the furrowed earth. Along the rough roadway, men and horses plodded ankle-deep in mud. Yet through the dark drifts of cloud that swept across the plains of northern Europe the first sunlight began to catch the flashes of white and gold among the massed richness of scarlet or royal blue uniforms.

Those who waited along the mile and a half of the ridge before Mont St Jean could hear clearly the music of the regimental bands from the opposing infantry columns on the plains below. The ridge itself was alive with the familiar sounds of the British army preparing for battle, the shouts and the bumping of limber-carriage wheels mingling with the distant tunes of the enemy. Drums beat to summon men to arms, and the regimental muster-rolls were called. The light of the summer morning grew stronger still. It was 18 June 1815, a day to be commemorated in England more intensely than any subsequent anniversary. To many, it was an obsession rather than a commemoration. A little before noon on this Sunday morning in 1815, the original Waterloo Day, the sky itself seemed to shudder with the reverberation of the main French artillery opening fire upon the British position. After the first spurts of flame the dark mouths of the cannon were masked by ragged drifts of smoke, and then grape-shot sprayed like hailstones among the British regiments on the low ridge.

The events of the next ten hours decided the fate of Europe, and seized the ambitions of some of the most influential men in England. The pattern of the battle was simple enough. The French launched two main attacks, an infantry attack at the beginning of the afternoon, and a cavalry attack two hours later. Both were repulsed. Then, with the arrival of Blücher's Prussians, Napoleon was outflanked, and Wellington's regiments swept down from their ridge upon the scattered columns of the Grande Armée.

But it was not the pattern of the battle which preoccupied the British nation so much as the quality of Wellington and his men. The exploits of the Scots Greys, the Union Brigade, and the Gordon Highlanders became the stuff of which the Waterloo legend was constructed. Those who remembered the battle would recall how, in the early afternoon, the four great columns of D'Erlon's infantry, 16,000 strong, were ordered into the attack by Marshal Ney. These were the victors of Austerlitz and Iena. With a great shout of *'Vive l'Empereur!'* they came forward, smashing through the first positions of the allied army, until they were poised to drive through the centre of the British line, where only the two ranks of the Gordon Highlanders, under General Sir Thomas Picton, stood between Napoleon and the open road to Brussels. Picton's men heard the familiar sound, the 'rum dum, rum dum, rummadum rummadum, dum dum,' of the French drums advancing, the cheering of the imperial infantry, and the gathering roar of *'Vive l'Empereur!'* which ran along the line like the crest of a breaking wave.

Picton, whose lesser eccentricities included leading his men into battle wearing his top hat and carrying an umbrella for a weapon, spurred his horse forward, leading the brigade straight into the oncoming mass of the French columns.

'Charge!' he shouted, 'Charge! Hurrah! Hurrah!'

The Gordons fired a volley into the blue-coated infantry, and in the return of fire a bullet struck Picton in the head. He fell dead from his horse. But though his men were too few to throw back the French advance, their ranked bayonets checked it for an instant. The British position at Waterloo, which had very nearly been overrun, was safe for a few moments, until D'Erlon's advance should recover its momentum.

What followed was, to many Englishmen, the most thrilling moment of the entire battle. From behind the lines on the British side of the struggling mass of infantry, there came an unmistakable bugle call. The ranks of the Gordons, as they strove to rally under the weight of the French attack, were suddenly thrown open. There was a mighty roar of cheering as the cavalry of the Union Brigade, under Sir William Ponsonby, and the Household Brigade, under Lord Edward Somerset, thundered down the slope towards the advancing French columns. It was the type of manoeuvre which could only be relied upon once in every battle, but Wellington had let loose his cavalry.

It was an unforgettable sight to those who witnessed it. There were three hundred Scots Greys on their heavy and powerful chargers, the Inniskilling Dragoons, and the Life Guards in their plumed helmets. As they hurled themselves upon the French formations, it seemed that there had never been a cavalry charge like it. The earth shook under the massed hooves of the heavy horses. Then, with the short barking cheer of the British dragoon regiments, the two brigades smashed and scattered D'Erlon's infantry. The Life Guards drove into the lines of the escorting French cuirassiers, putting them to flight in every direction as easily as though it had been a field day demonstration in Hyde Park. Within a few minutes, D'Erlon's columns had been overrun, and the French infantrymen, who had at first tried to engage the cavalry sabres with their own bayonets, now began to surrender as prisoners of the allied army.

By this point, the cavalry had done all that was required of it, but a cavalry charge was more easily launched than checked. Apart from the technical difficulties of halting it, the troopers were seized with the exhilaration of the speed and the triumph, which made them reluctant to break off the action abruptly. Somerset and Ponsonby, riding into an increasing storm of fire, were now leading their men at full gallop towards the main French position. A few men, like Sergeant Charles Ewart, were positively ordered back to the British lines in order to carry home triumphantly the captured standards of the French regiments, inscribed with the victories of Iena and Austerlitz. Yet a great many more were being urged on by regimental commanders like Colonel Frederick Ponsonby, who rode through the bullets until he had been shot through both arms, and then continued with the reins held between his teeth.

In some cavalry regiments the command changed several times in a matter of minutes, as first the colonel, then the major, and then the senior captain fell under the raking fire of the enemy. But once the leaders of the Union Brigade galloped into the French battery, they fell upon the gunners and put out of action fifteen pieces of artillery. All too soon, they discovered that no more than twenty of the 1,200 men of the Union Brigade had reached the French guns intact. Moreover, their retreat was cut off as the French infantry closed in upon them. Of the Scots Greys, who were foremost in the charge, there were eventually twenty-one survivors from a total of three hundred men. It was in vain that the rally or recall had been sounded by the trumpeters. The cavalry charge was, in military terms, almost an art form. To cut it short in such a manner was as unthinkable as to cut short a symphony or the performance of a great actor.

There was much more to the legend of Waterloo than the charge of the Scots Greys and their comrades. The laconic coolness of Wellington, and the desperately close victory which he had won were interminably discussed. Yet if one moment alone in the entire battle was to be chosen for its physical and emotional splendour, it seemed that it must be the charge of the Scots Greys. The regiment had been destroyed, Wellington and Europe had been saved for those few vital minutes, and it had all been done in such superb style.

Waterloo was the apogee of national self-satisfaction, and Wellington was the great hero of all time. Britain's troops had beaten the finest in the world, and it seemed incredible that any other nation would dare to challenge the army of the Iron Duke. As for the famous regiments of the British cavalry, they were almost beyond praise. Unrivalled in courage, invincible in spirit, irresistible in battle, they were the most glorious spectacle of British military prowess. The Duke himself had some reservations as to their conduct. He murmured that the British cavalry had a natural aptitude for getting itself and its commanders into scrapes. But he was obliged to add that they generally extricated themselves with courage of the highest order.[1]

For the rest of Wellington's long life the legend of Waterloo was bright and glorious. To wear the Waterloo Medal was to be one of a precious brotherhood whose prestige grew as time and chance reduced its numbers. There could surely never be such a war or such a battle again. Neither could there be quite such heroes as those who vanquished Napoleon: Wellington, Picton, Ponsonby, Uxbridge, and their gallant soldiers. It was possible that there might be men capable of such heroism if the chance arose, but in the political circumstances of Europe after 1815, it seemed unlikely that the opportunity would occur in the next generation.

No man was more enthralled by the victory than the Prince Regent himself, who had been safely in England during the battle. At dinner in Carlton House, having finished his iced punch and an entire bottle of sherry, the Prince would describe to his guests how *he* had led the charge of the Household Brigade at Waterloo. Those who had heard how the Prince's bulk prevented him from continuing to mount a horse, except by means of a ramp level with the saddle, were the most taken aback of all. Even when Wellington was a guest, the Prince described how he had 'completely bowled over' Marshal Ney's cavalry.

'I have heard you, sir, say so before', said the Duke coldly, 'but I did not witness this marvellous charge.'[2]

During the reigns of the Prince, as George IV, and his brother William, the Waterloo stories were retold and refurbished. At the accession of the young Victoria, twenty-two years after the battle, the army and the nation still looked to the same heroes for leadership and security in the more dangerous future of the mid-century. Until the death of Wellington, in 1852, Waterloo Day was celebrated with a commemorative intensity unrivalled since. Seventy years after the battle, 18 June was still officially 'Waterloo Day', a span which seems unlikely to be matched even by the Armistice commemoration of 11 November 1918. Almost forty years after Waterloo, the *United Service Gazette* was still proclaiming,[3]

> Were you at Waterloo?
> I have been at Waterloo.
> 'Tis no matter what you do,
> If you've been at Waterloo.

In such circumstances, there could be no more invidious fate in 1815 than to be a young man ambitious to perform prodigies of valour, eminently suited to a command in a crack regiment, physically handsome, courageous almost to a fault, a superb horseman, and yet just to have missed the battle of Waterloo. However, such was the plight of James Thomas Brudenell, only son of Robert, 6th Earl of Cardigan. His one ambition was to be a soldier, a leader of his men at such momentous battles as Blenheim or Dettingen, Fontenoy or Salamanca. Instead, the contemporary prophets offered him a century of peace and industry. There might, of course, be colonial skirmishes in India or Egypt, but these were hardly the wars of the great professional armies from which alone came the true deeds of glory.

It was particularly galling that the young Lord Brudenell should look so much the pattern of a proud cavalry officer. Tall and slender, with fair hair and whiskers, pale blue eyes and a great deal of natural charm, even his enemies agreed that in appearance he was the beau idéal of a light dragoon. The 6th Earl was unsympathetic to his son's military ambitions, both as a matter of taste and out of prudence, since James Thomas was the only son. The father suggested that the young man's public duty would best be discharged in the world of politics, where the heroes of the new peace might be found. But what consolation could there be in the interminable vapourings of the House of Commons and, later on, the House of Lords? What substitute could be found, for the trumpets of war, among the committees and reports of parliamentary administration?

To the 6th Earl, a man of gentle disposition and mildly progressive views, his son's lack of political enthusiasm was disquieting. A long period of peace was not the worst that the fierce young lord might have to endure. He had been born a soldier when soldiering seemed almost done, but he had been born as the future 7th Earl of Cardigan precisely at a time when hereditary power was growing suspect and the new century began to sing the virtues of the self-made man. The Victorian gospel of self-improvement was to offer little hope of salvation to a man who must inherit the great Northamptonshire house and estate of Deene, town houses in London, lands that stretched across three counties, and an annual income of £40,000, or about £500,000 in modern terms.

He might, of course, become a reformer like Lord Shaftesbury, whose long-established title in no way prevented him from becoming the people's hero. But he would more probably become one of the titled nonentities of mid-nineteenth-century politics, a minor figure among the Lords Aberdeen, Newcastle, Clarendon, and their cabinet colleagues. Perhaps he would rise no further than to be the parliamentary servant of such mediocrities.

In many respects, Lord Brudenell was a personable young man. Like his seven sisters, who were celebrated for their beauty, he had inherited more than his share of aristocratic good looks. But he was fiercely proud and self-confident in a manner more suited to the European courts of the eighteenth century than to the frock-coated decorum of Victorian politics. Matters that could not be settled by debate and compromise were to be decided by duelling pistols. It was, of course, the duty of a gentleman to interest himself in political affairs, as a general rule, and to attend the House of Lords occasionally if he succeeded to the peerage. But that, in the view of the young Lord Brudenell and his kind, was as far as the obligation went.

By the standards of the Brudenell family, the political and social changes of the early nineteenth century were hardly less than revolutionary. Time and progress had so far dealt gently with the owners of Deene. Set in the finest hunting country of the Shires, the great house had been there, in one form or another, since Domesday Book had been compiled. The Great Hall, built in 1086, had been modelled on Westminster Hall, since the house was at one time a hunting box for the Abbots of Westminster. Over the centuries, the building was extended, but always in a style which preserved its appearance of medieval harmony. A broad stone bridge bore the carriageway across water from the parkland to the towers and battlements of the house, with its tall chimneys and long windows. Across that bridge, as guests of the Earls of Cardigan, came royal dukes, foreign princes, and sometimes a high-class courtesan. But for all its external grandeur, in the intimacy of the courtyard with low archways and sundial, or in the smaller scale of the upper rooms, it seemed quite obviously a family house. Sir Robert Brudenell, a Justice of the King's Bench, had bought it in 1518, and when his descendant, Thomas Brudenell, declared for King Charles I against Parliament, the family had already been in tranquil and prosperous possession of Deene for nearly a century and a half. Sir Thomas spent twenty years as a prisoner of the victorious Cromwellians, but when he was released his loyalty to the throne was rewarded by Charles II. In 1661, the old man was raised to the peerage as 1st Earl of Cardigan.

By the year of Waterloo, the Brudenell estates included the great house; a hunting box called Brudenell House near Melton Mowbray; estates throughout Northamptonshire, Leicestershire, and the West Riding of Yorkshire; town houses in Carlton House Terrace and Portman Square (the latter with Adam ceilings and fireplaces); a stable of thirty or forty horses; splendid carriages with the arms of the Earls of Cardigan emblazoned on their doors; and a fine library of books and manuscripts. If the social revolution of the nineteenth century seemed a threat to the security and position of the family, the industrial revolution added to its wealth and power, for the Yorkshire lands were rich in coal.

Yet for all their accumulated wealth and their controlling power in the Shires of eastern England, the members of the family had never played a prominent part in the conduct of their country's affairs. Their names were not to be found among members of cabinets or in the memoirs of those closest to the court. In the world of great events, it hardly seemed to matter whether half a dozen Brudenells had been Earls of Cardigan or mere country squires. Their world of stables and gunrooms, the well mannered rivalry of huntsmen with the yelping packs of the Cottesmore or the Quorn on crisp winter mornings, the careful domestic accounts of the estate, seemed far removed from the real centre of power. This was deceptive, for such families in 1815 still constituted that widespread patrician support upon which the structure of government rested. It was not a question of parties, either Tory or Whig. Whatever such men called themselves, and whatever the ruling party might call itself, they were the fabric of the realm, which must outlive political factions or party enthusiasms.

It was precisely the assumption of such political and social indispensability which the reformers of the early nineteenth century had sworn to destroy.

The impetuous clash between such reformist aims and the military ambition of the young Lord Brudenell must seem to have been inevitable. The variety of charges and actions which brought him before an assortment of courts in the seventy years of his life may offer some indication of the impetuosity displayed on his part alone. Among the judicial accusations facing him were those of attempted murder; wounding; grievous bodily harm; 'criminal conversation' with other men's wives, and actions for damages or injury. Among the actions initiated by him, criminal libel and conduct unbecoming an officer and a gentleman stood high on the list. At little more than a ten-year interval, he was to be variously described as 'the plague-spot of the British army' and 'without doubt the most popular soldier in all England'. He was burned in effigy as a public enemy, and cheered through the streets of London as a popular hero. He was hated by more than his fair share of men, but loved by more than his share of women. The public controversies were only a superficial indication of the storms which raged around his darkening reputation. Yet he never lost his faith and his belief that, somewhen in his time, the call to glory would come. He was the last of a great line, and the only Cardigan to be a soldier. Despite the shadow of Waterloo, despite the new fashion for electing tradesmen to Parliament and singing the praises of peace, he would be a hero before he died.[4]

CHAPTER 2

THE YOUNG LORD

1

Though it would be wrong to suggest that Lord Brudenell's father never expected to become 6th Earl of Cardigan, he was none the less not in the most direct line of descent. He succeeded to the title in 1811, when he was forty-two years old, upon the death of the childless 5th Earl, who had been his uncle. Until the death of the old Earl, Robert Brudenell, 6th Earl of Cardigan, had lived in the style of a country squire at the Manor House of Hambledon, Buckinghamshire. He had always been known there as plain 'Mr Brudenell'.

His was not a life crowded with incident. Between the slopes of the long wooded range of the Chiltern hills and the willowy banks of the Thames as it wound from Oxfordshire into Buckinghamshire, he lived in the kind of good-tempered genteel tranquillity which was celebrated by Jane Austen's portraits of family life among minor landed gentry. He was known as the friend of the village, and had bought some land close by in order to let plots at peppercorn rents to the industrious poor, so that they might grow their own food. For a few years he did his duty as a Member of Parliament, voting generally on the Conservative side and stolidly opposing Catholic emancipation with the born suspicion of a Protestant English gentleman.[1]

Only once had the 6th Earl caused his family distress. In 1794 he had defied all their protests and married Penelope Ann Cooke, the beautiful but by no means rich daughter of George Cooke, a Middlesex gentleman. Her brother, Colonel 'Kangaroo' Cooke was to become the lanky aide-de-camp and confidential messenger of the Duke of

York as Commander-in-Chief of the British army. Whatever doubts may have been felt about the new Mrs Brudenell as future Countess of Cardigan, the Rector of Hambledon found her 'sweet', and reported her temper as 'mild and engaging'. It seemed that Robert Brudenell might be excused his determination to marry her. It was, after all, his one act of rebellion.[2]

By 1811, the couple had seven daughters: Elizabeth, Harriet, Charlotte, Emma, Mary, Augusta and Anne. For the provident squire of Jane Austen's novels, to unload seven frugally-endowed daughters on to the middle-class marriage market was a labour of hope rather than achievement. However, the Brudenell girls had certain advantages over Miss Austen's heroines. As daughters of a future Earl of Cardigan, they could expect dowries of about £20,000 apiece. Moreover, they were the inheritors of their mother's beauty as well as their father's money. The poet Thomas Moore thought them among 'the prettiest girls of the fashionable world'.[3]

There was one other child, James Thomas, born on 16 October 1797, after a first son had died in infancy. When his father inherited the earldom in 1811, James was a boy at Harrow, where his stay was as short as it was undistinguished. The houses of the school were still houses in the literal sense, where boys were the paying guests of their housemasters. It was a more gentlemanly and less earnest system of education than the English public school as later remoulded by Arnold at Rugby. However, until his departure from Harrow in 1813, the new Earl's son was known as Lord Brudenell, a courtesy title conferred upon him as his father's heir.

The young Lord Brudenell was regarded by his mother and his seven sisters with feelings hardly short of adoration. It was not merely that he was the heir and the hope of the family, but he looked so eminently deserving of adoration. If the English nation in the nineteenth century had been called upon to devise its own Apollo, he would have been tall, fair, blue-eyed, courageous, not over-intelligent, a superb rider, and a crack shot. Provided that he was not aggressively intellectual, an education at Harrow and Christ Church would have counted in his favour rather than against him. In terms of Matthew Arnold's *Culture and Anarchy*, he would have been one of the aristocratic Barbarians. 'The care of the Barbarians for the body, and for all manly exercises; the vigour, good looks, and fine complexion which they acquired and perpetuated in their families by these means— all this may be observed still in our aristocratic class.' Such was the race of young gods, of whom Lord Brudenell might have seemed the archetype.[4]

Between the ages of sixteen and eighteen, he lived at Deene, earning a reputation as a horseman which endured for the rest of his life. He rode, as one who later watched him on the battlefield remarked, not with foolhardy courage but with complete determination to overcome any obstacle or any foe. The finest riders in England were to be found in the Shires, generally among the fashionable hunts of the Pytchley and the Quorn, which numbered royalty as well as nobility among their supporters. Yet few of them could match Lord Brudenell's speed. His most bitter criticism of a horse, which had taken every timber obstruction in its path, was, 'It takes him a long time to get from one bit of timber to another!' While home from Harrow, he made a bet with his cousin Wilbraham Tollemache as to which of them should be in first after a run with the Quorn. When the hounds entered a broad stream, Brudenell, who could hardly swim a stroke, plunged in after them and surfaced, gasping, 'Mind, Wilbraham, I was in first!'

He never learnt to swim and came close to being drowned on several such occasions, but to 'funk' the ordeal was as unthinkable as turning back in the face of an impossibly high gate. 'He seemed', said his friend Whyte-Melville, 'to attach some vague sense of disgrace to the avoidance of a leap, however dangerous.' While hunting several miles from Deene, on the borders of Leicestershire, he came upon the highest gate in the county, which most sensible riders avoided. He might have opened it or gone round it. Instead, he spurred his horse and rode straight at it. The horse, Langar, was a fine one but those nearby could see that the animal had not jumped clear, and within a few seconds there was an appalling smash. Lord Brudenell was thrown over the gate and into the roadway beyond, where he was picked up and carried back to Deene. For twenty-four hours he lay unconscious and partially paralysed. When he recovered consciousness and movement, his first action on such occasions was to mount his horse and ride to the front again.[5]

In 1815, he was sent to Oxford, taking his own horses and servants with him. His two years at Christ Church were no more remarkable than those at Harrow. To less sophisticated young men, Harrow and Christ Church might stand as landmarks in their youthful career. To Lord Brudenell, they were incidents, sometimes agreeable and sometimes tedious, in a life whose real centre lay elsewhere. He left Oxford after two years without bothering to take the degree which he could have had by merely paying for it, and set off on the Grand Tour. A university degree was of no use or importance to a future Lord Cardigan. Instead, he visited France and Italy, where the peace of 1815 had opened up great possibilities for the education by example of young Englishmen abroad. More surprisingly, he also went to Sweden and Russia. Then, upon his return, the serious business of life began.

To return from Paris of the Grand Tour to London of the Regency was to leave the restaurants of the Rue de la Paix with their mirrors and gilding and exquisite cuisine for the plain cooking of Stephens's Hotel in Bond Street or Fladong's in Oxford Street. As Captain Gronow discovered, not only was the boiled potato universal, it was served with almost every course. But if London food was insipid, compared with that of Paris, its clubs and society were more colourful. Lord Brudenell was a member of White's and Boodle's, and a founder member of the Travellers' Club in Pall Mall, where a candidate for membership was required to have travelled at least five hundred miles from England.

Of all the clubs in Regency London, White's was the most celebrated, if only because pedestrians in St James's Street could see Beau Brummell and his admirers posing, and quizzing, and talking in the famous bow window, the centrepiece of the passing show. In politics, White's was Tory. Yet behind its decorous façade and in the elegant high-ceilinged rooms, men had won and lost fortunes of £200,000 at a time, playing faro or macao. Women were not permitted on the premises of such male societies, but at Almack's in St James's the most hard driven and cynical contracts of the patrician marriage market were supervised by Lady Jersey and her sister peeresses, to strains of the newly-introduced quadrille. Rules were strict at Almack's, and even the great Duke of Wellington himself was turned from its door on the evening that he arrived wearing trousers instead of knee-breeches.

The outdoor world was, for most men and women of fashion, that neo-classical sweep from Carlton House in Pall Mall, where the Prince Regent kept court, up the splendid arcaded bow of Regent Street and on across Regent Circus towards the Regent's Park with its ornate harmony of the great Nash terraces. Or for some there was the carefully civilized countryside of Hyde Park, where in the afternoon Brummell and his associates rode in the creations of their Bond Street tailors, blue coats with brass buttons, leather breeches and top-boots. The 'carriage company' in the Park consisted of the most celebrated aristocratic beauties of the day, from duchesses to the youngest daughters of peers. Conspicuous among the riders was the portly figure of the Prince Regent and his brother, the Duke of York. The middle and lower orders of society were not even present as spectators, for such places as the Park 'with a sort of tacit understanding were then given up exclusively to persons of rank and fashion'.[6]

There were genteel shops in Bond Street and Regent Street, theatres in the Haymarket, clubs in St James's, livery stables in Piccadilly and Oxford Street, and hotels or taverns in most major thoroughfares. Yet the West End of London was a residential haven, dominated by the town houses of the rich in their Georgian squares, and supported by the humbler dwellings tucked away in courtyards and mews. West of Mayfair and north of Oxford Street, a well-cultivated countryside of parkland and market gardens surrounded the metropolis with green and open views. It was in this London, formal in its manners but relaxed in the pace of its life, that the 6th Earl of Cardigan saw his son's future. A political career would not only be the discharge of the family's public duty, it would also make convenient use of one of those seats in the House of Commons which the family happened to have, so to speak, in its pocket. It would provide a distraction from the endless riding and hunting. The 6th Earl was not to know that his son had already sworn an 'inclination' for the army, but he was soon to find out.

The division of opinion between father and son was a symptom of their differing temperaments. From the 6th Earl's point of view, either there would be a major war in which a soldier son was likely to be killed, or there would be no such war and a military career would be a complete waste. In either event, the army was no place for his heir. But the difference between them was wider than that. Even after he had succeeded to the title and the estates, the 6th Earl continued to live very much as though he were still plain Mr Brudenell of the Manor House at Hambledon. He hunted occasionally, as though it were part of his social duty, but he was not at home among the 'slangy' and rather 'fast' hunting society, which made up a considerable proportion of the Quorn, the Pytchley, or the Cottesmore. He knew the value of money, by coming to it after many years, and by his care and prudence the revenue of the estates was actually increased.

In no aspect of this sort did his son resemble him. The young Lord Brudenell sought the kind of military career in which he must buy a commission in a fashionable regiment for anything over £10,000, and must then spend several thousand pounds a year, in addition to his pay, in order to maintain the style of living which his brother officers would consider appropriate to gentlemen. Hunting was an adjunct to military training in cavalry regiments, so his enthusiasm as a rider would be encouraged rather than checked. He would never, if possible, miss a meeting of the Quorn, which meant keeping a string of thoroughbred horses, bought high and sold again cheap at Tattersall's auction market near Hyde Park Corner. As a cavalry officer, he would have to provide his own charger as well, since only the subalterns of the shabbier regiments would think of using a cavalry horse as a hunter. Neither was it a case of buying and maintaining one charger. A peer's son in a smart dragoon regiment would have two or three horses for field days, and a small retinue of personal servants to attend to his regimental needs.

The 6th Earl must have looked with growing alarm upon his son's way of life. Even without the prospect of a military career, there were bills for hunting boxes, stables, carriages, tailors, clubs and dinners which would have done as a Lucullian feast for most contemporaries. Politics might require a certain amount of ready money but, before the Reform Bill of 1832, a man might buy up seats for himself and his supporters in Parliament without incurring anything like the debts which were now threatened by Lord Brudenell's military ambitions. Moreover, the advantage of a strenuous political career was that it would give the young man less time in which to bankrupt the Cardigan estates by his other extravagances.

Conveniently, the Marquess of Ailesbury, a cousin of the Cardigan family, owned the rotten borough of Marlborough. There were few electors in the town and they were all pledged to do the will of their lord. The Marquess agreed to let his young kinsman, Lord Brudenell, have the seat. On 18 February 1818, eight months before his twenty-first birthday, the young man went through the formality of being elected Member of Parliament for Marlborough. Yet though he might sit in the House of Commons as an acknowledged legislator of the nation, he was still Lord Ailesbury's man. He might boast of the freedom of the Commons, but his patron imposed certain limits upon that freedom. Chief among such limitations was that Brudenell must act like a right-minded English gentleman, supporting the Crown and the Established Church, resisting the seditious demands of the reformers, and opposing at all costs the sinister attempts at the emancipation of Catholics.

Happily, there was at least one area in which the political and military obligations of the Brudenells seemed to overlap. In the years 1815–20 there appeared to be an even chance of England being convulsed by widespread rebellion, and perhaps total revolution. The life of the old King, George III, who was confined as a lunatic in Windsor Castle, moved towards its pathetic close. His son had long been prepared for the metamorphosis from Prince Regent to George IV, which he underwent in 1820. But by 1817 the economic recession which followed the war had soured the triumph of Waterloo for many ordinary men and women. The government of Lord Liverpool found it necessary to prosecute as seditious libels the lampoons of William Hone, and such newspapers as Richard Carlile's *Republican* and T. J. Wooler's *Black Dwarf*. Dr James Watson and other agitators for political reform were charged with treason but acquitted. Yet by 1820 a number of men across the country, from Cato Street conspirators in London to Jeremiah Brandreth, 'the Nottingham Captain', and his confederates at Derby, were convicted and executed as traitors. In scenes more appropriate to Tudor England than to the threshold of the age of railways and photography, the men were drawn on hurdles to the place of execution, hanged, and their heads then cut from their bodies before the silent crowds.

But the traitors who had been condemned epitomized a more general mood of rebellion which stirred a little below the surface of English working-class society. Mrs Gaskell recalled her childhood in Cheshire,[7]

> when watchers or wakeners in the night heard the distant word
> of command, and the measured tramp of thousands of sad
> desperate men receiving a surreptitious military training, in
> preparation for some great day which they saw in their visions,
> when right should struggle with might and come off
> victorious: when the people of England represented by the
> workers of Yorkshire, Lancashire, and Nottinghamshire,
> should make their voice heard in a terrible slogan, since their
> true and pitiful complaints could find no hearing in
> Parliament.

The first line of defence against revolution would be the regular units of the British army, but these were too thinly spread to suppress a general uprising. In the nineteenth century, a large proportion of them would be required for duty in Ireland, either in Dublin or in such outlying garrison towns as Newbridge, Carlow, or Dundalk. Other regiments were needed in India, where another less-publicized war had been fought while Wellington was campaigning in the Peninsula. Regiments which were not on duty in Ireland or abroad, went the rounds of English garrison towns, spending a year or so in each before being moved on elsewhere. It was a convenient means of keeping military allegiances separate from those of local politics. A regiment might be posted from Uxbridge or Hampton Court to Manchester, Brighton, or York. It might equally well be sent to Cork or Cawnpore. But once it was shipped to India its men could expect to spend the next twenty years there.

Since the cavalry and infantry regiments could do little more than protect a few essential areas and people in the event of a general revolution, Lord Liverpool's government had encouraged the building up of yeomanry regiments in counties or areas which could be depended upon for their loyalty. Since 1794, this militia had been used in time of war to protect the country from invasion while the regular army was campaigning in France, Portugal, or Flanders. Now such a force was required to aid the army against the enemy within. The men were part-time soldiers, very much in the manner of the later Territorial Army or Home Guard, continuing to do their ordinary jobs while training as yeomanry cavalry or infantry. Their commanding officer was generally the local squire or lord of the manor, their social superior who became their military leader as a matter of course.

Though it hardly shared the aura of the Life Guards or the Hussar regiments, the system at least offered some step towards a military career for Lord Brudenell. In 1819, at twenty-one, he was already rather old to think of beginning an orthodox army life. By his age, a man in a fashionable regiment would have passed from cornet to lieutenant and then, as a rule, to captain. But at least the yeomanry offered a form of political action in military uniform. In November 1819 he wrote to his Member of Parliament, W. R. Cartwright, offering to raise a troop of yeomanry cavalry from among the tenants at Deene. He received a reply urging him 'to lose no time in taking the preliminary steps towards accomplishing your object'.[8]

His offer was also made to the Home Secretary, Lord Sidmouth, who consulted the Prince Regent on the matter. The Prince agreed that the offer should be accepted and, within a fortnight, forty-six tenants of the Deene estate had been measured for cavalry jackets and overalls on Lord Brudenell's urgent orders. The officers of the troops were expected to clothe and equip themselves, while the privates were to provide their own horses but their uniforms were paid for by the government. In addition, Lord Brudenell used his own money to provide the most handsome spurs and accoutrements, so that his yeomanry cavalry should appear the smartest troop of all. With the arrival of pistols, swords and belts from Weedon Barracks, the training of the tenants began.

Though devoid of military experience himself, there was no mistaking Lord Brudenell's youthful eagerness. The double column of part-time dragoons, looking more like over-dressed huntsmen than a cavalry troop, trotted and wheeled and charged across the green parkland of the estate, towards the trees of Rockingham Forest. A less war-like setting could hardly have been imagined.

It came to nothing. There was no revolution, and the yeomen of Deene never drew their swords in earnest. Their cavalry field days seemed merely an extension of the meetings of the Quorn or the Cottesmore. As the threat of civil war receded, it was to these more orthodox forms of equestrian sport that Lord Brudenell's attention turned. He took a share in the exclusive four-member club which rented the Old Club House at Melton Mowbray. Among his fellow members were the Regency wit, Lord Alvanley; the Honourable George Germaine, brother of the Duke of Dorset; and Thomas Assheton-Smith, one of the ablest horsemen of the earlier nineteenth century, a man who thought nothing of paying a thousand guineas a time for hounds at Tattersall's auctions. The Melton Club was the most aristocratic and expensive of those houses which wealthy huntsmen were accustomed to take over and turn into well-run establishments for their own private enjoyment.

C. J. Apperley, who as 'Nimrod' was the finest reporter of the sporting life of the time, recalled Lord Brudenell's superb horsemanship at the time of the Melton Club, when he rode with the Quorn under the mastership of the redoubtable old Squire Osbaldeston. The pace was enough to annihilate all but the finest riders, and as yet another hanger-on crashed over gate rails with a snapping of leg and collar-bone, Brudenell turned in the saddle and disdainfully surveyed the catastrophe and the horse running loose. 'Who is he?' he demanded disapprovingly of the huntsman. No one knew, and the hunt rode on. As Nimrod remarked, the pace had become far too exciting for Brudenell and the first flight men of the Quorn to turn back and offer help to a 'snob', as interlopers were called.[9]

While the prospect of revolution receded, Lord Brudenell started to build hopes of military glory on some forthcoming war with a major European power. The betting book of White's soon began to record his optimism.[10]

> Lord Brudenell bets Mr. Cornewall 10 gns. that England will be at war with some European power by this day three years.
>
> > Brudenell
>
> Decr. 20, 1822   H. Cornewall

> Lord Brudenell bets Mr. Greville 50 Guineas, that England is at war with some European power or America before this day year.
>
> Novr. 18th, 1823

The great European war was not so easily brought about. Yet there were other skirmishes to be fought nearer home. In 1823, Lord Brudenell stood upon the threshold of the first of those innumerable personal conflicts which were to make his name notorious.

Frederick Johnstone, who was born in 1791 and whose family owned an estate at Hilton, had been an acquaintance of the Brudenell family since childhood. He was a Captain in the 19th Lancers, and went on half-pay when the regiment was disbanded in 1821. In 1817 he had married Elizabeth, the eldest and most beautiful daughter of Admiral John Tollemache and his wife, Lady Elizabeth. Captain Johnstone's bride was twenty years old, and possessed of a dark but apparently rather delicate beauty. This was deceptive. She had an ungovernable temper and had inherited a full range of the Tollemache eccentricities. Her grandmother, Lady Aldborough, was a celebrated courtesan of her day, who had been the mistress of Lord Westmorland and whose jokes were so earthy that even Captain Gronow could not bring himself to repeat them. Her father, the Admiral, tolerated no opposition. During the peace negotiations at Amiens, a Frenchman had tried to interrupt his game of billiards, and the Admiral had simply picked him up and thrown him bodily through the window. His domestic behaviour was equally uninhibited. One evening after dinner, while the family sat in the drawing-room, his sister-in-law, Lady Emily Stratford, began to laugh at him. To her dismay, she was 'at once laid across his knee and flogged like a schoolboy'. The Admiral's mother-in-law, Lady Aldborough, was also present and protested vehemently against such an outrage, until the Admiral informed her in brisk naval language that if she complained again he would treat her in precisely the same manner.[11]

Captain Frederick Johnstone soon discovered that his young bride had inherited most of the quarrelsome characteristics of her father and grandmother. However, the newly-married couple were much in demand as guests in the society of the late Regency. They were frequent visitors to Deene, and to the great town house of the Brudenells in Portman Square. By this time, Elizabeth's parents had separated but the young couple went to live with Lady Tollemache and paid frequent visits to the Admiral. A child was born in the first year of the marriage but Elizabeth and her husband fought and argued so indiscriminately that the Admiral was consulted as to the best arrangements to be made for a separation. Lady Tollemache noticed that during these troubled months the young Lord Brudenell seemed to come rather often to her house, and that he always made courteous inquiries as to the welfare of her married daughter.

Matters improved a little in the summer of 1822, when Elizabeth was ill and Captain Johnstone showed great devotion in looking after her. Then, in January 1823, they were invited to go to Dorset as guests of Henry Sturt and his wife Charlotte, who was Lord Brudenell's sister. Elizabeth refused to go. Captain Johnstone went down to Dorset alone. It had become apparent by this time that the wealth of his own family could never match that of the Tollemaches, and Elizabeth was apparently indignant at the reduced manner in which she was expected to live. Frederick Johnstone had been with the Sturts for a week, when he received a letter from Admiral Tollemache bluntly informing him that Elizabeth had left London for Paris. She had refused to give any reason.

Johnstone hurried back to London and persuaded the Admiral to write to the girl, appealing to her to come home. Elizabeth replied that she was now living in Paris under the protection of her notorious grandmother, Lady Aldborough, and had no intention whatever of coming back or going to live elsewhere. Captain Johnstone set off for Paris at once, only to find that Elizabeth refused to see him. He asked his lawyers if it might be possible to 'get at her by force' and compel her to come home. He was told that it could not be done. Even if it had been permissible, the Dowager Lady Aldborough was a formidable *duenna*. Her resource and self-confidence were matched by the voice and vocabulary of a sergeant-major. Lady Louisa Molyneux reported seeing her 'rouged up to the eyes', and wearing a large opera hat, at a demonstration by an unfortunate hypnotist. At the most intense moment of his whole experiment, Lady Aldborough rose and, 'bouncing out of the room', denounced the whole thing as a fraud, with all the self-possessed stridency of which an English peeress was capable.[12]

Not surprisingly, young Captain Johnstone conceded defeat and returned home. He had hardly left Paris when he was replaced by Lord Brudenell, whose passion for Elizabeth reached a new intensity now that she was apparently available to him. For the young lord, the doors of Lady Aldborough's house stood open, and he began to make love eagerly to his friend's estranged wife. He was, after all, much more Lady Aldborough's idea of a lover for her granddaughter than Captain Johnstone could ever have been. He was handsome, athletic, impulsive, gallant, much richer, and one day he would be 7th Earl of Cardigan. Within a few weeks, Elizabeth was living openly with her lover in Versailles.

Towards the end of 1823, the couple returned to England, and lived together at an hotel in Bond Street. Brudenell had developed a quite uncontrollable passion for young Mrs Johnstone, and to the dismay of his family he seemed quite beyond caring for his own reputation or that of the title he would one day inherit. It is said that, as a man of honour, he offered Captain Johnstone 'satisfaction' with duelling pistols for having taken his wife from him. The Captain refused the offer, on the grounds that, in taking Elizabeth from him, Brudenell had performed the greatest service that one man might render another. It was a phrase which was to echo again, twenty years later.

However, honour and prudence both required that the Captain should seek more conventional remedies against his wife's seducer. He did this by bringing an action for damages against Lord Brudenell, for 'criminal conversation' with Elizabeth. The case was heard at the Sheriff's Court, in Red Lion Square, on 23 June 1824.

It was in everyone's interests that the action should succeed. Every divorce, until 1857, required its individual Act of Parliament to dis-

solve the previous marriage. It was expensive, slow, and made mistresses a far more convenient sexual comfort than second marriages
following a divorce. But even in order to obtain such an Act of Parliament, some good reason for the divorce had to be shown. The best
evidence of this was a successful action for damages brought against
the seducer of a wife, since this gave the court's legal sanction to the
plaintiff's parliamentary petition.

The whole of the proceedings in the case of Johnstone v. Brudenell
seemed to be in a very subdued tone, by the standards of such marital
scandals. Brudenell's counsel offered very little evidence and no witnesses. On the other hand, Captain Johnstone's counsel relied merely
on the evidence of Elizabeth's parents. The prosecution conceded that
the marriage had broken down before Lord Brudenell's appearance in
Paris. The defence counsel responded by admitting that Brudenell had
formed a 'violent and irresistible attachment for this lady', though
reminding the court that he had never laid a finger on her while she
was still living under her husband's roof. She was, indeed, 'a lady of
great beauty and accomplishments', which might increase the damages
to be awarded, but this had to be tempered by the certainty that Lord
Brudenell 'could not accuse himself of having had recourse to the
ordinary arts of the seducer'. The jury put their heads together, and
announced that Elizabeth's market value was £1,000, to be paid as
damages by Lord Brudenell to Captain Johnstone.[13]

With this verdict in his favour, Captain Johnstone could proceed
with the cumbrous legislation for a divorce. He was not, of course,
obliged to do this, since a man might simply collect his damages and
then continue to live with his wife. However, Elizabeth was already
in Lord Brudenell's possession and all the parties regarded a divorce
as the one acceptable solution. It took two years to get the legislation
through Parliament, after which Lord Brudenell married his mistress
in the chapel of Ham House, the Tollemache home near Richmond.
There was no question of the clergy refusing to marry a divorced
woman in such a case. As a matter of law, the clergy of the Established
Church were not relieved of the obligation to remarry divorced persons until the Matrimonial Causes Act of 1857. But in any case, the
great families of England had the gift of the livings of numerous
parishes, and any recalcitrant incumbent could expect to find himself
evicted very briskly indeed.

By 19 June 1826, the date of the wedding, Elizabeth was described
as 'being now single and unmarried'. It was not long before Lord

Brudenell began to wish that she (and he) had remained so. He now discovered that she had 'an ungovernable temper', which was quite a match for his own. She still considered herself free to take a lover, if she chose, much as her new husband regarded certain girls as being his own natural property. But for a woman to demand such equality of sexual opportunity was an unacceptable breach of the moral code. In all, the characteristics of the new husband and wife were so similar that they were destined for twenty years of married strife, which would make the Johnstone marriage seem almost idyllic by comparison.

Most important of all, the 6th Earl of Cardigan had been shown that any form of discipline must be welcomed if it would prevent his son's moral ruin. He withdrew his opposition to a military career, and the young Lord Brudenell turned eager and avaricious eyes upon the finest regiments of the British cavalry.

2

Though Lord Brudenell's mother died in 1826, she lived long enough to make use of one important family connection on her son's behalf. It remained necessary for an officer to buy his commission, and desirable that the investment should be made in a fashionable regiment of the cavalry or the Guards. Lady Cardigan's brother, Sir Henry Frederick 'Kangaroo' Cooke, was conveniently placed to ensure Lord Brudenell's preferment. The Duke of York, whose aide-de-camp Cooke had been, resigned as Commander-in-Chief after one of his mistresses, Mary Anne Clark, was discovered to be running a black market in military favours on the strength of her association with him. But he was, after all, the 'Grand Old Duke of York', who had led the British army bravely against the French in Holland, and there was a great deal of public fondness for him. Once the row died down and the parliamentary inquiry was over, he was quietly reinstated in his command and remained there until the Duke of Wellington succeeded him. Indeed, by 1820 he was heir to the throne of his brother, George IV, although in the event it was the Duke who died first, in 1828.

Kangaroo Cooke was approached over the matter of Lord Brudenell's commission, and with his aid the young man obtained the military patronage of the Duke of York himself. 'The Duke promised me my first commission in the 8th Hussars, and I was gazetted to a cornetcy in that regiment in 1824. His Royal Highness promised that if I would pay attention to my duties, he would push me on in the service.' With the possible exception of the Duke of Wellington, the new cornet could hardly have wished for a more influential military patron.[14]

The 8th King's Royal Irish Hussars was about half-way down the seniority list of British cavalry regiments, which ran from the Life Guards and the Blues (making up the Household Cavalry of the monarch) down to regiments like the 21st Hussars, which were raised and disbanded according to the changing requirements of war and empire. The 8th Hussars had been raised in 1693 by Colonel Henry Cunningham, and were first known as 'Cunningham's Dragoons'. The regiment consisted of Irish Protestants who had fought at the battle of the Boyne to defend the throne of 'King Billy' against any attempt to restore the deposed James II. It had then served in Spain during Marlborough's wars in the reign of Queen Anne. At the end of the eighteenth century it fought under the Duke of York in Flanders, took part in the capture of the Cape of Good Hope, and fought against the French in Egypt.

The 8th Hussars were known as 'The Cross Belts', from their privilege of wearing the sword belt over the left shoulder, which was conferred upon them after they had seized the belts of the Spanish cavalry at Zaragossa. The regiment was somewhat less flatteringly referred to in the British army as 'The Dirty Eighth'. In 1802, the 8th Hussars were sent to India, in the new tropical cavalry uniform of light blue with red facings and silver lace. They fought under General Lake in the second Mahratta War, and in most other Indian campaigns for the next twenty years. Lake was the partner of the future Duke of Wellington in a double campaign to rid India of French influence. Under him, the regiment fought at Leswaree and Agra, the site of the Taj Mahal, and in a series of battles which finally won the sub-continent for the British Crown. In 1822 its troopers returned to England, bearing proudly on their standards the battle honours 'Hindoostan' and 'Leswaree'. They were put into uniforms of royal blue with gold lace, and helmets plumed with red and white. They were also to be known as the King's Royal Irish Hussars.

Once Lord Brudenell had bought his commission as a junior officer, this remained his property, unless he were killed or dismissed after court-martial, in which event he or his heirs lost its value. Otherwise, he might sell it again at a price which would be well above the nominal value, in the case of a fashionable regiment. After serving a statutory period of a year, he could buy his way to the next rank, lieutenant, and so on to captain, major, and lieutenant-colonel, the commander of a regiment. If there were no vacancies in a particular regiment, he might exchange into another, or he might go on half-pay as an unattached officer until he could arrange an exchange with an officer who wished to sell out. Purchase was, of course, subject to the approval of the military authorities at the Horse Guards, and promotion by purchase ended at the rank of lieutenant-colonel. Officers might be promoted by an occasional general brevet, as when an heir to the throne was born or a war was in prospect. A few would win patronage and promotion by merit alone. But any man who counted on making a career without purchase would have been thought extremely foolish. The system had been designed to ensure that the British army was officered by gentlemen of sufficient means to make them proof against temptations to betray their loyalty for material gain, and of good enough family to guarantee the long-term social stability of the country's military power.

Liberal Victorian opinion was soon to announce vehemently that the purchase system was unfair, absurd and designed to put the army into the hands of aristocratic fools. The defenders of the system replied that since the pay of an officer was less than the interest on the price of many commissions, and since he provided his own horse, servants and uniform, the country was virtually getting its officers for nothing. Yet the system undoubtedly had its absurdities. Commissions were bought for infant sons, the youngest on record being two years old. General Wolfe had actively held his first commission at fourteen, and had been adjutant of the 12th regiment of foot at the battle of Dettingen when he was sixteen. Yet, said the defenders of the system, purchase had produced men of the stature of Wolfe, Marlborough and Wellington. It was also to produce Wolseley, Gordon and Kitchener. Indeed, a comparison of the Victorian army before and after the abolition of purchase in 1871 suggests that the only credible argument in favour of abolition was that it removed an injustice, not that it would produce better officers.

When Lord Brudenell joined the army in 1824, it still remained very much an agglomeration of individual regiments, each with its own peculiar traditions, history, rivalries and allegiances. As a regular or standing army, it had grown from Cromwell's New Model Army of

1645, but it was rare, except in times of war or emergency, for the various regiments to be grouped together into effective military brigades or divisions.

Yet the Napoleonic wars had brought at least one fundamental change to army life. Barracks had been built in various towns and cities to house the regiments when they did duty there, which was a remarkable change from the custom of simply lodging groups of soldiers, under a non-commissioned officer, in the nearest available inn or ale-house. But the new accommodation was less than luxurious, with four men to each crib or bunk, until in 1827 the Duke of Wellington ensured that each man should have a bed to himself. Yet in rooms little more than twenty feet square, a score of men and some of their women were expected to sleep, cook, eat and conduct their domestic lives. One pump supplied water for a whole regiment, so that disease spread often and rapidly. Rations for men and horses depended, ultimately, on what supplies a commissariat could procure in given circumstances. However, the standard daily diet was 1lb of meat per man with 1½lb of bread or 1lb of hard biscuit, and either one third of a pint of rum or a pint of wine. It was, of course, possible for a soldier in peacetime to supplement the diet from his shilling a day wage, or to spend the money on gin at the regimental canteen. However, his pay was often reduced, before he received it, by stoppages for uniform and equipment, or for barrack damages.

It is a commonplace that the discipline of the Wellingtonian army was of a stupefying brutality. Regiments were paraded in hollow square to witness the flogging or hanging of a culprit. William Cobbett was gaoled for seditious libel in 1810 when he wrote that sentences of a thousand lashes inflicted on British soldiers made even Napoleon's army seem more humane than that of George III. Captain Gronow, a tough but intelligent Guards officer, was strongly critical of such punishments, during which the man quite frequently died. Gronow suggested that if it was intended to punish a man with death, the court-martial should have the courage to sentence him to be hanged or shot, and not leave him to be beaten to death in this manner.[15]

If the men continued to admire their officers it was, in part, because sentences of this kind, though well-advertised, were comparatively infrequent. More positively, however, the army relied strongly for its morale upon the intense loyalty of each regiment to its own members and traditions. Successive generations of families, among officers and men, served with the same regiment, sons and daughters often marrying other sons and daughters of the regiment. Other regiments might be regarded as friends, rivals, or nonentities. In many respects the regiment was like a mobile estate, in which the lieutenant-colonel was lord of the manor, the major was his agent, while the captains and subalterns were his principal tenants and heirs. The private soldiers were the workers. As on a great estate, the owner might claim the obedience of those under him but they, in turn, were entitled to expect his care and protection. The first duty of an English gentleman, when he put on the uniform of the regiment and received the King's commission, was not the destruction of the enemy but the welfare of his men.

In a cavalry regiment like the 8th Hussars there were generally four or five troops, of forty or fifty men each, two troops making up one squadron. Each troop was commanded by a captain, with a lieutenant or cornet as his junior officer. Above the several troop captains there were, as a rule, two majors, the senior of whom would deputize for the lieutenant-colonel when necessary. The peacetime routine of most cavalry regiments was much the same. Morning stables, the grooming of horses by the men and their inspection by the troop commanders, would be followed by forenoon riding school, or a mounted parade, skirmishing drill, or by an occasional full-dress field day. The field day involved a full range of cavalry manoeuvres and ceremonial, from the formality of wheeling at the trot to sword exercise at full gallop. These morning parades began early and might last for four or five hours. Then the regimental office or orderly room opened at about eleven o'clock for the commanding officer or his deputy to deal with the administrative business of the day. At midday, the men cooked their own food, boiling the beef and drinking the broth as a soup. Half the day's ration was eaten then, the first half having generally been eaten for breakfast. For the officers, too, there was midday dinner in the mess. They received the same rations as the men but were, of course, better able to supplement them from their own funds. Unless a private soldier was able to buy more food with his own pay, he might wait from midday until the following morning for a meal. For all that, however, he was no worse off than many of his civilian contemporaries.

The afternoon was generally devoted to foot-drill for the cavalry, undertaken by troops rather than by the whole regiment together. Finally came evening stables, when a conscientious commanding officer went the rounds of all his troops to see the horses groomed and bedded down. Evening stables were not popular with junior officers, who generally liked to regard their work as finished by mid-day, and who complained bitterly when some regimental commanders required their presence at evening parades. It was almost as if the Horse Guards had deliberately contrived this late inspection to clash with more alluring social engagements.

Saturdays were sacred to the watering parade, when the cavalry horses were thoroughly washed and groomed, while a Sunday church parade was held either in the riding school of the larger barracks or at the nearest and most convenient church.

The life of a cavalry officer, either subaltern or regimental commander, was not as arduous as it might appear. He came of a wealthy family, otherwise he would not have been able to buy a commission in a crack regiment of hussars or lancers. It was expected that he would have commitments, as a Member of Parliament, as a landowner, or at least the son of a landowner, and as a huntsman. The last was, perhaps, the most important. Even after the First World War, one late Victorian soldier, Field Marshal Sir Evelyn Wood, was still warning the nation of 'remarkable instances of brain power being handicapped by want of horsemanship'. Horsemanship was all important and, 'we have one incalculable advantage which no other nation possesses in that our officers are able to hunt and than which, combined with study, there is during peace no better practice.' But the young subaltern of dragoons, in his scarlet or royal blue and gold lace, with his arrogant manner, immaculate whiskers and drawling slangy speech was as much an essential part of the dinners and balls of the London season in Pall Mall or Portman Square, as of the great hunts of the Shires, or the fashionable summer gatherings of well-born yachtsmen at Cowes. An understanding Horse Guards had so arranged matters that during much of the year no more than half the officers were required to be present with their regiments. In some cases they were hardly seen at all, except when the regiment was mustered at the end of each month, or when there was a half-yearly general inspection by the district commander.[16]

In certain respects, life in the regiment differed little for its officers from life outside it. The mess was rather like a small club or a large all-male family. When a score of officers assembled for dinner, their servants in attendance behind their chairs, the mess assumed the appearance of a formal family occasion in one of the smaller country houses. The food was the best and the wines the choicest that could be provided. Champagne was commonly drunk, since the Napoleonic wars and the Grand Tour had together given cavalry subalterns a taste for such luxuries. But even an officer who found this life too spartan for him was not unduly oppressed by it while serving with his regiment. He was not required to live in the barracks, and the mess of a cavalry regiment was quite likely to be found in the best hotel that Hampton Court or Dublin, Brighton or Edinburgh, could offer.

Officers were not only expected to hunt, in the manner described by Sir Evelyn Wood, but they were expected to provide themselves with horses and hounds for the purpose. Wellington and other British officers had even taken their hounds to war with them. In the winter of 1813–14, when the British and French armies decided with commendable urbanity to call a halt to the fighting until the spring should come, hunting had been a major pastime of the officers as the British regiments faced their placid enemy in south-west France. On one occasion, an unco-operative fox had actually made its way across a river and into French territory, followed by the entire pack of hounds. The British sent an officer across to parley. The French commander, with expressions of sympathy, opened his lines and allowed the hunt through.

If in his future career, Lord Brudenell was often to seem out of patience with later military ideas and standards, it is perhaps as well to recall the nature of the army, and particularly of its cavalry regiments, when he became an eager cornet in May 1824. At twenty-seven years old, he seemed to have joined a decade too late, but he was about to make up for lost time.

The 8th Hussars had a new lieutenant-colonel, Lord George William Russell, under whom it spent much of its time doing tours of duty under the eyes of George IV, both at Brighton and at Hampton Court or Hounslow, which were convenient barracks for Windsor. Lord Brudenell was soon recognized as a smart and zealous subaltern, who assumed immaculate military behaviour, as if to the manner born. Both in his regimental duties and in his social behaviour he was the perfect Hussar. Perhaps by civilian standards he was a little too ready to 'resent an insult' and call out his opponent with pistols upon the 'field of honour', but this was not remarkable by the standards of a fashionable regiment. Happily, the subalterns of the dragoons were such bad shots, and their pistols still so primitive, that it was rare for a man to be killed in a duel.

On hearing that Sir Gilbert Heathcote, Master of the Cottesmore, had insulted one of the Brudenell sisters, their indignant brother challenged him to a duel with pistols. The seconds paced out the ground, the two men raised their long-barrelled pistols and fired. They both missed, and honour was satisfied. By an odd coincidence, however, Sir Gilbert was the second cousin of Lord Brudenell's newly-acquired wife. As Lady Derby remarked, when Sir Gilbert had received Brudenell's shot, he should then have said; 'Now, my lord, I must beg you to receive my shot for your conduct to my cousin!'

'Damned fair, I think', noted Thomas Creevey. However, after the first exchange of fire and the glitter of homicidal determination in Brudenell's eye, young Sir Gilbert was probably quite glad to let matters rest.[17]

The crack of duelling pistols in Rockingham Forest, or on the grassland of famous meeting places like Wimbledon Common or Wormwood Scrubs, were the only shots fired in earnest which most aristocratic young officers of the British army heard for the next thirty years. For their more proletarian comrades who could only afford to serve in the heat of the Indian plains, or in the Afghan expeditions, it was of course a different matter.

Lord Brudenell's patron, the Duke of York, tall and portly like all his royal brothers, was growing into a shy but amiable old man. He had exchanged the iron duties of war for the domestic pleasures of buying a donkey and teaching his great-niece, the little Princess Victoria, to ride it. With a vague and benign approval, he observed the progress of the fierce young lord in the 8th Hussars. With the Duke's blessing, Brudenell bought his way up the military hierarchy with the maximum speed which the law allowed. In 1824 he was a cornet, in 1825 a lieutenant, in 1826 a troop captain of the 8th Hussars. His diligence and efficiency were beyond question. Other subalterns might complain at the bore of having to attend evening stables or act as orderly officer for the day, but neither high society nor parliamentary duty tempted Lord Brudenell from such things. As he later remarked, 'I was a Member of Parliament all this time, and neglected much of my parliamentary duties for the purpose of doing orderly duty as a subaltern officer in the 8th Hussars.' Fortunately, in the pre-Reform Bill House of Commons, so many other members were neglecting their duties for even less creditable reasons that

Lord Brudenell's lapses were unlikely to be the subject of much comment.

When the 8th Hussars went to Dublin, Captain Lord Brudenell was seconded to the staff of the commander of the army in Ireland, General Sir Charles Dalbiac, who had not only fought through the Peninsular Campaign as a major of the 4th Light Dragoons, but had taken his wife through the campaign as well. Lady Dalbiac was a formidable woman, who shared the hardships of her husband's life under canvas, and rode with him at the head of the regiment, as though bearing the King's commission herself.

Apart from his tour of duty with Dalbiac's staff, Brudenell remained a zealous troop captain of his regiment. When the new commanding officer, Lieutenant-Colonel the Honourable G. B. Molyneux, was on leave, and the Major was in bed with a cold, Brudenell as Senior Captain found himself in brief but complete command of a cavalry regiment. Though it was mid-winter in Dundalk, he at once ordered a field day and a review. Hours later the troopers and their horses returned, chilled by the cold winter mists of the Irish Sea and exhausted by the wheeling and charging over wet and muddied turf. Lieutenant-Colonel Molyneux came back to find his regiment hardly fit for duty. Lord Brudenell was carpeted and given such a reprimand that it seemed even his belligerent enthusiasm must have been checked.

This impression was inaccurate. The incident of the field day was no more than the merest taste of what was to follow. Captain Lord Brudenell tolerated no slackness, no softness, and no insubordination on the part of his men or his officers. The day of glory might come at any time. When it did, it must not be said that the British army flinched from the call to honour because it was the middle of winter in Dundalk. In August 1830, he bought the rank of major, and in December the same year he became lieutenant-colonel. Unfortunately for him there was no regiment whose commander was willing to sell out to him just then. He retired on half-pay and waited fretfully.

But while Lord Brudenell's military career was interrupted, his political future seemed even more uncertain. He had quarrelled with the Marquess of Ailesbury over the question of Catholic emancipation. When it was first proposed to remove the civil restrictions upon Catholics, Brudenell opposed the idea, but in the end he decided to support the Emancipation Bill of the Duke of Wellington's government. In the following year, 1829, the Marquess of Ailesbury turned him out of his parliamentary seat. Brudenell, as he never tired of reminding future Conservative leaders from whom he sought preferment, was then put to the considerable expense of buying another seat in the House of Commons. This time it was the old rotten borough of Fowey in Cornwall, for which he sat from 1830 until such constituencies were abolished by the Reform Bill two years later.

Even by 1830, it appeared that parliamentary reform must soon become a reality. The government of Lord Grey proposed a bill which, by abolishing such seats as Marlborough and Fowey, would redistribute votes and electoral power among the upper middle classes of the more populous areas. Only a minority of men, and no women at all, would receive the vote. However, its effect would be to produce an electorate, and perhaps a House of Commons, dominated by manufacturers and tradesmen, farmers and professional men. The power of the aristocracy in England was not to be overthrown by a revolution of workers but by the rate-paying strength of men successful in commerce and industry.

From the first, Lord Brudenell opposed the Reform Bill. When, despite Conservative opposition, it passed the House of Commons, the House of Lords threw it out in 1831. Then Lord Grey prevailed upon the new King, William IV, to threaten the House of Lords that if its members continued to thwart the will of the Commons then he, at Lord Grey's request, would use his royal power to create so many Whig or Liberal peers that the Bill would be forced through their Lordships' House by the weight of such numbers. The Lords, concluding that the Bill itself was preferable to having their House cursed with a permanent majority of reformers, at length capitulated. In the autumn of 1832, following the triumph of Reform, there were to be new elections, conducted according to the Bill's provisions. There was no longer a seat at Fowey for Lord Brudenell. He was obliged to stand for the Northern Division of Northamptonshire, in the face of strong and embittered Whig opposition.

English parliamentary elections in the years following the Reform Bill were not quite as farcically corrupt as Dickens's account of the Eatonswill contest in *The Pickwick Papers* but, for all that, they were quite bad enough. While Lord Brudenell was fighting for the Northamptonshire seat, Captain Gronow of the Guards was standing at Stafford. No sooner had he arrived in the town than a great crowd gathered under the window of his room at the Star Inn. The leaders of this crowd came straight to the point.

'Now, Gronow, my old boy, we like what we have heard about
you, your principles, and all that sort of thing; we will
therefore all vote for you if . . .' Here every man in the crowd
struck his breeches-pocket several times with his open hand.
After this expressive pantomime, the speaker continued, 'You
know what we mean old fellow? If not—you understand—you
won't do for Stafford.'

Captain Gronow, by his own admission, thereupon 'set to work to
bribe every man, woman, and child in the ancient borough of Stafford',
and was in due course elected.[18]

Northamptonshire North was a two-member constituency and, in
a tacit but civilized agreement, the Conservatives or Tories and the
Liberal Whigs had each put forward one candidate, so that it appeared
likely to be an unopposed election. After all the acrimony attending
the Reform Bill, it seemed that the first Northamptonshire election
under its provisions was to be an old-fashioned and gentlemanly
affair. Lord Brudenell was put forward for the Tories, and Lord
Milton, the son of Earl Fitzwilliam, for the Whigs or Liberals. Lord
Milton made much of his support for parliamentary reform, and his
thorough opposition to the institution of black slavery in the British
Empire. Lord Brudenell came forward, rather more astutely, as 'The
Farmer's Friend'. In other words, he favoured the retention of the
1815 Corn Laws, by which the importation of cheap foreign corn was
prevented in order to protect the British farmer. This policy was
favoured by the farmers themselves, supported by the Conservative
party, but opposed by Liberals, free-traders, and all who regarded
such laws as the means of denying adequate food to the poorly-paid
British workers. Ironically, it was to be a Conservative government,
under Sir Robert Peel, which abolished the Corn Laws in 1846. But in
1832, to be a 'farmer's friend' in rural Northamptonshire was to be
certain of a respectable number of votes.

The gentlemanly atmosphere of the contest was soon dispelled
when Brudenell persuaded his neighbour, Squire Tryon of Bulwick, to
stand as a second Conservative candidate and thus to attempt to win
both seats for the party. Lord Milton and the *Northampton Mercury*
accused him of trying to deprive the electors of a Liberal representative in the next House of Commons. *The Times* dreamed hopefully
of another 'popular and spirited candidate' coming forward to join
Lord Milton, in order that the electors should be able to defeat

Brudenell. It was duly announced that William Hanbury of Kelmarsh was to join Lord Milton.[19]

The two parties began to canvass the farmers and the other electors of the constituency in the autumn of 1832. The Conservative slogan was borne everywhere:[20]

> Brudenell and Prosperity!
> OR
> Milton and Ruin!
> To be or not to be *that* is the question!

With all the enthusiasm of a well-born Liberal reformer, Lord Milton strove to acquire the common touch and canvassed the electors personally. Brudenell did not regard it as his duty to go the rounds of voters personally and beg for their support. Nevertheless, in his election address he claimed that there was such general support for him 'as to leave no doubt on my mind that I shall have the honour of being returned as one of your Representatives'. There were those in the county who longed to see him proved wrong, but he spoke with the confidence of a man who, even a month before polling day, had already distributed £10,000 in what *The Times* euphemistically described as 'election expenses'.[21]

However, anyone who witnessed Lord Brudenell's entry into the market town of Wellingborough might have doubted the confidence with which he looked forward to the election. He and his party of supporters rode into the town to find their way blocked by a hooting and jeering crowd. When they dismounted and attempted to open a path through the mob, a riot broke out. As the little group struggled to make a way forward, its members were pelted on all sides by mud and stones. One of the stones, perhaps shied by an expert, caught Lord Brudenell on the back of the head, and this was the signal for a general attack. In a short while, Brudenell had received 'considerable personal injury', further disturbances had broken out in the neighbouring streets, the Riot Act had been read without effect, and the mayor had sent off express riders to call in the army from Weedon Barracks. Brudenell and his party, bruised and bedraggled, extricated themselves from the brawl and withdrew from the town of Wellingborough, 'soiled by Whig excrement, and covered by Whig spittle'.[22]

It was the worst riot of the election, though there was a similar outburst at Kettering, and most of the subsequent brickbats were verbal. Brudenell continued to be 'The Farmer's Friend'. On the question of slavery, which Milton had made a central issue of the campaign, he was cautious and unenthusiastic. Brudenell was 'most anxious to see the slave emancipated', but the slave 'in his present uneducated and ignorant state is unfit for freedom'. The solution was to cause 'his condition to be improved, so as to qualify him for emancipation'. And with that the momentous issue was put aside from the election campaign.[23]

On 15 December, a day of rain and early darkness, the candidates were officially nominated, for immediate election, at a public meeting or 'hustings' in Kettering. The High Sheriff demanded a show of hands, as a matter of formal tradition, and declared Lords Brudenell and Milton to be elected. Naturally, the other two candidates made a formal protest at this and so there had to be a ballot. This continued over several days, the progress being announced day by day, so that the public might know which candidate was in the lead.

In many respects, the hustings on nomination day marked the climax of the election campaign. The 'pebble pelting gentry', who had beaten up Lord Brudenell and his supporters at Wellingborough, were out in force. They massed several ranks deep in front of the platform, looking forward to a repetition of that earlier fracas. But Brudenell rode into the town at the head of 1,000 horsemen, who appeared to be his own uniformed yeomanry, in a display of paramilitary strength which provoked bitter comments from his critics. His 'private cavalry' rode in with a band playing and the blue pennants of the Conservative party fluttering. Their first action was to form a circle, three men deep, round the troublemakers who had gathered in front of the platform. With his most vociferous opponents isolated within this *cordon sanitaire*, Brudenell and the other candidates appeared on the platform. Lord Milton, still determinedly pursuing the issue of slavery, was accompanied by a flag, upon which appeared a Negro in chains above the slogan, 'Am I not a friend and a brother?'

Milton made a sharp little speech, accusing Brudenell of having gone creeping up the back-stairs of voters, instead of canvassing them like a gentleman. Brudenell got up, to a storm of mingled cheers and hisses, and indignantly denied the charge. Indeed, he announced that Milton had only resorted to such jibes to draw attention away from 'the back-stairs way in which he got into Parliament last time'. The querulous bickering continued. It may nevertheless have occurred to some of the crowd that, for all the talk of reform and emancipation, the two opposing candidates had far more in common with each other than with the great majority of Englishmen, who were to remain without a vote for half a century after the Reform Bill of 1832. The Wellingborough mob may have disrupted Lord Brudenell's canvass with their mud and stones, but they remained an unenfranchised mob, who could often be bought by either party for the price of a drunken spree.[24]

The voting took place during the following week. By Tuesday evening, Lord Milton and Squire Hanbury were ahead, but after Wednesday's polling, Lord Brudenell and Squire Tryon had just gone into the lead. Finally, a little before two o'clock on Friday afternoon, 21 December, the High Sheriff announced that Lord Milton and Lord Brudenell had been elected. In this constituency, at least, the result was precisely what it might have been if there had been no Reform Bill and no contest. Among the acclamations of their separate supporters, the two successful candidates were chaired shoulder high in two processions which, with a proper sense of decorum, moved off in diametrically opposite directions.

CHAPTER 3

CONDUCT UNBECOMING

1

In the life of Lord Brudenell, the Reform Bill and the parliamentary election of 1832 were as nothing compared to the really important event of that year. On 16 March he exchanged from half-pay into the 15th King's Hussars, and assumed the command of the regiment. Unlike the 8th Hussars, which had fought bravely but unobtrusively in India, the 15th had been in the thick of the most celebrated and glorious battles of recent times.

The regiment had been raised by Colonel George Augustus Eliott, in London, in 1759 during the most critical period of the Seven Years' War against France. Known as 'Eliott's Light Horse', it was officered by wealthy and adventurous young men like the Earl of Pembroke and Sir George Erskine. It incurred heavy casualties in the battle of Emsdorf, in 1760, but returned home with sixteen standards captured from the enemy, which were duly presented to George III at a parade in Hyde Park. Fighting against the French again in the 1790s, the regiment took part in the battle for Cambrai, during which it performed a classic and spectacular cavalry charge at Villiers-en-Couche which completely routed the French infantry and put their horsemen to flight. As the war moved to Spain and Portugal, the 15th Hussars fought with Wellington from Sahagun to Vittoria, and in 1814 crossed into France and defeated Soult's cavalry at the battle of Toulouse.

Inevitably, it was present at Waterloo, fighting as a front-line regiment in a long and bloody engagement with the French cuiras-

36

siers which occupied it for much of the battle. Afterwards, the courage and spirit of the 15th Hussars seemed almost beyond praise. Undeterred by the heavier squadrons of Napoleon and the rapidity with which their own officers were cut down, the troopers of the regiment rode and fought with a valour that ensured their reputation for years to come. At the fiercest moments of the battle, the command of the regiment changed hands several times within a few minutes. Its Lieutenant-Colonel, Leighton Dalrymple, had his left leg blown off by an artillery burst as the 15th Hussars went into the French fire. His second-in-command, Major Edwin Griffith, was cut down by French sabres as the two opposing cavalry detachments met head on. The senior Captain, Joseph Thackwell, at once assumed command of the regiment and led it onwards against the enemy until he was shot through the bridle hand by a French infantryman. It was eventually a junior Captain, Skinner Hancox, who brought the survivors of the regiment out of the battle.

The 15th Hussars came home to a grateful nation and an admiring Prince Regent. When the Prince became George IV, the regiment was chosen to provide his escort. In scarlet trimmed with ermine and pelisses braided with gold, royal blue overalls or trousers, scarlet shako or headpiece with matching plume, they made an impression of bright splendour against the pale elegant architecture of Georgian London, or among the oriental domes and archways of royal Brighton. Upon the scarlet saddle cloths was a simple gold monogram, '15 KH', and the lion and crown of England set within the circle of the garter. Upon the regimental standards, the gold emblazoning of battle honours told the regiment's history in summary. 'Emsdorf', 'Villiers-en-Couche', 'Egmont-op-Zee', 'Sahagun', 'Vittoria', 'Peninsula', and 'Waterloo'.

When Lord Brudenell assumed command of the regiment, which was then in barracks at Manchester, he might have considered himself to be in a delicate situation. With the exception of Emsdorf, all the battle honours had been won well within living memory. Indeed, there were many soldiers of the regiment who had served at Waterloo and in the Peninsula, if not at Villiers-en-Couche. Apart from fashionable affairs of honour with other rich young men, Lord Brudenell had never known what it was to be under fire. By spending tens of thousands of pounds, he was now promoted to the command of a regiment, over the heads of older men who had fought some of the bloodiest battles of history against the armies of Napoleon or Marshal Soult, while their new Lieutenant-Colonel was still a boy at Harrow or Christ Church. But the new commander was not inhibited by this consideration. It seemed to him that such men ought to be grateful for the privilege of having been present upon those fields of honour.

Two years of enforced retirement on half-pay had merely sharpened the young Lord's enthusiasm for making the 15th Hussars the smartest, most efficient and best disciplined regiment in the service. Joseph Thackwell, his predecessor, who had been promoted Lieutenant-Colonel after Waterloo, was an easy-going commander, but soldiering was about to become a serious matter for the officers who now fell under Lord Brudenell's orders. Regulations were to be observed down to the last dot and comma. Regimental field days and reviews, which were regarded elsewhere as rather special occasions, were to be held two or three times a week. Permission to marry, which officers and men must obtain from their commanding officer, was to be withheld rather than granted, since marriage might distract a man from his regimental duties. At all events, a soldier's first duty was to the regiment, and there were to be no more idle young men who joined the 15th Hussars with as little sense of commitment as when they joined a dining club.

Yet such military professionalism was to be accompanied by the most extravagant style of life. The mess was to be graced by French cuisine, champagne and the finest cellar that could be bought. At this level, the splendour with which important guests were entertained seemed just as important to the regimental reputation as the grooming of the horses or the smartness of the troopers at some grand review in Hyde Park, or in Phoenix Park, Dublin.

Lord Brudenell's Major was Walter Scott, the eldest son of the famous novelist. The father, mortally ill and still driving himself to write in order to satisfy the demands of family and creditors, expressed his disenchantment with his son's prospects in the 15th Hussars to his friend Daniel Terry.[1]

> Every one grumbles at his own profession, but here is the devil of a calling for you, where a man pays £3,000 for an annuity of £400 a year and less—renounces his free-will in almost every respect—must rise at five every morning to see horses curried—dare not sleep out of town without the leave of a cross colonel, who is often disposed to refuse it merely because he has the power to do so; and, last of all, may be sent to the most unhealthy

climates to die of the rot, or be shot like a blackcock. There is a per contra, to be sure—fine clothes and fame; but the first must be paid for and the other is not come by, by one out of the hundred.

During Lord Brudenell's first months of command, the younger Scott was much preoccupied by his father's last illness. The great man died in September 1832 and the Major, in turn, became Sir Walter Scott. Lord Brudenell himself had been less active in the regiment during 1832 than he would have wished, since much of his time and attention was required for the Northamptonshire election. Then, in 1833, the regiment was ordered to Dublin. Not only was this a city of fashion, where Major Sir Walter Scott and other officers took up residence in the finest houses near St Stephen's Green, and Lord Brudenell himself in Sackville Street, but the open grassland of Phoenix Park, the guard duties at Dublin Castle and the Bank of Ireland, offered opportunities for display and ceremonial which had been quite lacking in provincial and industrial Manchester. During the few weeks that the regiment was in Dublin, rumours of the extraordinary behaviour of Lord Brudenell began to reach the press. But when the 15th Hussars went to Cork, in the autumn of 1833, the rumours became court-martial charges. It was even whispered that there had been a mutiny.

On its way south, the regiment was stationed for a while at Newbridge, near the Curragh. With an enthusiasm which seemed to some observers to border on demonic possession, Lieutenant-Colonel Lord Brudenell ordered field days and full dress inspections on no less than four days a week. The superbly uniformed squadrons in their scarlet and blue with gold lace were kept charging and wheeling at the gallop across the broad expanse of the barrack field until every detail was perfect. Brudenell left nothing to his junior officers or NCOs. Most of the aristocratic cavalry commanders might keep their distance from ordinary troopers, but Brudenell pounced on malingerers, shouted reprimands at his troop captains and, as Sir John Fortescue remarked, behaved in general more like a sergeant-major than a commanding officer.

Not only were the field days intolerably frequent, they also lasted for far too long. The regimental office could never open for business on time, because the troopers and Lord Brudenell were still advancing and retiring alternately, in double lines of scarlet and gold. Hours later, the weary squadrons returned. Several of the horses actually collapsed during the drill, and most of them were so over-heated that it was impossible to take the saddle-cloths off them for two hours afterwards, in case they should catch a chill. Major Sir Walter Scott regarded the horses with utter dismay.[2]

'No regiment ever marched into Newbridge in better condition. I never saw such a squadron as I had command of when I left Newbridge, in regard to their low condition, and number of sore backs.'[3]

It was hardly the most promising start to Lord Brudenell's career as a regimental commander, but he could hardly be expected to consider it as his fault. The regiment had been slack and easy-going under old Lieutenant-Colonel Thackwell, a bluff and good-tempered officer who had succeeded to the command largely by being the senior survivor of Waterloo. Of course the horses collapsed and the men grumbled. To Lord Brudenell it was sure confirmation that they had not been trained hard enough or long enough. There was a remedy for that.

However, when the regiment reached its barracks near Cork, he made a temporary concession. The number of field days each week should be reduced from four to three, but the number of days spent in skirmishing drill must be increased from one to two. His troop captains were horrified. Field days were primarily intended as summer exercises, and it was now approaching mid-winter in Ireland. Yet the man they soon regarded as a mixture of villain and lunatic was proposing to take them out three times a week on these elaborate and ceremonial manoeuvres. The season of the year was irrelevant to Lord Brudenell. He had heard that the 15th Hussars might at any moment be under orders to embark for Portugal. The usurper Dom Miguel had seized the Crown, and the British government proposed to restore the exiled Queen, by force of arms if necessary. It was some comfort to an eager soldier to see the recurrent fallacy of 'peace in our time' undergoing one of its recurrent exposures.

But the Lieutenant-Colonel waited in vain for this particular call to glory. As the autumn turned to winter in south-east Ireland, the plight of Portugal's Queen was forgotten and his attention lingered increasingly upon one of his five troop captains, Augustus Wathen. Captain Wathen was an older soldier than Lord Brudenell, and had been present at Quatre Bras and Waterloo, though not in the 15th Hussars. He was by no means a poor man, since poor men did not become cavalry officers, but with Lady Wathen, his wife, he enjoyed the alternating comforts of a town house in Chelsea and the mess-room of a fashionable regiment.

To the fierce eye of Lord Brudenell, Captain Wathen appeared the prototype of the barrack-room lawyer. He announced that if men were allowed to behave as Wathen behaved, 'discipline would soon be subverted, and there would soon be regiments of lawyers instead of obedient soldiers.' But worse than that, it seemed that Captain Wathen was intent on inciting the men of his troop to denigrate their Lieutenant-Colonel. On ceremonial parades, when the Captain should have been riding in precise position at the head of his troop, he would amble off to one side, holding his sword limply as though it had been a lady's parasol. In a purple rage, Brudenell swore that Wathen had 'systematically thwarted and opposed me for two or three months together'.[4]

In his anguish, Brudenell began to deliver parade ground reprimands in a voice which was clearly audible from one end of the cavalry line to the other. Sir Hussey Vivian, Master General of Ordnance, had issued new instructions on cavalry drill. A troop captain was to ride in front of his column and to one side. But Captain Wathen, through absent-mindedness, would position himself in the old way, at the centre of the head of the column. To the Lieutenant-Colonel, such behaviour was deliberate and intolerable insubordination. It amounted almost to mutiny. He shouted and bawled at Captain Wathen, who was certainly a far better military theorist than a parade ground soldier. But no sooner had Wathen moved into the right position than Brudenell's voice was ringing in his ears again.

'Carry your sword, sir! Can't you carry your sword properly?'

And then there came a stand-up row in the middle of the barrack field, Brudenell swearing that he would demote Wathen and put one of the junior officers in command of the troop, and in command of Wathen himself. But these public rages were nothing compared to the treatment which Wathen received in the semi-privacy of the regimental office. Hardly a week passed without a fresh rumour running through the regiment of yet another 'turn-up', as it was called in cavalry slang, between Lieutenant-Colonel Lord Brudenell and his troop captain.

Soon it was not Captain Wathen alone but his entire troop who became the targets for Brudenell's anger. The men of the troop were more often on defaulters' parades for drunkenness or absence from roll-call than the men of the other troops. Drunkenness was a bad enough problem among troopers in England, but it was even worse in Ireland, where the men could buy more drink for their money. Then it was discovered that the majority of horses with sore backs proved to be in Wathen's troop. Lord Brudenell summoned him to the regimental office and proceeded to berate him.

'Your troop is the worst in the regiment. It must be your bad management.'

Wathen prudently remained silent, at which Brudenell demanded angrily, 'Well, sir, is it not so?'

The same scene, with minor variations was played repeatedly. It was in vain for Wathen to protest that he had been absent during the period when the horses had been found with sore backs. Brudenell with a gleam of maniacal triumph retorted sharply that in that particular month the condition of the troop had actually *improved*. To which he added a descant of rage at 'the idleness and want of care of their horses' which Wathen's example inspired in his men.[5]

The outside world began to hear stories of the state of affairs in the 15th Hussars, a comic opera whose star would make the most temperamental *prima donna* seem the soul of equanimity by comparison. Paragraphs on the subject began to appear in the papers, first in Cork, then in Dublin, and finally in London. Lord Brudenell found that his angry words, even when used in private to Captain Wathen, were now becoming public property. He swore that Wathen was not only scheming to thwart and oppose him, the man was also hand in glove with the scandalmongers of the gutter press. Brudenell had recently had occasion to horsewhip a Radical editor, John Drakard, for calumnies published in his *Stamford News*, and he was by no means a lover of the popular press.

The regimental wives proved as dangerous as their husbands in battles of this kind. Both Lady Wathen and Lady Elizabeth Brudenell were in Cork with the regiment, and Lady Wathen was adept at getting her side of the story into the newspapers. Brudenell found his conduct towards Wathen publicly denounced as 'disgraceful and dishonourable—replete with petty envy and vindictive spleen'. As for Lady Brudenell, said the press, though she might ride at the head of the regiment with her husband, the wives of the other officers regarded her as little less than a whore for her conduct towards her first husband. They refused to receive her in their homes and they rejected all invitations to visit her. The *New Weekly Despatch* gave its readers a potted history of her sexual escapades in the army, describing her as 'the wife of a gallant Major—the friend of another—the attaché of a third—and, at last, the lady of the Lieutenant-Colonel'. The paper added that it was the regiment's treatment of his wife which had enraged Lord Brudenell most of all, and which had driven him to take revenge upon Captain Wathen and certain other officers.[6]

2

The first crisis of the Wathen affair had come in September 1833, when after a more than usually spirited 'turn-up', Lord Brudenell had ended the argument by placing the Captain under close arrest to await trial on court-martial charges relating to a refusal to obey orders. The papers were sent to Lord Hill, Commander-in-Chief, at the Horse Guards. As Sir Rowland Hill, he had been one of Wellington's closest colleagues and best generals in the Peninsula, and had become Commander-in-Chief when Wellington resigned the post to be Prime Minister in 1828. By this stage in his life, 'Daddy' Hill, as the soldiers called him, was as much of a gentleman-farmer as a soldier. But there had been no wars and few rumours of wars, so that to be Commander-in-Chief in the tranquillity of the Horse Guards seemed likely to be an honoured and uneventful sinecure.

Lord Hill considered the state of affairs in the 15th Hussars. He ordered that Captain Wathen should be released from arrest, and decided that there would be no court-martial. Informally, he suggested to Lieutenant-Colonel Lord Brudenell that he and his officers should forget their old quarrels and learn to live together as brothers in arms. Lord Brudenell's retort was that though he might be ordered to release Wathen from arrest, no one could compel him to like the man.

On 20 October 1833, the officers of the regiment were assembled in the mess-room. Brudenell read out Hill's order releasing Captain Wathen from arrest. He also commented on the order at some length, 'stating that the General Commanding-in-Chief must have decided on some points under a wrong impression.' Then he delivered a string of unflattering comments on Wathen, finally turning to the Adjutant and saying, 'in a peculiarly ungracious manner' and with a 'supercilious wave of the hand', 'In consequence of this decision of Lord Hill's, release that officer from arrest.'[7]

Wathen had spent several weeks under arrest, and had previously intended to travel to London at that time in order to see a relation about a matter of his own preferment, which was probably an exchange into another regiment. As soon as he left the mess-room, he sat down and wrote to Lord Brudenell requesting leave of absence and suggesting that it would be convenient if it were granted in time for him to catch the next steamer from Dublin to Bristol. His answer came back with remarkable speed. The Adjutant was instructed by Lord Brudenell to inform him, 'in the most decided manner', that his request was refused. In the first place, Brudenell did not consider that the day upon which an officer's conduct was 'animadverted on in strong terms' was the proper moment for him to be granted leave of absence. In the second place, Brudenell did not consider Wathen's troop to be 'in good order', though the letter continued predictably with a taunt that the junior officers had managed to effect a considerable improvement in its condition while Wathen was under arrest. There was to be no leave for Captain Wathen. As surely as when he had called his man out upon the duelling ground, Lord Brudenell wanted a fight to the finish with his adversary.[8]

It was the unlikely subject of stable-jackets which turned the squabbles of the 15th Hussars into a national scandal. These jackets, scarlet or blue according to regimental uniform, were worn by men as an alternative to the more elaborate dress worn on field days. When the regiment was paraded on foot, its commander inspected the men's equipment, including their stable-jackets. If a jacket seemed past its best, it was sent to the regimental Quartermaster, who had it repaired if he thought it worthwhile. Otherwise, a new jacket had to be purchased. Each troop had a sum of money, supplied by the Horse Guards through the commanding officer, but some of the costs were stopped out of the men's pay. Consequently, a new issue of stable-jackets was not likely to be popular with the troopers. In the 15th Hussars the problem was aggravated because the men had scarlet jackets which were reckoned to be less hard-wearing than the blue ones, and which cost eighteen shillings to replace.

When a man was ordered to have a new stable-jacket, he was of course expected to sign his account. But the men of Wathen's troop began to complain that Lord Brudenell was making them buy new jackets on the slightest pretexts. As the mood of protest grew stronger, Private William Surret refused to sign his account. On 4 November the Adjutant approached Wathen and said, 'The Colonel wants you and Surret in the office directly. He is to come in his stable-jacket without waiting.'

The two men found their Lieutenant-Colonel in one of his worst rages of all, a state in which he was alleged to foam at the mouth quite literally. He cursed Surret for 'one of those lazy, idle fellows of his troop', and then broke out in uncontrolled fury.

'Do you choose to sign your account, sir? Now, I'll have you out before all the regiment. I won't wait for you to complain to the General, but I'll have you out—you shall complain—I'll force you—I'll oblige you to do so. If you were to go back for fifty years, such a troop could not be found throughout the service!'

After much more of this, some of it hardly coherent, Surret was dismissed and Lord Brudenell turned upon Wathen. But Wathen said calmly, 'Your lordship has made very severe animadversions upon my troop. After what you have said, and that in the presence of a private, I think it will be but justice to me that you should bring the state of it under the notice of the General at the inspection, and then make good the assertions you have put forth.'

'I shall do as I please', shouted Brudenell. 'You are not to dictate to me, sir!'

With that, Wathen was dismissed but only to be recalled a few minutes later.

'You addressed me in an improper manner, sir', announced Brudenell, 'when you were here just now. Now, sir, what do you mean by what you said?'

'My lord,' said Wathen, 'I am not aware I said anything improper.'

'Yes you did', said Brudenell abruptly. 'Do you *dare* to doubt my word, sir? This is what you said.'

With that he produced a sheet of paper on which the whole of the previous argument had been taken down. Wathen was shocked and dismayed at so unorthodox a proceeding. He maintained a quiet dignity, saying calmly, 'I was not aware that my words had been taken down in writing.'

'I daresay not, sir!' said Brudenell triumphantly. 'But I find it very convenient. Do you mean to deny that these were your words?'

Wathen looked up at this point and saw that the Adjutant, Lieutenant Hecker, was busily scribbling down the words of the present discussion.

'Under these circumstances', said Wathen, 'I think it better not to say anything further, than that I am not aware of having said anything improper.'

'Then, sir,' retorted Brudenell, 'I tell you that you did; and I now reprimand you for it. I desire you to be more careful for the future. I can tell you, that in regard to your troop, I shall adopt any course I think fit. I shall not, in order to *gratify your feelings*, report it to the General. I shan't do any such thing, but you may adopt any course you please.'

After this, Wathen understood that the interview was ended, and that he was dismissed. He turned to go.

'Come back, sir!' bawled Brudenell, pointing with his finger to the floor at his feet.

Wathen obeyed.

'Has your lordship any further commands?' he inquired.

'No', said Brudenell. 'You may retire.'[9]

By this time, the officers of the 15th Hussars seemed to consist of two parties: the first thought their Lieutenant-Colonel guilty of conduct unbecoming the character of an officer and a gentleman, the second merely thought that he was insane. If the second group were correct, then he had certainly behaved with the cunning proverbially attributed to certain madmen. It was now discovered that for more than a year he had been in the habit of having secret records made of all conversations which took place in the regimental office. Worse still, it was said that he used to hide one of his NCOs in a cupboard, where he might take notes of conversations without being seen. Major Sir Walter Scott, appalled at such revelations, declared that these practices were 'most painful and revolting to the feelings of the officers'.[10]

The week which began with Wathen and Surret in the regimental office on Monday 4 November, was to be one of the most memorable in the whole history of the 15th Hussars or in the life of Lord Brudenell. On the following Friday, Major-General Sir Thomas Arbuthnot arrived in Cork to carry out his half-yearly inspection of the regiment as district commander. One of his duties was to examine the accounts of each troop and to see whether they were in credit or debit. In consequence of the frequent issue of stable-jackets, Captain Wathen's account showed a debt of nearly £30. On the day before the Major-General's arrival, Captain Wathen claimed that he was summoned to the regimental office where Lord Brudenell taunted him savagely on the size of his troop debt. The implication was that Brudenell sneered at him as a pauper who could not afford to pay off the troop debt from his own pocket and who had no business to be in a smart and expensive regiment. He certainly promised to draw the attention of the Major-General to the manner in which the troop debt had been allowed to accumulate. Let Captain Wathen try exchanging into another regiment after that.[11]

On the morning of Friday 8 November, there was a full-scale inspection of the regiment in field order in the barrack field by Sir Thomas Arbuthnot. Following this, he turned his attention to the financial affairs of the 15th Hussars. The troop captains were summoned to the office to present their accounts to him, Wathen as the most junior being called last. General Arbuthnot found the account correct and satisfactory. But Wathen was ready for his revenge on Lord Brudenell. Instead of withdrawing he said, 'General, I understand Lieutenant-Colonel Lord Brudenell has made a complaint to you respecting the amount of the debt of my troop, and I wish to offer some explanation on the subject.'[12]

Wathen judged that Brudenell would not, in fact, have mentioned the subject, and in this he was right. General Arbuthnot inquired if the men of the troop had expressed discontent at having new stable-jackets issued to them, and Wathen said that they had. The General asked if the issue had been unusually large or frequent, to which Wathen also replied that it had. Finally, Arbuthnot asked if Wathen had told Brudenell of the complaints. Wathen said that he had.

'It is false!' protested Brudenell. 'He never mentioned a word to me about it!'

'Now, Lord Brudenell, pray do restrain yourself', said the Major-General, motioning with his hand for the Lieutenant-Colonel to be silent. And then Arbuthnot asked if Brudenell had told Wathen previously that new stable-jackets would be issued. Wathen said that he had not.

'It's not true, sir', protested Brudenell. 'He knew it perfectly well. There have been less jackets in my time than in any former period. I'll call the Quartermaster. This Captain talks about the custom of the regiment. The Quartermaster will tell you.'

Wathen attempted to withdraw from the argument, saying that the evidence in the accounts was quite clear enough. At this, Brudenell turned to Major-General Arbuthnot in new fury.

'This officer is making complaints about me. Now, sir, you allow him to go on in the same way you did the men in the field this morning. This is the most gross case of *mutiny* I ever knew.'[13]

Before any reply could be made to this, the discussion was interrupted by the news that another parade was formed up outside for the

General's inspection. That evening he dined in the mess, where the atmosphere was something less than relaxed. Before dinner, the captains of the troops were ordered to go to their men and inform them of his pleasure at the fine state of the regiment. When Captain Wathen reached his troop, he discovered that the Adjutant had been there first and had read out a quite different message, apparently concocted by Lord Brudenell and making Wathen's troop an exception to the general praise. Wathen thereupon addressed the men himself, informing them that Major-General Arbuthnot was extremely satisfied with their turnout and performance.

On Monday 11 November the inspection was resumed, when the General examined the men's kits. Brudenell accompanied him. As they reached Wathen's troop, Brudenell ordered Private William Hopkins to bring forward his old stable-jacket.

'This fellow came to me to complain of a new stable-jacket being ordered for him', he announced triumphantly to the General, 'and he seemed to consider that it was a violent grievance that I should order him a new one. Now look at it!'

General Arbuthnot tactfully agreed that since the pay of a cavalry trooper was so good, the man should buy a new jacket. Vindicated at last, Brudenell threw the jacket at the man, and turned to Wathen with a loud whisper.

'I can tell you, sir', he said exultantly, 'you shall have plenty more new jackets in your troop.'[14]

However much his officers might hate him, it seemed that Brudenell had won this particular battle. But he was about to make a catastrophic error. The next day, Tuesday 12 November, the Adjutant came to the mess-room after midday dinner to summon Captain Wathen to the office again. As usual, Lord Brudenell was waiting for him and demanded to know whether he had addressed his troop on any of the three previous evenings. Wathen said that between Saturday and Monday he had done no more at the evening parade than to read out the orders given to him.

'It's very extraordinary', said Brudenell. 'You may go, sir, and I'll send for you again.'

Wathen retired to his own room, only to be fetched back by the Adjutant a quarter of an hour later.

'It has been reported to me', said Brudenell with distaste, 'from three different sources in the regiment, that on Saturday night you assembled your men, that you addressed them, that you told them you were very much pleased with them, that the left troop of the line had been particularly admired, that you made some allusion about going on service, and had said your heart was with them.'

Wathen replied that this summary of his words was inaccurate, and that in any case he had spoken to his men at midday on Saturday and not in the evening. Brudenell demanded to know exactly what the Captain had said to his men, and Wathen repeated it. After cross-examining him upon it, Brudenell ordered him to repeat it a second time. Wathen noticed that the Adjutant was once again scribbling busily, and offered to write it himself.

'I am not to be dictated to, the way I am to command *my* regiment', shouted Brudenell. 'I choose to have it verbally and you'll state it all over again.'

Wathen refused to repeat what he had said, except in writing. He later recalled that Brudenell's face became red with anger and that he waved his arms about wildly, roaring, 'Now, sir, do you disobey my *commands*? I here most solemnly declare, that as I am commanding officer of this regiment, if you don't comply with my orders, you shall be placed under arrest.'

Wathen firmly refused to repeat his statement except in writing. Brudenell calmed himself a little, and finally agreed. Then, as Wathen began to move, he shouted, 'You shall do it in this office. *Come here, sir, you shan't go away!* Now sit down here and write it.'

Under the ferocious glare of his Lieutenant-Colonel, Wathen filled about two and a half pages, without finishing his statement. Brudenell demanded that he should hand it over at once. Wathen refused, on the grounds that he would not give up an unfinished letter.

'Then you can finish it after parade', said Brudenell.

'Very well, sir,' said Wathen, standing up and putting the letter in his pocket.

'You shall not take it out of the office!' exclaimed Brudenell. 'Give it to me, sir! Do you dare to disobey my commands?'

'My lord,' said Wathen, 'I cannot give up an unfinished document.'

'Then put it in the box till you come back from parade. I shan't read it. *The Adjutant* will be on parade with you, *all* the other officers will be there together, you will all leave parade together, so you can have no objection.'

'My lord,' insisted Wathen, 'I decline leaving my letter.'

'Then, sir, you disobey my positive commands—Mr Hecker, bring in some witnesses.'[15]

49

This instruction to the Adjutant could mean only one thing, the arrest of Captain Wathen on charges to be answered before a general court-martial. He was duly charged by Lord Brudenell with insubordination in addressing his troop in the words alleged, and in refusing to repeat them properly before his commanding officer. On reflection, Lord Brudenell also charged him with not having delivered the correct address to his troop on the day of the inspection, and with having imputed misconduct to his commanding officer by the 'invidious and improper manner' of his remarks to Major-General Arbuthnot over the issue of stable-jackets. The offences were arranged under the heading of six different charges, each of which alleged 'conduct unbecoming the character of an officer and a gentleman'. The papers were forwarded to the Horse Guards and arrangements were made for a general court-martial at Cork, which was to begin in December 1833 and continue into the new year. Whatever else might be alleged against Lieutenant-Colonel Lord Brudenell, he was not one to draw back on the brink of action. Indeed there were those who felt that this time he had gone over the brink, in every sense of the phrase.[16]

The court-martial opened in Cork on 23 December 1833, and created a sensation in the press which had hardly been paralleled in military affairs since the end of the Napoleonic wars. As courtroom drama, it could hardly have been better. Major-General Sir John Buchan sat as President with fourteen other officers, including the commanders of the 4th and 7th Dragoon Guards. The members of the court were immaculate in full dress uniform with swords. They sat along one side of a long table in the improvised courtroom of Cork barracks, attended by a civilian lawyer, David Walker, who acted as Deputy Judge Advocate-General. To one side of them, at a little table, sat Captain Wathen, deprived of his sword, but the very picture of courage, worthiness and affronted honour. At another little table, on the far side, sat the prosecutor, Lieutenant-Colonel Lord Brudenell, handsome, arrogant and vindictive. Every newspaper correspondent who could attend, and every spectator who could be squeezed into the room, seemed eager for one of the most bizarre trials of the century.

The majority of those who read the extensive press reports of the case regarded the cavalry regiments, in all their peacock splendour, with a blend of fascination and disapproval. In either view, such a prodigious washing of dirty linen before the newspaper public made excellent copy. Yet to Lord Brudenell's supporters the proceedings soon took on an ominous tone. The Northamptonshire election had been something of a routine duty, but it now became obvious that, when speaking in public on matters so dear to him as the honour and discipline of his regiment, he was quite incapable of hiding his true feelings. When, in his opening address to the court, he stood erect in his splendid scarlet and gold uniform to describe how Captain Wathen had opposed and thwarted him, he seemed to relive all his previous anger, and his voice rose to an indignant shout. At other times, he appeared to be overcome with emotion and seemed to shed tears. It was a display which appalled his friends and delighted the growing number of his enemies.

Lord Brudenell called Sir Thomas Arbuthnot and a procession of other witnesses in an attempt to prove that Wathen's men had never complained about the issue of stable-jackets but that the Captain had made up the story in order to disparage his commanding officer. Both Sergeant Walter Clarkson and Corporal John Denby of Wathen's troop swore that their Captain had not told the truth in saying that his men complained. There had been no complaints in the troop. However, when Wathen cross-examined Corporal Denby he produced a quite unexpected piece of evidence. Denby had been courting a girl called Amelia Teeter, and had unguardedly told her that Wathen had stopped his promotion and that, in his turn, he would stop the Captain's. It seemed likely that Wathen owed this information to his wife and that Lady Wathen had coaxed it out of the girl. At all events, its effect was to destroy Denby's story. Brudenell's NCOs were assumed to be giving evidence to the court on his behalf in expectation of being promoted afterwards by their grateful Lieutenant-Colonel.

Independent witnesses, like Major Sir Walter Scott, readily agreed with Wathen that such practices as the secret writing down of officers' conversations were 'most painful and revolting'. Lord Brudenell rose to the bait at once. Having produced Scott as one of his own witnesses, he now disowned him in front of the court, accusing him of 'private feelings of hostility towards me', of which he had been 'totally unaware' until that moment. To a later generation, accustomed to such novels as Herman Wouk's *The Caine Mutiny*, it might have seemed on this occasion that Lord Brudenell was showing the classic symptoms of paranoia. However, in 1833 the question for the court-martial to decide was whether Wathen was a born rebel or whether his Lieutenant-Colonel was a born persecutor.[17]

Throughout the dark and wintry days of early January, the court met by candlelight in the crowded barrack courtroom. It was on 13 January that the prisoner rose to address the President and the other members in his own defence. It was said that his speech had been written for him by Lady Wathen, but at all events it was a model specimen of advocacy. Throughout, he was modest and forgiving, hoping that in defending his own honour he would not be guilty of casting the least slur upon his prosecutor. It was not his aim to be vindictive but only to clear his name and reputation, which must be the dearest ambition of any soldier. When he came to describe his previous military career, he produced testimonials and good wishes from some of the most respected regimental commanders in the British army. And, of course, he described his presence at Waterloo. As he did so, in his quiet and dignified way, it was reported that old soldiers in the courtroom wept silently at the sight of so fine a man and so courageous a soldier standing before them, ignominiously deprived of his sword and of his honour by his aristocratic persecutor. The lines of the verse were not spoken, but no incantation was needed to invoke the Waterloo magic.

> Were you at Waterloo?
> I have been at Waterloo.
> 'Tis no matter what you do,
> If you've been at Waterloo.

There was no need to ask where the young Lord Brudenell had been on 18 June 1815, when so many brave men had given their lives for their country. The press had been busily spreading the answer to that particular question ever since the Wathen affair became public.

Captain Wathen spoke for well over two hours. On 16 January, Lord Brudenell replied, making his third address altogether. After that the proceedings were over, since courts-martial did not retire to consider their verdict immediately. It was usually two or three weeks before their findings and the verdict were announced from the Horse Guards. In this case, there was no doubt that Captain Wathen had done most of the things alleged against him. Major-General Sir Thomas Arbuthnot had himself prepared a separate report 'describing in the *strongest possible* terms the extreme impropriety of that officer's conduct' during the two days of the inspection. The question for the court was whether such conduct constituted a breach of the Articles of War, as the army's disciplinary code was called. The issue was complicated by the extraordinary behaviour of Lord Brudenell during the proceedings, and by revelations of a state of hostilities in the 15th Hussars which no other regimental commander had ever been able to bring about.

It was at the beginning of February 1834 that the first news of the verdict and findings leaked out. Captain Wathen had been acquitted of all the charges against him, 'honourably' acquitted, as the Adjutant-General of the Horse Guards insisted. The full text of the finding was dispatched at once to Ireland, and arrived in Cork while Lord Brudenell and his officers were at dinner in the mess. He studied the document, and his officers studied his changing face with increasing alarm. The verdict was monstrous, but what followed was enough to choke him with rage. For he, Lieutenant-Colonel Lord Brudenell, was now accused by the Adjutant-General and the court-martial of conduct 'revolting to every proper and honourable feeling of a gentleman'. And all this merely because he had ordered a record to be kept of what went on in the regimental office.[18]

There was no acknowledgment of the efficiency and warlike determination with which he ruled the 15th Hussars. Instead, he who had sworn to make the regiment one of the glories of the British army, was condemned by the Horse Guards for having created disunion and injured the service. But worst of all, there was a succinct command from William IV himself, a single sentence which turned anger to despair. Lieutenant-Colonel Lord Brudenell was to be dismissed from the 15th Hussars.

CHAPTER 4

PISTOLS FOR TWO

1

'His Majesty has been pleased to order, that Lieutenant-Colonel Lord Brudenell shall be removed from the command of the 15th Hussars.'[1]

Brudenell, who had been assured by his friends in the regiment that Captain Wathen would be either cashiered or 'in some way degraded in the service', read the Adjutant-General's message with an expression of incredulity. He had brought the prosecution against Wathen, as he understood it, with the backing of General Arbuthnot. But there was even worse to come. Lord Hill, as Commander-in-Chief, had added an order that the news of Lord Brudenell's disgrace should be read out at the head of the 15th Hussars, and of every other regiment in the King's service.

Though dinner was not yet finished, Brudenell got to his feet and rushed from the mess-room, muttering something about having to see the General. As an afterthought, he ordered a messenger to be sent at once to Fermoy to fetch back Major Courtney Phillips, the nearest available field officer, who would have to take command of the regiment in the absence of its Lieutenant-Colonel. As the puzzled junior officers finished their dinner, more of Brudenell's instructions were issued from the orderly room. The next day's cavalry exercise was cancelled and in its place there was to be a parade of all officers at 7.30 a.m.

Some suspicion of the truth grew among the captains and sub-alterns, when at midnight with rain falling heavily and the roads of southern Ireland almost impassable, Lord Brudenell mounted his horse and rode out of the barracks at a gallop towards Fermoy. Through the rain and the total darkness of the country lanes and tracks, he crossed the hills and rode down into the town. From Fermoy, he crossed a further range of hills and stopped the morning coach for Dublin near Clonmel. To have covered the sixty miles at night and in such conditions was, if nothing else, a considerable feat of horsemanship. As the 15th Hussars heard the findings of the Wathen court-martial, Brudenell continued his hectic journey by the Dublin stage, which arrived in the city that night. Lady Brudenell had sailed for Bristol two days earlier, and her husband followed almost at once.

Lord Brudenell's town house, in Carlton House Terrace, was equally well-placed for the Horse Guards or the fire-blackened remains of the Houses of Parliament. Believing that he had been caught between 'a Conservative Horse Guards and a Whig Government under Lord Grey', he decided to confront them both. He demanded, and got, interviews with Lord Hill at the Horse Guards, with Lord Melbourne, the Home Secretary, and with Lord John Russell. Lord Hill probably would have helped the angry young Lieutenant-Colonel but could not. Having held his post as Commander-in-Chief since Wellington became Prime Minister in 1828, this comfortable old Tory saw himself cast for a moderate and uncontroversial role in military affairs, at a time when the army was politically unpopular. To reinstate Lord Brudenell was the surest way of bringing political uproar and public debate to the calm of the Horse Guards, from whose windows 'Daddy' Hill could watch the cattle grazing in St James's Park.[2]

Lord Melbourne, an indolent but affable Home Secretary with an engaging habit of receiving important visitors while shaving, was a Whig by name and a Conservative by nature in the Grey government. He might have no objection in principle to helping Brudenell, but for a fear of political unpopularity and a hope of becoming Prime Minister before the year was out. That Brudenell should then have approached Lord John Russell, champion of the Reform Bill, is some measure of his desperation.

All this time, correspondence streamed between Carlton House Terrace and the Horse Guards, as Brudenell continued to draw official and royal attention to the injustice which had been done him. The first recipient of most of these protests was Lord Fitzroy Somerset, Secretary to the Horse Guards. Somerset, later Lord Raglan, was a youngish Major-General who had lost an arm while serving on Wellington's staff at Waterloo. A rather diffident, though pleasant, personality, he was in private a resolute defender of the army's rights against its Radical critics. His political sympathies lay with Brudenell, whom he was later to hold in high regard as a soldier.

When Brudenell's first interview with Lord Hill proved fruitless, he wrote to Somerset on 14 February 1834, 'to urge another request upon the attention of the General Commanding-in-Chief'. Since he had been condemned in the findings of the Wathen court-martial for 'practices revolting to every proper and honourable feeling of a gentleman', let such allegations be proved or rebutted by a court-martial on himself. The same day, he addressed a memorial to William IV, making the same demand of the King and complaining that he, Brudenell, 'has yet to learn that the assignment of discreditable motives . . . by vague and indefinite phrases, is either prescribed by custom or sanctioned by justice'. Before either of the two demands could be answered, he followed them up by insisting that even if it were technically impossible to court-martial him, at least a court of inquiry should be set up to investigate the whole affair.[3]

Lord Hill, appalled at the prospect of a second public performance by Lord Brudenell, either before a court-martial or a court of inquiry, advised the King to dismiss the request. On 22 February, a message was brought across to Carlton House Terrace from the Horse Guards. It was from Lord Fitzroy Somerset, conveying the King's refusal to allow a court-martial or an inquiry. However, the King acknowledged that the evidence at the Wathen court-martial seemed 'less unfavourable' to Brudenell than the court had allowed. Above all, the King was impressed by the fierce young Hussar's newly acquired 'temperate and judicious manner'. Brudenell replied sharply that the language of the court had opened the way to 'attacks upon my character and conduct full of falsehood, of injustice, and of malignity'. He would bear these attacks 'with patience', so long as he was assured of being able to vindicate himself before a competent tribunal. Otherwise, his 'distress' would be aggravated, and his correspondents could imagine for themselves what might happen then.[4]

Lord Fitzroy Somerset replied quickly, emphasizing how impressed Lord Hill had been by the 'very temperate manner' of the reformed Lord Brudenell, how happy Lord Hill would be 'in the opportunity of bearing testimony thereto', if only that temperate manner were to continue. It was left to Brudenell to picture the consequences of issuing challenges or threats at this delicate stage of the exchanges.[5]

Yet there was one other public figure, a name of more significance than any other, who was now involved in the squabble. Almost as a matter of right, Brudenell took his grievance to the Duke of Wellington. Though holding no military or political appointment at the time, the Duke's influence and advice were accepted everywhere. Even after his unpopularity as the great opponent of the Reform Bill, he was, as he said, 'getting up in the market again'. So the Duke listened to Lord Brudenell's complaint and then, in blunter terms, gave him the same advice as Lord Hill had done, telling him to 'remain quiet' for the time being, if he intended to have any further military career. It seemed that the 'quietness' was to last for a year or so, until the public had forgotten the Wathen episode. Then means might be found of doing something for Lord Brudenell.[6]

The return of the heir to Deene was something less than a hero's homecoming. John Drakard, the veteran Radical publisher, had not forgotten their last encounter. Then Brudenell, in a violent rage at Drakard's libels upon him, had ridden to Northampton, hunted out the unfortunate publisher, and horsewhipped him in the public view on the town racecourse. Now *Drakard's Stamford News* greeted the dismissed commander with the assurance that his disgrace would be 'hailed with delight', and his conduct with 'universal disgust'. Even by the despised moral values of the army, Brudenell seemed 'as deficient in military valour as he is in the celebrity of his military career'. Returning to the affair of the horsewhipping, the aggrieved old journalist added warningly, 'We could say more upon the meanness of demeanour which has characterized Lord Brudenell but we are averse to mix up private injury with public matters.'[7]

Brudenell's disgrace was welcomed with prim satisfaction by his more earnest critics and with warm enthusiasm by his Radical enemies. Regarding him as congenitally stupid and easily provoked, they found him the perfect aristocratic victim for their baiting. Strutting like 'a game cock trimmed and spurred', as John Mills described him, he was easily made a figure of fun. Yet Brudenell had his own estimate of the hostile journalists. One fought a gentleman, but one horsewhipped a libellous scribbler.[8]

There was plenty of scribbling. Yet much as Brudenell's fingers may have itched to thrash the editors of the *Morning Chronicle* or the *Stamford News*, he obeyed Wellington's advice to 'remain quiet', or 'temperate', as Lord Hill preferred to call it. Indeed, this advice was confirmed in a letter which arrived at Deene from Queen Adelaide, King William's dumpy consort with her sausage-roll curls, her cautious

fondness for the King's illegitimate brood of Fitzclarences, and her
fears of meeting the fate of Marie Antoinette at the hands of the
English Radicals. The letter of sympathy for old Lord Cardigan's
family also refers to Brudenell's eldest sister, Harriet, Countess
Howe.[9]

> The King begg'd me to say that he feels most deeply with his
> family, laments the Events which have taken place, but cannot do
> anything for Ld. B. *at present*. But I am certain he is *most* anxious
> to serve him. Tell Lady H. from me to *entreat* her brother to
> bear his trials patiently at present and things may become better
> for him but any violent act of his might make his case much
> worse than it is and could do no good. Assure her also how much
> the K. and I feel for her and Ld. B. on this occasion and how
> sorry we are for what has happened.

The prospects for the future might be even more hopeful than the
letter suggested, since Harriet's husband, Lord Howe, had been
Chamberlain to Queen Adelaide, and though forced out of his place
by Lord Grey for opposition to the Reform Bill, he had remained at
court as the Queen's friend. More than a friend, some said. 'Oh Lord
Howe, wonderful are thy ways', murmured Lord Alvanley, when a
false rumour spread that the Queen was pregnant.[10]

The command of the 15th Hussars passed to Lieutenant-Colonel
Lovell Badcock, but though deprived of his regiment Lord Brudenell
still held his rank in the army as a half-pay officer, unattached to any
unit. Moreover, the months of 'quiet' had their political diversions.
Lord Grey's government split in July 1834 over the question of imposing a Coercion Act upon Ireland. William IV sent for Lord Melbourne,
who agreed to form a government, though now that he was actually
faced with being Prime Minister he thought the whole thing 'a
damned bore'. At least it was not a prolonged bore, since his
administration was rather peremptorily dismissed by the King in
November, and the Duke of Wellington was called in until Sir Robert
Peel could be fetched back from Italy. However, Peel's Conservative
administration was a minority government, and by January 1835 there
had to be a general election.

In Northamptonshire's Northern Division, there were two seats
and two candidates, Lord Milton and Lord Brudenell, Whig and
Conservative respectively. After the hatred and violence of the 1832

contest, it seemed that gentlemanly feelings had prevailed. On 13 January 1835, in bright winter sunshine, the rival processions of the two candidates, preceded by brass bands and banners, moved through the flag-hung streets of Kettering from the White Hart Hotel to the market place, where a platform with a booth upon it had been erected. Brudenell was hissed and jeered by a large section of the crowd as he passed by, though the farmers cheered him as a man who stood for protection and guaranteed corn prices. Every window overlooking the market place was 'thronged with ladies', eager for a sight of the handsome young Lieutenant-Colonel of dragoons who had been the cause of so much scandal. As he passed beneath their windows they cheered him repeatedly and Brudenell, looking up, gallantly acknowledged their appreciation.[11]

For all that, Brudenell's proposer and seconder were almost inaudible through the hissing and groaning of his opponents. When one of them managed to make heard the claim that Brudenell was 'a gallant defender of his country', a voice from the crowd roared back, 'Captain Wathen, to wit!' and there was turmoil again. Brudenell got up and said how good it was that the King had dismissed the Whigs. 'Yes, and disgraced you!' roared the crowd. And so it went on until Brudenell rather lamely asserted that Conservative principles were 'daily' becoming more popular, and then sat down among groans, hisses, and shouts of, 'You know better!'[12]

As a first public appearance since the Wathen affair it was hardly a vindication of Brudenell's popularity. He was, of course, carried shoulder-high round Kettering by his own party and fêted by supporters first at the White Hart and then at the George. Yet it was all a synthetic and ludicrous celebration of having won an uncontested election.

But though there had been no opponent for Brudenell's seat, there had been an anti-Brudenell and anti-Conservative influence at work in Northamptonshire. It was none other than Dr Thomas Arnold, Headmaster of Rugby, and patenter of that most popular product of Victorian upper-class education, the Christian Gentleman. Neither by nature nor by reputation did Lord Brudenell match Dr Arnold's ideal. In any case, the complete Christian Gentleman would probably have to be a Whig or a Liberal. Arnold's influence in Warwickshire and neighbouring Northamptonshire was growing and had to be discredited.

If a man could not be physically disabled, then the custom of British nineteenth-century elections was to destroy his character. The chosen weapon in this case was the *Northampton Herald*, the organ of local Conservatism generally and Lord Brudenell specifically. So, in defence of Brudenell, the *Herald* revealed the secret vice of Dr Arnold, which was a mania for whipping little boys. With appropriate examples, the *Herald* showed that once the fit seized him, it mattered little whether the boy was guiltless or even disabled. When it discussed Arnold's political arguments, the paper did so in images of his alleged obsession.[13]

> No mortal man is half so arbitrary, or half so ludicrously consequential as your Whig pedagogue . . . nothing so contracts the mind, or so warps the judgment as the command of a rod in such hands. Such a man has no idea of an opponent in politics or in religion, except as a boy to be disbreeched and placed in a passive attitude on a flogging block.

With this image of the good doctor planted firmly in the public mind, the *Herald* and the Brudenell party could lay to rest the election of 1835. By the standard of the time, it had been a good clean fight.

After so much 'remaining quiet', it seemed to Lord Brudenell that the time must have come for him to be given another regiment. It was some mark of royal favour that he had been invited to hunt with the King's staghounds in the New Forest in 1835. One of the other guests, Assheton-Smith, was a first-rate horseman and Brudenell chose this occasion to show that he, as a rider, could 'cut down' Assheton-Smith or anyone else who needed 'cutting down'. Throughout dinner on the eve of the hunt, the two men sat glaring at one another. On the following morning, Brudenell set off after the hounds, as if riding a race. For all that Assheton-Smith attempted, he could not get past Brudenell, who scornfully rode both his rival and his rival's horse to a standstill. It was, perhaps, the most satisfying day of the whole year. No uncontested election, with or without Dr Arnold, could compare with the pleasure of annihilating the prestige of one of the finest horsemen in England.[14]

In June, the *Naval and Military Gazette* reported that Brudenell was to be given command of the 90th by an exchange with Lieutenant-Colonel Arbuthnot. 'We have repeatedly alluded to the harsh proceedings adopted towards this gallant and talented nobleman', added the *Gazette*, 'and we should rejoice in his restoration to the service.' Nothing came of the rumour, though Brudenell visited the Horse Guards, convinced that there could no longer be any reasonable objection to his reinstatement. Lord Melbourne would not object, nor would the rest of the Whig administration, which had succeeded Peel's government soon after the January election.[15]

With growing impatience, Brudenell wrote to Wellington, intimating that his period of 'remaining quiet' was now over, and that it was high time that the Horse Guards, Wellington, and everyone else, should fulfil their obligations towards him. 'You entirely misunderstood me', replied the Duke bluntly, 'if you suppose that I ever fixed, in my own mind, much less stated to another, a period after which you should be recalled.' As for the notion that the present Prime Minister and his cabinet had forgiven the arrogant young dragoon, Wellington briskly scouted that. 'I cannot but think you are mistaken respecting the feelings and sentiments of the Ministers in your case.'[16]

Having been carefully snubbed in almost every other quarter, Brudenell finally brought his influence to bear upon that scene of rather dowdy country-house life, which constituted the court of William IV. Here he had a strong ally in his favourite sister, Harriet, the eldest, tallest, and most beautiful of the Brudenell girls. She was likely to be a good advocate, being as strong-minded in her way as her adored and adoring brother. From religious conviction, she spent her Sundays in seclusion. When William IV arranged an outing for that day, she abruptly refused to go. Queen Adelaide was astonished and urged that even she would not have refused the King. 'Madam,' said Harriet firmly, 'his Majesty is *your* husband.'[17]

At Harriet's insistence, the Queen accompanied her to plead Lord Brudenell's case before the King. But William remained unmoved by their entreaties and tears. Much as he dreaded these scenes, he knew from past confrontations that Lord Melbourne and even Lord Hill at the Horse Guards could be obstructive. If he had to squabble with them, it would not be over so unpromising a case as that of Lieutenant-Colonel Lord Brudenell.

The news that came back to Carlton House Terrace was not encouraging, but Brudenell had other friends at court, one of whom was as close to William IV as the Queen herself. Lord Adolphus Fitzclarence was a hunting friend of Brudenell's and seventh of the King's ten illegitimate children by the actress Dorothy Jordan. Adolphus had now been given command of the royal yacht, a task in which he distinguished himself by losing his way in the North Sea and mis-judging the harbour of Rotterdam, so that the Dutch royal yacht had to be sent out to take off the Queen.

To all these voices around the King was added the appearance of the old Earl of Cardigan himself, who had begged William IV for a private audience. To him, the disgrace of the family in the dismissal of his heir was a grief not to be overcome. Making the most of a father's last effort to save his erring son, the 'venerable old Earl' was reported to have thrown himself upon his knees before the King, and 'implored his Majesty to wipe off the disgrace which had been inflicted on his family by the forced resignation of his heir. The tears of the aged nobleman effected what we are assured others had attempted in vain.'[18]

William IV, that most affable of English monarchs, whose less regal habits still included spitting out of the window of the royal coach and wiping his nose on the back of his forefinger, was won over by the sight of the old man's despair. He raised the Earl to his feet, and talked comfortingly to him. Having on previous occasions refused to interfere with what he called 'Lord Hill's righteous judgment', he now went so far as to say that 'if Lord Hill advised with him', he would give his 'favourable consideration' to the case. The old Lord Cardigan went to the Horse Guards and Lord Hill went to St James's Palace. Hill was hesitant, but the King seemed to have made his wishes clear and, after all, the tranquillity of the Horse Guards might best be preserved by yielding to royal whims. So Lord Hill gave way, remarking, 'I have consented to this step because I am unable to endure the distress of this noble family, and because I hope the author of their distress is now sensible that he cannot be permitted to follow the dictates of his ungovernable temper. I trust this lesson has not been thrown away.'[19]

There followed some months of formal courtesies. On 19 January 1836, Lord Brudenell paid an official visit to Lord Fitzroy Somerset at the Horse Guards. Two days later he was back again to attend Lord Hill's Thursday morning levee. In private he began to drum up more support for his cause by writing to a number of senior army officers and inviting them to comment upon his case. Some of them may have been taken aback when their replies were published and copied in the newspapers. However there was a general feeling in the army that the young Lieutenant-Colonel of the 15th Hussars had been too harshly condemned in 1834. Lieutenant-General Lord Stafford now offered to defend him if anyone should criticize his reappointment. Major-General Sir Frederick Ponsonby, approached twice, gave it as the opinion of officers of all ranks that the severity shown against Lord Brudenell had gone far enough. Sir Hussey Vivian, Master General of Ordnance, wrote via Sir Henry Hardinge that he would be delighted to see Lord Brudenell reinstated, and had said as much to Lord Melbourne.

By this time, Lord Melbourne, Lord Hill and the King may all have decided that there was more to be endured by resisting Brudenell's demands than by yielding to them. They would have been wrong, but they were men inclined to whatever course of action offered a prospect of immediate calm and leisure. Therefore, on 30 March 1836, a tall, slim Lieutenant-Colonel of Hussars, golden-haired and splendidly moustached, a pugnacious glitter in his blue eyes, strode into a royal levee in St James's Palace. The decision had been taken.

The regiment was the 11th Light Dragoons, which had been in India since 1819, stationed at Meerut and Cawnpore. The price paid was reported as £40,000, the entire annual income from the rents of the Earl of Cardigan. When the lieutenant-colonelcy of a cavalry regiment could command such a sum, it was as well for Lord Brudenell that he was, as the *United Service Gazette* described him, heir to 'one of the most princely fortunes of the British empire'.[20]

In the moment of silence before the storm broke, *The Times* hopefully suggested that the House of Commons should not interfere in 'the official responsibility of the Commander-in-Chief, in the distribution of military employment'. On the other hand, said the paper, Lord Hill should be held responsible for ensuring that Lord Brudenell's future behaviour was better than his past.[21]

It would not do. From the *Morning Chronicle* and the Radical press came a burst of carefully-meditated outrage. The *Chronicle* was aghast at Brudenell's appointment, in view of 'the unfitness of his Lordship to command a regiment'. The editor deplored a political system which allowed Lord Hill to make such a choice without the permission of either the House of Commons or the cabinet. Remembering its allegiance to the Whig administration, the *Chronicle* observed piously, 'It is quite clear that Ministers would never have given a regiment to Lord Brudenell.' Lord Hill and the Horse Guards must be brought under the control of the elected representatives of the people.[22]

The Conservative press, led by the *Morning Post*, rallied to justify both Hill and Brudenell. 'Party passions have long laboured to blight the character and mar the prospects of a brave and honourable man', said the *Post* of Brudenell, and this was certainly true. It was Lord Brudenell's disadvantage to be a Conservative, added the *Post*. Suppose he had been a Whig or a Radical, and suppose he had been similarly dismissed from his command in 1834. What would the *Morning Chronicle* and Radical politicians have said then? 'What a story would this have been for the Roebucks and the Wakleys! How would Sir William Molesworth have denounced the atrocious tyranny of the Horse Guards!' This was no doubt true, but when the *Post* went on to describe Lord Brudenell's meekness under censure, how in his modesty 'he impugns no man's motives; he courts no man's favour', this must have provoked derisive laughter in St James's Palace and the Horse Guards.[23]

Two of the most celebrated Radicals in the House of Commons began a campaign to stop Lord Brudenell's appointment. One, Sir William Molesworth, was a wealthy young man who loved the human race in principle rather more than he liked any of its members in practice. The other, Joseph Hume, was a veteran Scots Radical, of whom it was said that he spoke 'longer, oftener, and worse', than any other private Member of the House of Commons. Molesworth, seconded by Hume, brought forward a motion demanding a select committee to 'inquire into the conduct of the Commander of the Forces in appointing Lieutenant-Colonel Lord Brudenell to the Lieutenant-Colonelcy of the 11th Light Dragoons'.

On the evening of 3 May, when the motion was to be debated, Lord Brudenell took his place in the makeshift House of Commons, which consisted of a large committee room that had survived between the Thames and the ruined walls of the old Houses of Parliament, destroyed by fire in 1834. Though the massed candles glowed on oak panelling and benches covered with green leather, there was only a small iron-railed gallery above and no thick hangings behind which, in the old days, elderly members could sleep undisturbed and from which younger members emitted cock crows and horselike whinnyings when they decided that it was time for the night's proceedings to end.

As the earlier debates on the evening of 3 May were concluded the House began to fill and when Sir William Molesworth rose there were almost four hundred members present. He spoke long, and for most of the time rather badly, apparently uncertain whether to attack Brudenell, Hill, or simply Hill's action in reinstating Brudenell. His supporters dutifully called out, 'Hear, hear!' at regular intervals but only towards the end of his speech did he make a point which, though not particularly relevant to his own motion, was of the greatest relevance to the officers of the 11th Light Dragoons.[24]

> A more gallant regiment does not exist in his Majesty's service, nor one that has better served its country—in Egypt, in the Peninsula, at Waterloo, with the army of occupation in France, thence, seventeen years ago, to India, at Bhurtpore, and elsewhere, it has distinguished itself. Some of its officers have been nearly as many years in the army as the Noble Lord has lived years in this world. The two majors have served with this regiment since the years 1806 and 1811. With what feelings will they view the advancement over their heads of this young officer, who has never heard the sound of a musket, except in the mimic combats of a review; who entered the army in 1824, with unexampled rapidity obtained an unattached lieutenant-colonelcy in 1830, in 1832 the command of a regiment, in 1834, two years afterwards, was removed from that command for alleged misconduct,—and now in 1836, two years more, is deemed the fittest and most proper person to command their regiment?

Joseph Hume seconded the motion and then Lord Brudenell rose. With a personal charm which he showed more easily in the presence of the opposite sex, rather than in all-male assemblies, he made a moderate and sensible speech. Those who had read of him only through the *Morning Chronicle* would have been particularly impressed, while the hearts of Molesworth and Hume grew heavy. They had been promised an arrogant, swaggering young dragoon, who was guaranteed to be congenitally stupid and a prime target for their attack. What they had was a modest, debonair young man, who spoke moderately and argued sensibly. He humbly accepted the verdict of the Wathen court-martial and his own responsibility in the affair. Yet he showed by documentary evidence that officers dismissed as he had been were usually reinstated after a period, and there was no indication that his own removal had ever been intended as permanent. To this appeal, he added letters from senior army officers supporting his new appointment. The Commons warmed to him, and even began to cheer. Finally, Lord Brudenell tactfully proposed to withdraw from the House so that the members might continue to discuss his case as freely as they wished.[25]

> Before I withdraw, I must return my best thanks to the House for the kind attention with which it has listened to my statement of details, which must necessarily be very uninteresting to a great majority of the House, but which to me is of the greatest importance, as being intimately connected with my honour and character as a soldier and a gentleman.

As he withdrew from the chamber, he was loudly cheered on all sides, and the applause lasted for some time after he had actually left. For Molesworth and Hume, the initiative was irretrievably lost. They had been manoeuvred into an impossible position, and were left to reflect that perhaps, in political skirmishes, experience of cavalry tactics might be as relevant as superior intellect. Hume got up, after Brudenell's dignified and triumphant withdrawal, but even his most valid points began to sound carping and small-minded. He was interrupted constantly by cries of 'Oh!' and 'Divide!' Sir Henry Hardinge, for Brudenell, was loudly and almost continuously applauded. Molesworth tried to withdraw the motion before it was taken to a division. 'The Noes have it', said the Speaker. But one of Brudenell's supporters, Captain the Honourable Cecil Forester, of the Blues, immediately shouted, 'The Ayes have it.' Not that he wanted the Ayes to have it, but this was a way of forcing a vote. The vote was taken. Forty-two members were for Molesworth's motion and three hundred and twenty-two for Lord Brudenell's reappointment.

The *Morning Chronicle* was furious that its parliamentary protégés should have been so heavily and publicly defeated. It rounded on Forester and Brudenell's friends who had forced the vote, when the Radicals wanted to withdraw the motion. 'Young gentlemen of fashion', said the *Chronicle* bitterly, 'who are in the habit of sneering at the business-like habits and plebeian vulgarity of the real representatives of the people.'[26]

Arrangements had been made for Lord Brudenell to sail to India in HMS *Tyne* but his departure was delayed, in the first instance, by the Commons debate. This was perhaps as well, since after an unhappy voyage as far as Malta, the *Tyne* had to be laid up while the numerous colonies of rats were smoked out of the ship.

By the end of May, it was rumoured that Brudenell would not be going to India at all but would stay in England and join his new regiment on its return, in a year or two. This report in the *United Service*

Gazette provided some sardonic amusement for those who recalled that only two weeks earlier the same paper had been singing Brudenell's praises as a man who had deliberately volunteered to serve in India, 'whose climate is even more fatal to Europeans than the chances of war, and more feared than the dangers of the battle-field.'[27]

However, the new Lieutenant-Colonel of the 11th Light Dragoons was heavily engaged for the London season and was a guest at a drawing room held by the Queen on 28 May in honour of the King's birthday. In the courtyard of St James's Palace, the Life Guards were drawn up in their state uniforms and the band of the Foot Guards played. Even under William IV and Queen Adelaide, the glitter and gossip of the London season was a stronger attraction than a dusty exile on the banks of the Ganges. Finally, on 9 July, it was announced that Lord Brudenell 'intends to join overland, to avoid the monotony of a sea voyage'. With any luck, he might arrive just as the 11th Light Dragoons were about to start for home. In August it was suggested that he might like to accompany the newly appointed Governor of Madras, Lord Elphinstone, in the yacht *Prince Regent,* which was being sent as a present from William IV to the Imam of Muscat. Nothing came of this, which was fortunate, since the Imam sulked and raged on receiving his present, because it was not, as he had been led to hope, a *steam* yacht.[28]

In September, Lord and Lady Brudenell travelled to Dover and crossed to France, where they were guests of the French Dauphin, the young Duc d'Orléans, at a lavish military review at Compiègne. From there they travelled to Italy, from Italy to Malta, and so to Alexandria. Even without a canal the first steamships, which began operating between Suez and Bombay at the time of the Brudenells' arrival, had made this the fashionable route to India. It involved a bone-shaking dash across fifty miles of the Isthmus of Suez in a vehicle which looked rather like a horse-drawn omnibus with canopies projecting over the windows. Finding that a coal ship had just unloaded, Brudenell promptly hired this unlikely vessel to carry him and his wife to Bombay. The boat moved sluggishly through the fierce, prickling heat of the Red Sea, taking seventy-three days to reach Bombay. Its passengers had ample time to realize that a short sea route was hardly preferable unless it was also fast.

In nineteenth-century British India, the arrival of Lieutenant-Colonel Lord Brudenell to take command of the 11th Light Dragoons offered a rare social, as well as military, opportunity. Sir Robert Grant, Governor of Bombay, had retired to the Mallemista Hills, but Porell Palace, just outside the city, was put at Brudenell's disposal and he was entertained 'with great hospitality' by Sir John Keene, Commander-in-Chief of the Bombay Presidency. The Brudenells spent several weeks in Bombay, visiting Kirkee and Poona, before hiring a small boat to take them down the coast of India and round the tip of Ceylon to Madras. At Madras they found another eager host, Lord Elphinstone, who insisted on taking them over the presidencies of Madras and Mysore, as well as to Seringapatam and the ruins of the fort which Wellington, as a young Colonel, had helped to storm in 1799. From Madras, Brudenell hired a private boat for Calcutta, where yet another reception was prepared by the Governor-General, Lord Auckland, who had provided apartments for the Brudenells in Fort William. Even on the final stage of their journey up the Ganges to Cawnpore, the steamer had only got to Allahabad when they were detained for two weeks as the guests of the Civil Governor.

During the wanderings of the Brudenells, the 11th Light Dragoons had been ordered home from their eighteen years in India. When their new commander arrived in the autumn of 1837, more than a twelvemonth after setting out from Dover, his regiment was within a few weeks of moving out. However, as he wrote with a flourish of satisfaction, 'I got the command of the 11th Light Dragoons at once from Colonel Brutton, who retired from the service. I thus gained my object without the slightest assistance from the Horse Guards, and I here had the command of a Brigade in the field—the 11th and two native regiments.'[29]

Raised by Phillip Honywood in 1715 to defend the newly-installed George I against the threat of a Stuart invasion, the 11th Light Dragoons was a regiment which had seen its due share of battles. As 'Honywood's Dragoons' at Preston, and as 'Lord Mark Kerr's Dragoons' at Culloden, it had fought for George I and George II against the armies of the Pretender and his son, Charles Edward. After the second Jacobite uprising, when the officers of the British army were required to show their loyalty to the House of Hanover by drinking the sovereign's health after dinner in the mess, an exception was made for the 11th Dragoons. Because of their service to the Crown, they were given and retained the privilege of never drinking the loyal toast and of remaining seated when their regimental band played the national anthem. The names upon their regimental standards—'Egypt', 'Salamanca' (added in 1840), 'Peninsula', 'Waterloo', 'Bhurtpore'—gave some indication of the battle honours which the 11th Dragoons had earned. In the last of these engagements, in 1825, eighty men of the regiment and eighty men from the 16th Lancers had volunteered to storm the defences of the citadel of Bhurtpore, held by the usurper Doorjun Saul against the British-protected heir of the dead Rajah. Colonel Brutton, who had been a Major in the regiment at that time, was mentioned in Lord Combermere's dispatches for his 'conspicuous gallantry on numerous occasions' in the heat and slaughter. No wonder that some members of the regiment failed to share the jubilation of Lord Brudenell, the St James's Street hussar, at having 'got the command' from Colonel Brutton. Brudenell's popularity was not helped when it became known that Brutton's only official recompense for all his service was a pension of £100 in recognition of the number of times he had been wounded in action. Of those who remained in the regiment under Lord Brudenell, both the Majors, Jenkins and Rotton, and the Riding-Master, Lieutenant Bambrick, were among that select and diminishing band of warriors who wore the coveted Waterloo Medal.

Yet there was another side to the coin. Brudenell's enemies were quick to maintain that the 11th Light Dragoons had been a fine and a happy regiment until he assumed command. The truth is rather broader. Army life in India was often a hell on earth for both officers and men. It brought out the worst in soldiers of every rank. As Brudenell arrived in India, the tensions within his 'brigade' provoked Lieutenant Rose of the 11th Dragoons to quarrel with Lieutenant Frazer in command of the 7th Native Light Cavalry. Insisting that this was an affair of honour, Rose challenged his adversary to a duel, in the best Dragoon tradition. Pistols were produced and the two men shot at each other until a bullet from Frazer's gun smashed Rose's thigh bone. Honour was satisfied.[30]

Lieutenant Forrest of the 11th was more fortunate. After a 'misunderstanding' at a regimental ball at Meerut, he insisted on calling out an officer of the Cameronians. Once on the 'field of honour', however, the marksmanship of both duellists proved so abysmal that neither could hit the other. In 1837, when they were shipped back to England, the transport carrying the men had to put into Table Bay for two of their officers to go ashore and settle a matter of 'honour'.

'One was hit in the leg, not dangerously', reported the *United Service Gazette*.[31]

Less belligerent comrades, especially when left alone in charge of Native Infantry or Native Cavalry, were often quick to take to the bottle. There was a steady succession of courts-martial on officers for being on duty in a state of *delirium tremens* or, as in the case of Lieutenant De Fountain, for getting aggressively drunk and having to be forcibly ejected from another officer's quarters where they were making a nuisance of themselves. Typical of cases of this sort, at the time of Lord Brudenell's arrival in India, was that of Lieutenant S. J. Carter, charged with 'having at Sedasheghar, on 6th of April 1837, when in command of a detachment of the 2nd regiment N.I., commenced a course of hard drinking, continuing the same until the 17th day of the same month, so as to render himself frequently quite senseless, and altogether unfit for duty.' To this was added an accusation of addressing Indian soldiers in indecent language and appearing on parade before them 'in a disgraceful state of intoxication'. The army could not afford to dismiss every officer who had drinking bouts in India but Carter's was a bad case and he was cashiered.[32]

Neither were some of the other reports of the army in India during 1837 more encouraging. A correspondent of the *Naval and Military Gazette* reported on 30 September, 'At the mess it is where the mask drops, and the true character appears.' At least this made it easier to get rid of undesirable soldiers, but those officers who were to spend their whole careers in India, as employees of what was then still the East India Company, seemed beneath the notice of a gentleman. Such a man 'may indulge in low propensities, *in his own bungalow*, for years, with impunity. Individuals of this class are cut by Queen's officers.' As Sir Richard Burton discovered five years later, the rarity of white women in India led to the triumph of their 'coloured sister'. 'I found every officer in the corps more or less provided with one of these helpmates.' When cousin Fred, a young army officer, boasted to the narrator of *My Secret Life* at about this time of having bought three Indian girls to entertain him in his bungalow, he was not necessarily boasting or exaggerating the truth. Indeed, the native Indian press itself had already begun to publish derogatory accounts of the dinners and balls held by British officers.[33]

> Having stuffed themselves with the unclean food and many sorts of flesh, taking plenty of wine, they made for some time a great

noise, which doubtless arose from drunkenness. They all stood up two or four times, crying 'hip! hip!' and roared before they drank more wine. After dinner they danced in their licentious manner, pulling about each other's wives. . . . Captain —— who is staying with Mr. ——, went away with the latter's lady (arm-in-arm), the palanquins following behind, and they proceeded by themselves into the bungalow; the wittol remained at table, guzzling red wine.

The behaviour of the common soldiers seemed a match for that of their officers. In Lord Brudenell's new regiment, the limelight shone most brightly on Private Samuel Gullivour who was sentenced to seven years' transportation by a court-martial at Meerut for trading in silver plate stolen to order from the regiment by its Indian servants. In general, the humidity and the rainy season led to long periods of exemption from parades, weeks spent in unenclosed barracks where it was impossible to prevent the smuggling in of spirits. The *Madras Conservative* reported on 20 September 1836 that regimental life had deteriorated still further with 'the introduction of gambling-houses, to which the soldier eagerly resorts'. The paper added that courts-martial in some regiments were now running at the rate of a dozen every month. If drinking and gaming were beyond the control of the military authorities, at least those authorities offered alternative attractions for the men. Indian women were requisitioned, as if they had been army equipment, by official requests such as that 'for extra attractive women for regimental bazaar, in accordance with Circular Memorandum 21a'. Yet 'Indian service' was not generally popular, and in February 1837, a correspondent of the *Naval and Military Gazette* summed up the general feeling of the army in India.[34]

At the present moment such is the degraded state of the army in India, and the feeling against serving in that country, that none but needy adventurers and seedy boys can be procured for the King's regiments there.

Lord Brudenell, with memories of the Life Guards in their state uniforms drawn up in the courtyard of St James's Palace, or the splendid precision of the French cavalry proudly displayed to him by the young Duc d'Orléans, was abruptly confronted with the realities of foreign service. To say that he did not like what he found is something of an understatement.

In the first place, he was presented with a regiment which was about to disintegrate. To allow for more frequent sickness and a higher proportion of invalids, regiments in India were larger than when stationed at home. Many of the 11th Dragoons knew that what awaited them at home was their discharge and, in many cases, hunger. Of the 450 men under Lord Brudenell's command, 154 volunteered to remain behind in India with other regiments. At least the slackness of military routine in India helped to compensate them for the hazards of the climate. Of some 300 men who returned to England, more than 100 faced discharge and a quarter of the officers were to be put on half-pay.

When a cavalry regiment was ordered to India, the 'fashionables' among the officers swiftly exchanged into another regiment which was remaining in England. They bought the commissions of men who were about to return with regiments from India (but who now stayed there in consequence of the exchange), or they bought commissions from those in England who had found that they could not stand the expense of soldiering at home and had no alternative but to accept an exchange and serve in the cheaper conditions of Meerut or Cawnpore. As the 11th Light Dragoons prepared to leave Cawnpore, there were officers like Harvey Tuckett, who had fought at Bhurtpore and was still a Lieutenant twelve years later, who knew that returning to England meant having to sell out to affluent and arrogant young men of the Brudenell stamp. Tuckett was already on the path to the bankruptcy court, where he arrived in 1842, and his personal hatred of the new Lieutenant-Colonel was never concealed.

Stories about Lord Brudenell's conduct on joining the regiment at Cawnpore, many of them from the pen of Lieutenant Harvey Tuckett, began to reach the offices of the Bombay newspapers. In less than a month, his lordship was said to have placed more than a hundred men on the defaulters' list and to have held eight courts-martial, though this was still fewer than some regiments were accustomed to. It was reported that he was angry at what he regarded as the lenient sentences imposed by the officers of the regiment sitting on the courts-martial. He summoned them and warned them that if they continued in their policy, he would report them to Sir Henry Fane, Commander-in-Chief in India, and to Lord Hill at the Horse Guards. That evening a trooper of 'twenty years' service' was said to have been flogged and the rest of the regiment drilled on foot for an hour afterwards.

That Lord Brudenell was hated by some of his officers was to be proved by subsequent events. That he was hated by all of them, or that he was hated by the private soldiers remains open to question. Despite the rumours that came from Cawnpore in November and December 1837, there was a different view, expressed by a correspondent to the *Naval and Military Gazette* in September 1840, when Brudenell had become Earl of Cardigan.[35]

> Ask the men of the regiment their opinion of Lord Cardigan; I'll be bound nine out of ten would say 'Give us his Lordship for a Commanding Officer;' and soldiers now-a-days are not so illiterate and undiscerning as they once were, but, for the most part, men of talent and good sound judgment. Only point out to the Hussars the abuses and tyranny used towards them in India, previous to the noble Earl taking up the command of the regiment, and they would instantly say 'Ay, Lord Cardigan did not command us then.'

As on so many other occasions Cardigan was, for many people, what their side of the press made him, a sneering and barbaric aristocrat or a noble patrician who nevertheless understood and was admired by the common man.

In December 1837 the 11th Dragoons left Cawnpore to embark for England at Calcutta. Lieutenant Tuckett's pen seemed as busy as ever. 'He wrote several slanders and calumnies about me, while the Regiment descended the Ganges', said Lord Brudenell indignantly.[36]

Brudenell himself did not 'descend the Ganges' with the regiment, having a full round of social engagements elsewhere. Travelling by dak, a carriage pulled by relays of horses or, if necessary, by relays of men, the Brudenells visited Sir Henry Fane, Commander-in-Chief, in his camp near Delhi. From there they went to view the splendours of the Taj Mahal, and then to shoot tigers with Colonel Arnold of the 16th Lancers, near Meerut. Not until the 11th Light Dragoons were ready to embark for England did their Lieutenant-Colonel return to Calcutta. He watched them board the *Repulse* and the *Thames*, an East Indiaman now somewhat the worse for wear, for the long voyage round the Cape. He inspected the vessels, and took leave of his men: 'with every good wish for a happy meeting in England, whither his Lordship intends to travel overland', said the *Calcutta Courier*. In the light of their new commander's message, on his appointment, insisting on 'order, discipline and efficiency' which he expected in those who served under him, the 200 men on board the *Thames* had an unpleasant surprise waiting as the evening came. Apart from the almost uneatable salted food, someone had forgotten to provide any hammocks or blankets and the first stage of their voyage, 700 miles to Madras, was accomplished without either beds or bedding.[37]

Five hundred Indian bearers were waiting on the road to convey the Brudenells and their effects from Calcutta to catch the Suez steamship at Bombay. However, the bearers waited in vain. A week later Lord Brudenell was still in Calcutta. While there, he attended a concert by Mrs Goodall Atkinson, to which he had been invited on the strength of his reputation as a lover of music. His host afterwards inquired eagerly how he had enjoyed the recital. 'Oh,' said Lord Brudenell disdainfully, 'you know I have just come from England, and cannot, therefore, be supposed to relish the performances of an Indian actress or singer.' There was an outraged silence. 'He forgot', said the *Indian News* indignantly, 'that Mrs. Atkinson had also come from England.' This was true, but it was also true that by the 1830s English military and civilian life in India was, for Lord Brudenell and for a great many observers, lax in its standards of behaviour and inferior in its culture.[38]

Before Lord Brudenell returned from India, he received two messages. The first was that his eldest and most beloved sister, Harriet, Countess Howe, had died suddenly in October 1836, five weeks after the birth of her last child. The other message also concerned a family bereavement and was more significant, if less poignant. On 14 August 1837, at his town house in Portman Square, Robert, 6th Earl of Cardigan, had quietly succumbed to advancing age. He had never been much in the public eye and the newspapers hardly bothered to notice his death. But without knowing it, James Thomas Brudenell had already been for several months the 7th Earl of Cardigan. It was the title by which he was to be best known and most notorious.

The Earldom of Cardigan brought with it the estate of Deene and other lands in Northamptonshire and Leicestershire, coal mines in Yorkshire and the mansion and stables in Portman Square, together with horses, carriages, wines and the other trappings of wealth accumulated over several centuries. The income from the estates was some £40,000 a year. The 7th Earl was going to need every penny of it and a great deal more beside.

On his arrival in England in June 1838, the new Lord Cardigan was forty-one years old. He remained upright and slim-waisted, the 'beau idéal' of a gallant dragoon, as his contemporaries called him. Yet he was no longer a young man in physique, much less so in disposition. The golden hair was receding a little and his voice had acquired something of a sergeant-major's bark, which impressed many of those who met him quite as much as his slightly wilting good looks.

And still the hour of glory had not come, nor was there any sign that it would. From time to time the press speculated on the possibility of war with France, but it never seemed likely. There was trouble in Canada with the American 'banditti' over the common frontier with the United States, but it came to nothing. Cardigan, the 'beau sabreur', his life devoted to preparing the finest men of the British cavalry for deeds of imperishable glory, found himself marooned in a time of peace and in the languors of middle-age. This was, of course, true of many British field officers in the twenty years or so after Waterloo but most of them adapted themselves more easily to the situation than Cardigan. Some may have consoled themselves with thoughts of what their descendants might accomplish in their place. But Cardigan was the last of his line, having no children and being most unlikely to have any at this stage of his married life.

During his absence in India there had been another death, that of William IV in June 1837. A year later Cardigan arrived in a London that was preparing for Victoria's coronation on 28 June 1838. The parks were covered with the white tents and banners of the artillery, and with a collection of booths and stalls. The hot streets were thronged with visitors and the pavements were impassable for the timbers which workmen were hammering into place to provide stands for the spectators of the royal procession. Two weeks before the coronation, the 11th Light Dragoons disembarked after their long voyage from Calcutta and began their next tour of duty at Canterbury.

Cardigan returned to Deene, and was received at a triumphal banquet by 450 Conservative gentlemen. Among all the toasts and congratulations, however, there was an unwelcome theme. His political admirers saw in the 7th Earl not the commander of some glorious cavalry action against the armies of France or Russia, but a political policeman whose dragoons would keep order among England's industrial workers or agricultural labourers. A further unintended slight came from the *United Service Gazette*, which suggested that Cardigan's most useful role would be that of speaking up for the army in the House of Lords.

Having paid £40,000 for his command, and having endured, if only briefly, the rigours of service in India, it seemed to Cardigan that he had earned some reward. He approached Wellington and suggested that the Duke might care to obtain for him a post in the household of the young Queen. The Colonelcy of the Household Cavalry, perhaps? With habitual bluntness of style, Wellington replied that such offices were only to be held by men who had seen active service. Preferment, let alone glory, seemed as far off as ever.

Though Cardigan always returned to Canterbury to muster his men on the last Thursday of the month, he spent a good deal of his time in the Shires, though not necessarily at Deene, which was in the turmoil of having all those modern comforts installed which the old 6th Earl had managed to do without. The new Earl spent part of the family fortune on costly experiments in hunting the 'carted stag'. The stags were transported to the scene of the meeting and then released. In this type of hunt it was not intended that the stag should be killed and every effort was made to prevent it happening. Stag-hounds were used principally to pick up the scent and direct the huntsmen. From 1839 until 1842, Cardigan kept a pack of stag-hounds in Leicestershire, and these became the envy of British nobility and European royalty. He also presented a complete pack to the 11th Light Dragoons while the regiment was stationed at Canterbury.

He had become, in the judgment of some of his contemporaries, perhaps the finest horseman of his day. The physical challenge which war might otherwise have presented continued to be provided by the hardest runs in Northamptonshire or the grassy uplands of High Leicestershire. He rode at fences or jumps which few other men contemplated. If he came to grief, he reacted not with the petulance and spite which his enemies attributed to him but, according to Whyte-Melville, with 'a perfect good humour and *sang froid*'. Some of the falls, however, caused sufficient concussion and paralysis to make the suppression of petulance quite involuntary. 'Unless very much hurt, however,' said Whyte-Melville, 'he was sure to show to the front again, as soon as he regained the saddle. To be "soft", as he called it, was a weakness of which he would have been heartily ashamed in himself, and sufficiently intolerant in another.'[39]

At Canterbury, the squabbles of the regiment continued. The anti-Cardigan faction informed the *Morning Herald* that he was employing 'a system of annoyance' to drive certain officers from the regiment.

'Fudge from beginning to end', said the *Naval and Military Gazette*, having discovered the author of the story. Fudge or not, Cardigan sent his second with a duelling challenge to the *Herald*'s military correspondent. It seemed, however, that the only 'military correspondent' was a retired officer who lived in the country and made a small living by editing army news for the paper. Both he and the *Herald* were eager to apologize in print.[40]

Deprived of a chance to try out the new duelling pistols made for him when he went to India, Cardigan hurried to Canterbury to confront his regimental enemies, only to find that most of his officers supported him over the *Herald* incident. Lieutenant Tuckett, having lost this particular battle, sold out and went on half-pay.

In October, about a third of the officers were enjoying 'the sports of the field and the magnificent hospitality of Deene Park'. They included Captain R. A. Reynolds. Returning to Canterbury, Cardigan provided stags, as well as hounds, and the hunts organized for his officers became one of the most prominently reported social events in the area. He was now reputed to be spending £10,000 of his annual income on the regiment, adding £10 to the sum allowed for each new horse, and preparing to spend a small fortune on having his troopers dressed by Bond Street tailors.[41]

In a remarkably short time, his enthusiasm and his insistence imposed a striking professionalism on what was, in many respects, a freshly-raised regiment. In January 1839, he entertained the Duke of Cambridge (one of the last surviving brothers of George IV) at Deene. Six months later, the Duke repaid this hospitality by reviewing the 11th Light Dragoons in the barrack field at Canterbury on 10 June, 'a day as lovely as any that ever broke from the heavens'. A crowd of 3,000 elegantly dressed ladies and gentlemen watched on foot or from their carriages. The regimental band played 'military airs' as nearly 300 troopers in their scarlet tunics advanced and manoeuvred in ceremonial and battle formations. The precision and intricacy seemed worthy of the finest riding-schools in Europe. That evening the Duke was Cardigan's guest at dinner in the mess, where the regimental silver and the finest wines that Deene or Portman Square could offer did justice to the occasion. The Duke of Wellington inspected the regiment twice in 1839, though on the second occasion he spent much of the time paying compliments to Lady Cardigan. He was not shared with the other officers but dined with Cardigan alone. Not surprisingly, when a grand dinner was given for Wellington, as

Warden of the Cinque Ports, in the autumn of 1839, it was the band of the 11th Light Dragoons which played during the meal, and it was Cardigan who sat at the principal table close to the Duke. There was no more talk of 'remaining quiet' now. The impetuous young Lord Brudenell had been forgiven.[42]

Even the major scandal of 1839 in the regiment seemed only to show that Cardigan and his officers were brothers in arms. On 5 July, six officers of the regiment, led by Captain R. A. Reynolds, had been out riding across the fields from Canterbury towards Herne Bay. On their return, they were crossing a hayfield near the barracks, when the owner's father, a miller and Radical magistrate by the name of Brent, tried to stop them. According to Captain Reynolds, he called them 'blackguards', but according to Alderman Brent he only called them that after he had 'civilly remonstrated' with them for damaging the crop and breaking down the hedges by their trespass. Brent added, 'I was met by an insulting laugh in reply. I then requested their names and was told by one of them "Snooks", who called out to the others to "come on".' According to Brent, the officers tried to ride him down and he snatched Cornet Brotherton's horse by the curb rein. According to Brotherton, Brent began the scuffle by snatching his bridle 'in a most insolent manner'. Then, 'as I had not at the time either whip or stick in my hands with which to administer to Mr Brent the chastisement which his brutal assault would have warranted, I spurred my horse and rode at him, as he himself describes, till I got him up against a wall; when he let go my bridle.'[43]

The Radical press, particularly the *Morning Chronicle* and the weekly *Examiner*, seized on this aristocratic outrage by Cardigan's officers. Since the victim was a Radical and a magistrate too, they could hardly have done otherwise. In Canterbury itself, the *Kent Herald* gravely took up Brent's cause, while the Conservative *Kentish Gazette* described him as a pugnacious nincompoop, who had recently had to send express to Dover for a waggonload of rifles to protect himself from the wrath of his fellow-citizens.

Brent tried to get into the barracks to confront Cardigan, but the gate was slammed in his face. He wrote to Cardigan and received no reply. He complained to Lord Hill at the Horse Guards and, this time, received a reply from Cardigan offering to see him.

The *Morning Chronicle* opened the attack upon Cardigan (who was on his way to Scotland to shoot grouse) on 12 August, alleging that he had 'a very imperfect idea of what is due from one gentleman to another'. Cardigan replied in an irate letter, which was perhaps meant as a personal communication to the editor rather than for publication. He had indeed seen Alderman Brent, who had demanded from any one of the six officers involved 'that satisfaction . . . which one gentleman usually requires of another'. Whatever Brent's intention, these words had only one meaning for Cardigan, who promptly sent a message challenging him to a duel on behalf of the regiment. But, as Cardigan regretfully discovered, 'That he is a magistrate there can be no doubt —that he is a gentleman is quite another question.' In other words, Alderman Brent had refused to fight. As for the editor of the *Morning Chronicle*, Cardigan concluded,

> With regard to the opinion which you have so unwarrantably published to the world in the leading article of your journal, viz., 'that I have a very imperfect idea of what is due from one gentleman to another,' I have only to reply that such an assertion is an *infamous* and *scandalous falsehood*, and that it is fortunate for you that you are the anonymous editor of a newspaper.
>
> I am, Sir, your most obedient servant,
> CARDIGAN, Lt.-Col. 11th Light Dragoons.

'After so unbecoming a threat,' wrote the editor of the *Chronicle* nervously, 'were his lordship to forget himself further, we should have no hesitation in handing him over, with the least possible ceremony, to a police officer.' But the editor of the *Chronicle* was to escape horsewhipping, as John Drakard had not. The only penalty incurred, according to the *United Service Gazette*, was that certain regiments now refused to have the paper in the mess.[44]

Despite the efforts of both sides, the affair speedily turned into a joke. An announcement purporting to come from Lord Fitzroy Somerset at the Horse Guards, appeared in the press on 22 August.

> Her Majesty has been graciously pleased to permit the 11th Regiment of Light Dragoons, in addition to other honourable distinctions, to bear on their standards the name of 'SNOOKS'.

This was followed the next day by an anguished letter which protested that 'that which is fun to the military may be death to me'. It was from Thomas Snooks, a greengrocer of Canterbury.[45]

As the *Morning Herald* somewhat cynically observed, the real concern of the Radical press was not with the rights of Alderman Brent but with the opportunity of 'vilifying a Conservative nobleman'. According to the *Herald*, 'Had it been a lady's reputation instead of a hay-field, the 11th Dragoons might have ridden over it rough-shod with impunity.'[46]

Cardigan was, as he said, 'accustomed to be dealt with by a portion of the public press with great severity'. Yet among lesser men than the editor of the *Morning Chronicle* his stock had risen. For an Earl to lay aside his rank and offer to fight a miller made him a 'sportsman' in the eyes of many ordinary people, and not a bad sort at all. However, the Radical press omitted to publicize the end of the story, when Cardigan reviewed the situation, decided that he had been in the wrong, and sent the six officers to apologize to Alderman Brent.[47]

As the gloom of scandal darkened round the figure of Lord Cardigan, it was not he alone but the whole reputation of the army, particularly of the fashionable cavalry regiments, which was under scrutiny. When two officers of the 11th Dragoons fought a duel with pistols in the barrack field at Canterbury, or when a trooper was drummed out of the regiment, it rated a paragraph in the papers. In 1839 and 1840 the press turned its attention to the behaviour of cavalry officers and it rarely had to look far before it struck scandal. Throughout the 1830s there had been plenty of young dragoons in London with time enough to make a public nuisance of themselves. Sir Robert Gill would amuse himself by going into Mr Harbottle's, a corset-maker's shop in the Burlington Arcade, and asking the young lady behind the counter for stay-laces. The girl, overcome by embarrassment at a gentleman mentioning these intimate accessories, would rush to fetch Mr Harbottle. He would find young Sir Robert flourishing one of the female undergarments and asking some 'cursed impertinent question'. The troublesome visitor was eventually dragged off, shouting, 'I am *Sir* R. Gill, and you are *Mr* Harbottle, *stay-maker*!'[48]

But by 1840 'military outrages' or 'aristocratic outrages', as the Radicals called them, were of a more serious kind. Captain Clark of the 9th Lancers was arrested for horsewhipping a toll collector who had the impudence to ask for the toll at Hammersmith gate, when Clark drove his four-in-hand through. Earl Waldegrave and a high-spirited party of brother officers were prosecuted for beating a policeman unconscious after a fancy-dress ball. At Wigan, when the Hon.

Adolphus Fraser was arrested for debt, the Hon. E. S. Plunkett of the 86th regiment staged a riot and rescued him by force. These 'Waterford capers' as they were called, after the notorious Marquis of Waterford, came to a head when Captain Clark and a party of junior officers from the 9th Lancers visited Hounslow on a Sunday night. They arrived at a house of dubious reputation, 'kept by a female named Robottom', but were refused admission. Having nothing better to do, they drove into the town, tearing off the gate of the hayfield and throwing it into the crop. They raced through the streets, pulling down barbers' poles, ringing handbells, wrenching off the knockers from front doors and throwing them through their owners' windows. The baker's wife missed death by a couple of inches when the brass knocker smashed through the window and landed on the pillow of her bed. The behaviour of the 9th Lancers makes the conduct of the 11th Dragoons in the Snooks affair seem civilized by comparison.[49]

On 30 August 1840 the *Examiner* summed up the exasperation of the Radical press in an article entitled 'Military Licentiousness'. After 1815, said the *Examiner*, men who were good enough to fight ('food for powder'), but not ornamental on parade or capable of meeting the expenses of a fashionable mess-room, were weeded from the army, leaving it as the monopoly of 'the aristocracy and the Plutocracy'. Was it not time that Lord Hill weeded out some of the Hussars and Lancers?

> We specify Hussars and Lancers, because with the exception of the rescue outrage at Wigan, we find that the greater number of offences against the peace and decency of society have been committed by individuals of those rich and generally aristocratic bodies; from the insult at Canterbury to the tricks at Hounslow . . . the offenders have usually been Dragoons.

All this was true, and many of the well-heeled cavalry regiments in the early Victorian period deserved the unenviable reputation which they acquired. Yet before the major scandals of Cardigan's career broke upon the public, the army was already at the centre of a press war, in which the lines were as carefully drawn as upon any battlefield. To read Cardigan's story solely in the pages of papers like the *Morning Chronicle* (which wrote about him most because they liked him least) would be like gathering one's knowledge of the Poor Law and the workhouse system exclusively from the pages of *Oliver Twist*.

Being who he was and what he was, there was little that Cardigan could have done which would have pleased the editors of the *Morning Chronicle*, or its evening counterpart, the *Globe*, let alone a weekly paper like the *Examiner*. The Radical press saw in the army an influence hostile to political liberalism and an instrument which could be used, in the last resort, as the means of suppressing democratic movements. Cardigan's wealth alone was not a disqualification but had he combined, with his command of the 11th Dragoons, all the finer qualities of Lord Shaftesbury and William Wilberforce, he would still have had some way to go before satisfying the *Morning Chronicle* or the *Globe*.

It is equally true that because he represented the Conservative landed interest, his actions were, as a rule, favourably reported by the *Morning Post* and its evening counterpart, the *Standard*. The *Times* belonged to neither party and was quite capable of criticizing both Cardigan and the Radicals.

Of the military papers, the *United Service Gazette* kept closer to the official views of the Horse Guards and was more inclined to condemn Cardigan's actions, though not in such instances as the Snooks affair. The *Naval and Military Gazette* supported Cardigan at almost all times, often reporting news favourable to him which was ignored elsewhere. The paper had a reputation for taking up the cases of officers whom it considered badly treated by the Admiralty or the Horse Guards, and even after the Wathen trial it had suggested that Cardigan had received something less than justice.

The reputation of some papers, like the *Age*, was such that it was an honour for Cardigan to be attacked by them. Its editors, Charles Westmacott and Barnard Gregory, who speculated in property as well as slander, were renowned for digging up scandal about well-known families and then offering to withhold publication for a fee. Cardigan's physical chastisement of journalists seems entirely appropriate here. Indeed, Serjeant Ballantine recorded his own delight at seeing Westmacott in the dress circle at Covent Garden, 'howling under the horsewhip of Mr Charles Kemble, whose daughter he had foully slandered'.[50]

Yet whatever the battle lines in this press war, the reputation of the army was such that 1840 was almost the worst conceivable year for Cardigan to embark upon some of his greatest indiscretions.

2

The year began promisingly enough. Not only was Lieutenant Tuckett out of the 11th Dragoons, but he and his sort had been replaced so far as possible by more agreeable companions of Lord Cardigan's choice, young men who represented, like their commander, the landed interest and the Conservative cause. Among them were Captain John Douglas of the 79th, and subalterns like the future Sir Charles Jenkinson of Hawkesbury. The cornets and lieutenants were men of eighteen or so, while captains who had purchased their rank as quickly as possible were in their early twenties. There was a considerable age gap between them and their thirty-three-year-old Lieutenant-Colonel.

Early in 1840, the attention of the whole nation was turned towards Dover, where, on 7 February, Prince Albert of Saxe-Coburg landed on his way to London to marry the twenty-one-year-old Queen Victoria. The escort that awaited him was the band and troopers of the 11th Dragoons, superbly turned out and drilled, under the command of Lord Cardigan. Cardigan and the Prince were not unknown to one another, since Albert's father, Prince Ernest, had accompanied Wellington on his inspection of the regiment the year before. So, on his first night in England, the future Prince Consort dined with the commander of the 11th Dragoons. When the wedding was over, Cardigan was received at Buckingham Palace by the Queen, whom Creevey had described as a 'homely little being', who laughed and ate heartily though tending to gobble her food and to display 'not very pretty gums'.[51]

Before the summer came, it was announced that the 11th Light Dragoons were to become Hussars, which marked their social rather than military advancement. They were to be known as the 11th (Prince Albert's own) Hussars, and the Prince himself was to be their honorary Colonel-in-Chief. There was to be a new uniform, in keeping with the splendour of an Hussar regiment. Moustaches were to be worn.

Cardigan had let his house, 17 Carlton House Terrace, to Prince Louis Napoleon, the future Napoleon III, who had come to London after the failure of his military *coup* in Strasbourg, and who, before his next adventure, became a well-known figure at the dinners and race meetings of English metropolitan society. Cardigan had little use for the house in Carlton House Terrace, since he was now in possession of the family mansion in Portman Square.

By the middle of March, the attention of the newspapers was drawn towards the comforts of Deene. The bells of the Northampton churches pealed, and the band of the 11th (Prince Albert's own) Hussars marched musically and majestically through the streets on its way to the Cardigan estate. All this was in honour of a very special house party, including the father of Prince Albert, Prince Ernest of Saxe-Coburg (whose sexual reputation and financial extravagance were a match for Cardigan's own), the Barons de Grubia and de Lowenfels, Lord Adolphus Fitzclarence, and Lord Alfred Paget, Equerry-in-Waiting to Queen Victoria. Among the other guests was Maria, the young Marchioness of Ailesbury, cousin to Lady Cardigan and mistress of Cardigan himself.

'The mansion of the noble Earl of Cardigan has been throughout the week the scene of magnificent hospitality', exclaimed the *Northampton Herald* in a tone of goggling incredulity. On 19 March Cardigan and his guests were out with Lord Lonsdale's Cottesmore hounds. They drew Ranksborough gorse successfully but then contrived to lose the scent, 'owing to some of the field wishing to show off', said *Bell's Life in London*, in a disapproving reference to the Cardigan style of riding. Next day it was the turn of Cardigan's rival, Thomas Assheton-Smith, to provide the sport and no less than 3,000 spectators assembled to watch the royal and noble occasion. But the 'showing off' of the day before had taught the foxes a lesson and after some desultory milling about the hunt broke up in the afternoon without finding a scent.[52]

Apart from the splendours and comforts of Deene, Cardigan imported a new pack of stag-hounds for his guests and two 'remarkably fine' stags were seen by the citizens of Northampton as the animals were transported through the streets of the town to the start of the hunt. Cardigan and his visitors made a 'splendid assemblage' at the Northampton Races and the Pytchley Hunt Ball, Prince Ernest driving in one of the Queen's carriages and the horses being decorated with blue ribands. Everywhere, the band of the 11th Hussars provided the music for these occasions, reminding those who heard it that there was no regiment in the Queen's army to compare with Lord Cardigan's own. Then, having exhausted the pleasures of Deene, the party moved on to Badminton and the Duke of Beaufort's family, one of whose most notable members was, of course, Lord Fitzroy Somerset. It seemed a very small, not to say exclusive, world.

Cardigan spent much of the London season in his Portman Square house. He was the Queen's guest at a royal concert at Buckingham Palace in June. Victoria may well have thought, as she watched him listening appreciatively to Mozart and Donizetti, that this could hardly be the same rich barbarian whom his enemies described. Three weeks later he was invited back as one of the guests at the state ball in the lavishly renovated palace. 'Bad taste and every species of infirmity', said Thomas Creevey of the décor. 'Raspberry-coloured pillars without end that turn you quite sick to look at.' The Yeomen of the Guard lined the Marble Hall and on the grand staircases of what Regency survivors despised as 'The Brunswick Hotel', was a profusion of elaborate floral decorations. Cardigan had come without his Countess, but while the band of the Coldstream Guards played quadrilles, he was not without company: the Duke of Wellington, the Duke of Cambridge, Lord Somerset, Lord Adolphus Fitzclarence, Lord Alfred Paget, and, of course, Maria, the young Marchioness of Ailesbury. It was like Deene, on a somewhat grander scale.[53]

As for the 11th Hussars, there was hardly more than a whisper of criticism during the warm, dusty days of early summer. There had been opposition to the appointment of Prince Albert as Colonel-in-Chief, but this was inspired by dislike of the Prince as an interloping foreigner, rather than of the regiment. He was sneered at as a fortune-seeking pauper Prince, and mocked for his German accent and manners. The *Age* reported with glee how he had gone to Madame Tussaud's to see the wax model of the royal wedding, and how he had come out and expressed loud satisfaction with 'the marriage grope'. The *Age* provoked ribald speculations upon the topic of Prince Albert's marriage grope.[54]

In keeping with their new status, the 11th Hussars were to have a new uniform, said to have been devised by the Prince himself. It was, without doubt, the most remarkable of any in the British army. There was a shako with a crimson and white plume, a short royal blue jacket, crimson overalls or trousers, and an abundance of gold trimmings. *The Times* was aghast at the sight. 'The brevity of their jackets, the irrationality of their headgear, the incredible tightness of their cherry coloured pants, altogether defy description: they must be seen to be appreciated.' Some of those who did see them reported that they looked more like a *corps de ballet* than a cavalry regiment. It was said that for some unexplained reason they were being called 'Cherubims'. This was not quite accurate. The phrase shouted at them in the streets, as they swaggered by in the short blue jackets and crimson tights, was 'Prince Albert's cherry-bums!' Deaf to such plebeian insults, Cardigan sent his men to Mr Sporrer of Bond Street for their uniforms, which must have accounted for a good proportion of the £10,000 a year of his own money which he spent on equipping and mounting the regiment.[55]

There was some criticism by now of Cardigan's inordinate vanity. Having produced the smartest regiment in the army, it was said that he would send some of his men to London with five shillings and a day's leave. They were to station themselves along Piccadilly and down St James's Street so that they might salute him as he passed, turning his walk or ride into a semi-royal progress and drawing the London crowds to witness the passing of the splendid 7th Earl of Cardigan. If the ritual showed his vanity, it again earned him the reputation of a 'sportsman' among his soldiers, to whom the five shillings was worth almost a week's wages.

Yet something had gone badly wrong in the regiment. Only a handful of people, so far, knew the details but the rumours were beginning to spread. When Private William Bennett of the 11th Hussars appeared at Kensington magistrates' court, accused of assault on Hugh Percy Holden, a man of respectable appearance, the only witnesses were another private of the regiment and a pair of prostitutes who had been in the street with them. Holden had provoked the fight, said Bennett, by his remark to the two soldiers. Yet Holden had said nothing about 'Prince Albert's cherry-bums'. He had simply said, 'Black Bottles!'[56]

On 18 May 1840 Major-General J. W. Sleigh, Inspector-General of Cavalry, reviewed the 11th Hussars at Canterbury. He had been Lieutenant-Colonel of the 11th when it had won its battle honours at Waterloo and he had been made a Companion of the Order of the Bath for his distinguished conduct there. Yet however much Sleigh's courage was admired in the regiment's final charge upon the French artillery positions, he was not a universal hero. He dealt severely and decisively with junior officers. There was a sensation over his court-martial of Lieutenant Wood of the 11th in 1817, and a row with the Horse Guards in 1837 when he placed Brigadier Willshire, an officer serving in India, under arrest without the proper authority. It was said that two-thirds of the officers in the 11th Dragoons had resigned in 1819 rather than serve with Sleigh in India, but the truth is that most of them would have chosen to avoid serving in India in any case.

General Sleigh was impressed by the 11th (Prince Albert's own) Hussars on 18 May and, after a two-hour review, he warmly congratulated Cardigan on their appearance and performance. That evening, Sleigh and his party were the guests of Cardigan and his officers in the mess. A regimental dinner was generally a more intimate occasion than might be imagined. There were usually between twenty and thirty officers in the regiment, some of whom would have other duties to attend to and, at times, almost half the officers might be on leave. The average number at dinner would probably be between twelve and twenty, attended by their mess servants. The atmosphere was rather that of a family or country house dinner than of an institutional meal. There were rules of conduct for the mess table, voted on by all the officers, and maintained by the mess president. The mess president of the 11th Hussars was Captain Inigo Jones, a friend, or 'toady' as his critics said, of Lord Cardigan.

Dinner on 18 May was a particularly splendid occasion with as many of the officers present as was possible. The sparkle of the mess silver and the choice wines symbolized a final rejection of those 'Indian' habits which were quickly acquired by even the best regiments in the heat and tedium of Meerut or Cawnpore. In the East, even bottled porter was called for in the mess, while Abbott's or Hodgson's pale ale appeared at dinner with a piece of wet cloth wrapped round the bottle to keep it cool.

Cardigan and his guests enjoyed the most expensive 'delicacies of the season', followed by champagne. Then, almost at the end of a perfect day, a mess waiter came forward at the summons of a youthful Captain who looked little more than a schoolboy, J. W. Reynolds. There, among the fine linen and elegant silverware, the waiter placed on the table a large black bottle. Cardigan stared and General Sleigh stared. It was, in fact, a bottle of Moselle, which Reynolds had called for on behalf of those who preferred it to champagne. But as Cardigan's rage grew, the precise shape and contents were beyond his perception. He knew instinctively that it was 'one of those horrid bottles of porter for the Indian fellows'. The brash young Captain had disgraced him and the regiment in front of the Inspector-General of Cavalry. It might as easily have happened in front of the Duke of Wellington or Prince Albert.

When preparing for a turn-up, Cardigan was given to twirling his moustaches compulsively, and his whiskers must have received considerable attention as he sat, distracted by fury, waiting until dinner was over so that he might deal with Captain J. W. Reynolds.

Whether or not black bottles should be allowed on the mess table was, strictly, a matter for the mess to decide, not the commanding officer. Dinner was regarded as coming within the scope of polite manners rather than military discipline. Reynolds was therefore astounded the next morning when Captain Inigo Jones, president of the mess committee, confronted him in the mess-room with a message from Lord Cardigan.

'The Colonel has desired me, as president of the mess committee, to tell you that you were very wrong in having a black bottle placed on the table at a great dinner like last night, as the mess should be conducted like a gentleman's table, and not like a tavern or pot-house.'

Jones later claimed that he had not used the term 'pot-house', but whatever the language its effect was to send Reynolds at once to demand an interview with Cardigan. The interview was refused. But Reynolds was not to be denied. He collected two friends, Captain J. H. Forrest and a visitor, Captain Carmichael Smyth of the 93rd Highlanders. The three of them marched into the mess-room and confronted Captain Jones.

'Captain Jones,' said Reynolds, 'I wish to speak to you about the message you brought to me this morning. In the first place, I do not think you were justified in giving it at all. As a brother captain, having no possible control over me, it would have been better taste if you had declined to deliver it.'

'I received it from the commanding officer', said Jones dutifully, 'and as such I gave it. And if you refuse to receive it from me, I will report it.'

By now it seemed that everyone's honour had been impugned and that the 11th Hussars had yet another occasion for getting out their duelling pistols. But Reynolds had a quarrel to settle with Cardigan.

'Do not misunderstand me, Captain Jones, I have received and do receive it, but the message was an offensive one. And I tell you, once for all, that in future I will not allow you or any man to bring me offensive messages.'

'If I am ordered to give a message, I shall give it', said Jones, and he walked out of the mess-room to report the conversation to Cardigan. Almost at once, Captain J. W. Reynolds was summoned to the orderly room, where he found Cardigan, Jones, Major Jenkins and the Adjutant, Lieutenant Knowles, waiting for him. Cardigan began to berate him.

'If you cannot behave quietly, sir, why don't you leave the regiment? This is just the way with you Indian officers, you think you know everything. But I tell you, sir, that you neither know your duty nor discipline. Oh yes! You do know your duty, I believe, but you have no idea whatever of discipline, and do not at all justify my recommendation.'

There was a pause.

'Well,' said Cardigan abruptly, 'I put you in arrest.'

In the horrified silence which followed the explosion of this particular bombshell, the other men in the room must have realized that there was now no hope of preventing the storm in a black bottle from becoming a public sensation. Jones hastily offered to shake hands with Reynolds, perhaps hoping to soothe Cardigan. But Reynolds refused, saying that there was no occasion for it.

'But I say you have insulted Captain Jones!' thundered Cardigan. Reynolds persisted in refusing to shake hands and was placed under close arrest in his room, though allowed to take two hours' exercise each day in the barrack yard. He demanded to know the charge against him and was told that it was one of having addressed Captain Jones in an insulting and threatening manner. On the evening of 22 May Cardigan travelled from Canterbury to Portman Square. On the following day he drove to the Horse Guards to report Reynolds's conduct to the Commander-in-Chief.

Lord Hill was appalled. The squabble had all the makings of another Wathen scandal. But there was a way out, if it was taken in time. He instructed the Adjutant-General to write a memorandum, giving Reynolds a chance of acknowledging his 'error' before the case was 'officially reported in writing'. If this acknowledgment was made, the matter could be dropped. Reynolds made some acknowledgment but not enough to satisfy Cardigan, who summoned him to the orderly room and for two hours subjected him to 'a most harrassing and inquisitorial conversation', the object of which was to make him shake hands with Captain Jones.

'Well then,' said Cardigan finally, 'will you shake hands with him?'

'No, my lord. I have already told you I will not, and my reasons for declining.'

'Will you drink wine with him?' asked Cardigan.

'Certainly, my lord.'

'Will you ask him again?'

'Certainly, my lord. If a gentleman asks me to drink with him, I shall ask him again.'

'Will you ask him to-day?'

'No, my lord, I will not.'

'Will you ask him in a week?'

'No, my lord, I will not. I will ask him in no specified time.'

So it went on. Reynolds, who had been released by Cardigan from close arrest, was then put back under open arrest. However, it was only the Horse Guards who could release him from that. Reynolds addressed to them a series of protests and complaints against Cardigan. On 29 May the Adjutant-General ordered his release, though with a censure upon his conduct. On 9 June, three weeks after the splendid review, General Sleigh was back with the 11th Hussars. The officers were assembled in the mess to hear him read out an official letter from the Horse Guards, censuring Reynolds and vindicating Cardigan. Reynolds's motives were described in it as 'pernicious and vindictive'. Reynolds angrily demanded to have such charges proved or dis-proved by a court-martial, but Sleigh cut him short, telling him that he had already 'forfeited the sympathy of every officer of rank in the service'.

There it seemed the matter might end. But Henry Harvey, the uncle and guardian of John Reynolds, was not prepared to drop the case, even though Lord Hill might 'consider the matter to be settled'. Harvey wrote to Lord Hill, to Macaulay, who was Secretary at War, to the Prime Minister, Lord Melbourne (from whom he got nothing but a one-sentence acknowledgment), and to Prince Albert. None of them was prepared to become involved in the matter.

Then Reynolds himself sent in his papers to the Horse Guards and requested permission to sell out. Fearing that this too might be the means of publicizing the black bottle affair, Lord Fitzroy Somerset invited another of Reynolds's uncles, Captain Basil Hall, the traveller and writer, to meet him privately after hours at the Horse Guards and then at his home in Great Stanhope Street. They discussed whether Reynolds might be persuaded to remain in the regiment, but Captain Hall pointed out that the impediment to this was Cardigan. 'The Earl's conduct was overbearing, and his language abusive. On hear-ing this, Lord F. Somerset inquired if the Earl was in the habit of swearing at the officers; and had the *satisfaction* of having it explained to him, by Captain B. Hall, that a commanding officer might be abusive without resorting to oaths.'

Reynolds himself was summoned to an interview with Lord Somerset at the Horse Guards and over the next few months an agreement was reached that he would withdraw his resignation upon the following terms: 'a recantation of the censure given by General Sleigh on the black bottle affair; six months' leave of absence (which had been previously refused by the Earl of Cardigan), two years at the senior department of the Military College, and a distinct and express understanding that Captain John Reynolds should never again be required to serve for a single day under the Earl of Cardigan.'[57]

The terms were steep but it seemed the only way to prevent a public scandal. Already Reynolds's guardian was prepared to make public the reason why Cardigan had refused leave to his nephew.[58]

> A regimental court-martial having taken place, of which my ward, Captain John Reynolds was a member, the sentence on revision was not in accordance with his lordship's wishes. Soon afterwards Captain (then Lieutenant) Reynolds applied for leave of absence, when Lord Cardigan answered, 'No, sir, I will not give you leave; how can you expect me to do so when you oppose me?' And on being asked in what manner Lt. Reynolds opposed him, Lord Cardigan said, 'You were a member of the court-martial, which would not revise its sentence according to my wishes.'

Even in the regiment itself there was a gloomy awareness of the speed with which the rumours of its squabbles were beginning to spread. When Cardigan reprimanded one of his troopers who had hit a guardsman, the trooper was taken aback. 'My lord,' he said indignantly, 'he called me a Black Bottle!'

By the summer of 1840 the jealousies and factions among the officers of the 11th Hussars were more pronounced than they had ever been in India or England. Among a score of officers, the anti-Cardigan faction was led by Captain J. W. Reynolds, Captain R. A. Reynolds (who was no relation) and Lieutenant W. C. Forrest. Among Cardigan's supporters were Captain Inigo Jones, Captain Douglas, Lieutenants Smith, Cunningham and Jenkinson, who were of course regarded by their enemies as Cardigan's 'toadies'. Though the

Radical press supported the Reynoldses and Forrest, the truth was, as the *Morning Post* pointed out, Cardigan's enemies in the regiment were 'as much Tories as he is himself'. Yet whatever the precise lines of battle, the hostilities of the small and aristocratic world of the 11th Hussars were conducted with a claustrophobic ferocity.[59]

One of the continuing squabbles in the regiment was over the way in which Cardigan had sneered at Reynolds as an 'Indian officer', and over the arrogant manner in which he was alleged to have told Lieutenant Forrest that he was 'too Indian' for promotion. When this became known the press received dozens of letters on the subject, one of which demanded that a meeting of all officers who had served in India should be called (including, presumably, the Duke of Wellington), who would demand that the Commander-in-Chief should order Cardigan to apologize publicly for the insult to so many brave men.

Yet others were quick to point out that the term 'Indian officer' did not imply disparagement of those who had served in India. 'So far from the use of this term being peculiar to Lord Cardigan,' wrote a correspondent to the *Morning Post*, 'it is often applied, not to the *person*, so much as the *discipline* which he maintains.' Another of the paper's contributors pointed out that in India, where each officer generally called for beer or wine, as he pleased, dinner in the mess was 'more like a club or tavern dinner (I do not use the word offensively) than like a gentleman's table in England'. Reynolds, in this sense, had acted the part of an 'Indian officer'. Moreover, with all their admirable qualities, officers serving the East India Company were impatient of authority and much given to 'appealing to Government, or to the public, through the press, against the decisions of their military superiors.' Who more 'Indian' than Captain J. W. Reynolds in that respect?[60]

On the whole, the press and the public were to decide the matter according to their views of Cardigan. Yet there was a general and undeniable prejudice against service in India, which was now to be conveniently overlooked by his enemies. This distaste for Indian service was evinced by the speed with which officers exchanged into other regiments when their own was ordered there, as well as by the ease with which those who were compelled by circumstances to spend their active lives there were condemned as 'adventurers' or men of 'low propensities'.

As the rumours spread, there was some doubt as to the exact colour of the bottle and 'Black Bottle Reynolds' vied with the alleged 'buzzing' of 'Bluebottle Cardigan' in stories of what was now being called 'The Battle of the Moselle'. Yet throughout July and August the press remained almost unanimously silent about the affair. There were rumours of disagreements among the officers of the regiment, and when the senior Captain, Tomlinson, resigned his commission, it was said to be the consequence of a quarrel with Cardigan upon a matter of 'table etiquette'. However, it proved to be the consequence of advancing age and increasing deafness. The *Kent Herald* picked up the most nearly accurate version of events, when it reported at the beginning of June that 'two of the officers in the regiment having quarrelled, and a challenge following, the matter was reported to the Earl of Cardigan, who placed the offending party in confinement for a short time. The friends of the Earl say that he could not have acted otherwise.' It was, at least, part of the truth.[61]

Hopes rose that the Black Bottle and Captain J. W. Reynolds might be safely forgotten when the 11th Hussars were ordered to march from Canterbury to their new quarters in Brighton. 'Deeply do we regret your departure from our ancient city', read the message from 400 citizens to Lord Cardigan, who replied that he and his men were 'highly gratified' by such appreciation. It was also highly gratifying that the regiment had been chosen as the guard for the Royal Pavilion, built by Nash as a domed oriental palace by the sea for George IV. It had been popular with William IV too, and it might now become a fashionable retreat for Victoria and Albert. It certainly offered a mixture of gaiety and splendour, majesty and frivolity, which seemed peculiarly well suited to the 11th (Prince Albert's own) Hussars. Brighton in the 1840s, with its Theatre Royal and its Chain Pier, its race meetings and the parade of carriages and phaetons along its drives, seemed certain to be the resort of the royal and the famous. On 25 June two troops of the 11th Hussars marched out of Canterbury to Chichester, which was also to be garrisoned by part of the regiment, as an outpost. The main body of men followed later, led by the celebrated band, then the familiar figures of Lord and Lady Cardigan on horseback, leading their dragoons. A little black and white butcher's dog, which had attached itself to the regiment, trotted between them. The 'Major', as the dog was called, was reputed to be the reincarnation of some drum major of the regiment who had returned in canine form. But for the fact that he was still alive, it might more appropriately have been the angry spirit of Lieutenant Harvey

Tuckett, who was sitting in his East India Merchant's office in London, on half-pay, and biding his time.[62]

The death of its patron monarch, George IV, in 1830 had left Brighton, ten years later, as a still fashionable and already well-appointed resort. Around the open lawns of the Steine were grouped the dwellings of the comfortably rich and the more-or-less well-known citizens. The cluster of buildings was inward looking, excluding all suggestion of the sea, a few yards further on, with a proper eighteenth-century regard for the need to keep Nature in its place. At the north end, furthest inland, stood Sir Charles Barry's neo-Gothic church of St Peter, light and tastefully ornate. On the east side stood a terrace of fine houses. To the west were the bay-windowed front of Edlin's Gloucester Hotel, the domes and turrets of Nash's Royal Pavilion, and a house close by, where Mrs Fitzherbert had died in 1837. At the south end of the Steine, with its back to the sea and facing St Peter's in the distance, stood the most fashionable hotel in Brighton, the Royal York. The whole ensemble seemed like a village green copied on a grandiose scale.

Behind the Royal York, and a little to the east, the Chain Pier hanging like a series of suspension bridges from its supporting chains, offered an airy ironwork promenade for the 'fashionables' of the town and their visitors. On either side of Brighton new developments were appearing. To the east, Kemp Town, to the west, on the boundaries of Hove, Brunswick Square. This development of the 1830s, built round three sides of a wide lawn, with the fourth side open to the sea, was originally called Brunswick Town. Behind its bow-fronted, late Georgian mansions were humbler buildings in little streets, where those who catered for the needs and the whims of the wealthy had their homes.

The 11th Hussars marched from Canterbury to Preston Barracks, which was a mile and a half out of Brighton on the road to Lewes When the remaining squadron of the regiment rode in, under Major Rotton, they were quartered in Church Street, close to the Royal Pavilion itself, and were permitted by the Queen to use the royal stables (now the Dome). Cardigan and his officers moved into the Royal York Hotel, as the fashionable world streamed into Brighton for the races. The Duke of Beaufort, the Earl of Chesterfield, Lord Jersey and many others were soon recognized by the gossip writers of the press. Yet the course itself had another use. On the stretch of downland known as the Race Hill, the 11th Hussars wheeled, and cantered, and charged under Cardigan's orders. It had been arranged that Prince Albert would come to Brighton with the Queen to inspect his regiment in September.

In the summer evenings crowds of a thousand or more, the women in fancy straw bonnets and blue or green dresses which were decreed to be the fashion, came to hear the band of the regiment as it played on the open lawn of the Steine or on the Chain Pier. Some no doubt came for a chance to see Lord Cardigan and his officers who were frequent visitors to the concerts. As an attraction, the band was as popular as Charles Kean, who after remarkable displays of temperament was now offering *Shylock* and *Richard III* at the Theatre Royal, a few hundred yards away. Every day the summer crowds were joined by new arrivals, brought from Charing Cross or Regent Circus by coaches like the *Sovereign*, the *Regent* and the *Magnet*, which left London at almost every hour. In Brighton itself, at the top of Trafalgar Street, the building of a strange looking temple was evidence of how close to completion the London to Brighton Railway had come.

The servants at the Royal York Hotel were kept busy by the series of dinner parties given by Lord and Lady Cardigan for the officers of the 11th Hussars, occasions which were eagerly noticed by the fashion columns of the Brighton newspapers. Then, in order to entertain on a still more lavish scale, Cardigan moved out of the Royal York and leased the finest available mansion in Brunswick Square. From here he was able to set out with a large party of *'élégantes'* by private train from Brighton to the Swiss Gardens at Shoreham, the party being accompanied on the train and at the gardens by its own quadrille band. Cardigan and his guests then spent the remainder of the afternoon and the evening dancing and eating a lavish dinner provided by the officers of the regiment. Back in Brighton again, there was a select dinner party for thirty friends at Brunswick Square the next day, attended by the band of the 11th Hussars who played during the meal, and afterwards provided the music for dancing until two o'clock in the morning.

The visitors to Brighton were fascinated to see the officers of the 11th Hussars 'cut a dashing appearance' along the King's Road or the Marine Parade in their smart drags and cabs. Yet even more impressive was the sight of Lord and Lady Cardigan in an 'elegantly-styled chariot', with two liveried servants on horseback behind, the

Countess driving by means of an 'ingenious contrivance' which enabled her to attach the whip to her parasol. Some observers remarked how closely the general appearance of the Cardigan ensemble matched that of Queen Victoria herself.

Yet the greatest success of the Brighton summer was the regiment itself as it proceeded, mounted and in full dress uniform, from the barracks to the Steine, out on to the sea front by King's Road, eastward to Kemp Town, and so to the Race Hill for field exercise. Not only were the uniforms gorgeous beyond belief but Cardigan had not begrudged a penny even where the 'horse furniture' was concerned. The passers-by stared in wonder at the rich crimson of the saddle cloths with the initials of Victoria and Albert in gold, and there in frosted silver the battle honours of the regiment: 'Egypt', 'Salamanca', 'Peninsula', 'Waterloo', 'Bhurtpore'.

On the Race Hill, high above the town, the squadrons pranced and wheeled under the barked commands of the Earl of Cardigan. 'Columns will change front to the right, and form line of contiguous columns on the first regiment of the first brigade! Columns will wheel simultaneously by threes to the left, and the whole will wheel sharp to the right!' But what stirred the hearts of the spectators most was when the band played the *Keel Row* and the splendidly groomed horses and riders, recognizing the regimental signal, broke into a trot; and then at the regimental canter of *Bonnie Dundee* they moved at the double over the pale green turf; and, finally, with a 'Charge! Hurrah!' the flower of the British cavalry, the Earl of Cardigan at its head, sabre blades held out at eye-level, swept in magnificent order over the downland, tilting at the only visible enemies on that peaceful horizon, the Sussex windmills.

The greatest triumph of the regiment on that particular spot was the occasion of Brighton races in early August. Thirty-four races were run for record stakes of £13,000. The officers of the 11th Hussars contributed £20 of their own, as well as riding their own horses in the races. Captain Douglas, Cardigan's protégé, won the hurdle race on the second day 'at a slapping pace' on his bay gelding Kildare. The grandstand was filled with 'fashionable company', including Cardigan himself, and there was a half-mile line of the carriages of the wealthy, complete with their servants and picnics. Yet with that strange social mixture of the Victorian racecourse there were also gypsies, cardsharps and thimble-riggers, and a special tent for the *rouge-et-noir* table. With all this and the crowded refreshment booths, it was as much a fair as a race meeting.

After the races, Lord and Lady Cardigan parted from one another. Lady Cardigan went south to Wiesbaden, while Cardigan went north to Scotland with Lord Adolphus Fitzclarence to shoot grouse. With his volatile temper, Cardigan was as perfect a butt for the jokes of his friends as for the jibes of his enemies. Men like Fitzclarence ragged him as they might have done when they were schoolboys. On the way back from Scotland, while Cardigan was standing guard over the carriage and a pile of game, outside the Garve Inn, Fitzclarence persuaded one of the pot boys to see how many of the birds he could steal by outrunning and outwitting the watchful Earl. At the boy's approach, Cardigan warned him off sharply. When the boy retorted by snatching up a brace of birds Cardigan set off after him at a tremendous pace, among the laughter and applause of the spectators. The boy led him round and round a circuit, flourishing the stolen game triumphantly in a quite superfluous effort to urge Cardigan on. The chase passed through stables, up into hay lofts and down again, and each time they passed the carriage another brace of birds was removed. His friends, convulsed with laughter, then saw that Cardigan, half out of his mind with fury, had snatched up a knife and 'literally foamed with rage'. At last, 'regularly done up with passion and fatigue', he tried to save the remainder of the birds by throwing them in through the door of the carriage, unaware that to the anguished amusement of the onlookers, the pot boy was simply removing them by the opposite door. However, the joke had its point and when the press heard of it there appeared another facet to the image of Lord Cardigan, that of a murderous clown.[63]

If Cardigan 'literally' foamed at the mouth, it would not have surprised Captain R. A. Reynolds, who was writing to Lieutenant Moysey, 'I am tired of soldiering under this mad man. Cardigan has grown very much more mad than he ever was and I do assure you that on Friday last at a field day he ought to have been confined.'[64]

Cardigan returned to Brighton. On Tuesday 25 August he held a dinner party and ball at 45 Brunswick Square. Among the guests on this occasion were Mrs Cunynghame, one of the Brighton 'fashionables', and her daughter. Neither Captain J. W. Reynolds nor

Captain R. A. Reynolds was invited, though other officers of the regiment were. R. A. Reynolds happened to be on regimental duty in Chichester, but even had he been in Brunswick Square with time on his hands, he would not have seen the inside of Cardigan's mansion in the present state of relations with his commanding officer.

Miss Cunynghame, in conversation with Lord Cardigan, said with innocent surprise that she did not see the Captains Reynolds among the guests.

'I have not invited them', said Cardigan with gruff displeasure.

Miss Cunynghame inquired why, and Cardigan became gruffer.

'Because I don't happen to be on good terms with them, and I fear if you are very anxious to see them you are not likely to meet them here.'

Miss Cunynghame was intrigued, and pressed the point further. According to some of those present, Cardigan's voice was clearly audible above the conversation and the regimental band as he delivered his final judgment on the Captains Reynolds.

'As long as I live, they shall never enter my house!'

On the following day, Wednesday 26 August, a young lady who was acquainted with Lieutenant Cunningham of the 11th Hussars, spoke to him in Sussex Square, where the regimental band was playing.

'What a very curious woman Mrs Cunynghame is', said the young lady.

'Why?'

'I heard Mrs Cunynghame ask Lord Cardigan several times why the Captains Reynolds were not at his party. Lord Cardigan gave her no answer for some time. At last he replied that they should not come to his house as long as they lived. I thought Mrs Cunynghame must have known that he was not on terms with them.'

Though the story referred to *Mrs* Cunynghame, it was claimed that it was her daughter, not she, who had spoken to Cardigan about the Captains Reynolds. At all events, when Cunningham returned to his room that evening he received a chance visit from R. A. Reynolds. The two officers and Mr Lewis, Cunningham's brother-in-law, began to discuss Cardigan. 'He is not very fond of you,' said Cunningham to Reynolds, and repeated what the girl at the band concert had told him.

Captain Reynolds began to laugh.

Brighton Barracks, Aug. 27, 1840

My Lord,—A report has reached me that on Tuesday last, at a large party given by your lordship, when asked why the Captains Reynolds were not present, your lordship replied—'As long as I live they shall never enter my house.' I cannot but consider this report highly objectionable, as it is calculated to convey an impression prejudicial to my character, and I therefore trust your lordship will be good enough to authorise me to contradict it.—I am, my lord, your lordship's obedient servant,

RICHARD ANTHONY REYNOLDS

The Right Hon. the Earl of Cardigan,
    45, Brunswick-square, Brighton.

On the morning of Friday 28 August the 11th Hussars paraded for field exercise on the Race Hill. Cardigan raised his sword and summoned Captain R. A. Reynolds, Captain Jones, and the Adjutant, Lieutenant Knowles. They rode out about a hundred and fifty yards in front of the rest of the regiment. Cardigan addressed Reynolds.

'I yesterday received a communication from you, to which I beg to inform you I have no reply to give, inasmuch as I consider your letter one of an improper nature for you to address to me. And I have to request in future that all letters addressed by you to me may be strictly official, with my military rank affixed to the address and your own to the signature.'

Then Cardigan, who had kept his sword raised, lowered it as a sign for the three officers to return to their positions. Reynolds attempted to argue.

'To your troop, sir!' barked Cardigan.

As soon as the field exercise was over, Captain Inigo Jones, whose troop was on squadron duty at the Royal Pavilion, rode up to Reynolds and said,

'What is all this about?'

Reynolds told him, and Jones advised him to drop the matter, since it would be impossible to prove what was said or not said at Cardigan's ball. However, before he could reach the Pavilion, Jones met Cardigan in the street.

'In order to explain what took place to-day at drill', said Cardigan, 'read this letter.'

It was the letter of 27 August from Reynolds to Cardigan.

At about two o'clock, when the men were just coming back from their dinner, Jones reached the Pavilion stables and found Reynolds there, grumbling that he had been insulted by Cardigan and swearing that he would write another letter. Jones tried to dissuade him, saying that it might cost him his commission, but Reynolds refused to listen. He wanted the satisfaction which one gentleman owed to another, and he wrote to Cardigan the same day, demanding it.

> Your Lordship's reputation as a professed duellist, founded on having sent Major Jenkins to offer satisfaction to Mr. Brent, the Miller of Canterbury, and your also having sent Captain Forrest to London to call out an Attorney's Clerk, does not admit of your privately offering insult to me, and then securing yourself under the cloak of Commanding Officer; and I must be allowed to tell your Lordship, that it would far better become you to select a man whose hands are untied for the object of your reproaches, or to act as many a more gallant fellow than yourself has done, and waive that Rank which your Wealth and Earldom alone entitle you to hold.

The letter was, as the Horse Guards General Order of 20 October put it, 'calculated to excite' Lord Cardigan. To refuse a challenge might be the action of a coward, but to fight Reynolds would be a breach of military law and etiquette. Cardigan had Captain Reynolds placed under arrest to await a general court-martial. The terms of the arrest, however, were in keeping with Brighton gentility. There was to be no prison cell for Reynolds, who came of a wealthy Huntingdon-shire family. He merely moved out of the Royal York Hotel, where most of Cardigan's supporters lived, to Edlin's Gloucester Hotel. The contending parties confronted each other across the grassy expanse of the Steine, while the expensive carriages rolled by and the band of the 11th (Prince Albert's own) continued to play. After this, how-ever, there were no more references to a regimental inspection by Victoria and Albert, even though Cardigan's stock remained high for a few days longer.[65]

'The Earl of Cardigan, at the head of his regiment on his beautiful Arab steed, looked well', reported the *Naval and Military Gazette*, 'He bears good nature and kindness in his eye, and his men all speak in his praise . . . but trifles are constantly harrassing the gallant soldier. The present arrest, I hear, is all about a chit-chat, grounded on what some queer old woman, not worth a charge of a *copper cap*, has thought fit to whisper.' The paper, which published this report under a pseudonym, also deplored letters attacking Cardigan which had begun to appear in the *Morning Chronicle*. They were signed, 'An Old Soldier'. Let him be man enough to put his own name to them, the *Gazette* demanded. But after the letter published on 4 September 1840, there was no need for Lieutenant Harvey Tuckett to do that.

> Lord Cardigan has now insulted the senior captain of the regiment—*a private insult*; and, when called upon for redress, has again claimed his privilege as a commanding officer, and placed Captain —— in arrest for resenting such insult. Many a gallant officer has waived the privilege which nothing but wealth and an Earldom obtained for Lord Cardigan.

The similarity of thought and phrasing between this and the second Reynolds letter was remarkable. However, the 'Old Soldier' addressed his letter to 'The Officers of the Army', and its implication was clear. The bold, aggressive Earl of Cardigan, who prided himself so greatly on his military valour, was actually afraid to fight, and so hid himself behind army regulations. If there was anything calculated to heat Cardigan's blood beyond endurance it was this charge of physical cowardice. He asked Captain Douglas to act as his second.[66]

The editor of the *Morning Chronicle* was approached for the name of the author of the letters and readily gave it. Cardigan then instructed Captain Douglas to go and 'demand satisfaction from Mr Tuckett'. On 11 September Tuckett agreed, asking only for time to go into the country to consult his second, Captain Henry Wainwright, formerly aide-de-camp to Sir Willoughby Cotton in India.

On 12 September Douglas met Wainwright, who demanded in writing the reason for Cardigan's challenge. At half-past two that afternoon, Douglas handed him a note.

> Lord Cardigan yesterday authorized Captain Douglas to require of Mr. Tuckett to afford him satisfaction in consequence of a letter of which Mr Tuckett has avowed that he was the Author, and which appeared in the *Morning Chronicle* of the 4th inst. signed 'an Old Soldier'—many parts of which contained matter entirely false, and the whole of it was slanderous insulting and calumnious.
>
> London Sept. 12th 1840   Cardigan.

At five o'clock on the same afternoon, a carriage containing Lieutenant Tuckett and Captain Wainwright drew up at the northern corner of Wimbledon Common, some ten miles south-west of the centre of London. Almost simultaneously a second carriage, containing Cardigan, Captain Douglas and Sir James Eglintoun Anderson of Burlington Street, who was Cardigan's surgeon, stopped by the palings of Earl Spencer's park, a little distance away. Tuckett and Wainwright got out of their carriage carrying a case of Nock's duelling pistols Cardigan had brought a brace of Manton's pistols, made for him just before his departure for India. They were silver-mounted and the case itself bore his crest in silver. His enemies alleged that his pistols had hair triggers and rifled barrels, making them more deadly than those of Tuckett.

Captains Douglas and Wainwright measured out twelve paces, close to the spot where duels, fatal and otherwise, had been fought, including one between Cardigan's acquaintance Prince Louis Napoleon and the Count de Léon. Then as Cardigan and Tuckett prepared to face one another, there was a sudden alarm that they were being watched. In a grotesque charade to disguise their intentions, the five men, two of whom were about to attempt murder against each other, had to spend several minutes 'rollicking in the grass'. Then, as soon as it seemed safe to do so, Cardigan and Tuckett went to their places, facing one another and each holding his first pistol.

They aimed and fired almost together, but both of them missed Tuckett took his second pistol and fired at Cardigan, missing again Cardigan might have fired his second pistol in the air and ended the matter, but he did not. He aimed at Tuckett, fired, and saw Tuckett fall. Sir James Anderson hurried over to where the Lieutenant lay. He was unconscious and bleeding from a wound made by the bullet as it entered below the ribs and came out close to his spine.

But as Cardigan stood in the September evening with the smoke drifting from the barrel of his pistol, there was another man who was moving even faster than the surgeon. It was Thomas Dann, who lived in the mill on Wimbledon Common. He had seen almost everything that happened and was only fifteen yards off when the second shots were fired. Dann arrived in time to take the pistol from Lord Cardigan's hand. He would have arrived even earlier if he had not gone back to his house, in the first place, for his staff: for Thomas Dann was a constable.

Yet Dann knew his place. He politely asked the culprits to pack their pistols into the cases, and then he took possession of them. Tuckett recovered consciousness and was helped back to the mill. On being shown the Lieutenant's card, Dann agreed to let Sir James Anderson take him home and put him to bed. Captain Wainwright disappeared too, though apparently without Dann's authority. Then, with a certain sense of occasion, Constable Dann arrested the 7th Earl of Cardigan and Captain Douglas. Both were put into a post-chaise and escorted by Dann to the station-house of the Metropolitan Police, 'V' Division, at Wandsworth.[67]

For Cardigan, caught in the act of attempted murder, the journey must have been a disturbing one. Only three years earlier, Parliament, in its attempts to put an end to the practice of duelling, had provided heavy penalties for those who took part in 'affairs of honour'. A man who shot his opponent, as Cardigan had done, even though the wound was not fatal, faced death by hanging. Until 1868 there was only one procedure for hanging a man or a woman and in the metropolitan area it generally took place outside Newgate Prison at eight o'clock in the morning, in front of a large and excited crowd, many of whom had waited all night in order to be sure of a good place. A drop was used, but anyone believing that this caused instant death would have been regarded as a fool by those Victorians who had actually witnessed Courvoisier's death struggle in the year of Cardigan's duel. Worse still, there were cases in which the hangman was alleged to have played the buffoon with the corpse as it hung there, boxing it on the ears, spinning it round, and shaking hands with it.

Of course, the final act would have to be preceded by the rare and ornate ritual of a notorious nobleman being tried by his peers in the House of Lords. Within the previous century, the Lords had sent Lord Ferrers to the gallows and Lord Lovat to the block, and had promised to brand the bigamous Duchess of Kingston with a hot iron if there was any more trouble from her. Such a trial in itself would be a nine-days' wonder, since there had not been one for sixty-four years. But after the scandals of the 11th Hussars, it would have been difficult to stage a more sensational Victorian spectacle than the public execution of the villainous Earl of Cardigan.

CHAPTER 5

BY GOD AND MY PEERS!

1

Whatever Cardigan's apprehensions may have been, he gave little sign of them. Inspector John Busain was on duty in the whitewashed office of the Wandsworth station-house when the pony-chaise drew up outside. It was just before six o'clock on the evening of the duel. He heard a tap on the window and, turning round, saw Cardigan standing outside. Captain Douglas stood behind Cardigan and Constable Dann was not yet in view. Busain had never seen Cardigan before but, noting that this was evidently a gentleman of some importance, Busain bowed to him.

As Busain opened the door, Cardigan said disdainfully, 'I am a prisoner, I believe.'

'Indeed, sir? On what account?'

Cardigan entered the office.

'I have been fighting a duel, and I have hit my man. But not seriously, I believe. Slightly, merely a graze across the back. This gentleman also is a prisoner; my second, Captain Douglas.'

Cardigan reached into his pocket and pulled out several cards, some of which fell to the floor. He handed one to Busain. On it was written, 'The Earl of Cardigan, the 11th Dragoons'. Busain needed no further introduction, in the light of the 'Black Bottle' and 'Indian Officer' stories that were circulating. Referring to Cardigan's admission of having fought a duel, he said, 'Not with Captain Reynolds, I hope?'

'Oh, by no means', said Cardigan scornfully. 'Do you suppose that I would fight with one of my own officers?'

Constable Dann arrived with the two cases of pistols and Cardigan claimed the one which bore his crest in silver. The other case was never claimed. Inspector Busain took both cases home and kept them in his own bedroom.[1]

Matters began to improve for Cardigan. His offence was now described as an 'intent to murder', rather than 'attempted murder'. Intent to murder was still a felony, carrying a prison sentence, but it did not carry the death penalty. There was some controversy over whether to allow bail to Cardigan and Douglas. Inspector Busain would have hesitated to lock a peer of the realm in a common cell with the usual collection of drunks and vagrants. So, although one of the magistrates, Captain Page, opposed it, both prisoners were allowed bail. When they appeared at Wandsworth magistrates' court on Monday 14 September, the amount of this bail was set at £1,000 for Lord Cardigan and £500 for Captain Douglas.

Since the magistrates were only concerned with committing the two men for trial by higher courts, it was the press rather than the law which first pronounced judgment on Cardigan. On the evening of 16 September the *Globe* devoted most of its first two pages to an article, 'Earl Cardigan and the 11th Hussars'. It was a complete exposure of the whole 'Black Bottle' incident and its associated scandals. The account was so detailed that it occupied the first two pages on the next evening as well. It reproduced the letters from J. W. Reynolds, Cardigan, the Horse Guards, Reynolds's uncle, Henry Harvey, as well as the conversations between Reynolds and Cardigan. The entire feature was copied with delight by the *Morning Chronicle* and by the other leading papers, though the *Standard*, which was generally sympathetic to Cardigan, described it as 'evidently a very partial report'.[2]

The public reacted to the story with amusement or outrage, according to personal taste. Gentlemen at their London clubs, who chose not to have their wine decanted, were asked if they would have it 'out of the "Cardigan". The term "black bottle" will soon be obsolete.' Overnight, it seemed, the 11th Hussars and their Lieutenant-Colonel became the subject of gossip, satires and songs which brought impersonations of the Earl of Cardigan to the music hall stage.[3]

> Oh! list a moment while I sing
>   The glory and renown, sirs,
> Of one whose deeds have won much fame,
>   For good Prince Albert's own, sirs.

A pattern of nobility,
 A model of an officer;
In manners quite a gentleman,
 In temper a philosopher,

Sore trouble once upon a time
 He gave to him who reared him,
When for some noble deeds of his
 The good old king cashiered him.
That is, he would have been cashiered,
 But petticoats held sway, sirs;
And so they gently let him down,
 And put him on half-pay, sirs.[4]

While his fame was sung from the stages of the 'chanting cribs' and 'penny gaffs', the Earl of Cardigan found himself front-page news, even without the story of the duel. The *United Service Gazette* washed its hands of him publicly on 26 September.

How many more courts-martial his Lordship may have in *petto*, it is, of course, impossible for us to guess; but if he regulates his future by his past behaviour to his officers, none but the sychophants and tale-bearers who may be employed to do his bidding, can hope to escape.

To talk of a 'cabal' against such a commanding officer is absurd. Let him cease to trample on the feelings of his subordinates, and abrogate a little of that aristocratical *hauteur* which characterises his demeanour towards them, and all cause of complaint on his part or their part will, we are satisfied, be at an end.

But for every reader of the *United Service Gazette*, there were probably hundreds of men and women who heard of Cardigan's fame in the halls of Southwark or Blackfriars.

Though thick his blushing honours fell,
 Yet panting to be glorious,
With great success he strove to be
 For *odd tricks* more notorious!
To see how courteously he warm'd
 The military hot-house,
And taught his subalterns to shun
 The manners of a pot-house.

While comic songs like 'A Military Mess' became the favourites of the moment, the full story of the pending court-martial on Captain R. A. Reynolds, and of Cardigan's duel with Lieutenant Tuckett, became public. With the news of the duel, the sense of outrage on the part of even the most unsensational newspapers seemed to have no limit. Coming on top of the other revelations about the 11th Hussars, it drove *The Times* to recommend prison with hard labour for Cardigan, even though he had not yet been tried and convicted.[5]

> A little 'ungentlemanly' prison discipline would be the best thing in the world for gentlemen of the Cardigan school; the terror of cropped heads, oatmeal diet, and the treadmill, would be more effective in aristocratical circles than hanging. Our readers will remember that this penalty was strictly enforced upon the gentlemen who assisted as seconds in the last lamentable affair on Wimbledon common, of which a linendraper named Mirfin was the victim. . . . Let that case be remembered on the present occasion, and let equal justice be dealt to rich and poor, the peasant and the noble. Let not occasion be given to any to say, that to break the laws with impunity is a luxury reserved for legislators, officers in her Majesty's service, and peers of the realm; or that the same offence which was visited as a felony upon the associates of the linendraper Mirfin is excused as an act worthy of a man of honour in the Earl of Cardigan.

Lord Cardigan had been granted bail, but he was constantly reminded by the press that his liberty was temporary and his chances of prolonging it slender.

Yet even before *The Times* had a chance to get its indignation into print, Lord Cardigan had become involved in another regimental 'turn-up'; not in the mess, this time, but in the streets of Brighton and before the very eyes of the astonished citizens. His adversary on this occasion was Lieutenant William Forrest, a friend of the Reynoldses, and the man whom Cardigan was alleged to have described as 'too Indian' for promotion.

On 17 September 1840 Lieutenant Forrest locked his room at the Cavalry Barracks and rode into Brighton, where he relieved Lieutenant Cunningham on the Pavilion Guard at three o'clock. At half-past five, Cardigan, driving his phaeton in the street, saw Forrest, pulled up his horses and got out of the carriage. He called Forrest across to him.

'What do you mean, sir, by locking your door and taking away your key?'

Forrest admitted that he had done so, although a temporary room was provided at the Foot Barracks in Church Street for officers on Pavilion Guard.

'Do you suppose, sir, that you can hold two rooms?' snapped Cardigan.

Forrest protested that the room in the Cavalry Barracks was his own room, whereas the one that he occupied in Church Street for the week of his duty was a guard room. It was inconvenient not to have a room in the Barracks where he could change for mess.

'Oh!' barked Cardigan, 'you mean to come the letter of the law with me, sir, do you? I can tell you this, sir, that were I to do so with you, I should find more faults than I do, which are now a great many. What were you doing in the mess-room this morning after the Stable Trumpet had sounded?'

Forrest retorted that he had neither stable nor servant at the Pavilion and was obliged to bring his horse back to the Barracks himself. He had then gone into the mess-room to get some breakfast.

'Do you suppose, sir,' demanded Cardigan, 'that it is necessary for an officer to eat after Field Exercise?'

Forrest again asked to be allowed to keep his room at the Barracks.

'Well, sir,' said Cardigan triumphantly, 'I, as Commanding Officer of this regiment, order you to give up the key of your room. And that instantly!'

Forrest saluted and withdrew to the Pavilion Stables. About three-quarters of an hour later, he was confronted there by Cardigan again, who was now accompanied by Lieutenant Knowles, the Adjutant. Cardigan demanded, in front of Knowles, what Forrest meant by locking the door of his room. Forrest repeated his previous explanation.

'This is some plan of yours, sir!' shouted Cardigan. 'And I would tell you that "Military Lawyers" do not get on in the service. I could understand you feeling inconvenienced if you had been accustomed to live in two or three suites of apartments in St James's, but really for a cavalry officer to require two rooms is ridiculous.'

Forrest remarked that if he had been asked for the loan of his room, he would have had no objection to Lieutenant Jenkinson or any other officer using it while he was on Pavilion Guard for the week. Cardigan's wrath exploded.

'What—I—sir, as Commanding Officer, ask you for the loan of your room! Why, if I choose I can keep you down here for a month, and you have no business to go into the Barrack Yard at all except for your breakfast and dinner. I again order you to give up the key to your room to Lieutenant Jenkinson before night. Do you understand the order?'

Forrest replied that he did, and the interview ended. Unimportant as the subject of the quarrel seems, it took the intervention of the Commander-in-Chief of the army, Lord Hill, to part the combatants. Lieutenant Forrest was officially ordered by the Horse Guards to surrender the key of his room and was reprimanded for his conduct. He obeyed the command but insisted on sending the Adjutant-General a transcript of Cardigan's remarks made on the afternoon of 17 September. Since this had to be forwarded to the Adjutant-General by Cardigan himself, it was not calculated to sweeten relationships within the 11th (Prince Albert's own) Hussars.

Of course, the Forrest incident reached the press, where it was published alongside stories of 'Black Bottle' Reynolds, Captain R. A. Reynolds, and Cardigan's duel with Lieutenant Tuckett. 'What great events from trivial causes spring!' said *Bell's Life in London* wearily, and turned to its staple diet of the turf and the field. Yet worst of all, the wicked Earl who had fought a duel and shot his man, was now about to court-martial Captain R. A. Reynolds for attempting to do exactly the same thing. The injustice of it seemed beyond question, and those who had thought Cardigan a sportsman when he offered to fight Alderman Brent on behalf of the regiment, thought so no longer. Cardigan, in the peacock arrogance of the 11th Hussars uniform, or in 'frock-coat, check trousers and chimney-pot hat, complete with eye-glass and dundreary whiskers', held his critics in contempt. To the sober warnings of the middle-class press or to threats of violence from any class, he remained equally indifferent, displaying that 'aristo-cratic *hauteur*' which the *United Service Gazette* so much deplored. Perhaps it was as well for his peace of mind that he was capable of such patrician detachment, while field officers and press reporters converged upon Brighton. There, on 25 September, the sensation of the season was to open: the court-martial on Captain R. A. Reynolds.[6]

With the coming of the autumn rain and the darker evenings, the court-martial was a boon to Brighton society and its guests, as the *Sussex Advertiser* remarked.

The idlers at this place ought to feel obliged to Lord Cardigan and his antagonists for finding them an interesting topic of conversation, while they were constrained to stay indoors during the equinoctial storms that raged the greater part of last week, and to tell the truth the squabbles of his Lordship have been the all-engrossing theme of conversation in every company both public and private that met here during the last ten days.[7]

Not everyone was staying indoors. The *Brighton Guardian* reported that Captain R. A. Reynolds, at Edlin's Gloucester Hotel, was receiving numerous visits from the gentry to wish him well at his trial. As the 11th Hussars marched down the Steine it was said that they performed an automatic 'eyes right' in the direction of Reynolds's window.

On the morning of 25 September Lieutenant Forrest's phaeton drew up outside the Gloucester Hotel to take Reynolds to the barracks. The crowd waiting outside was rewarded at last by a glimpse of the thirty-four-year-old Captain, who made a particular impression on the female spectators. His figure and movements in the splendid full-dress uniform of the 11th Hussars showed 'all the vigour of youth'. His face was 'the deep bronzed colour of one who has been for many years exposed to the burning rays of the Indian sun . . . His hair and mustachios are jet black; and these, with the dark flashing eyes of one who has encountered many a peril . . . exhibit him to be what he is —a brave and gallant "Indian officer".' This romantic paragon of a gallant Hussar was swept off to the Cavalry Barracks in Lieutenant Forrest's phaeton to find an immense crowd of journalists and sight-seers pressing into the corridor and round the windows of the hospital ward which had been turned into a temporary courtroom.[8]

The President, Major-General the Honourable Sir Hercules Pakenham, and thirteen other officers, assisted by the Judge Advocate, formed the court. They sat at a table running about half the length of the ward, while in opposite corners at the far end of the room sat Reynolds and Cardigan, each with his legal adviser. The court was staffed by several NCOs of the regiment, standing at attention by the main table. The presiding officers and the two parties in the case all appeared in full regimental costume which presented 'a truly magnificent and imposing spectacle', said the *Naval and Military Gazette*, whose reporter was one of the crowd which pressed forward as far into the room as the sentries permitted them to go. Those who had not managed to push their way in, collected outside in the rain and pressed their faces against the windows. It was almost like a siege.[9]

The charge was read, accusing Reynolds of conduct 'unbecoming an Officer and a Gentleman, prejudicial to the interests of the Service, subversive of Good Order and Military Discipline'. Then Cardigan, as prosecutor, opened his case. He spoke rapidly and excitedly, detailing the history of his feud with R. A. Reynolds. When he came to the second letter from Reynolds, imputing cowardice to him, Cardigan was 'all but overwhelmed with emotion', according to the *United Service Gazette*. He was unable to continue for some moments and began wiping his eyes. According to some spectators, he actually wept with rage. The members of the court watched impassively.[10]

Cardigan then had to appear as a witness and was soon being cross-examined by Reynolds. Reynolds had no direct defence to the charge, since he could hardly deny sending the letters to Cardigan. Instead, he attempted to justify his conduct by showing that Cardigan had ruled the regiment by arrogance and insult, and had provoked the challenge. With Cardigan in a particularly excitable state, the court ruled this line of argument out of order. However, the ears of the press and the public were keen to hear more. Then, after a long examination and cross-examination of Captain Inigo Jones, the President announced that 'owing to circumstances' it was desirable to adjourn the court for four days.[11]

When the court sat again on 29 September Reynolds asked for more time to prepare his case and there was another adjournment until 1 October. In the meantime, the press continued the debate. The President of the court-martial had asked the reporters not to prejudge the case, but with the columns of the London and the Brighton newspapers filled with daily editorials and strings of letters on the subjects of the Black Bottle scandal and Cardigan's alleged insults to 'Indian officers', it was difficult to keep the court-martial out of it.

One interesting piece of information to be published on 26 September was that Reynolds himself had written to Prince Albert on 31 August asking for a court-martial 'to prevent my being condemned unheard, or sacrificed to the power of the lieutenant-colonel, the Earl of Cardigan'.[12]

By the time that Reynolds opened his defence on 1 October, the curiosity of the public seemed close to hysteria. At the brief session on 28 September the President had deplored the press treatment of the case and had mentioned the possibility of prohibiting further reporting. This, of course, increased the fascination of the trial still further.

On 1 October a crowd of quite unexpected size and determination besieged the temporary courtroom at Brighton Barracks. They surged down the corridor, tore the door of the room from its hinges and smashed the glazed panels on either side of it. Fortunately for the members of the court they were already at their places. A group of brother officers from the 11th Hussars stood round Captain Reynolds, offering him encouragement and wishing him well. Cardigan sat alone. Order was imposed in the courtroom at last but the atmosphere soon became suffocating. Instructions were given to open the windows, but as the sergeants and corporals of the 11th Hussars did this, the crowd outside the building swarmed forward and pushed themselves in through the window spaces.

There was an intent silence as Reynolds began to speak. The court had ruled that Cardigan's behaviour as commanding officer was not an issue in the case, but Reynolds continued to argue that 'Lord Cardigan's conduct towards me and the other officers of the regiment has been very irritating and offensive'. It had been so irritating and offensive that even if it did not excuse the letters which Reynolds had written, it must at least mitigate the severity of any sentence passed upon him. The point was that whether or not Reynolds was legally correct, he and most of the onlookers felt that he was morally right. To see Cardigan, who had shot a man in a duel less than a month before, prosecuting a subordinate who had challenged him to a duel, offended a basic sense of justice. Reynolds concluded his speech. 'I hope by your verdict of "not guilty" you will prove to Lord Cardigan, that wealth and rank do not license him, although the commanding officer of a regiment, to trample with impunity upon honourable men, who have devoted their lives to the service of our country.'

The words were well chosen. As Reynolds sat down, the room rang with applause and cheering for several minutes. Sir Hercules Pakenham, at last able to make his voice heard, called, 'Clear the court this moment! I will have no such ebullitions!' However, there was no way in which the court could be cleared, and the trial proceeded with the spectators still in possession of their places.

For the remainder of that day, Thursday, the whole of Friday, and Saturday morning, Reynolds produced his witnesses. Some, like Major Jenkins, Major Rotton and Lieutenant Cunningham, were called simply as to matters of fact. Others, like Major Morse Cooper (who claimed to have sold out of the regiment rather than serve any longer under Cardigan) and Captain J. H. Forrest, were called to give evidence of the feuds and rancour which Cardigan had inspired among his officers. In every case this evidence was interrupted by the Judge Advocate, as the court's legal adviser, and was ruled inadmissible. Of all these witnesses, the one who created the biggest stir among the sightseers was the 'fine young officer' Captain J. W. Reynolds, now famous wherever the English newspapers were read as the hero of the Black Bottle incident.[13]

After the court had heard testimonials to the character of R. A. Reynolds, Cardigan made his final address on Monday 5 October. It was a better performance than his opening speech. Reynolds, for the benefit of the press and his audience perhaps, had warned the court-martial that 'the public also take a lively interest in your proceedings . . . and they will look with a vigilant eye to the result of this case.' It was not the most diplomatic of suggestions and Cardigan seized upon it in his reply. 'I will not follow the prisoner's example by reminding you that the eyes of the public are upon you, because that is a consideration which I should be as ashamed of urging, as you would of being influenced by.' Popular or not, Cardigan's was the kind of sentiment which Sir Hercules Pakenham and his colleagues approved.[14]

Finally came the anti-climax. The court-martial deliberated, reached its decision, and announced nothing. Not until the findings had gone to the Horse Guards and had been approved by the Queen would the result be known. The *United Service Gazette* criticized the Judge Advocate for prohibiting the evidence of Cardigan's behaviour. Without this legitimate and relevant testimony, the trial was a 'mockery'. The *Morning Chronicle* obligingly supplied some of the evidence which Major Morse Cooper had been prevented from giving. Apart from all the other squabbles in the 11th Hussars, there had apparently been another, in which Lord Cardigan had called one of his officers a liar and bloodshed had only been prevented by the intervention of Captain R. A. Reynolds.[15]

Of course Cardigan denied provoking the anger of his officers. He specifically denied ever having said at his ball, of the Captains Reynolds, 'So long as I live they shall never enter my house.' This could only be confirmed or rebutted by Mrs Cunynghame, who had left her house in Brunswick Square and gone to the Continent before the court-martial, so that she would not be called as a witness. On 4 October, she wrote from Paris to the *Globe*, protesting that she had no part in the affair and 'never knew such a man as Captain Reynolds existed'. This was answered by another letter to the paper from 'Alpha', explaining that it was *Miss* Cunynghame who had made the statement repeated at the court-martial, 'so that the only difference is, that it is the daughter is the mischief-maker instead of the mother'. Unfortunately, Miss Cunynghame was in Paris with her mother and not available to give evidence either.[16]

At Brighton, the 11th Hussars continued to provide ceremonial pomp as well as courtroom rhetoric. Led by their band performing 'popular airs', they rode down the Steine, west to Brunswick Square, along the King's Road, where the autumn seas broke against the Chain Pier, and then past the empty royal apartments of the Pavilion and back to their barracks on the Lewes road. The visitors to Brighton stood and stared in amazement at the regiment, which afforded them 'a military spectacle they are not soon likely to forget', said the *Sussex Advertiser* proudly, though its choice of phrase was perhaps a little unfortunate at that moment. Sometimes the regiment was led by Cardigan himself but more often by Major Jenkins. Cardigan's time was spent chiefly in London, where he was not the immaculate commander of dragoons but the murderous aristocrat of the Wimbledon Common duel.[17]

The Radical press had not quite recovered from its indignation that Cardigan should have been allowed bail instead of being confined in Horsemonger Lane Gaol, to which he stood committed. Captain Page had continued to argue in favour of gaoling Cardigan during the months before his trial, but he had been outvoted by the other two Wandsworth magistrates.

As more details of the duel were revealed, it seemed that there was no limit to Cardigan's viciousness. When the police took both sets of duelling pistols to be examined by gunsmiths, Tuckett's pistols, made by Nock, were found to be of the ordinary kind. However, according to a letter in the press from John Field, one of the gun-makers who examined them, Cardigan's pistols had both hair triggers and rifled barrels. The wicked Earl had apparently taken a mean and unsporting advantage of the impoverished Lieutenant. When the pistols were produced at the magistrates' court hearing on 28 September, Cardigan handed his pair to the bench and invited the magistrates to see for themselves that there was no rifling inside the barrels and that there were no hair triggers.

This gesture went for nothing when Inspector Busain's letter to Captain Page was reprinted in the *Globe*. 'I have had the pistols examined by Mr Parker, an eminent gunsmith in Holborn', wrote Busain, 'Capt. Tuckett's are of the commonest and plainest kind of duelling pistols. His Lordship's on the contrary, are of the best kind, with stop locks, hair triggers, and French rifle barrels, rifled from the breech to about an inch from the muzzle, and will hit with unerring precision when fired by a steady hand.'[18]

Cardigan might well offer the pistols for the inspection of the bench, said his enemies, since the rifling of the barrels stopped short of the muzzles and would not appear on casual examination. Manton and Hudson, the Dover Street gunsmiths who had supplied Cardigan's pistols before he left for India, wrote to the press, certifying that the pistols were 'in every respect similar to other duelling pistols of their manufacture for the last half-century'. It was soon pointed out that this was not the same as swearing that the pistols did not have hair triggers or rifled barrels.[19]

It was suggested that the pistols might be left at the United Service Club for a while, so that public curiosity as to their manufacture might be satisfied by independent witnesses. The suggestion was not taken up because, in any case, the pistols were in the possession of the police. The most favourable construction put upon Cardigan's conduct was that he used pistols of a superior kind to Tuckett's without knowing of their superiority. But few people seemed to be interested in favourable constructions. There was some interest in the image of Cardigan, the maligned Lieutenant-Colonel. But in an age when melodrama was the popular art, there was a general eagerness to see the moustache-twirling, heartless aristocratic villain of the stage come to life in the person of the 7th Earl of Cardigan.

Among this public excitement it was in vain for the *Naval and Military Gazette* to suggest that the editor of the *Morning Chronicle* had been irresponsible in printing Tuckett's letters which provoked the duel. Nor did those who read eagerly the scandals of the 11th Hussars pay much attention to the *Morning Post*'s protest at the *Globe*'s two-day exposure of the regiment's squabbles at a time when its commander might be facing trial for felony or even a capital charge. Cardigan the villain, as much as Cardigan the hero, existed for many people as the product of the newspapers. When the grand jury refused to sanction a prosecution against Tuckett or Wainwright over the duel but endorsed the charges against Cardigan and Douglas, there were few protests. Tuckett and Wainwright were colourless figures: it was Cardigan that the public wanted to see.[20]

The truth of even the most routine matters remained the property of the press and appeared in correspondingly varied accounts. The *Brighton Herald* reported that when Cardigan returned from the magistrates' court at Wandsworth, he went straight to Brighton Barracks and found the gates open and the sentry asleep at his post. The sentry was woken by Cardigan's irate bawling and was consigned to Lewes prison the next morning. This story was widely reprinted. However, according to the *Naval and Military Gazette*, the truth was that the sentry had left his post unmanned and was sleeping in front of a fire in the guard room. He was not sent to Lewes prison but punished by several days' confinement to barracks. Of course, those papers which criticized Cardigan's treatment of the man would have been the first to seize on any story that he was leaving the barracks unguarded and generally ignoring his military duties. To that extent, his actions had by this time become almost immaterial to his reputation.[21]

On Monday 19 October, Cardigan and Captain Douglas appeared at the Central Criminal Court, which was obliged to pass Cardigan's case on to the House of Lords. That evening the two men shared a box at Drury Lane Theatre for one of the Concerts d'Hiver, as the promenade concerts of the winter season were known. They were not noticed except by a few members of the audience and one or two gossip columnists. Public reaction to Cardigan on such occasions was still confined to curiosity. All that was to change on the following day, when Cardigan had some business at the Horse Guards, and when Colonel Cochrane, Assistant Adjutant-General, travelled down to Brighton with the court-martial finding. He read it out to Reynolds that afternoon, in Reynolds's room at the Gloucester Hotel, in the presence of Major Jenkins and Adjutant Knowles. Then it was issued to the press, and national indignation was given full rein.

> The Court, having duly weighed, and most maturely considered, the whole of the Evidence adduced on the part of the Prosecution, together with that advanced by the Accused in support of his Defence, is of opinion, that he, Captain Richard Anthony Reynolds, of the 11th (Prince Albert's own) Hussars, is *Guilty* of the Charge exhibited against him, which being in breach of 'The Articles of War,' The Court does in virtue thereof Sentence

him, the said Captain Richard Anthony Reynolds, of the 11th (Prince Albert's own) Hussars, to be *Cashiered*.[22]

Reynolds received the news 'with great firmness, and to the last was in good spirits'. Tory though he was, he became more firmly than ever the hero of the anti-Cardigan Radicals. On the evening of the announcement, a band came and played outside his hotel window for some hours. On the following day, without making any kind of public statement, he left Edlin's Gloucester Hotel and drove in his buggy to London, where he took up residence at the Union Hotel in Cockspur Street. Whatever his supporters might have envisaged, their sunburnt Hussar with the dark flashing eyes was keeping himself to himself.[23]

Cardigan was satisfied that he had been vindicated by the result of the court-martial, but even moderate and judicious press opinion now began to express astonishment that such a man should be left in command of a regiment. 'Smart and zealous officer though he undoubtedly be,' said the *United Service Magazine* sadly in November 1840, 'Lord Cardigan is disqualified from the command of others by the due want of control over himself.'

Yet it was not moderate opinion which was most noticed. The press war over Cardigan and the 11th Hussars, which had taken the form of minor skirmishes since the middle of September, broke out in earnest once the result of the Reynolds court-martial was announced. The *Morning Post* attacked the *Morning Chronicle*, while the *Globe* attacked the *Morning Post*. The *Standard* and *The Times* attacked other papers, and sometimes one another, rather less predictably. In Brighton, the anti-Cardigan *Brighton Herald* and the pro-Cardigan *Brighton Gazette* fought their local battle, while the *Naval and Military Gazette* was described by the *United Service Gazette* as 'a drivelling weekly newspaper, in Lord Cardigan's pay'. The *United Service Gazette* was already in the grip of a criminal libel action on another matter, but the editor did not propose to let that emasculate his style.[24]

Walter Savage Landor, who took up Reynolds's cause, might have seen a certain irony in his own remarks. 'If anything at the present day is glorious to our literature, it is the manly and strenuous concordance of those who the most powerfully influence the public mind. Such as the writers of newspapers.' A reading of a cross-section of the press certainly suggests discord on the topic of Cardigan rather than concord.[25]

The Times, the *Morning Chronicle*, the *Globe* and the *United Service Gazette* led the attack on the court-martial finding and the malign influences of Lord Hill at the Horse Guards and Lord Cardigan at Brighton. The papers were incredulous at the court-martial ruling that Reynolds's behaviour could not be excused by any 'private irritation' which he might have suffered from Lord Cardigan. Such a ruling, said the *United Service Gazette* had 'excited but one feeling throughout the army; a feeling of unmitigated indignation and disgust'. The *Globe* attacked Lord Hill for refusing either to investigate regimental complaints against Cardigan or to condone the attempts of officers to seek justice for themselves in the face of their commander's insults. 'The wrongs of honour must therefore remain unheard and unredressed altogether,' said the *Globe*. In the view of Landor, the court-martial ruling gave Cardigan *carte-blanche* to ill-treat officers whom he disliked until they resigned their commissions, losing a good deal of money in the process. 'A superior has only to spit in their faces if he wishes with impunity to filch from their straitened uniforms some thousand pounds.'[26]

A prime target for the Radical press was the Horse Guards, specifically Lord Hill and Lord Fitzroy Somerset, who were both accused of shielding the Earl of Cardigan from public anger. There were 'obligations of a very peculiar nature existing between Lord Fitzroy Somerset and the Earl of Cardigan', said a correspondent of the *Morning Chronicle* knowingly. Later, in the face of protests, the paper withdrew this insinuation.[27]

The editorials of the leading newspapers seemed to be taken up with the subject of Lord Cardigan as the major topic of the autumn. On the following pages, column after column was given up to news items about him and to letters on his behaviour from such pseudonymous correspondents as 'A Citizen', 'An Old Adjutant', 'Not One of the 11th, I Thank God!' or 'A Lover of Justice, a Hater of Tyranny, and an Admirer of the Gallant and Noble Spirit Which Beats in the Bosom of Captain Reynolds'.

For their part, the *Morning Post* (described by the *United Service Gazette* as the 'Cardigan organ-in-chief') and the other pro-Cardigan papers could only repeat that the court-martial had acted correctly. Had the Horse Guards or Cardigan behaved otherwise in this case they would, indeed, have been liable to censure. The *Brighton Gazette* even went so far as to advertise the present happy state of affairs in the regiment. 'Prince Albert's own Hussars consist of 335 men, of whom

110 are at the Chichester Barracks, and the rest, 225, at the Cavalry Barracks in Brighton. Out of the latter number there are only four on punishment drill, and one in the Hospital. There is also only one sick horse.'[28]

The report sounded factual enough but it made very little difference at a time when the public believed only what it wanted to believe about Cardigan and the regiment. However, a pamphlet now appeared, attacking R. A. Reynolds as a snob who sneered at the social origins of other officers in the regiment. Cardigan, on the other hand, was 'beloved' by the common soldiers, one of whom he had raised from the ranks to be his Adjutant, Lieutenant Knowles. Knowles had indeed been a sergeant-major in the 11th before he was commissioned. However, the *United Service Gazette* remained unimpressed and suggested that Cardigan must be employing his butler to write his propaganda for him. Whatever the authorship, a copy of this particular pamphlet was sent to Prince Albert, on Cardigan's behalf. On 10 November there was a chilly snub from Windsor Castle, signed by the Prince's private secretary, declining to have anything whatever to do with the publications of either side in the dispute.[29]

By the end of October the press war had inspired penny subscriptions and public meetings in support of Captain R. A. Reynolds. There were reports of large and violent demonstrations against the Earl of Cardigan. Lord Melbourne, the Prime Minister, wrote to Lord Hill and demanded a full report on the 11th Hussars and their commander.

On 23 October, the day after the departure of Captain Reynolds for London, Sir John Macdonald, Adjutant-General, described by the *United Service Gazette* as 'the most notorious tuft-hunter in Great Britain', for his obsequious search for the company of the titled and the noble, arrived in Brighton. He went straight to the Barracks and summoned all the officers of the 11th Hussars, including Cardigan, to the mess. The doors were then locked.[30]

'I have been ordered by the General Commanding-in-Chief to come down to Brighton', said Macdonald, 'to call together the officers of the 11th Hussars, and to express to them his lordship's feelings upon recent transactions in the regiment.'

Macdonald began by delivering a reminder from Lord Hill that all officers were bound, by the terms of the Mutiny Act and by army regulations, to obey their commander. If there were any complaints to be made against that commander, they must be made in the proper manner.

'But the General Commanding-in-Chief trusts that the officers will not be too ready to draw conclusions from, or impute motives to, looks or casual expressions in conversation, that complaints when made will be susceptible of proof, and that the harmony of the service will not be disturbed on light or imaginary grounds.'

There was one other hope of Lord Hill's, the sincerity of which was beyond question. He trusted, said Macdonald, 'that all that has passed will be buried in oblivion, and that henceforward the officers of the 11th Hussars will serve together with cordiality.'

To many of those present it must have seemed that Lord Hill's memorandum might have been written at Cardigan's dictation. Indeed, it was reported that Cardigan began to show visible signs of delight as his officers were reprimanded for ignoring the obedience due to an officer of superior rank. Yet Macdonald had only read the first half of the memorandum and, tuft-hunter or not, he was obliged to continue to the end.

Cardigan was now ordered to remember in future that he commanded a regiment only recently returned from a long period of service in India, 'in which the habits and customs of the service must differ from those in European service'. So much for the 'Indian officers'. Cardigan was ordered to view the errors of his officers with 'indulgent moderation', and to set an example in 'moderation, temper, and discretion, blended with the zealous activity and ability for which he is noted'. Cardigan was never to forget that those placed under his command 'are officers in the service of her Majesty, gentlemen of education as well as himself'. According to the *Brighton Herald*'s informant, Cardigan's face changed colour at this point and he began to squirm in anguish at the rebukes delivered to him in front of his subordinates 'whom he had so frequently treated with arrogance, repression, and insult'.[31]

The most predictable reaction was, perhaps, Cardigan's own, when he was shortly afterwards heard to remark, both in front of his own officers and at a large dinner party, that Lord Hill was 'much more fitted to fatten bullocks on his pet farm than to have the command of an army.' Both sides of the press felt cheated, the *Morning Post* because Lord Hill had not supported Cardigan sufficiently, and the *Morning Chronicle* and the *Globe* because Cardigan had got off too lightly.[32]

Lord Hill had hoped that the troubles of the 11th Hussars would now be forgotten. The Radical press promised him that they should not be. The irresistible force of enlightened democratic opinion would smash the power of Lord Cardigan and, if necessary, the power of Lord Hill as well. To begin with, there was the plight of Captain R. A. Reynolds and the £6,000, the value of his commission, of which he had been robbed by being cashiered.

'Public demonstrations in favour of Captain Reynolds are sheer humbug', said the *Spectator* irritably, though the paper was no friend of Cardigan's.[33] Humbug or not, the demonstrations continued.

On 23 October there was a public meeting at the Lord Nelson Inn, Southwark, which deplored the treatment of R. A. Reynolds, and the slights cast upon officers who had served in India, by Lord Cardigan. It was resolved that a subscription should be launched to provide an annuity for Captain Reynolds, and J. West Shrewsbury, a notary of Chancery Lane, was appointed honorary secretary. On 29 October, he invited the co-operation of all the other Reynolds meetings across the country, in order to produce the promised annuity.

On 2 November there was a rival meeting at the British Coffee House in Cockspur Street, which was crowded to capacity for the occasion. Mention was made of raising money. However this money was not to be presented to Reynolds, since that might be an insult to a proud man, but would be used to defray the costs of any legal action which might prove necessary in order to secure justice. Before long, it was clear that the meeting was far more concerned with Cardigan than with Reynolds. Mr Robinson of Croydon proposed an official inquiry into the state of affairs in the 11th Hussars.

'I am sorry to say there are many Cardigans in this country', he announced, and there was a roar of approval. 'The whole of the court-martial that has lately sat at Brighton are composed of Cardigans!' There was great cheering at this, and the discussion of Reynolds's case continued. However, according to the chairman, they were still 'fighting shy of the question'. The second resolution soon altered that. Among tremendous applause it was proposed 'That it is both the interest and the duty of the British nation to procure the dismissal of the Earl of Cardigan (tremendous cheering) from the army.' A third resolution proposed to petition the Queen to reinstate Reynolds and dismiss Cardigan.[34]

Money for the Reynolds subscription had begun to arrive at the offices of the *Morning Chronicle* and the *Globe*, accompanied by letters of sympathy for the gallant Captain and expressions of disgust at Lord

Cardigan's behaviour. The rich sent their guineas and the less rich sent their shillings. All over the country, 'from Dover to John o' Groats' House', as one observer described it, the Radicals adopted their unlikely hero and his cause. A shilling subscription was opened in Huddersfield and a penny subscription in Hull. Other subscriptions were organized from Manchester to Maidstone, and there was another public meeting, at Marylebone, on 2 November, at which it was demanded that Reynolds should be restored to his rank by royal authority. Reynolds might, of course, be reluctant to accept any of the money collected on his behalf, but the fund could still be used in support of legal action to show both Cardigan and the Horse Guards that the will of the people was not to be defied.

On 3 November the Radicals were amazed, though they ought not to have been, by a letter from Reynolds himself, which appeared in most of the leading newspapers. Writing from his home, Paxton Hall in Huntingdonshire, where he was able to live quite comfortably without the aid of penny subscriptions, Reynolds admitted publicly that he had 'grievously offended' against army regulations by challenging Cardigan to a duel, and had thus incurred his punishment. Though the loss of his commission was bitter to him, 'no degree of provocation can ever justify a subordinate in breaking from the strict line of respectful submission'. Reynolds almost echoed the words of the court-martial finding and, to the horror of many of his supporters, began to eat humble pie with all the relish of a gourmet. He paid tribute to the 'perfect uprightness' of the officers at his court-martial, and then made his last public statement.

> Such being my views of this matter, I hope and trust that my assertion will be received as sincere, when I state it as my most anxious desire that no subscription of any kind be entered into on my account. But I am, if possible, even more anxious that no attempt should be made to influence the Crown on my behalf. I have said already, and I repeat it with the most unaffected sincerity, that I am not a fair judge in my own cause, neither do I conceive that the public can be so.[35]

As the *Morning Post* had remarked, Reynolds was as thorough-going a Tory as Cardigan, a landowner who rode with the Fitzwilliam Hunt. He was unlikely to consent to becoming a mascot of the Radicals. After two years of 'remaining quiet', he was gazetted a Captain in the 9th Lancers in 1842.

The pro-Cardigan papers were delighted at his rebuff to the Radicals and their penny subscriptions. 'Captain Reynolds refuses the money', said the *Naval and Military Gazette*. 'Into whose pocket will it be transferred?' The editor reiterated the suspicions of *The Times* that 'Fraud may be lurking under all this humbug.'[36]

In general, the press let Reynolds down lightly, observing how noble his letter was, when set beside Cardigan's conduct. However, there were those who felt that Reynolds had betrayed a first-class crusade against the abuse of military power. The *Sun* described him as 'the now subservient and obedient craven of the Horse Guards', whose only hope was another commission in the 11th Hussars, since no other regiment would tolerate him. Other attacks were less directly personal. 'His disposition to kiss the rod', said the *Examiner* solemnly, 'does not remove the public quarrel with the rod.'[37]

If Cardigan appeared indifferent to public scorn and the threat of three years on the treadmill for shooting Lieutenant Tuckett, it was in part because he had other matters on his mind. He and Lord Eglinton, who had been spoken of as a possible husband for Queen Victoria before Albert's triumphal arrival, had taken the Billesdon kennels for the hunting season. Moreover, in 1840 the Earl of Chesterfield resigned the mastership of the Pytchley, and Cardigan made his bid to succeed to one of the greatest positions in the social and sporting life of Victoria's England. But his chances had been spoilt by Chesterfield who, as master, had insisted on an almost regal standard of dress and entertainment, making membership extortionately expensive. The members feared that Cardigan might be even worse, in this respect, and so it was 'Gentleman' Tom Smith who succeeded Chesterfield. This was a severe disappointment to Cardigan. He had paid some thousands of pounds at Tattersall's auctions for the best hounds of Harvey Combe, dogs which had come originally from the redoubtable old Squire Osbaldeston.

However, November was the month of the Pytchley dinner and it was also that time of year when up to half the officers in the regiment were permitted by the Horse Guards to be absent on leave. Five officers, Captains Douglas and Vivian, Lieutenants Cunningham, Jenkinson, and Weguelin, accepted an invitation to accompany Lord and Lady Cardigan on a shooting party at Deene. 'Toadies!' chorused the *Morning Chronicle* and the *Globe*.

Shortly before the party was due to leave Brighton, according to the *Morning Chronicle*, Cardigan appeared in a box at the Theatre Royal. As soon as he was recognized there were hisses and groans, and for half an hour it was impossible to begin the performance. After sitting impassively in his box throughout this storm of threats and insults, Cardigan at last withdrew to the accompaniment of three cheers for Captain Reynolds and 'three groans for the Earl of Cardigan'. Yet according to the *Brighton Gazette*, Cardigan was actually in London at the time. The disturbance in the theatre, said the paper, was started by a 'stranger, who made his appearance in the "slips", accompanied by a lady of a certain description.'38

Indifferent to public demonstrations, Cardigan responded by ordering a special performance at the Theatre Royal, Brighton, on 30 October, 'under the distinguished patronage of the Earl of Cardigan and the officers of the 11th Hussars'. The regimental band would be in attendance, presumably to drown any hissing or groaning that might break out. According to the *Globe*, Cardigan had personally bought up all the tickets for the performance with a view to 'packing the house with his hirelings'. The *Brighton Herald* accused him of deliberately 'choosing the moment of his shame to blazon forth his name and influence in the full face of the world'.39

Yet on 30 October itself, there was an announcement from the theatre. The patronage of Lord Cardigan and the 11th Hussars had been postponed, 'in consequence of the very dangerous illness of Major Jenkins'.

Jenkins, the most senior officer in the regiment after Cardigan, was fifty-two years old and had been in indifferent health for some time. He suffered an apoplectic seizure on Wednesday 28 October. For the whole of Thursday and Friday nights, Cardigan sat up with him, while Jenkins's eldest son (a young clergyman at Oxford, about to be elected to a Balliol Fellowship) was sent for. The departure of the shooting party for Deene was postponed. The Major became delirious and on the Saturday morning he died.

On the following Wednesday, 4 November, to the beat of a muffled drum and the regimental band playing the 'Dead March in Saul' over and over again, the coffin was carried by troopers of the regiment from Brighton Barracks to St Peter's church. The 11th Hussars marched in double file with arms reversed, followed by the band, the coffin, four officers carrying the pall, and the Major's black horse with its master's riding boots slung round its neck. Behind the horse marched the officers of the regiment, two by two, with the Earl of Cardigan and the Adjutant bringing up the rear. Behind them came the black, ornate mourning coach with the Major's eldest son and the colonels of three other regiments, and finally a private carriage carrying the Major's doctors. The unusual pomp of the solemn occasion ensured that every window and balcony along the route was crowded, while carriages and pedestrians lined the road, and a great crowd surrounded the procession at St Peter's church.

There is no doubt that Cardigan behaved well towards Jenkins, and towards his family, who were found to be in considerable financial difficulties, having forfeited the value of his commission by his death. Cardigan therefore paid the expenses of the funeral, bought the Major's horse for the use of William Jenkins, the eldest son, and as William was about to return to Oxford, Cardigan 'begged his acceptance of a sum of money for his immediate use, pending the settlement of the Major's affairs'. When they parted, Cardigan said, 'Pay me again when you are a bishop, but not before.'

As the *Naval and Military Gazette* remarked, 'It is a great pity that such hard-hearted tyranny as this is not more general.' Cardigan also paid £400 to be elected a Governor of Christ's Hospital, in order that he might give his nomination to the youngest orphan of the Jenkins family.[40]

Of course, it would not do. Cardigan's enemies, setting aside the post-mortem evidence of apoplexy, enlarged heart and diseased kidneys, decided that Jenkins's death had been caused by the dishonour which the commanding officer had brought upon his regiment. It was said that in his delirium the dying Major had cried out repeatedly, 'Poor Reynolds! Poor Reynolds!' Jenkins had lost the power of speech long before then, but that was not the point. As the *Brighton Gazette* remarked, there were those who now credited Lord Cardigan with crimes of every description, from setting fire to Plymouth Dockyard to being the hitherto undetected murderer of Mr Westwood of Prince's Street several years earlier.[41]

The alacrity with which Cardigan flew to his duelling pistols was certainly matched by the speed with which he gave away his money. On hearing of an officer who had been offered a commission in India but had not the money to accept it, Cardigan, on impulse, wrote him a cheque for £2,000 at once. Though the Pytchley had rejected him as master, in favour of 'Gentleman' Tom Smith, this did not prevent Cardigan from giving the hunt £1,000 a year to keep it solvent. The problem, however, was not to decide whether he was either generous or arrogant, he was both generous *and* arrogant.

Neither the press nor the public was much interested in subtle distinctions. When Cardigan returned from the shooting party, he was hissed and booed at railway stations and obliged to drive through London with the blinds of his carriage drawn down. Everywhere, it seemed, there was jeering, groaning, and shouts of 'Black Bottle!'

While Major Jenkins was being buried in St Peter's churchyard on 4 November, other citizens of Brighton were preparing their Guy Fawkes celebrations for the following day. These celebrations began when the Guy was carried in procession through the streets to the scene of the bonfire. On 5 November 1840, the traditional Guy in, cloak and high boots, was nowhere to be seen. In its place was a dummy dressed in the uniform of the 11th (Prince Albert's own) Hussars. The dummy carried a black bottle, marked 'Moselle', and, much to the amusement of the crowd, a brace of pistols labelled, 'Not hair-triggers'. Even the less boisterous bystanders had broad grins upon their faces, according to the *Brighton Herald*, whose correspondent observed, 'The people had turned satirists, and had given up the satisfaction of burning a Pope for the pleasure of roasting an Earl.'[42]

The pleasure of roasting Cardigan, metaphorically, seemed inexhaustible. When he attended a concert at Drury Lane Theatre on 22 December there was a sudden shout of 'Black Bottle!' from the pit, and fingers were pointed at his box. Cardigan continued to sit disdainfully in his place while a general hissing began. Soon there were shouts of 'Shame!' and 'Turn him out!' as well as other 'significant sounds'. Cardigan sat through the tumult for some time but it was evident that no performance could begin while he was in the theatre. Moreover, the boxes at Drury Lane were accessible from the main body of the theatre by way of a door, and there seemed to be a growing danger that Cardigan might be mobbed. At length he got up, walked to the front of the box, put on his greatcoat, bowed to the angry crowd below him, and was escorted from the building 'amidst one universal roar of disapprobation'. According to the *Morning Advertiser*, the 'yells, hissing, and discordant sounds were deafening'.[43]

A few weeks later, Cardigan reappeared at a Drury Lane promenade concert, occupying the box usually reserved for Queen Adelaide, and accompanied by several friends. He was not recognized until the interval.

At the end of the first act a few young gentlemen gathered into a corner of the stage and began hissing. It soon spread, and in about ten minutes there was a complete uproar, every eye in that vast circle fixed upon one spot; necks craning, bodies twisting round pillars, vermicular, all to gaze upon or to cast insult at, one small party.

From nine o'clock until eleven it was impossible to hear a note of the music but Cardigan refused to be budged, throughout what the *Morning Chronicle* depicted as an 'indescribable uproar'. Some of those present, more angered by the uproar than by Cardigan, began to cheer him in a counter-demonstration. However, as the *Globe* added, 'When the performance was over numbers of persons rushed out of the pit to give him, which they did, a lusty parting groan in the street.'[44]

It is perhaps worth mentioning that audiences at the Drury Lane promenade concerts were somewhat less than genteel. In August 1840 there had been a riot when a gentleman in one of the tier boxes began to amuse himself 'by imitating the music'. There were shouts of 'Turn him out!' and the police were called. On their arrival, the man threw himself into the pit, whose occupants suddenly changed sides and began to defend him from the police. In a vain attempt to restore order the manager commanded the orchestra to play 'God Save the Queen', but it was drowned in the uproar.

Yet, by any standards, Cardigan was a special case, as Macaulay conceded.[45]

> Could Lord Cardigan go to a theatre that he was not insulted ? Could he take his place in a railway train without having a hiss raised against him ? Was there ever a case in which a man was more violently and intemperately assailed ? Without wishing to assert that Lord Cardigan is faultless (on that point I do not give an opinion)—if he had been Hare, the accomplice of Burke, or any other person impugned on the most criminal charge, instead of being accused with faults of temper and manner, could stronger or more violent, or more intemperate means be taken to mark the public aversion ?

But, of course, Lord Cardigan was impugned on no less than three criminal charges: intent to murder; intent to maim; and inflicting grievous bodily harm. He was soon to answer these charges before his peers. In the meantime, there was another regimental 'turn-up'.

This time it was the surgeon of the 11th Hussars, Dr Sandham, who provided Cardigan's antagonist. On 8 December, as the regiment left St Peter's church in Brighton after the Sunday morning service, the clasp of Dr Sandham's cap became unhooked and he stopped to adjust it. Then, in order to catch up with the rest of the regiment, he left the church and the churchyard by a side entrance.

When the men had reached the barracks and been dismissed, Lieutenant Knowles, the Adjutant, confronted Sandham.

'It is his lordship's order that you fall in with the troops.'

'I am unable to understand the drift of his lordship's commands', said Sandham, 'seeing that I have invariably obeyed them to the very letter.'

'It is his lordship's order', said Knowles, and walked off.

Since Cardigan had not yet left the scene of the parade, Dr Sandham approached him.

'My lord, I have been ordered to fall in with the troops.'

'Those are my orders, sir', said Cardigan briskly.

'But I don't understand them, my lord.'

'They are my orders, sir! Did you not come out at the small gate?'

'I did', said Sandham.

'I order you in future to come out of the large gate.'

Sandham withdrew to his room, where some of his brother officers called on him and inquired what the trouble had been.

'I came out of the small gate instead of the large one', said Sandham simply.

Before Sandham had time to leave the barracks, the Adjutant summoned him to another confrontation with Cardigan.

'Your conduct was highly improper and reprehensible in having made such a statement to the young officers who have just left you', Cardigan announced to him.

Sandham tried to explain that he had made no complaint to them but had merely described his own fault.

'Be quiet, sir!' snapped Cardigan, 'I shall not listen to any reply!'

'My lord,' insisted Sandham, 'I have not failed to use my best endeavours to please your lordship, but I now find that it is impossible to do so.'

'Well, sir,' rejoined Cardigan, 'you had better state that fact in writing. And now, sir, *leave the room!*'

With his commander's final shout echoing after him, Sandham went off and stated the fact in writing to Lord Hill. Cardigan went to the Horse Guards with his own version of the dispute. The result of his interview there was not encouraging.

> Lord Hill regrets to find that his recommendation to the Earl of Cardigan on a previous occasion has not had the effect of preventing applications to the Horse Guards by way of complaint of the Earl's conduct.

'We think', remarked the *Morning Chronicle*, which had ferreted out this private reprimand, 'that his lordship would best consult his own dignity, comply with the wishes of the army in general, and more particularly of his own regiment, and would conciliate the feelings of the British public towards himself, were he at once, by retiring from the army, to restore that harmony and good fellowship again to the 11th Hussars, which, until his lordship joined the regiment, previously existed.'[46]

Lord Hill, at least, had little hope that Cardigan would take such advice. However, a conviction and prison sentence by the House of Lords would have the same result in practice.

There were successive press rumours of officers seeking to sell out of the 11th Hussars rather than serve any longer under Cardigan. Captain J. W. Reynolds had already stated his terms to the Horse Guards. Now it was said that Captain Vivian wished to leave, which Captain Vivian denied in a letter to the press. Since he had been one of the 'toadies' in the shooting party, it seemed unlikely that he would go. Captain Sandham was said to be selling out. Yet a man with thirty years' service hardly seemed likely to do so in consequence of a single quarrel with his commanding officer. Even Captain Douglas, Cardigan's protégé, was named as a discontented junior officer, though he seems the most unlikely candidate of all.

Most of these rumours had no foundation, but Major Morse Cooper, formerly of the 11th Hussars, created a small press sensation by describing how he had sold out and gone on half-pay because he could no longer tolerate Cardigan's sneers and arrogance. The effect of his revelation was rather spoilt when the *Morning Post* published a letter of Cooper's, written after he had sold out, asking Major Jenkins to exchange, so that he might rejoin the regiment.[47]

Anecdotes of Cardigan's heartlessness were widespread in the weeks before his trial. It was said, for instance, that when the father of Captain R. A. Reynolds was dying, Reynolds had asked for leave. 'If your father is *really dying*, you may go to London', said

Cardigan, 'but you must return to the review the day after tomorrow.'

Reynolds senior died, his son travelled back all night to the regiment, and was present with his squadron at the review. On a similar occasion, in the 15th Hussars, Cardigan is alleged to have remarked, 'If I give —— leave, I shall have some officer's father *dying every day!*'[48]

As such stories as this went the rounds of clubs and mess-rooms, the *Globe* suggested that Cardigan should be elevated in the peerage to the rank of Marquis of Carabas and 'Baron Blackbottle', but there were other voices which remained loyal to him. On 16 January 1841, the *Naval and Military Gazette* published two letters written anonymously by private soldiers of the 11th Hussars. The first praised Cardigan as a 'working soldier', unlike many of his fashionable junior officers. 'The men of the regiment saw with what disgust they left the sofa and the cigar for the litter and stench of a stable.' Cardigan, it seemed, had found his men more reliable in matters of military routine than their officers. He had even chosen for his Adjutant a man who had risen from the ranks. That was the cause of the trouble.

The second letter was shorter and more specific.

> Sir,—It is determined by the men of the 11th Hussars to destroy every paper they meet with, in spite of ownership or position, that has anything in it reflecting on Lord Cardigan, and to thrash any fellow for the future who takes the liberty of speaking disrespectfully of him. Your obedient servant.
>
> ONE OF PRINCE ALBERT'S OWN.

The *United Service Gazette* deplored such 'ruffianly threats', and the poor taste of the *Naval and Military Gazette* in printing them, whether the letters actually came from the 11th Hussars or not. The *Britannia*, too, was shocked by the 'ruffianly language', and disgusted that private soldiers should be allowed to take part in the quarrels of their officers.[49]

The tranquillity of Lord Hill's Horse Guards had gone for ever. Indeed, he was now given to public outbursts on the subject of the 11th Hussars. One evening after dinner he was sitting next to Lady Langdale as she cracked a walnut. The skin of the nut was so beautifully variegated that she exclaimed it was just like the uniform of the 11th Hussars.

'I am thoroughly sick of the 11th!' protested Hill desperately. 'And of all that belongs to it!'[50]

Prince Albert was sick of the regiment, too, and was making

preparations to wash his hands of it before Cardigan's trial came on. Cardigan was summoned to Windsor in the New Year. 'His Lordship', reported the *Alligator*, 'looked exceedingly ill, and appeared careworn and out of spirits.' The interview with the Prince was brief. Cardigan, who had arrived in Windsor before breakfast, was back at Slough railway station with time to spare before the late morning train left for London. He went into the first-class waiting room, to escape the sightseers, and picked up one of the morning newspapers provided there. It was covered with news of the forthcoming trial, the regiment, the 'turn-up' with Dr Sandham, Morse Cooper's letters, and similar items.

'Damn these papers', growled Cardigan, throwing it down in a rage. 'I'm sick of them!'[51]

The public waited for Prince Albert to resign, which he did; for Lord Hill to resign, which death was soon to anticipate, and for Lord Cardigan to resign. But resignation was not one of Cardigan's virtues.

Cardigan returned to Deene for Christmas, where there was a large house-party including Lord and Lady Lucan, his sister and brother-in-law, and another sister, Lady Augusta Baring. He went through the Christmas ritual of giving away a bullock to each of the five neighbouring villages, with bread and ale to every villager. Twice a week throughout the winter, free soup was to be supplied to all who wanted it. At the end of December he went to Brighton to muster the regiment, for what seemed likely to be the last time, and he attended a subscription ball at the Ship Inn in the evening before travelling back to Deene.

Both Queen Adelaide and the Duke of Wellington issued statements disclaiming any responsibility for Cardigan's having been reinstated in the army after his dismissal from the 15th Hussars. They had neither desired it, apparently, nor interceded in any way on his behalf. These disclaimers were a certain indication that the time of the trial was at hand and they seemed to most observers a clear sign that, in the light of the evidence, there was only one possible verdict.

Since the fire of 1834 the House of Lords had met in the Painted Chamber. Though the furnishings were ornate, the benches covered in crimson and bound with brass, six richly gilt chandeliers on long lacquered chains lighting the house, it was still much smaller than the old chamber. £2,400 had to be spent on improving the accommodation for Cardigan's trial, but that was only the beginning of the expense involved in the ritual pomp of trying a nobleman before his peers. Three hundred peers and 340 spectators were to be crammed into the chamber by means of enlarging the galleries. A new gallery was to be built to provide seating for the royal family and for the families of peers. All peers were to attend in full ceremonial robes and wearing their orders of knighthood. The date for the opening of the trial was to be Tuesday 16 February 1841.

Both sides in the coming legal battle began to prepare their cases. Counsel for the Crown was to be the Attorney-General, Sir John Campbell, later Lord Campbell, a forceful and ambitious Scots politician who alienated many of his contemporaries by his undisguised urge for self-advancement. As Attorney-General, Lord Chief Justice and Lord Chancellor, he earned the reputation of being one of the most redoubtable lawyers of his time. As an author he was celebrated for his *Lives of the Lord Chancellors*, a vast and intimidating work which according to the reigning Lord Chancellor, Lyndhurst, had added 'another terror to death'. In middle-age, Campbell with his tall forehead and parrot-beak nose looked rather like a Roman senator in frock-coat and trousers. Even had he been a less able lawyer and a more indifferent personality, the case against Cardigan was virtually proved before the trial began.

Cardigan's counsel was Sir William Follett, a younger man than Campbell and a former Solicitor-General in the short-lived government of Sir Robert Peel in 1834-5. Though only forty-three years old, Follett was already suffering the first symptoms of an illness which was to kill him within four years. By 1843, the lower part of his body was paralysed and he conducted his last cases by sitting in a high chair. He was Campbell's opposite. His manners and address were graceful, though he spoke without rhetoric or gesture. His lucidity of mind earned him the reputation of being one of the best intellects of his day. In the view of many contemporaries, had Follett lived, he would have become one of the great Victorians. In appearance he was tall and slim with a fine brow and grey eyes. Follett had fought Campbell before, appearing for George Norton in the celebrated divorce action of 1836 when Lord Melbourne was cited as co-respondent. Campbell had won.

As the day of the trial approached, Cardigan prepared for the worst. One of the penalties inflicted on a peer of the realm found guilty of felony was the confiscation of his estates by the Crown.

Cardigan temporarily transferred the whole of his wealth to his nephew, the eldest son of Lord Howe. The stamp duty alone on the transfer was £10,000, but it was a small price for securing the family estates in the event of the 7th Earl's conviction. Even in the eighteenth century it had sometimes been possible for a condemned peer to plead his clergy and so escape punishment, but now, as the Radical press gleefully pointed out, this medieval ruse of benefit of clergy had been abolished. Once Cardigan was convicted the public would expect to see him punished.

Because the trial had been delayed for five months after the duel, the significance of it had been temporarily forgotten and the peril in which Cardigan stood from the law had passed from the public mind. In the first days of February 1841 the public mind roused itself, to alarm or satisfaction according to its political mood. John Wilson Croker, an old-style Tory and former Secretary to the Admiralty, wrote to Sir William Follett a few days before the trial.[52]

> If you find it necessary to parry an attack on the general system of duelling, I would have you strongly to lament that the law connived at it, and that the custom, stronger even than law, had so sanctioned it, that one would be dishonoured who should decline. Let the House propose and pass a distinct law against the practice, but not attempt to do it by a sidewind, against one who was a peer, and therefore in a special degree bound to stand, as *they* were all trying *him, on their honour*—against one, too, who was a soldier, and was challenged in his military character by a soldier; and finally against, not the aggressor, but the challenged.

Moreover, Croker added, no less than six prime ministers of the past one hundred years had fought duels, as well as a number of present members of the House of Lords itself. But the truth was that this was no defence to the charges against Cardigan, and Follett made no use of the argument.

2

On the afternoon of 15 February, the day before the trial, two men called upon Lord Cardigan at his Portman Square house. They were Sir Charles Rowan and Richard Mayne, Chief Magistrate and Commissioner of Police for the Metropolitan area. They had come to offer him police protection against the expected attacks of the crowd as he drove to the Houses of Parliament. Cardigan thanked them but said that he was quite able to look after himself.

By eight o'clock the next morning, spectators were swarming through the streets of Westminster towards the parliament buildings. Strong forces of Metropolitan police, both uniformed and in plain clothes, had been deployed in the area. At ten o'clock a battalion of the Scots Guards was called in to secure the approaches to the House of Lords. The carriages of the noble and the famous, their servants in state liveries riding on the outside, began to roll past. Soon there was a line of them stretching down Parliament Street towards Whitehall. The Lord Chief Justice arrived first, shortly followed by Lady Cardigan. The diplomatic corps was led by the ambassadors of France, Prussia, Austria, Russia and Brazil. There was one royal duke, Cambridge, but the Queen had announced that neither she nor Prince Albert would wish to attend upon so painful an occasion as this. The royal carriages were there, however, crowded with the Queen's Ladies-in-Waiting who had come to see the show.

At half-past ten the other carriages were drawn on one side, as if the Sovereign might perhaps be coming after all. A splendid carriage with liveried coachmen and footmen thundered down Parliament Street, the horses moving almost at a gallop, as though they were pulling the four-in-hand of some Captain of Dragoons. There was no time for the crowd to hiss or cheer. The coach had passed by the time they realized that its solitary occupant was the Earl of Cardigan, on his way to the most expensive trial of the century.

In the crowded chamber the benches, galleries and floor were newly covered in crimson cloth. Against this the robes of the peers in their cocked hats and orders of knighthood made a brilliant display. It looked more like the scene of a coronation than a criminal trial. Those members of the House of Commons who could press their way forward were allowed standing room just below the bar of the house. The throne, of course, remained empty but just below it a chair of state had been provided for Lord Denman, the Speaker of the Lords. In the absence of the Lord Chancellor, who was ill, Denman was to preside over the trial as Lord High Steward.

Just before eleven o'clock the medieval pageantry of the procession began. Lord Denman was preceded by the purse-bearer, the Sergeant with the mace, and Garter King-at-Arms carrying the sceptre. There was also Black Rod, who held the slender white staff symbolizing the royal command to the Lord High Steward to preside over this trial. Once the trial was over the staff would be snapped in two and the Queen's commission would be dissolved.

After prayers, the royal commission was read, followed by the three counts of the indictment, which accused Cardigan of intent to murder, intent to maim and inflicting grievous bodily harm upon, Harvey Garnett Phipps Tuckett. Then proclamation was made for the Yeoman Usher to bring the prisoner from the ante-chamber to the bar of the house. Cardigan came forward and bowed once to the Lord High Steward and once to the peers on either side. The bows were returned with a rustling of robes. A stool was provided for him at one side of the bar of the house, close to his counsel. At the other side of the bar sat the counsel for the Crown.

Cardigan was arraigned on the three charges.

'How say you, my lord,' asked the Deputy Clerk of the Crown, 'are you guilty of the felony with which you stand charged, or not guilty?'

'Not guilty, my lords,' said Cardigan firmly.

'How will your lordship be tried?' inquired the Deputy Clerk.

The traditional response was, 'By God and my Peers.' But Cardigan, having a proper sense of the importance of the British aristocracy in such matters, said simply, 'By my peers.'

'God send your lordship a good deliverance.'[53]

In the anxious silence of the spectators, who had come to witness the downfall of the notorious Earl of Cardigan, Sir John Campbell rose to open the case for the Crown.

Like most accomplished lawyers, Campbell had something of the qualities of the actor, and could cast himself in whatever role seemed best suited to his case. As prosecutor, he could be the outraged guardian of social morals or common decency; as defender, he might appear in the guise of a champion of innocence-in-peril; in courts of appeal and in the argument of legal technicalities, he was a reasonable man addressing other reasonable men. It was this last role which he chose for his appearance before the Lords. Histrionics might impress ordinary jurors, but not peers of the realm.

Campbell needed no histrionics. If his opening address was in a low key, the evidence upon which it rested was irrefutable. He had only to outline the law of duelling, the facts of the case, and then to remind the assembled peers that they were bound to find their verdict as strictly as any court of justice and that they were 'bound by rules of law, and under a sanction as sacred as that of an oath'.[54]

Then Campbell listed his witnesses, explaining that neither Tuckett nor Wainwright would be among them. Although the grand jury had sanctioned no prosecution against them, they might lay themselves open to other charges by giving evidence to the Lords, and that, said Campbell, would not be 'decorous'. He did not mention that Tuckett, in any case, had retired abroad for the duration of the trial.

With his plea for a conviction amply supported by evidence, Campbell could afford to give away a few inessential points. He willingly accepted, for instance, that Cardigan had not meant to take an unfair advantage of Tuckett by having duelling pistols of a superior kind. 'Nothing but what was fair and honourable was intended', Campbell remarked, but that was not the point for consideration.[55]

> But although moralists of high name have excused or even defended the practice of duelling, your lordships are to consider what it is by the law of England. My lords, by the law of England there can be no doubt that parties who meet deliberately to fight a duel, if death ensues, are guilty of the crime of murder; and, my lords, it will be my duty to state to your lordships a few of the leading authorities upon that subject.

These authorities entirely supported the argument put forward by Campbell, showing that Cardigan must be guilty of intent to murder.[56]

> Then, my lords, however painful the consideration may be, does it not necessarily follow that the first count of this indictment is completely proved? The circumstances, my lords, clearly show that the Earl of Cardigan and Captain Tuckett met by appointment. Lord Cardigan (the ground being measured out) twice fires loaded pistols; he takes deliberate aim; he wounds his antagonist. He must be supposed to have intended what he did. If, unfortunately, death had ensued, would not this have been a case of murder?

If the first count, charging Cardigan with intent to murder, was proved, then, in Campbell's view, 'with regard to the second and third counts of the indictment, I know not what defence can possibly be suggested.' Finally, Campbell envied Cardigan for having secured as his defender, 'my most able and ingenious and honourable friend, Sir William Follett'. There was a sting at the end of this compliment, however. 'But, my lords, notwithstanding the learning, the ability, and the zeal of my honourable and learned friend Sir William Follett, I know not how he can at all persuade your lordships to acquit upon any one count of the indictment.'[57]

The first of the prosecution witnesses was Thomas Dann, who had arrested both Cardigan and Captain Douglas, and had seen most of the duel. He now identified Cardigan as one of the duellists and was preparing to identify Tuckett by the visiting card which had been given him after the duel, and in consequence of which he allowed Sir James Anderson to take Tuckett home and put him to bed. As Sir John Campbell's junior, Waddington, was about to read out the name on the card, Follett jumped up in some agitation.

'Do not read that card yet!'[58]

A legal battle began, which Follett seemed certain to lose, as to the admissibility of the visiting card to prove the identity of Tuckett as the wounded man on Wimbledon Common. The more agitated Follett became, the more determined Campbell grew to introduce this card in evidence. It seemed the obvious way of proving that the man whom Cardigan had wounded was Tuckett. However, the Lord High Steward postponed legal argument on the point until later in the case.

A matter of seconds later, Follett was on his feet again, objecting to the way in which Waddington was leading the witness by his questions. Follett's own cross-examination of Dann was skilful enough but Dann had some experience of giving evidence in court and he was not to be shaken in his story. The story was next confirmed by Dann's son, and then by Dann's wife. Mrs Dann was a less experienced witness than her husband and, at last, Follett made some progress in his demonstration that none of those who had given evidence could possibly have identified the duellists at 220 yards, the distance between the mill and the spot where the duel was fought. Follett's style, never hectoring and always gentle, brought Mrs Dann to a standstill.[59]

> *Follett*   I observe that you have all, you and the other witnesses before, said that the distance from your house to this spot was two hundred and twenty yards; has it been measured?
> *Mrs. Dann*   I think it has.

Follett   And could you at the distance of two hundred and twenty yards see the persons knocking pistols?

Mrs. Dann   Yes; I had a commanding view where I stood.

Follett   What do you suppose to be the distance from where you are standing now to the end of this house?

Mrs. Dann   I do not know. I should not have thought it had been more than a hundred yards; not at first, when I saw them.

Follett   You should not have thought what was more than a hundred yards?

Mrs. Dann   Not the distance from the mill to where the gentlemen were standing.

Follett   But you say it was two hundred and twenty yards?

Mrs. Dann   That is what I have been told.

Follett   At the distance of two hundred and twenty yards, could you see persons knocking and hammering?

Mrs. Dann   Yes, I could.

Follett   Could you distinguish their features?

Mrs. Dann   I could see their countenances.

Follett   Could you distinguish the countenances or features of any of the gentlemen standing at the other end of this house?

Mrs. Dann   I mean, I could see if they were red or pale when my husband went to them.

Follett   Can you see whether the gentlemen standing at the other end of this house are red or pale? (*Laughter*)

Mrs. Dann   Yes, I can. (*Renewed laughter*)

Follett   You are sure you can; are you quite sure of that? Look; can you distinguish whether the gentlemen are red or pale at the other end of the house?

Mrs. Dann   I can see better on the common, where I am more accustomed to look. (*Laughter*)

Follett   Can you see better in some places than in others?

Mrs. Dann   I have been there a good many years, and I can discern anything sooner than a stranger might.

Follett   Therefore that is the place where you see best, is it?

Mrs. Dann   I think it is.

Follett   Upon the common, where you see best, can you distinguish the features of gentlemen two hundred and twenty yards off, and whether they are red or pale?

Mrs. Dann   They looked to have red faces in the sun.

Follett   All the gentlemen had red faces, had they?

Mrs. Dann   No; I do not know that all of them had.
Follett   Had they all red faces?
Mrs. Dann   No.
Follett   How many had red faces? (*No answer*) Can you tell me who has been telling you this story, or who has been examining you upon this subject?
Mrs. Dann   No one.
Follett   No one! Have you never been examined as a witness?
Mrs. Dann   No.
Follett   Were you not before the grand jury?
Mrs. Dann   Oh yes, I was; I forgot that.

Follett worked meticulously, eroding the credibility of the witness, but it was of little use to Cardigan's defence once Campbell had established the evidence of Dann and his son. Dann had actually removed the smoking pistol from Lord Cardigan's hand and no questions about Mrs Dann's remarkable eyesight could alter that.

Campbell next called Cardigan's physician, Sir James Eglintoun Anderson. Before he gave evidence, he was warned by the Lord High Steward, 'that you are not bound to answer any question which may tend to criminate yourself'. Sir James took this advice to heart. Having said that he was a physician and that he lived in New Burlington Street, he declined to answer any further questions relating to the duel or even to his acquaintance with Tuckett. Amid roars of laughter, he parried Campbell's inquiries by saying in response to each one, 'I decline to answer the question.' He was permitted to withdraw, having added nothing to the Crown's case but not having weakened it either. Inspector Busain gave evidence of the scene at Wandsworth station house, and two of Tuckett's business acquaintances identified Tuckett as the man who lived at 13 Hamilton Place, New Road.[60]

Campbell had stated his case and produced his witnesses. All that remained was to decide whether Tuckett's visiting card, handed to Dann on Wimbledon Common, should be admitted as evidence to prove the identity of the man shot by Cardigan. Follett continued to object and then said, 'Will you let me look at the card?'

It was handed to him. Apparently resigning himself and Cardigan to an inevitable fate, he withdrew his objection to the card being read. It was handed in as evidence and the words upon it read.

'Captain Harvey Tuckett, 13 Hamilton Place, New Road.'

Though Tuckett's official half-pay rank was that of Lieutenant, he had held a temporary captaincy in India and had adopted it as his style. On the other side of the card someone had written in pencil, 'Captain H. Wainwright'.

Sir William Follett asked, 'Is that your case, Mr Attorney-General?'

Ignoring Follett, Sir John Campbell addressed the peers: 'This, my lords, is the case on the part of the prosecution.'

With the satisfaction of a task accomplished, he sat down and closed his case. By this time it was late in the afternoon. When Follett rose to address the house he had no witnesses, no evidence, and apparently no defence for Cardigan. It took several moments for the significance of his opening words to be fully appreciated.

> That being the case on the part of the prosecution, I shall venture to submit to your lordships that no case has been made out which calls upon the prisoner at the bar for an answer; and I think your lordships will see at once that my learned friends have failed in proving an essential part of their case.[61]

As a matter of fact, no one saw anything of the sort until Follett began to explain it to them. What they saw then was that throughout the prosecution case, Follett had been leading the Attorney-General into a very simple and quite inescapable trap. It had seemed that all Follett's efforts were concentrated on demonstrating that Dann, his wife and son could not have seen what was going on upon Wimbledon Common at a distance of 220 yards. He had shaken Mrs Dann's story but the Crown case, otherwise, seemed intact. Follett had also given the impression that the introduction of Tuckett's visiting card as proof of identity would be the death of Cardigan's hopes. Campbell had been all the more determined to use it and, in fact, had made it the foundation of his case so far as the identification of the wounded man was concerned.

Follett patiently explained to the peers why there was no case for Cardigan to answer. The indictment, in all three counts, charged Cardigan with crimes against Harvey Garnett Phipps Tuckett. The visiting card identified the man shot in the duel as Captain Harvey Tuckett. The Crown had introduced no evidence to prove that the two were identical, though anyone who had read a newspaper in the past five months would know that they were. At no time had it been shown by the prosecution evidence that the man shot by Cardigan bore the names of 'Garnett Phipps'. 'I think your lordships will see', said Follett calmly, 'that there is no evidence whatever to prove that the person at whom the noble Earl is charged to have shot upon the 12th of September was Mr. Harvey Garnett Phipps Tuckett.'[62]

Sir John Campbell, angry and incredulous, got up to answer Follett. He could, of course, have called a dozen witnesses to prove Tuckett's full Christian names, if he had known of Follett's tactics beforehand. But he had been induced to close his case, so that it was now too late to do anything about it. However, Campbell did not propose to give up without a struggle.[63]

> Now, my lords, how does the case stand? My learned friend withdrew all objection to the reading of the card. Well, then, the gentleman who was wounded, at whom the Earl of Cardigan shot on the 12th of September, was a Captain Tuckett. It was Captain Harvey Tuckett. We have got so far as to one of his names. Now, my lords, how does it stand with regard to the rest? Am I obliged to call the clerk of the parish where he was baptised, in order to prove his baptismal register? Am I obliged to call his father or his mother, or his godfathers and godmothers, to prove the name that was given to him at the baptismal font?

With the desperation of a man who sees certain victory slipping away from him, Campbell began to lose his grasp of logic and to suggest that his case might be proved by having shown that Tuckett had been in the 11th Hussars, a regiment commanded by the Earl of Cardigan. Follett irritated him still further by murmuring calmly from time to time, 'There is no proof of that whatever,' or 'You really are quite mistaken.' For some time the Attorney-General thundered on, but he did so, as Follett observed, in the manner of a man who knows that he has lost his case.[64]

The spectators were cleared from the galleries and the Lord High Steward addressed the peers, while Cardigan waited in his ante-chamber. Lord Denman emphasized that the proof of names was an integral part of the case and that, in his view, an ordinary jury would acquit a prisoner in the present circumstances. Then the spectators, but not Cardigan, were re-admitted.

The result of a trial by peers was not, of course, decided by a unanimous verdict but by a vote, each peer giving his decision in turn, beginning with the most junior. The Lord High Steward rose and faced the junior baron.

'John, Lord Keane, how says your lordship; is James Thomas, Earl of Cardigan, guilty of the felony whereof he stands indicted, or not guilty?'

Lord Keane rose in his place, uncovered his head, laid his right hand upon his breast and said clearly, 'Not guilty, upon my honour.'

As the barons, viscounts, earls, marquesses and dukes rose to give their verdicts, bobbing up one after the other, there was almost complete unanimity. Only William Harry, Duke of Cleveland, could not bring himself to give an unqualified verdict and said, 'Not guilty *legally*, upon my honour.'

Cardigan was brought to the bar again and Lord Denman, ignoring the Duke of Cleveland's reservation, addressed him.

'James Thomas, Earl of Cardigan, you have been indicted for a felony, for which you have been tried by your peers, and I have the satisfaction of declaring to you that their lordships have pronounced you not guilty by an unanimous sentence.'[65]

Cardigan bowed to the Lord High Steward, and to the peers on either side. Then he withdrew. The Lord High Steward rose and took the slender white staff which Garter King-at-Arms had carried before him to symbolize the royal authority of the proceedings. Lord Denman broke the staff in two and the Queen's commission was dissolved. The spectators filed out from the scene of medieval pageantry into the gas-lit February evening with its horse-drawn omnibuses and penny steamers on the Thames. The whole performance had cost some £4,000, but those who witnessed it were inclined to agree that, both as spectacle and as drama, it had been worth every penny.

The press behaved true to form. The *Morning Post*, the *Standard* and the *Naval and Military Gazette* thought the result of the trial very satisfactory. To the *Morning Chronicle*, however, it was a 'solemn farce', while the *Globe* complained that 'The public has been mulcted in a sum of £3,000 or £4,000 for its apathy, in having tolerated the restoration of the Earl of Cardigan to a position where to insult, and be insulted, has been his vocation.' The newspapers continued their bickering of the autumn and the *Morning Post*, which appeared at breakfast, usually found the evening *Globe* snapping at its heels by dinner time. 'The poor *Po* has, I fear, cracked', wrote one *Globe* correspondent triumphantly, 'and leaked out all its patronage of that much injured pet of the Horse Guards, Lord Cardigan.'[66]

On 18 February Lord Adolphus Fitzclarence gave a dinner party in his suite at St James's Palace to celebrate the acquittal of Lord Cardigan. It was a suitably military occasion and the other guests included the Duke of Cambridge, his son Prince George (the future Commander-in-Chief), and Lord Fitzroy Somerset. Not everyone saw reason to celebrate, however. The night after his acquittal, Cardigan and his Countess went to a promenade concert at Drury Lane. All too soon, Cardigan was recognized by 'suckers of oranges, and adults with inflamed countenances'. Soon there were shouts of 'Black Bottle!' and general uproar. The yells and hisses continued for half an hour. Cardigan sat in his box, apparently indifferent to the display, while Lady Cardigan appeared to be rather amused by the whole thing.[67]

On 5 March when the Radicals in the House of Commons urged the Melbourne government to take some action against Cardigan, Macaulay as Secretary-at-War replied that there were no grounds either for court-martialling him or dismissing him from his command. Whatever Cardigan's faults, the government would not be blackmailed into getting rid of him by demonstrations at theatres or railway stations.

Captain Douglas was tried at the beginning of March but it was a pure formality after Cardigan's acquittal. Cardigan's estates were now transferred back to him, since he was out of danger, and it was pointed out that the £10,000 in stamp duty which this precaution had cost him was more than enough to meet the expense of the trial. To that extent, justice had been done in a somewhat circuitous manner.

The last murmurs of debate died away in the Commons on 8 March and by 10 March the Earl of Cardigan's name had almost disappeared from the columns of the newspapers. The public was certainly entitled to feel that it had earned a rest from having his misdeeds detailed in column after column, morning and evening. That rest was to last for just six weeks.

CHAPTER 6

CRIMINAL CONVERSATION

1

On 22 March 1841 the squadrons of the 11th Hussars began to march out of Brighton Barracks for the last time. After Cardigan's acquittal, the regiment had been ordered on 'Queen's Duty', to provide escorts for royal journeys and state visits. The new Headquarters were to be at the Hounslow Barracks, with detachments at Hampton Court, Kensington and the Royal Military College at Sandhurst. As the Kensington squadron passed through Hyde Park on 23 March, the carriageway was lined by spectators who had gathered to admire the men's 'fine soldier-like bearing, and the handsome appearance of their accoutrements'.[1]

For all the national hostility towards Cardigan, there was general regret in Brighton society at the departure of the regiment. Cardigan and his officers had been welcome guests at balls and parties, bringing a dash and a vitality to even the most unpromising occasion. At a ball to raise funds for the hospital, their enthusiasm and the splendour of their full-dress uniforms had transformed a dreary civic function into the most lively social event of the winter. 'We have seldom known a ball go off better in Brighton,' remarked the *Brighton Gazette*, 'a circumstance which it is only fair to add was mainly due to the spirit with which the officers entered into the evening's amusement.'[2]

Yet there were also less happy memories which inevitably attended the departure of a cavalry regiment for its new station. Junior officers had run up bills with local tradesmen and could not, or would not, pay them. Cornet Pitt's last appearance in Brighton was not among the swirling dresses and glittering chandeliers of Brunswick Square but before the court to which his exasperated creditors had finally brought him. Like most subalterns in the more expensive cavalry regiments, Pitt was under twenty-one, and his guardian shrugged off the matter of the debts by saying that they had been incurred by an infant and were therefore not recoverable at law. It was a customary and sometimes reliable line of defence in such actions.[3]

Cardigan's private soldiers had few facilities for running up debts, but they were capable of making a nuisance of themselves in other ways. The departure of the regiment for its new station was notoriously the time for celebration, aided by supplies of gin still freely available in the regimental canteen. By the time that the squadrons of the 11th Hussars were ready to move out, there was at least one man, Private William Rogers, who was still incapably drunk. Rogers was twenty-six years old, had served five years in the regiment, and was under the immediate command of Cardigan's sworn enemy, Lieutenant W. C. Forrest.

Drunkenness was a perennial problem among the common soldiers, though it was not an offence which Cardigan as a rule treated with particular severity. However, he was determined that there should be no drunkenness while the 11th Hussars were on Queen's Duty. Rogers was tried by a district court-martial at Hounslow on 8 April and was sentenced to receive one hundred lashes. The finding and sentence were confirmed, and the confirmation was delivered to Hounslow on 11 April. It was customary for the commanding officer to make arrangements for the sentence to be carried out forthwith. That was what Cardigan did.

Unfortunately, 11 April 1841 happened also to be Easter Sunday. With supreme insensitivity, Cardigan saw no reason why that should interfere with the normal process of military discipline. Even more incredible was the place chosen for the punishment, the Riding School at Hounslow, where the Easter Morning service had just ended. According to the earliest accounts, the first blows of the drummers' whips almost merged with the final cadences of the Easter prayers. It seems more likely that the regiment was dismissed after the service and paraded again about half an hour later to witness the punishment. At all events, Rogers was stripped, fastened to the triangles, and flogged by two drummers, standing to right and to left, striking alternate blows.

On Wednesday 14 April, the story of the hundred lashes reached the columns of the *Morning Chronicle* and soon became the topic for editorials in newspapers of every opinion. Lord Hill read the story in the *Chronicle* and, with feelings of familiar gloom, ordered the Adjutant-General to write to Cardigan and find out the truth of the matter. The Adjutant-General wrote and received a puzzled but decidedly unrepentant confirmation of the story from Cardigan. Hill, dreading another public row, went to the Duke of Wellington for advice. With the Duke's aid he drafted a memorandum to Cardigan, which he hoped would meet the occasion.[4]

> It is well known that it is not the practice of this country to carry the penal sentences of the law into execution on the Lord's-day: neither is it the practice of the Army, whether employed abroad or at home.
>
> The General Commanding-in-Chief is therefore surprised that an officer in the situation of Lieutenant-Colonel commanding a regiment should have carried such a sentence into execution on Sunday.
>
> The General Commanding-in-Chief desires that it may be clearly understood that the sentences of military courts are not to be carried into execution on the Lord's-day, excepting in cases of evident necessity, the nature of which it cannot be requisite for him to define.

This reprimand was issued as a General Order on 22 April, but it was too mild and certainly too late to prevent public controversy. Victorian opinion was affronted by the Easter Sunday flogging as much as by any of Cardigan's actions. The *Morning Post*, which had once been his most influential defender, now joined the ranks of his critics and announced that his conduct deserved 'unqualified censure'. *The Times*, which had carefully kept free from either camp on most previous occasions, denounced him most vehemently of all.[5]

> What, then, is to be done with this inveterate offender, this plague-spot of the British army, who seems to exist for the single purpose of setting public opinion at defiance, and bringing discredit upon the unwise clemency which restored him, after one well-merited disgrace, to employments for which he is by temper and character thoroughly disqualified.

Like the *Globe* and certain other papers, *The Times* argued that Cardigan was not merely a savage brute and an arrogant wastrel, he was guilty of one of the greatest acts of sacrilege in modern times.[6]

We doubt if in the whole series of 1800 years which have elapsed since the great Event which the church commemorates at Easter, anything parallel to this act has before occurred; and under all the circumstances we can hardly speak of it as less than diabolical.

It was vain for Cardigan's few remaining supporters to protest that he was not the satanic beast of the newspapers' descriptions, and that, far from being an officer who resorted to corporal punishment at every turn, there had not been an instance of it in the 11th Hussars for at least two years. The subject was too emotive to be so easily dismissed. For ten years almost the entire press had campaigned against military flogging as a disgrace to a civilized nation. When in opposition, the Whigs and their supporters demanded its abolition. When in power, they swore that the army could not be governed without it.

There had been several *causes célèbres* in the previous decade, when such punishments were carried out within sight or earshot of the civilian population. The sentence executed on Private John Hutchinson at St George's Barracks, Charing Cross, in July 1834, was clearly heard by the protesting inhabitants of Westminster. The only consequence was that the drums were ordered to beat to drown the man's cries. When he was taken down, he looked, said *The Times*, 'as if he had been flayed alive'. Even in the military hospital at Grosvenor Place, the sultry weather made it impossible to keep the flies from swarming on his open wounds.[7]

In the following year, a Royal Marine, Private Thomas Ramsby, died after a flogging, and the coroner's jury insisted on fixing the responsibility upon the court-martial. When the regimental surgeon, who had been present during the punishment, told the court that Ramsby 'stood it like a Briton', he was jeered by the spectators. Nonetheless, a further attempt in 1836 to abolish such punishments was defeated in the Commons by 212 to 95. In March 1836, a special commission of inquiry reported that flogging was an irreplaceable part of British army discipline.[8]

By 1841, the kind of sentence carried out on Private Rogers at Hounslow was still commonplace. Two days earlier, a soldier at Dover Barracks had received exactly the same punishment for the same offence. Since it was Good Friday, rather than Easter Day, and since the infamous Earl of Cardigan was not involved, the *United*

Service Gazette (which was shortly to denounce Cardigan's conduct) approved the Dover flogging.[9]

Being who he was, Cardigan could hardly have involved himself in a more damaging controversy. The argument passed from the press to Parliament, though not before certain figures were made public relating to the 11th Hussars' two years at Canterbury. During that period, when there were 335 men in the regiment, there were no less than 105 courts-martial, 748 defaulters, and 90 men in Canterbury gaol. No wonder, added the *United Service Gazette*, that the Commander-in-Chief had admonished Cardigan for his conduct as Commanding Officer.[10]

On 13 May 1841, the Radicals in the House of Commons moved for an official inquiry into Cardigan's behaviour, with a view to having him expelled from the army by parliamentary vote. Macaulay, for the Melbourne government, refused to agree to such a proceeding. The motion for an inquiry was lost by 135 to 58. To Melbourne, who was facing defeat on other issues, the weakness of the anti-Cardigan vote was a small respite. Yet the vote was weak because it seemed already to be generally known that Cardigan had been officially given the choice of resigning from the army or of being dismissed peremptorily. It was said that he had agreed to go and was to be allowed to resign in his own time, so long as that time was no more than a few weeks.[11]

> The noble earl has consequently received notice to quit; but is to be allowed the grace of having himself originated his retirement. The Sunday flogging affair has proved the last drop to the full cup of official endurance.

Elsewhere, the *United Service Gazette* summed up Cardigan as a convicted adulterer, a violator of the Sabbath, and the 'scourge and detestation' of the regiments with which he served. The paper dismissed him with an epigram.[12]

> Prostrate in prayer the Colonel lies,
>   While vengeance from his eye-balls flashes.
> First to his God for mercy cries,
>   Then gives his man a hundred lashes.[13]

Yet it was neither the press nor Parliament which was to decide Cardigan's fate. And even though he might seem to have forfeited Divine favour, there might be hope in Victorian diplomacy.

Melbourne's cabinet had met on 24 April 1841 to discuss the problem of Lord Cardigan. Afterwards, Melbourne had written to the Queen.[14]

> We have had under our consideration at the Cabinet the unfortunate subject of the conduct of Lord Cardigan. The public feeling upon it is very strong, and it is almost certain that a motion will be made upon it in the House of Commons for an Address praying your Majesty to remove him from the command of his regiment. . . . It was thought proper that Lord Melbourne should see Lord Hill, and should express to him the opinion of the Cabinet, that it was necessary that he should advise your Majesty to take such measures as should have the effect of removing Lord Cardigan from the command of the 11th Hussars. The repeated acts of imprudence of which Lord Cardigan has been guilty, and the repeated censures which he has drawn down upon himself, form a ground amply sufficient for such a proceeding and indeed seem imperiously to demand it.

The decision of the Melbourne cabinet had been taken on a day when the editorials of the Saturday weekly press were calling for Cardigan's dismissal. But the cabinet decision had been taken without reference to Lord Hill or the Horse Guards. The Horse Guards owed allegiance directly to the Crown and not to the cabinet. When Melbourne called on Lord Hill that afternoon and told him of the cabinet's wish, he found the Commander-in-Chief 'deeply chagrined and annoyed'.[15]

In Lord Hill's view, Cardigan's conduct was a military problem. It was not, and could not be, the business of the civil government. However, he promised to consult the inevitable oracle, the Duke of Wellington. Melbourne summoned another cabinet meeting for the following day, Sunday 25 April, at four o'clock in the afternoon. In the morning he called upon Hill again and received the Duke's opinion, to be laid before the cabinet later that day.[16]

> The opinion of the Duke is that the Punishment on Sunday was a great impropriety and indiscretion upon the part of Lord Cardigan, but not a Military offence, nor a breach of the Mutiny Act or of the Articles of War; that it called for the censure of the Commander-in-Chief, which censure was pronounced by the General Order upon which the Duke was consulted before it was issued, and that according to the usage of the Service no further step can be taken by the Military Authorities.

In other words, the Horse Guards refused to be dictated to by men who were not their masters, either in the cabinet or in the House of Commons. The only course left open to the government, short of capitulation by Lord Hill, would have been for Melbourne to ask the Queen to order the Horse Guards to dismiss Cardigan. But for an administration which was on the point of collapsing to attempt this, in the face of joint opposition by Wellington and the Horse Guards, was not in the realm of practical politics. The Duke had no illusions as to his own power in the matter. As he wrote to Lady Wilton on the day following the cabinet's surrender, Cardigan's fate had been in his hands.[17]

> I have been for the last days up to the ears as usual in Lord
> Cardigan's last indiscretion. I had first to settle it for Lord
> Hill to draw the order. I have since settled it with the
> Government. . . . This is no small Affair settled.

So after all the storming editorials, the threats of an official inquiry, the promises of a resignation, the row between cabinet and Horse Guards, the bewildered public realized by the end of the spring that the unspeakable Earl of Cardigan was to remain Lieutenant-Colonel of the 11th (Prince Albert's own) Hussars.

Surprisingly, perhaps, Cardigan was prepared to acknowledge that over the Easter Sunday flogging he had been in the wrong, technically at least. Then, once the immediate anger of press and parliament had died down, it was time for him to do what he had been trying to do ever since the regiment's return from India, establish a place in society which befitted the 7th Earl of Cardigan.

It was not enough that a man should belong to such clubs as White's or Boodle's. A soldier of any reputation at all must also belong to the United Service Club, the most famous of all military clubs, founded at the time of Waterloo. In the summer of 1841 he was proposed for membership with the tacit support of Wellington and the active support of a number of friends. The election took place on 6 July and when the result was announced, Cardigan discovered that he had been blackballed twenty-eight times. The *United Service Gazette* was delighted by such an unprecedented humiliation, and marvelled at the impudence of such a man in presenting himself for membership of a respectable club. 'The number of ostracisms recorded against his lordship may, therefore, be taken as a tolerable example of the estimation in which he is held by the unbiassed members of the club.'

Not apt to be halted in his purpose by a single snub, Cardigan mustered his friends in greater strength and tried again. On the second occasion, the members relented somewhat towards the 'Honourable Damnable', as he was known, but he was still black-balled eighteen times. 'Courage, my Lord, courage! "Once more unto the breech!"' jeered the *United Service Gazette*, suggesting that if Cardigan's popularity grew at this rate he might one day find himself blackballed no more than nine or ten times in the London clubs.[18]

The sequel came on 2 December 1848 with the announcement in the same paper that Cardigan, unable to gain admission to any established military club, had started one of his own in St Martin's Lane, the Military and County Service Club. 'A home for the black-balled', said the paper scathingly, and denounced it as socially obnoxious and commercially fraudulent. Ultimately, Cardigan was obliged to found the St James's Military Club, which foundered in 1852 in some £20,000 of debts and a great deal of publicity. The eighteen principal creditors met on 1 November 1852 and held him personally responsible for £10,000 of the club's debts. They allowed him the option of either discharging this amount within twelve days or else being sued for it. In the end the members were obliged to combine together for no more agreeable purpose than that of paying off the huge debts incurred by their club. Indeed, Cardigan's custom had hardly been any more welcome than his debts, according to the *Freeman* in 1843. 'Ask the traders in London, with whom Cardigan deals, their opinion of his lordship, of his penurious and grinding-price habits', suggested a correspondent, writing from the comfortable seclusion of the United Service Club on 7 October.[19]

Though the fashionable military world might snub him, Cardigan had something to hope for from the new Conservative government of Sir Robert Peel, which had succeeded the Melbourne administration in the autumn of 1841. Indeed, Peel took office to the accompaniment of a reminder from Cardigan that when the ailing Lord Westmorland should die, there would be a vacancy for a Lord Lieutenant of Northamptonshire. Soon after returning from India, Cardigan had informed Peel that following the next Conservative election victory he would expect some recognition of his services to the party. The time had now come for the payment of that political debt.

Lord Westmorland died on Wednesday 15 December 1841. As soon as the news reached Deene, Cardigan travelled to London and demanded an interview with Peel, 'upon the subject of my anxiety to be appointed to the vacant Lord Lieutenancy of the County in which I reside'. During the interview, he reminded the new Prime Minister of the support which he had given the Conservative party and the gratitude which it owed him.[20]

Having returned to Deene, it crossed Cardigan's mind that he had forgotten to mention to Peel the financial loss incurred when he had been deprived of his parliamentary seat at Marlborough in 1829, and had had to buy another one at Fowey. He wrote on 23 December informing Peel of this. He was not to know that Peel and the Home Secretary, Sir James Graham, were already doing their best to persuade Lord Exeter, Lord Lieutenant of Rutland, to take the vacant Lord Lieutenancy of Northamptonshire as well. Exeter was reluctant but finally agreed. Peel wrote to Cardigan on 6 January 1842, telling him that Lord Exeter's name had already been submitted to the Queen.[21]

Cardigan drove at once to London and tried to confront Peel. However, he was put off with an interview with the Home Secretary instead. Sir James Graham told him bluntly that he disapproved of his conduct as Lieutenant-Colonel of the 11th Hussars and considered him a most unsuitable person to be Lord Lieutenant of a county. Cardigan protested to Peel that in the whole of his military career he had only once been pronounced in the wrong by his 'Military superiors'. He accused Peel of bowing down to 'the rancour and persecution of the public Press'. He had been unjustly deprived of an honour, 'to which I may safely say it is generally considered I have the strongest pretensions'. Peel replied calmly that unsuccessful competitors were bound to feel some disappointment. Cardigan was not so easily pacified. He announced that Peel was guilty of 'inflicting upon me (to say the least of it) a *marked slight*, and, as it were, affixing a stigma upon me in my own County'. Such was the bitter reward of a man of flawless character, apart from 'one single act of indiscretion in the honourable service of the command of a regiment'. As for Lord Exeter, he was a man who had honours enough already, did not want to be Lord Lieutenant, and did not even live in the county. 'I think you will find', answered Peel coldly, 'that Burleigh is within the County of Northampton.' As a matter of routine, Cardigan then complained to the Duke of Wellington and received a rather distant expression of sympathy.[22]

Worst of all, the world heard of the snub and Greville, as a fellow member of White's, was well aware that Cardigan seemed more broody and irritable than ever. The Home Secretary, who had borne the impact of Cardigan's disappointment, assured Greville that 'Cardigan was very angry that he had not got it'. Indeed, it was even possible to feel that Cardigan might have had a very good claim to the honour, but for his conduct and reputation during his command of the 11th Hussars.[23]

At the beginning of March 1842, he wrote to Peel again. There was a vacancy in the Order of the Garter and he wanted it. Here was Peel's chance to show that the choice of Lord Exeter as Lord Lieutenant of Northamptonshire had not been a deliberate slight. Peel was shocked, so shocked that he wrote to the Queen about this direct application. The peers with the strongest claims had, said Peel, 'behaved very well with respect to it', and would never have dreamt of writing to the Prime Minister and demanding the honour. However, this was a mere beginning. On three separate occasions when vacancies occurred in the Order, Cardigan wrote to the Prime Minister, demanding the honour for himself as a natural right. Peel did not even include his name on the short-list of seven which was submitted for Victoria's approval.[24]

Yet the Queen had some reservations about Peel's treatment of Cardigan. Prince Albert had resigned as Colonel of the 11th Hussars, though the regiment remained 'Prince Albert's own'. Victoria knew Cardigan well enough to guess his likely reaction to this.[25]

> The Queen fears, indeed knows, that Lord Cardigan will be deeply mortified at the Prince's leaving the Regiment, and that it will have the effect of appearing like another slight to him; therefore, the Queen much wishes that at some fit opportunity a mark of favour should be bestowed upon him . . .
> The Queen hopes Sir Robert will think of this.

Sir Robert thought, and did nothing. The end of his government came more than four years later, in June 1846, and he had still done nothing. However, in the autumn of 1846 there was a brevet on 9 November and a mass promotion of officers. Cardigan, who had been a Lieutenant-Colonel for somewhat longer than usual, was promoted to Colonel. After the rapidity of his early career, this was his first rise in rank for sixteen years. It seemed likely to be his last. Even at

Victoria's bidding, the political and military leaders of England had done all that they proposed to do for Lord Cardigan.

Cardigan enjoyed ample opportunity for bringing himself to Victoria's attention in 1841–2. In the summer of 1841 it was the 11th Hussars which escorted the Queen to Nuneham, Woolwich and Woburn. When the King of Prussia came to Windsor in January 1842, for the christening of the infant Prince of Wales, it was the 11th Hussars which escorted him. The regiment was inspected in the presence of Victoria and Wellington who, whatever their misgivings over Cardigan, were never less than flattering about the appearance of his regiment. In April 1842, after a review by Prince Albert on Wimbledon Common, the Queen wrote enthusiastically to Peel of her admiration for the 'beautiful order' of Cardigan's men.[26]

Other social events of 1842, as spectacular in their way as any military review, kept Cardigan in the royal view. When starvation faced many classes of industrial workers, the Queen decided to organize relief by means of that most Victorian of entertainments, the fancy dress ball. Cardigan attended the first ball for 'distressed trades', held in May 1842 at Buckingham Palace. He appeared as the Chevalier de Bayard and acted as trainbearer to the Duchess of Cambridge, who had got herself up as Anne de Bretagne. These fancy dress occasions were attended by leading political and military figures, who showed an endearing willingness to appear ridiculous in a good cause. At the *bal poudré* of 1845, they were required to appear in costumes of the reign of George II. Sir Robert Peel was most imposing in a powdered wig, but Wellington appeared in trousers so vast that he looked like an aged Pantaloon, recognizable only by his famous nose. Palmerston arrived in clothes that were too tight and gave him the appearance of a gaunt acrobat, while the more diminutive figure of Lord John Russell was enormously padded out, like a belligerent Tom Thumb. On that occasion, Cardigan paraded as an officer of the 11th Dragoons at Culloden, ready to cut down the rebels with what the *Annual Register* called a 'true jack-boot stride and swagger'. Wellington, not to be outdone, went as 'Butcher' Cumberland himself.[27]

Amid the dying echoes of the Easter Sunday flogging rumpus, the officers of the 11th Hussars had begun to make themselves comfortable in their new station. The best and most expensive hotel in the neighbourhood being the Mitre, at Hampton Court, they took it over and treated it as a regimental mess. The style of a cavalry regiment on Queen's Duty was even more costly to its subalterns than Pavilion Guard at Brighton. The pay of a Lieutenant was about £160 a year, but it was common knowledge that no young man could think of entering the 11th Hussars, the 13th Light Dragoons, or the 17th Lancers, or even an infantry regiment like the 79th, without a parental allowance of at least £300 to £500 a year more. In none of these regiments, according to the *United Service Gazette*, 'can a gentleman of moderate means hope to remain without running deeply into debt: let him essay it and persecution must be the consequence.' According to the editor of the paper, the 'persecutor' of impecunious young officers in the 11th Hussars was Cardigan himself. He was said to despise young men who could not 'emulate' his own expenditure.[28]

Neither was it enough that a young man in the 11th Hussars should be able to eat, drink and dress in the right style. As *Fraser's Magazine* pointed out, there was an obligation on an officer in a 'fast' regiment to hunt and even to involve himself in racing horses like a peer of the realm. For all that, his knowledge of the turf was 'gained not more by experience in horseflesh and acquaintanceship with jockeys, than from *Bell's Life*, and those welcome, green-coated periodicals, the *Sporting Magazines*.'[29]

By the time the 11th Hussars reached Hounslow, there were young officers like Lieutenant John Cunningham, one of Cardigan's 'peculiar pets', as the *United Service Gazette* called him, who were heading for a spectacular financial smash. Cunningham's pay was £160 and his allowance from his father was £300. On this, he was living at the rate of £4,000 a year, raising much of this by loans which, effectively, cost him £8,000, a sum nearer to £80,000 by modern values. Cunningham had been a guest at Deene and had caught Cardigan's enthusiasm for stag-hunting. His stag-hounds cost him £800 and his two race-horses, which he entered at Epsom and Hounslow, another £160. He ran up bills of £118 for the hire of horses and £202 for cigars. He owed £435 to his jeweller, principally for presents to ladies, £360 for hosiery and £660 to his six different tailors.

Worst of all was the eagerness for ready money, which led Cunningham and other young officers to sign loan bills indiscriminately. Yet when Cunningham signed a bill for £250 to be repaid within a few months, he did not expect to get £250. A cavalry subaltern was too bad a risk for that. Bills were 'discounted', and

Cunningham's signature for £250 only raised £125, for which he would soon have to repay double. Another bill for £250 produced £188. The only way to get the sums he really needed was to sign bills for larger and larger amounts, until his credit was exhausted and both he and his family were in the hands of his creditors. He signed two bills for £500 each, receiving £300 for one and £290 for the other. He kept no accounts and had no idea of his total debts. It was not surprising that rumours spread in the regiment that Cunningham was going to smash. The money-lenders might know this too, but they looked forward to being repaid when the young man's family was obliged to realize some or all of its assets to prevent him from being disgraced. If Cunningham's debts were general knowledge, they were accompanied by rumours that Cardigan himself, for all his £40,000 a year, was obliged to money-lenders of a very superior and discreet kind.

But for the time being Cunningham's stag-hounds were a great attraction in the regiment, as J. Anstruther Thomson discovered, when he and his brother officers of the 13th Light Dragoons were invited to dinner by the 11th Hussars at Hounslow in the winter of 1841–2. There was hard frost, and hunting had been impossible for some time. The hounds, which Cunningham kept at Jim Parson's public house at Kingston had been idle.

After dinner, the junior officers adjourned to someone's room and continued the conviviality in their own style, laughing, shouting and preparing to spend the night in 'chaff'. At three in the morning it began to rain and someone realized that the hunting weather had returned. Unfortunately, there was a watering parade that morning, so it was agreed that Thomson and John Vivian should wake Cardigan and ask for the officers to be excused the parade.[30]

> We knocked at the door and a gruff voice said, 'Come in.' He was sitting on the side of his bed, with a shawl dressing-gown on and his hair all dischevelled and standing on end. He had not slept a wink we had made such a row. We stated our request, and he said 'Certainly, certainly,' and so we thanked him and retired. In the morning he put his head cautiously outside the door and said 'Have all those d——d fellows gone ?'

Whatever Cardigan's disagreements with his officers in other matters, there was rarely any trouble over hunting. The one exception to this was a regimental 'turn-up' in 1841 over the question of hunting badgers. Cardigan disapproved of this, and most of those who heard of the latest 'shindy at Hounslow' supported him.

In October 1842 the money-lenders and creditors of Lieutenant Cunningham closed in. As a means to force payment by his family, there was a threat to prosecute him for incurring debts without any reasonable expectation of paying them. Cunningham's father was unimpressed by such blackmail and argued successfully that the means used by the money-lenders to ensnare his son were nothing less than extortion. The extravagance of John Cunningham, however, was remarkable even at a time when the improvidence of cavalry officers was a commonplace of society. In two years, on an allowance of £300 and pay of £160, he had managed to incur debts of £17,226.

The moral indignation of the press was turned against Cardigan. Cunningham was the young man whose evidence had been vital to him at the court-martial of Captain Reynolds. Cunningham had been a member of shooting and hunting parties at Deene. Cardigan must have known that the young man was living far beyond his income. Yet no advice was given and Cardigan remained apparently indifferent to the rate at which the Lieutenant was 'running to ruin'. Indeed, his only reaction to the bankruptcy of young men like Cunningham was to make his junior officers sign an undertaking that they would not sell their commissions for less than £5,500, though the normal rate was £3,225. There was to be no repetition of the Cunningham case. The 11th Hussars must be put beyond the reach of all those 'who have not large fortunes'. Cardigan angrily denied these stories, but the press remained unconvinced.[31]

The 11th Hussars, with a French messman and Continental cuisine, was a by-word for military extravagance. The cooking seemed as much a part of regimental life as the cavalry uniform and, in its way, every bit as expensive. Each major review was followed by a *déjeuner*, given by Cardigan or his officers in a large marquee near the review ground. After the Wimbledon Common review before Prince Albert on 10 May 1850, Cardigan provided a banquet for no less than 250 'nobility, gentry, Officers &c.' in a marquee whose interior appeared more like the state apartments of Buckingham Palace than a tent. At the same time, he provided the entire regiment with a special dinner in the barracks at Hounslow.[32]

Junior officers of the regiment were also expected to provide *déjeuners*, prepared by the French messman, for distinguished guests. *Haute cuisine* was a commonplace of mess life. *Fraser's Magazine* described the cultivated disdain which even the most junior subaltern of eighteen or nineteen soon learnt to show in the mess towards the finest and most expensively prepared food.[33]

> You shall see a languid boy, who a year ago was flogged at school, ring the bell for the mess-waiter and tell him, 'For God's sake to bring something with plenty of cayenne in it.' The same evening, perhaps, at mess, as the side dishes are one by one uncovered, he lifts his eyebrows, pulls down the corners of his mouth, and cries, 'Oh my God!' and this although he may have lived, up to the previous month, on plain joints and suet-puddings. Perhaps he leans forward, with his elbows on the table, and with exquisite resignation, begs the president to 'show up the bill of fare.' It is astonishing how soon a mere child falls into these habits. His mess table, though he wouldn't acknowledge it for the world, groans with a dinner infinitely better than he ever sees at home; and all is served up upon the richest plate.

By the end of April 1842 there were more urgent duties awaiting the 11th Hussars than those of acting as royal escort. The unrest of the 'manufacturing districts' of the north, and the threat of revolution in Ireland created a demand for military supervision which the army was hardly equipped to provide. At the same time, the disaster at Cabul and the outbreak of the Sikh wars made the dispatch of re-inforcements to India a matter of urgency.

At the end of April the 11th Hussars marched to Yorkshire, where Chartist leaders like Feargus O'Connor and papers like the *Northern Star* had already promised a 'warm reception' for any attempt by the army or the police to 'put down the cause of the people by physical force'. Among stories of strikes, lock-outs, vitriol attacks and worse, the industrial workers had taken to the streets of towns like Halifax, and had fought the soldiers and the police. The Metropolitan Police were called in to restore order in the centre of Birmingham, while in Ireland the rebels published articles in papers like the *United Irishman* on the techniques of vitriol throwing and unhorsing mounted troops.[34]

By August 1842 the situation in the industrial north had become serious enough for most of the 11th Hussars to be withdrawn from their regimental Headquarters at York and billeted in the worst affected towns like Halifax, Rochdale and Glossop. Cardigan did not regard it as part of his personal duty to assist in breaking up 'assemblies of rioters' in narrow streets or in escorting Chartist prisoners from one gaol to another. Leaving such matters to his junior officers, he began to make arrangements to hunt the Lancashire country during the coming winter.

He spent most of the uneasy summer of 1842 in London, giving dinner parties at Portman Square for the Duke and Duchess of Beaufort, the Earl of Chesterfield (late Master of the Pytchley), Lord Adolphus Fitzclarence, and Maria, Marchioness of Ailesbury. It was his inveterate critic, Lieutenant (now Captain) W. C. Forrest, who led his men against overwhelming, if ill-equipped, numbers at such unsung battles as that of North Parade, Halifax. There, Captain Forrest's troop was caught between two mobs, the first coming over the top of the hill and into New Bank, the second a column of marchers from Lancashire who swarmed through the town from King's Cross, at the west. The Riot Act was read and the people ordered to disperse, but it was Forrest's troop in the end which had to clear the streets.

Not surprisingly, the troop was unpopular and there was a bloody skirmish at Elland, when they were attacked by a crowd with a salvo of bricks and stones. Hardly a trooper was left unscathed and there was a fierce mêlée in the narrow street, during which three of them were unhorsed and beaten by the crowd. Riderless horses galloped loose, Hussars with blood running down their faces struggled to force their way through the packed crowd towards the fallen troopers. Civilians were ridden down by the cavalry horses. Finally, Forrest gathered his men and ordered them to charge while firing over the heads of the crowd, in which manner they cleared a space and rescued the three men who had been unhorsed.[35]

Forrest emerged as the hero of the anti-Chartists, the gallant Hussar who had saved Elland and Halifax from a fate worse than the French revolution. But the praise for the brave soldiers of the 11th could hardly include Cardigan. He was not at Halifax, not even at York, where command of Headquarters was delegated to Brevet Lieutenant-Colonel Rotton. After a summer at Portman Square, he was spending the autumn at Deene, visiting his regiment only when it was necessary to muster it.

By the spring of 1843 even the riots in the northern industrial cities were overshadowed by the news from Ireland. With the formation of Peel's Conservative government in 1841, Daniel O'Connell, the veteran nationalist, denounced once and for all the 1801 Act of

Union which had formally united England and Ireland as a single state, abolishing the Irish parliament and making the people subject to rule from Westminster. Repeal of this Union, and the granting of independence to Ireland, became the minimum demand of O'Connell and his followers. In practical terms, the Irish situation was aggravated by the famine of the 1840s and the widespread acts of violence against employers and their sympathizers.

English readers were horrified at reports of the murder and maiming of the 'industrious poor' by dissident workers. 'Outrage in Ireland' became an almost daily headline in the London press, as when two dutiful workers in Ballyhooley were dragged from their beds, beaten unconscious, and revived to 'the most agonizing torment' by vitriol poured over their heads. With a fractured skull and their eyes destroyed, they had little hope of surviving their appalling injuries.[36]

In April 1843 three infantry regiments due to return from Ireland were ordered to remain. The 60th Rifles and the 15th Hussars were dispatched to join them. On 25 April the 11th Hussars, under Cardigan's command, left York for Liverpool. They embarked at once for Dublin. Throughout the latter half of April and early May, one detachment of troops after another disembarked at the North Wall, in Dublin, and was marched away along the bank of the Liffey to join the growing numbers at the Royal Barracks near Phoenix Park.

If Cardigan's conduct in having Private Rogers flogged for drunkenness during a regimental move seems severe, the disembarkation of the British army in Dublin may explain the severity. When the first battalion of the Rifle Brigade swarmed off the paddle-steamer which had brought them, it was evident, as *The Times* delicately phrased it, that 'teetotalism did not appear to be in universal fashion among the corps'. A dozen or more of the first soldiers were so drunk that they had to be put in carts for the journey to the barracks. Among those still capable of marching, there was a lively interest in the Dublin street girls. Fighting broke out among the rearguard of the 60th Rifles, and one man managed to knock out three of his comrades before the constabulary intervened and carried him off 'struggling manfully to the last', to the police office.[37]

The behaviour of British officers in Ireland could match that of their men. After one of them was taken to court by an Irish creditor, the creditor's nephew was later sent to the barracks to collect the debt. The boy was shown into a room full of officers, given the money, and told that he would now discover the fate of those who dared to take a British officer to court. He was seized by the private soldiers, dragged to a communal pump, and held under it until he nearly drowned. In this state he was returned to his uncle. It required all the Duke of Wellington's influence to quieten the scandal. Some observers decided that before law and order could be brought to Ireland, it must first be imposed upon the British army.[38]

Cardigan had made himself comfortable at the Bilton Hotel in Sackville Street, a street so broad as to give almost the impression of a spacious eighteenth-century square with tall, elegant houses. For the next three years the regiment spent its winters in Dublin and much of the summer at the Curragh Camp. Cardigan divided his time between Ireland and England, being seen a great deal at the theatre and at private parties during his visits to the regiment. His conduct in Dublin society produced fewer shrugs of disapproval than his behaviour in the regiment. A brawl at the theatre between a civilian and one of his officers was broken up by Cardigan's appearance in the box, which was reckoned to his credit. On the other hand, as guest of honour of the 4th Dragoon Guards, he was said to have kept the entire company waiting for their dinner from 7 until 10, and then to have sent an abrupt note saying that he was too busy to come.[39]

Cardigan's view of the Irish problem was that its solution required only a little simple and direct action by resolute men. The first step must be to silence the agitator O'Connell, who had been allowed to act with too great impunity by the Peel administration. In the autumn of 1843, O'Connell was to address a great crowd of supporters at Clontarf, on the northern outskirts of Dublin. Cardigan went to London and, in an interview with the Duke of Wellington, offered to be 'the personal arrestor' of the Irish hero on that occasion. The exact words of the offer were reported as, 'Leave him to *me*, and I'll *nab* him at the outset. My life on it!'

The Peel government rejected the brave offer but the 'nabbing' story became another public joke at Cardigan's expense. Of course, some Irishmen found it irritating rather than amusing. 'If I were near,' vowed the correspondent of the *Freeman*, 'and saw Lord Cardigan approach O'Connell, I would risk my life to make SOME-BODY the richer of an earl's coronet.'[40]

Distant though Cardigan was from his regiment for much of the time, the internal squabbles of the 11th Hussars cast a certain gloom over the fine autumnal rides of Northamptonshire and Leicestershire, and soured the gaiety of the waltzes and card parties which followed the early dusk of winter afternoons at Deene. Moreover, with the death of Lord Hill in 1842, the Duke of Wellington, who had ceased to be Commander-in-Chief on becoming Prime Minister in 1828, was appointed Commander-in-Chief for life. He was seventy-three years old and it seemed like a final and short-lived honour conferred upon the greatest Englishman of the century. It might have been conferred less readily if his contemporaries had known that it was to last for another ten years. Indeed, Wellington might have accepted with less enthusiasm, had he known how much of his time and patience were to be squandered on Lord Cardigan and the 11th Hussars. Within a few months of assuming his command, the aged Duke was commenting bitterly, 'It will be quite a pleasing occupation to command the army if I am to have many such commanding officers as Lord Cardigan!'

The Duke took office on 15 August 1842. By the end of October, Captain W. C. Forrest was sparring with Cardigan over the matter of his leave. He had been granted leave by the Major-General commanding the Yorkshire district and then told that he could not proceed on leave until relieved by Lieutenant Harrison at Barnsley Barracks. On 28 October he wrote impatiently to Cardigan and demanded an explanation. In place of an explanation, he was told not to proceed on leave at all until further notice. The feud dragged on until Forrest had gone on leave to escort his pregnant wife to friends, where she was to stay while her child was born. When Forrest's leave expired, the child had still not been born. Despite Cardigan's refusal to extend the leave, Forrest remained with his wife. When he finally reached the regiment again, there was a memorable 'turn-up'.[41]

However, Cardigan was already involved in another long-range quarrel with Captain J. W. 'Black Bottle' Reynolds (on leave of absence at Sandhurst) over the drunkenness of the batman provided for him by the regiment. Cardigan insisted on forwarding all the papers in the matter to the Duke at the Horse Guards. Wellington replied, urging him to drop the matter, 'for my sake, as I really have not leisure time to consider all the nice details of these trifles'. The affair of Forrest's leave came on top of this, with a mass of carefully documented accusations and counter-accusations. This was too much for the Duke's self-restraint and he issued an ultimatum to Cardigan and the officers of the 11th Hussars.[42]

The Duke observed that in the whole course of his experience, he had never known the time of the Staff of the Army to be taken up in so useless a manner as in the present instance, that if any other Regiment in Her Majesty's Service gave such trouble and could not be commanded without such voluminous correspondence and such futile details, an additional Staff would be necessary for conducting the affairs of that one Regiment. The details of the foolish quarrel of the Officers of the 11th Hussars amongst themselves had gone to such an extent that if they continued His Grace would think it necessary to submit to Her Majesty some plan to relieve the department from such an intolerable annoyance.[43]

Worst of all, the Forrest story reached the press, though in a predictably elaborate form. The *Court Journal* published an account, belatedly, on 28 December 1844. The facts were dressed with an unmistakably Victorian garnish of melodramatic pathos.

A report, which deeply affects the character of a noble Lord in command of a cavalry regiment now quartered in Ireland, has just reached us. . . . An officer in Lord ————'s regiment lately asked for leave to go to England to attend his wife's dying moments, which leave was, of course, granted. At the expiration of the time given, the lady still lingered on, though without the slightest hope of recovery; and the unhappy husband begged for a further leave, to remain to receive her parting breath. This request, ever held as sacred and undeniable, was refused—nay, treated as a subterfuge by the noble lord. The officer was forced to return to his quarters, death released the wife from her sufferings, and her eyes were closed by the hands of strangers.

The *Court Journal* did not know, or perhaps did not care, that Mrs Forrest had been pregnant, not dying, and was yet to accompany her husband to the Crimea and back. The paper went on to chastise, with suitable piety, the 'unchristian and unfeeling manner' of Lord Cardigan in this matter. Since this was one occasion when he could fight with the law undeniably on his side, Cardigan collected the necessary affidavits and, in January 1845, brought an action for criminal libel against the paper, to which no defence could be offered.

The truth about Cardigan's behaviour was hard enough to establish when newspaper reports were flatly contradicted, but the contradictions were not always absolute. In 1842 it was reported that Cornet

Tynte had resigned as Adjutant of the 11th because Cardigan had made him act as a private spy upon those officers suspected of missing evening stables. The incident had ominous similarities to certain stories about the Wathen affair. Tynte wrote an indignant denial to the press, maintaining that he had never spied 'privately' for Cardigan. Whether he had spied officially was not clear.[44]

No sooner had the 11th Hussars reached Dublin in 1843, than Wellington was confronted by more complaints about Cardigan's conduct. On 29 August, at a field day in Phoenix Park, Cardigan ordered one of his subalterns forward to receive some orders. According to witnesses, 'the young dandified subaltern lounged listlessly and at a creeping pace towards the front ranks'. Cardigan shouted at him to go back and come forward again 'in a more soldierlike fashion'. However, 'the lounge to the front was repeated' and Cardigan, beside himself with fury, told the young officer to consider himself under arrest. It then required the officer commanding the field day, Lieutenant-General Sir Edward Blakeney, to ride down to the scene of the disturbance, admonish the subaltern and release him from arrest.[45]

Two days later, there was another field day and another incident. After several hours of cavalry drill, Cardigan ordered the brigade to dismount and it seemed that the field day was at an end. The grooms had led away several of the officers' horses when Cardigan suddenly gave the order to remount. Cardigan galloped up to Lieutenant Harrison, who was standing without a horse in the middle of the cavalry formation, and demanded an explanation. Harrison explained that the grooms had taken his horse back to the stables but assured Cardigan that he had sent a message after him to have the horse fetched again.

'Go for him yourself, sir!' barked Cardigan. Harrison, in an ill-suppressed rage, obeyed the order. However, as soon as the field day was over, he approached the Adjutant and demanded an interview with Cardigan. At the interview, Harrison accused Cardigan of trying to bring him into contempt before the rest of the regiment, and warned him that if he ever behaved in that manner in future, he would not obey any order so given. There was then a short but fierce argument, at the end of which Cardigan put Harrison under arrest. According to the *Dublin Mercantile Advertiser*, it took another personal intervention by Sir Edward Blakeney to get him released.[46]

On 11 October Lieutenant Weguelin, an officer of seven years' service, was ten minutes late for morning stables as orderly officer. He conscientiously reported this to the Adjutant and was dismayed when, shortly afterwards, he was arrested on Cardigan's orders, the third officer of the regiment to be arrested in little more than a month. He was released on the following day on the orders of Major-General Wyndham commanding the Dublin garrison. However, Cardigan assembled all his officers in the mess-room that afternoon and berated Weguelin in front of them. One of the captains wrote to General Wyndham, complaining of Cardigan's language in the drill field. The officers of the regiment were then paraded again by Cardigan and addressed in terms which even made the language of the drill field sound courteous by comparison.

Complaints over the bickering and the arrests, many from Cardigan himself, began to pile up on Wellington's desk at the Horse Guards. The general officers in Ireland, who had to keep releasing subalterns arrested by Cardigan, were growing weary of the 11th Hussars. There were also official complaints about Cardigan's language and his manner of publicly reprimanding his officers. In an effort to reduce the torrent of complaints, the Duke laid down a special procedure to be followed by disgruntled officers of the 11th Hussars.[47]

> In future should any officer of the Regiment address any complaint or remonstrance to Lord Cardigan, such letter, together with a copy of the proposed reply from the Lieutenant Colonel is to be submitted to the General Officer who should be so unfortunate as to have the Regiment under his command.

But the Duke also proposed something else, a course of action so unprecedented as even to stun the most belligerent members of the regiment.[48]

> The constant disagreement between Lord Cardigan and the officers serving under him having been brought to the notice of the Commander-in-Chief the Duke of Wellington, he proposes, should these dissensions continue, to put a stop to them by dispersing all the officers through various regiments in the service.

To break up a crack cavalry regiment was an unheard of proceeding but after a year as Commander-in-Chief, the Duke had reached the end of his rather limited patience. He must have thought, from time to time, that for all Cardigan's discipline the behaviour of the regiment on active duty left something to be desired. In September 1843, for instance, when a squadron was sent to deal with the expected riots in Meath, the only violence came from the troops themselves. Officers and men alike were said to have got fighting drunk at the carmen's stages and the small public houses, to have drawn their swords and fought both the police and an infantry regiment. The wounded were brought in by drays to the hospital, as if from a battlefield.[49]

Yet the Duke's threat appeared to have a temporary effect upon the behaviour of Cardigan and his officers. Then, after some months of tranquillity, the usual troubles began again. The surgeon and the paymaster both left the regiment, the latter after a public row with Cardigan over not wearing his uniform to church. Since the Black Bottle squabble of 1840, the regiment was losing almost a third of its officers every year. For those who remained, there was the ever-present possibility of sudden arrest and, in 1850, Cardigan even arrested his second-in-command, Major Inigo Jones. 'What a chapter might be written on the arrests in this Regiment since it fell into the hands of its present Commandant!' said the *United Service Gazette* wistfully.[50]

Not least in that chapter would have been Captain the Honourable Gerard Noel, MP, son of Lord Gainsborough. Cardigan was reported to have arrested him twice in a short space of time, once for being late for stables and once for being absent to attend a parliamentary debate. In both cases Captain Noel was set free by the area commander but not before Cardigan had made him march at the rear of the regiment, deprived of his sword, as a public signal of disgrace. Perhaps it was only coincidence that the Noel family had been among Cardigan's rivals for the coveted Lord Lieutenancy of Northampton-shire.

Shortly after the second arrest and release, Cardigan noticed during a field day that Noel was not positioned on the precise spot where he should have been.

'Captain Noel, go to your troop, sir!' he shouted.

'I am with my troop, sir!' replied Noel determinedly.

'You are not, sir,' bawled Cardigan. 'None of your London manners here!'

Noel left the field day in great indignation. He went to see Cardigan and demanded first an explanation and then an apology. There was a noisy argument, which ended with Cardigan's voice, clearly audible to all those in the vicinity.

'Get out of my room, sir!'[51]

It was said that Noel had demanded of Cardigan that satisfaction which one gentleman owed another, and that Cardigan seemed likely to give it. When this story of an impending duel reached Wellington, he intervened personally and rapidly to prevent it.

'Lord Cardigan's affair', he confessed to Miss Burdett-Coutts on 15 November 1848, 'gave me a great deal of trouble. . . . The truth is that Capt. Noel was bringing the affair originating on the Parade to be a Private quarrel, which would have brought it to a duel. This course occasioned my Interference and the particular mode of it.'[52]

However, there was to be no respite for the Duke. Long before death relieved him from his life-appointment, it seemed that two commanders, Lord Londonderry and Lord Cardigan, had become the twin scourges of his semi-honorific post. One day, in the Duke's later years, the Adjutant-General went into his room to find Wellington sitting at the table 'with a large pile of correspondence spread out before him'. He was evidently in a bad mood and, looking up, demanded what the Adjutant-General had brought him this time. It was a complaint from Londonderry about certain regimental appointments and it had arrived, inopportunely, when the Duke was in the middle of settling Cardigan's latest rumpus.[53]

> His Grace seized the papers which were before him with both hands, dashed them down with a thump upon the table, and throwing himself back in his chair and crossing his arms on his chest, exclaimed, 'By ———, these two lords, my Lord C[ardigan] and Lord L[ondonderry], would require a commander-in-chief for themselves; there is no end to their complaints and remonstrances.'

By 1850, Cardigan's quarrels had so exasperated the Duke that Wellington wrote an official warning to him. If there were any further incidents of this kind, he would have Cardigan confined to his headquarters, where at least his improprieties would not be in the public view.

As if to oblige the Duke, Cardigan picked his next and most embittered quarrel with his brother-in-law, the Earl of Lucan. The marriage of Lucan and Anne Brudenell had reached the point of separation. Cardigan played the part of an outraged brother over Lucan's treatment of his sister, and there seemed likely to be a violent sequel. Once again, it was left to Wellington to intervene, and to prevent a family squabble from becoming a public entertainment. Cardigan's feud with Lucan was to become the most protracted and the most savage of any in his life. By his own death in 1852, the Duke was at least spared the fruition of new 'complaints and remonstrances', upon the field of Balaclava.

But whatever his officers or his commander-in-chief might feel about him, Cardigan remained a popular figure among his troopers. While the regiment was in Dublin, Trooper Pennington returned from leave several hours late. He was put in the guard-room to await an appearance before his Colonel. Next morning, in the orderly room, Cardigan, 'Rhadamanthus-like', was sitting in judgment upon offenders.

'What have you to say?' he growled at Pennington.

'Nothing, my lord, but it shall not occur again.'

The expression of contrition, which was the very thing Cardigan missed among his officers, was well-chosen. Pennington saw an 'expression of gratification' flit across the stern features. Cardigan turned to the sergeant and demanded what Pennington's previous character had been. On hearing that it had been very good, he turned again and stared fixedly at Pennington for several minutes.

'Fall away!' he said at last, and the case was dismissed.[54]

Pennington's experience was one of many pieces of evidence which bore witness to the feelings of the common soldier for Cardigan. Though he had never fought a battle, he was already regarded by many troopers of the 11th Hussars as one of the great cavalry commanders of his day, a notion which was abhorred as the most dangerous lunacy by his officers and by the exasperated Horse Guards. Cardigan owed his continuing command to official reluctance to disturb the social order of the army by dismissing a Lieutenant-Colonel who was also an earl, and to official optimism that he would never be required to fight in earnest.

2

Throughout the 1840s, sinister rumours and scandalous anecdotes circulated about Lord Cardigan. In the autumn of 1841, the clubs and dinner parties of the West End shuddered at the story of another duel, in which the homicidal Earl was said to have shot Colonel Wood, MP for Middlesex, in the head.[55] The United Service Club may have blackballed him more than forty times but he was as much talked of there as anywhere, particularly as regards his sexual reputation. According to one story, which circulated in the Club smoking room, one of the Captains of the 11th Hussars had come to the orderly room with a request for short leave. Cardigan refused the request, 'something about an inspection' being given as the reason for the refusal. When the request was repeated, frowns began to gather on Cardigan's face. Finally, the young Captain said in desperation, 'The fact is, sir, I must have leave. I have arranged to elope with Mrs ———.'

Cardigan's frowns cleared like an April storm.

'My *dear* fellow, why didn't you say so before? Of course, you may have your leave. A most Hussar-like action!'[56]

When such stories circulated freely, it came as little surprise to readers of the more scandalous papers, like the *Age*, to learn in 1843 that Cardigan was about to be sued by Lord William Paget for £15,000 damages for 'criminal conversation' with his wife, Lady Frances Paget.

According to Lord William, he had been suspicious of his wife's relationship with Cardigan for some time. In the summer of 1843, he had employed a private investigator, Frederick Winter, to watch the pair. The place where they were to be watched was in Lord William's town house, in Queen Street, Mayfair. On the first floor there were two adjoining drawing rooms with folding doors between them, which were generally left open. There was a sofa in both the back and front drawing room. On Saturday 5 August Winter was installed under the sofa in the back drawing room, unknown to Lady Frances. Shortly afterwards, Cardigan arrived and sat down with her on the sofa in the front drawing room. Then the folding doors were closed and, on this occasion, though Winter heard the murmur of conversation and some resounding kisses, there was insufficient evidence on which to base proceedings.

That night, Lord William and his wife went to the opera, occupying Cardigan's private box. On the following day, Lord William pretended that he was going to take his son to Woolwich. Winter was given a bottle of sherry and concealed under the sofa in the back room again, while Lord William waited in a hansom cab in Berkeley Square. Just before six in the evening, Cardigan arrived again, and this time the folding doors remained open. The blinds in the front drawing room had been drawn down against the afternoon sun and when Lord William's valet went to raise them, Cardigan said gruffly, 'Never mind, they will do very well.'

Once Cardigan and Lady Frances were alone, Winter heard her say, 'Are you come again?'

'Yes', said Cardigan. 'How do you do? Where is Lord William?'

On hearing that Lord William was at Woolwich, Cardigan began 'kissing and toying' with Lady Frances. They talked of the opera, Cardigan remarking that he would have appreciated it far more if he had been able to enjoy 'a little closer acquaintance' with Lady Frances in his private box.

Cardigan was immaculate in full dress cavalry uniform and, according to Winter, the couple were at one point actually upon the sofa under which he was hiding. Yet he dared not put his head out for fear of having his cheek grazed by Cardigan's spurs. Even when the couple were in the other room, their kisses were loud enough to be heard distinctly by the spy. Winter alleged that there was then a creaking of sofa springs and a cracking of military boots. This was accompanied by heavy breathing. 'The breathing was hard like persons distressed for breath after running.' He slithered forward on his stomach until he could peep round the edge of the folding door. What he saw of the state of dress and the situation of the couple left 'no doubt that a criminal connection had taken place between the parties'.

Lady Frances suggested that Cardigan might find a place for a respectable man in the Post Office whom she knew. Cardigan said he could not, 'he was not in very good favour with the present Administration'. His counter-proposal was that Lady Frances should feign a headache and, instead of dining with Lord William at Lady Richmond's, should spend the evening with him.

'Don't you know Lord William better than that?' said Lady Frances. 'If he should call and find me not there, he'll go stark-staring mad, and go to all the policemen in the town!'

Then she whispered something to Cardigan.

'Oh, indeed I am!' said Cardigan, 'I never loved anyone as I do you. Is not Lord William very kind to you?'

'Oh no', said Lady Frances plaintively. 'He is very unkind. He calls me all the damned bitches he can think of.'

'Does he?' said Cardigan. 'That is very wrong of him.'

Criminal connection 'occurred a second time'. Finally, Winter heard Cardigan moving about the front drawing room, 'as if he was adjusting his dress'. Lady Frances pulled up the blinds and, after Winter had been under the sofa for two hours, Cardigan left.

Winter hurried to Berkeley Square, where Lord William was still sitting in the hansom cab awaiting the outcome of the vigil. When he heard the news, he jumped from the cab, rushed home, blacked Lady Frances's eye, and began proceedings against Cardigan for criminal conversation with her. Then, according to the *Freeman* on 8 September 1843, Lord William had second thoughts and sent a note to Cardigan, calling him out, 'either in England or on the Continent', promising that if Cardigan offered 'this satisfaction', the prosecution would be stopped. Cardigan denounced the charges against him as 'a foul conspiracy', and declined the duel on the grounds that since the Tuckett scandal he was not 'a free agent' in such matters.

The more sensational newspapers had the time of their lives, not always at Cardigan's expense. 'Sofa virumque cano', said the *Age*, whimsically parodying Virgil. But on 24 September the *Age* crisply denounced Lord William Paget, alleging that he had been prostituting Lady Frances to Cardigan, in order to extort a substantial sum by way of damages. The paper described the whole affair as 'a plant', and urged Cardigan to bring a prosecution for conspiracy. In fact, it was Lord William who prosecuted the *Age* for criminal libel. The paper retaliated by revealing Lord William as a beater of women and as the man who had stood in a bedroom doorway in Paris, and coolly watched a bill-broker, Cassidy, beat up Caroline Bellew.[57]

Yet the most extraordinary events of Paget *v.* Cardigan were yet to come. The case came on for trial before Lord Chief Justice Tindal and a special jury in the Court of Common Pleas on 22 December 1843. That morning, Winter accompanied Lord William's solicitor as far as Holborn. Then saying that he would be at the court first, Winter set off at a rapid pace. In court when the case was called, it was announced that the special jury need not wait. The record had been withdrawn. Winter, the star witness for the plaintiff, had disappeared. 'The announcement', said *The Times*, 'came like a thunderclap on all present.' Lord William swore that Cardigan had bought Winter somewhere between Holborn and the court. He wrote a letter to Cardigan which even the *Age* would only publish in an expurgated version.[58]

238, Oxford Street,
22d Dec., 1843
20 past 10, A.M.

MY LORD,—My Solicitor, Mr. Bebb, has this instant made known to me that my principal witness, Winter, who was with him until within a few minutes of the opening of the Court at Guildhall, had suddenly disappeared.

My Lord, I charge you with the *wicked and infamous crime* of having bought him, and sent him 'out of the way.'

Having done so, you may go forth to the world and declare your innocence, and legally speaking you are so; but you are not in my opinion, one jot the less of a scoundrel for having debauched my wife, nor of a liar and a coward for having acted the part you have done.

> I am my Lord, yours, &c.,
> (Signed) WILLIAM PAGET

The Earl of Cardigan.

In his indignation, Lord William, as a sailor, wrote to the First Lord of the Admiralty, demanding that some disciplinary action be taken against Cardigan and, since Cardigan was a soldier, Lord William addressed a similar request to the Duke of Wellington at the Horse Guards. Both recipients blandly replied that Lord William must seek redress in the appropriate courts.

Then Winter was found again by Lord William, persuaded to testify, and the case was on once more. It was heard in the Court of Common Pleas on 27 February 1844 with a great crowd of spectators trying to fight their way in to hear the details of the scandal. 'The court was crowded throughout the day to suffocation,' reported *The Times*, whose representative had at first been refused admission. 'Every seat was occupied and the passages were so densely thronged that it was almost impossible, even for the privileged few, to obtain either ingress or egress.' Whatever Cardigan's grosser failings, he seldom failed to pack a courtroom.[59]

Sir Thomas Wilde, for Lord William, presented the evidence of the seduction, while the Solicitor-General appeared for Cardigan. Winter was severely cross-examined, both as to his evidence and as to Lord William's character. Lord William, when in London, spent most of his evenings smoking and drinking at the White Bear in Piccadilly or at Dubourg's in the Haymarket. He had lived for some months at the White Bear, arranging to have street girls brought in for the night. When he was on naval duty at Portsmouth and Lady Frances had come to join him there, he had installed a common prostitute in the bedroom of the hotel on the night before her arrival. Whatever Cardigan's faults, he began to appear almost a figure of chivalry by comparison with the brutal and brutish Lord William Paget.

By the end of the Solicitor-General's closing address, the effect of Winter's evidence seemed insignificant. The jurors were not prepared to award £15,000 damages to Lord William on the strength of the character which he had been given. Indeed, they gave a verdict for Cardigan without leaving the court. There was a sudden burst of applause, which the criers found it almost impossible to subdue. For Cardigan, this was an unprecedented but no doubt gratifying display of sympathy.

Among other rumours, Cardigan's name was linked with that of Maria, the young Marchioness of Ailesbury, who was celebrated as one of the great beauties of Victorian society. Maria, with her rather severe features softened by cascades of golden ringlets, seemed to fascinate older men, military and otherwise. The 1st Marquess of Ailesbury was a sixty-year-old widower when she was married off to him and, though he lived to be eighty-three, his waning powers made the young Marchioness the natural prey of men like Cardigan. Wellington himself had wanted to marry her, when he was in his sixties and she was hardly twenty. He rode to the house of her father, the Hon. Charles Tollemache, and was met by the joyful announcement that Maria had just become engaged to marry the Marquess of Ailesbury. The Duke remounted at once and galloped away, muttering audibly, 'Too late! Too late!'[60]

Maria was the cousin of Cardigan's wife and was a frequent, unescorted guest at Portman Square and Deene. Before the outbreak of the Crimean War, both Cardigan and the second Lord Wilton were fierce rivals for the favours of the young Marchioness. Wilton was known as a notorious womanizer, as well as Commodore of the Royal Yacht Squadron and a prominent member of the Quorn. If Cardigan could rival Wilton as a huntsman, so he could as a yacht owner. He spent £10,000 on the building of the latest kind of steam yacht, which he proposed to use on his crossings to Ireland. During Cowes regatta, when Maria and the rest of the fashionable world came to the resort, Cardigan arrived on the *Dryad* and dropped anchor off Calshot. Wilton sailed in with the *Xarifa*, a schooner which he had bought in 1835 and which had been used as a slave trader.

Wilton had apparently come to regard Maria as his property, and was not best pleased when she agreed to have lunch with Cardigan on board the *Dryad*. Wilton's gloomiest suspicions were realized when sunset, midnight, and sunrise came without any reappearance of the young Marchioness. The visitors at Cowes were then diverted by a 'turn-up' between Cardigan and Wilton over their rights in the lady, a quarrel quite loud enough to reach the ears of Elizabeth, Countess of Cardigan.

Elizabeth, however, was unlikely to have been surprised at the news that her cousin Maria had spent the night with Cardigan on his yacht. The Cardigans were not seen much together any longer, not even for the sake of propriety. Each had long since found the other's temper unendurable and certainly they had both found other sexual partners. Of the two, it was Cardigan himself who seemed to provide the greatest challenge in this respect. Women were charmed by the appearance of the tall, wasp-waisted *sabreur*, who even at fifty remained the epitome of elegance and vitality. Whatever his behaviour with tiresome subalterns, once he was in the presence of a woman he became the gallant and chivalrous, if covetous, knight. The more desperate of his female admirers actually sent *billets doux* to Deene, begging for an 'interview' with him.

When some of these sexual begging-letters fell into Elizabeth's hands, she forged a reply on Cardigan's behalf, agreeing to come to the lady on condition that she would send her servants away and keep the place in darkness, since he was too well known otherwise to avoid recognition. The terms were agreed, and Elizabeth then sent Cardigan's agent, an imposing and virile gentleman who was delighted by such opportunities for seduction in the dark. When the trick had worked, Elizabeth let the story be generally known, enjoying complete vengeance and incurring life-long enmity.[61]

By 1846, however, she was prepared to leave Cardigan completely and live with a lover. The man in question was a British Admiral, John, 9th Baron Colville, who was more than twenty years older than Cardigan. He had been Lord-in-waiting to Prince Albert for a brief period and now spent his time travelling from one fashionable resort to another, moving from Bath to Cheltenham, and then on to Brighton. He seemed to his contemporaries a man of no pretensions or distinctions. For all that, it is said that he felt in honour bound to offer Cardigan both an apology and 'satisfaction' in the form of a duel. Cardigan replied, echoing the words of Elizabeth's first husband to him twenty years earlier. He reassured Colville, telling him that in taking Elizabeth off his hands he had performed 'the greatest service one man may render another'. There was no duel.

Some of the unhappy ladies who had longed for 'interviews' with Cardigan at Deene now had their requests more readily granted. As his second wife later recalled, this was the time when he was 'consoled by many fair friends'. Of course, he was still rich and, therefore, 'certain ladies were always ready to stop at Deene without their husbands', even if only as a means of getting Cardigan to pay one or two of their outstanding bills. At fifty years old, nursing the first symptoms of mild but chronic bronchitis, and an unpleasant but by no means fatal inflammation of the bladder, it seemed that he was already in semi-retirement. He visited his regiment less and less frequently, especially when the 11th Hussars went back to Ireland for a second spell in 1852–4. Yet though his health showed minor imperfections, the semi-retirement had its compensations.[62]

When the 11th Hussars were first ordered to Ireland in 1843–6, Cardigan sold his hunting stud at Tattersall's for just over £2,300, though he bought new horses for hunting in Ireland. The financial loss was considerable, since he received less than half what he had paid for some of the finest horses. Moreover, two of his best hunters were soon killed in Ireland, one of them in a hunting accident while being ridden by Lieutenant Peel of the 11th Hussars, son of Sir Robert Peel.[63]

However, Cardigan's economies were never more than temporary and the style of his life at Deene was little affected by them. The house parties, at which he entertained the Duke of Cambridge, the Prince of Mecklenburgh Strelitz, who was to marry Princess Augusta of Cambridge, or cronies like Lord Adolphus Fitzclarence, were almost royal occasions. First thing in the morning, Cardigan and his guests would be out with the Quorn, the Pytchley, or the Cottesmore hounds. After dinner, depending on which guests happened to be present, there would be either dancing or cards. The band of the 11th Hussars provided Cardigan with his own private orchestra, both for the balls held at Deene, or simply as a pleasing distant accompaniment for those guests whose tastes ran to faro or baccarat. To the newspaper public, the house parties began to sound like a cross between a Buckingham Palace state ball and a gambling hell, garnished by sensational rumours of Cardigan's amorous adventures.

The hunting field alone continued to provide Cardigan with the type of challenge which he might otherwise have found in leading his regiment in battle. Whyte-Melville, who had often been one of his hunting companions, concluded from this, 'The foundation of Lord Cardigan's whole character was valour. He loved it, he prized it, he admired it in others, he was conscious and proud of it in himself.' He certainly appeared to find some disgrace in a man avoiding even the most perilous jump, and was notorious himself for riding his horse at the deepest and broadest brooks, without being able to swim a stroke. He was twice saved from drowning, in the most desperate circumstances.[64]

In the years following the Crimean War, it was sometimes put about that Cardigan had been loved and respected by all his tenants at Deene. This was less than accurate. He had a reputation for tolerating no kind of objection from those around him, which made him sometimes disliked and sometimes ridiculous. During a shoot at Deene with Lord Westmorland, there were so few birds that Cardigan, cursing his keepers and ordering them out of the way, directed the beaters himself across a new covert. Then the sky seemed to fill with birds and the shooting party massacred them systematically. Only afterwards would Cardigan listen to his dismayed keeper, who explained that his lordship had beaten in the wrong direction and had just blasted out of the sky Lord Berners's entire stock of pheasants.[65]

It was just before another shooting party that the birds were mysteriously disturbed and flew off in all directions before a shot could be fired. Eventually, the beaters flushed from the covert 'a very aged yokel gathering sticks'. Cardigan threw down his guns and prepared to chastise the culprit verbally and even physically.

'My lord,' said the old man reproachfully, 'I am your lordship's hereditary mole-catcher.'

He then made a dignified withdrawal, leaving Cardigan 'senseless and wordless with wrath', and with no idea as to whether he had ever had an hereditary mole-catcher or not.[66]

By the end of the 1840s, relations between Cardigan and his tenants were not improving. When Charles Payne, the huntsman of the Pytchley, had run a fox to ground near Deene and was preparing to dig it out, Cardigan ordered him to stop.

'He has been killing some lambs, my Lord, and the tenants are complaining.'

'Tenants complaining?' shouted Cardigan. 'The land is mine; the woods are mine, and the tenants are mine; and my tenants are not in the habit of complaining about anything.'[67]

Dislike of Cardigan reached such a point with some of his tenants that they were said to have agreed on a plan to drown or half-drown him in Staunton brook during a ride to hounds. As they approached the brook at an unjumpable spot, two would ride on either side of him, as close as possible, while another would ride hard at his back. Then as the other two pulled him from his horse into the water, the third horse and rider would jump upon him.

Though the particular scheme never worked in all these details, there was, perhaps, some gratification for disgruntled tenants in the sight of their lord floundering in water up to his neck, unable to swim, and shouting mournfully, 'Will no one assist to save the seventh and last Earl of Cardigan?'[68]

Like so many of their compatriots, the tenants of Deene appear to have indulged in a hatred of Cardigan before the Crimean War which was as irrational in its way as their adulation of him afterwards. It is a matter of record, for instance, that apart from his regular gifts of food to the poor, he allowed the poorest of the local inhabitants 2s. 6d. a week of his own money, and that he clothed the local children who attended a school which was also maintained by his financial assistance. If this seems less than munificent in twentieth-century terms, it was more than adequate in the eyes of many Victorian landowners.[69]

In May 1846 the 11th Hussars had returned from Ireland and for the next two years were stationed at Coventry, with detachments at Manchester. From 1848 until 1850 the regiment was back at Hounslow, where its duties were principally those of escorting Queen Victoria between the Palace and the railway stations, and appearing in the Lord Mayor's Show. In 1850 the 11th was sent to Norwich, where it remained until the posting to Ireland in 1852. By this time, Cardigan had virtually handed over the regiment to his new second-in-command, Brevet Major Douglas, his companion in the Wimbledon Common duel.

For all the disputes with his officers, Cardigan's supporters were quick to notice the loyalty which he inspired among his men. The *Coventry Standard* reminded its readers of his generosity towards old soldiers who had fought in past campaigns. One of these was an ancient veteran of Wellington's first battles in India. The old man was destitute when discovered by Cardigan, who promptly gave him the monopoly of the sale of oranges and fruit in the barracks, as well as providing him with food and clothing. When the old man died, he was buried with military honours at regimental expense.[70]

A letter from another old soldier to the *United Service Gazette*, on 12 October 1850, insisted that for all the adverse publicity, Cardigan was the hero of the ordinary trooper, for his generosity to his men, for his kindness to their families, and for his determination to promote men from the ranks. There was soon to be another instance of this in the 11th Hussars, when Sergeant-Major Dungate was promoted to cornet. But even so, it seemed something of an exaggeration, to most readers, for the *Naval and Military Gazette* to claim that every man of his regiment would follow Cardigan to 'victory or death'.[71]

Neither victory nor death seemed particularly relevant to the life which Cardigan was leading in the final years of peace. As often as possible he was out with the Pytchley or, as the guest of others, with packs like the Warwickshire Hounds. In the autumn he would go to Paris, combining his visit with the sports of the field. He became a welcome visitor to the new Emperor, Napoleon III.

In London he engaged in political debate and speculation, sometimes in the House of Lords but more often at White's, where he argued over issues great and small with men like Charles Greville and Lord Adolphus Fitzclarence, in the expensive calm of St James's Street.

In the House of Lords, he defended British soldiers who had fought against Irish rioters at Six-Mile Bridge and had then been prosecuted for the injuries which they inflicted. He attacked Lord John Russell's government for reducing the strength of the army and the navy, and then proceeding to quarrel with every other major power until Britain was 'almost without a friend or an ally upon the whole Continent of Europe'. In 1853, he began a one-man campaign to abolish the Lord Lieutenancy of Ireland, whose real power had been abolished anyway by better communication between London and Dublin, and whose tenant had been reduced to a mere ceremonial 'King Charming'.[72]

In the privacy of White's, he bet Lord Adolphus Fitzclarence £100 in 1846 that Lord Stanley (later Lord Derby) would be Prime Minister before the ungrateful Sir Robert Peel ever regained office. Peel died and Derby later became Premier. He bet Fitzclarence and Lord George Paget £50 each that the duty on corn would be restored before 1855. (He lost the bet.) Yet perhaps the most interesting wager at White's was one not made by Cardigan himself.

'A. bets B. £100 to 10 that Lord C. does not command a Household Cavalry Regiment within 5 years from this date. May 24, 1850.'[73]

Since the command of a Household Cavalry Regiment would go to an officer who stood high in royal and official favour, most members would probably have given even longer odds than 10–1 against Lord Cardigan.

Even for a Lieutenant-Colonel of Hussars, whose life seemed to be a succession of dinner parties at Portman Square, hunting parties at Deene or Melton Mowbray, summer days at Cowes, and field days in Phoenix Park, the darkening prospect for peace in Europe was no longer a mere subject of speculation. The westward expansion of the Turkish Empire had long since reached its limit. As the tide of that expansion ebbed eastward again, newly independent governments rose in its deserted provinces and the eyes of the great European military powers roved covetously over the decaying imperial domain of the Sultan.

Ever since Napoleon and Tsar Alexander had met at Tilsit, Russia had made clear that she regarded Constantinople as part of her legitimate area of political influence, if not as part of her territory. In January and February 1853, Tsar Nicholas discussed the Turkish problem, or 'Eastern Question', with the British Ambassador to St Petersberg, Sir Hamilton Seymour. The Tsar played repeatedly on the cliché of Turkey as 'The Sick Man of Europe'. 'I repeat to you', he told the Ambassador, 'that the sick man is dying, and we can never allow such an event to take us by surprise. We must come to some understanding.' The 'understanding' which Russia offered was that Britain should take Turkish territory in Egypt and also the island of Cyprus, leaving Russia a free hand elsewhere.

What Britain and France understood was quite clear. At the very least, the Tsar proposed to hold political control over the government of Turkey. At the most, he would annex the Black Sea territories from the Russian frontier to Constantinople, seizing the Dardanelles and giving Russia free access to the Mediterranean. The British route to India via the Isthmus of Suez would be at the mercy of the Russian fleet. It might prove impossible to prevent the Russians from occupying the Balkans almost as far north as Venice, and Palestine as far south as the frontier of Egypt. Victorian England might be faced by the greatest land empire in the history of the world, its frontiers standing upon the Pacific and the Adriatic, upon the Arctic Ocean and the Sinai Desert. Without a secure route to the East, and with the possibility of Russian expansion southwards through Afghanistan, the entire British position in India might become untenable.

Against this alarmist view of the Russian threat, men like the Prime Minister, Lord Aberdeen and Lord Fitzroy Somerset who, as Lord Raglan, succeeded to the office of Master of Ordnance at the Horse Guards in 1852, balanced the horrors of war, which each had experienced at first hand at Leipzig and Waterloo respectively.

Nor was there any strong sympathy towards Britain's potential ally in the war, the French Empire of Napoleon III. Since his seizure of power through the revolution of 1848 and the establishment of the Second Empire in 1852, Napoleon was widely regarded in England as a tyrant with blood on his hands, who endeavoured to secure his position in France by spectacles of military glory in the French colonization of northern Africa.

However, France revived her claim to be Protector of the Holy Places in Palestine, which were under Turkish rule. The Turks accepted this, and the privileges of the Holy Places, which had passed to Orthodox monks, were transferred to the Latin monks at French insistence. The Tsar intervened, as champion of the Orthodox Church and ordered the Turks to restore the *status quo*. He also demanded to be recognized as protector of the 40 per cent of the Sultan's subjects who were an oppressed Orthodox minority in a Muslim state. In May 1853 the Sultan refused to recognize the Tsar as protector of the Turkish Orthodox community. On 2 July the Russian army crossed the frontier into Turkey and occupied the Danubian provinces along the Black Sea. After more diplomatic exchanges, Turkey belatedly declared war on Russia on 23 October but for the present there were no further military operations.

On the day before Turkey's declaration of war, British and French warships entered the Dardanelles, 'for the security of British and French interests, and, if necessary, for the protection of the Sultan'. However, there were those in England, including the Queen, who still doubted the wisdom of an unconditional alliance with a decaying, despotic power. Others had an even more powerful dislike for the alliance with Napoleon III, whose sole aim, they judged, was to win political prestige for himself by Britain's recognition of him as a trusted ally.

However, on 13 December 1853 news of a naval engagement at Sinope on 30 November reached the British press, and public opinion swung irrevocably in favour of the alliance and of war with Russia. On

30 November six Russian battleships under Admiral Nakimoff had found the Black Sea squadron of the Turkish fleet lying unprepared for battle in the harbour of Sinope. The Russian ships shelled the Turkish squadron at point blank range, blasting every vessel to pieces and wiping out 4,000 men.

Throughout the autumn of 1853 there had been public meetings and public debate over the Eastern Question in London and the major British cities. As late as 12 December, *The Times* was of the opinion that peace could be, and ought to be, concluded between Turkey and Russia. The *Morning Chronicle* and the *Manchester Guardian* were determinedly anti-war. Then, on 13 December, came the news of Sinope. The hopes of such bodies as the Quaker-sponsored Peace Society, whose supporters included Bright and Cobden, were destroyed in the popular feeling of outrage at the mean-spirited and brutal action of the Russian navy. Those papers which had urged peace now ceased to do so, and some very energetically demanded war. By 20 December, for instance, the *Morning Chronicle* had abandoned all hope of a negotiated settlement and was publicly hinting that the British squadron in the Black Sea ought by now to be avenging the defeated Turks. 'To stop the unprofitable contest by striking down the aggressor with a blow is as plain a duty towards humanity as it was to send succour to Sinope.'

After this, even those who still regarded conflict with Russia as undesirable began to accept it as inevitable. The demands of the editorials, the heroics and patriotic caricatures of *Punch*, the public expressions of feeling and the private policies of men like Lord Palmerston, all seemed to combine to make the outbreak of war a mere matter of diplomatic timing. Even while Lord Aberdeen and the press were talking of such peace hopes as remained, plans were being announced for the dispatch of a British army to Turkey. Cardigan's brother-in-law, Lord Lucan, was to command the cavalry, and, under him, Cardigan was to command the Light Cavalry Brigade with the rank of Brigadier-General.

An ultimatum was issued to the Tsar by the British government on 27 February 1854. Unless the Russian army was withdrawn by 30 April from the Danubian provinces of Turkey, which it had occupied in July 1853, Britain and France would go to war in support of the Sultan. By the end of March the ultimatum was still unanswered, though it was reported that 50,000 Russian troops had been moved into the occupied territories and were positioned for a possible drive towards the Dardanelles. On 28 March Britain and France declared war upon Russia.

In Dublin, two squadrons of the 11th Hussars were put under orders for service with the expeditionary force, which was to be led by Lord Raglan himself and accompanied by HRH the Duke of Cambridge, cousin of the Queen. The 11th made plans to care for the wives and families of those men who were to serve with their own regimental commander in the Light Cavalry Brigade. Cardigan and his officers celebrated their departure from Dublin by a farewell banquet for Sir Edward Blakeney, who commanded the army in Ireland. Yet many of the most spectacular of the celebrations had actually preceded the declaration of war. Both White's and Boodle's anticipated the event with 'grand farewell entertainments' for the Duke of Cambridge and Lord Raglan some weeks before the outbreak of war.

On 4 March, at Boodle's, the tables glittered with a profusion of gold and silver plate, when a sumptuous dinner was provided for fifty-four gallant and distinguished guests. Raglan, as Commander-in-Chief of the expeditionary force, was unable to be present, but the Duke of Cambridge and Lord Cardigan were both there. Cardigan took the chair, with the Duke on his right as the principal guest. After dinner, loyal speeches were made and loyal toasts were drunk. 'The subject of the approaching struggle with Russia was of course alluded to, always with cheers, and in hopeful and confident terms.'[74]

CHAPTER 7

GOING TO THE WARS

I

The farewell dinners to the commanders of the British expedition continued during a period of six weeks in the early spring of 1854. By way of accompaniment, there were scenes of fervent popular support for the war as the most famous names among British regiments, the heroes of the Peninsula and Waterloo, marched off to battle. 'Never such enthusiasm seen among the population', wrote Charles Greville despondently in his diary. 'Cold I am as a very stone to all that; seems to me privately I have hardly seen a madder business.'

On 27 February a great crowd began to gather silently during the coldest hours of the winter night, outside the Wellington Barracks in Birdcage Walk. Men and women waited patiently for the dawn. Soon after six o'clock, the Queen was picked out at the balcony window of Buckingham Palace and there was a storm of cheers from the crowd below. When Victoria unfastened the window and stepped on to the balcony with Prince Albert, the twelve-year-old Prince of Wales, and several of the other royal children, the throng in the Mall began roaring its approval, waving hats, sticks and handkerchiefs enthusiastically. At seven o'clock the barrack gates were thrown open and the Scots Guards marched out in slow time, the regimental band playing at the head of the column. The Queen took the young Prince of Wales to her side and began to explain the regimental ceremonial to him. When the Guards entered the Palace forecourt to give the royal salute, even the band playing the national anthem was drowned by the massed cheering of the crowd. The regiment itself, with bearskins held in the air, gave three cheers for the Queen before marching away in an extended column towards Waterloo Station and Portsmouth. As they disappeared from sight, the spectators still heard the echoes of the regimental band and the plaintive notes of its melody, 'O Where, and O Where is my Highland Laddie Gone?'[1]

All over England the same enthusiasm was evident. In London, there had been a similar demonstration when the Coldstream Guards marched off to war. In Manchester, which had long been the citadel of free trade and anti-war sentiment, Sergeant-Major Timothy Gowing of the Royal Fusiliers recalled that when the regiment marched from its barracks to the railway station, there was such a crowd that 'one could have walked over the heads of the people, who were wrought up to such a pitch of excitement as almost amounted to madness'. The band played 'The British Grenadiers', 'The Girl I Left Behind Me' and 'We Are Going Far Away'. All along the route to the station, the Manchester crowd shouted their encouragement to the soldiers.

'Pur them, Bill! . . . Remember Old England depends upon you! . . . Give them plenty of cold steel, and then pur them! . . . Keep your pecker up, old boy—never say die! . . . Leave your mark upon them if you get a chance!'

There was a pause while families took brave or tearful farewells of husbands, sons and brothers. Then the band struck up, 'Cheer, Boys, Cheer', and the Fusiliers marched briskly away. At Winchester, almost the entire population turned out to cheer the soldiers. In Portsmouth, as the regiments approached the dock gate, the streets were thronged by pretty girls and by citizens shouting, 'Stick to them, my boys! . . . Give it to them, if you get a chance! . . . We'll not forget you!'

The troops marched into the dockyard and, as the gates closed behind them, a thousand cheering voices shouted, 'Farewell, God bless you!'

And the men of the regiments, as they boarded the transports, 'cheered heartily for Old England and England's Queen'.[2]

Without doubt, the most spectacular of all departures was that of the Brigade of Guards, the conquerors of Napoleon and the finest troops in Europe. It is some measure of the calamities which lay ahead that when Lord Rokeby went out to command the Guards in the following winter he was presented not with a brigade of 3,000 men but with some 400 ill-clad and starving soldiers. Some had not even soles to their boots but walked barefoot on the snow. After a few moments it was apparent that this was all that remained of the Brigade of Guards, and Lord Rokeby wept at the sight of them.

Two squadrons of the 11th Hussars sailed from Kingstown for Turkey, under the command of Major Douglas. Another of Cardigan's Light Cavalry regiments, the 13th Light Dragoons, left Portsmouth in May. The cavalry horses were hoisted aloft in a canvas sling, by convicts pulling on a rope, and then swung aboard the transports. There were fewer tearful farewells as the troopers boarded the transports, possibly because most of them, like Sergeant Albert Mitchell, had seen enough of 'the partings of soldiers and their wives and mothers at embarkations', and simply wrote to their families, explaining that they were going to Turkey and would be back soon.[3]

Many of the transports were elderly sailing ships which had done more than their share of service on the long route to India. Hardly had they put to sea when the troubles began. Horses became seasick or developed the 'staggers'. The men were generally seasick too, and had no appetite for food. Perhaps this was as well, since the provisions for the voyage included barrels of peas, hard as bullets and clearly marked '1828'. Fortunately for the men of the 13th Light Dragoons they had officers who cared enough for the regiment's welfare to go ashore at Malta and obtain, at their own expense, fresh meat, vegetables, eggs, oranges and even cigars for the troopers.[4]

In the light of criticisms later made of Cardigan for his alleged indifference to the problems of transport and supply, it is worth recalling that on 23 February 1854 he had warned the government of the muddle and hardships to which cavalry regiments would be liable. He criticized the foolish policy of sending out cavalry and artillery in sailing vessels, which would leave many of the horses unfit for service, and he urged the authorities, in planning the movement of the army, 'to take advantage of those inventions, which art, science, and ingenuity have lately brought to light in this country'.[5]

It was not until the following year that the government took such advice to heart and, belatedly, produced a dramatic improvement in the health and capability of the army in the Crimea. For the time being, they were content to buy up the two fastest P & O steamships, which had proved too expensive for the company to run, and to use these in a limited capacity. The *Himalaya*, 3,438 tons, was the largest and fastest ship afloat, and one of the earliest screw steamers. The *Simla*, 2,400 tons, had been built the previous year but was already regarded by P & O as unacceptably expensive. The *Himalaya* combined sail and steam, having the appearance of a three-masted East Indiaman with a short funnel amidships. It was said that her captain could handle her as easily as if she had been a rowing boat, but her most impressive characteristic was speed. While the 13th Light Dragoons spent almost eight weeks on the voyage to Turkey, the 320 men and horses of the 5th Dragoon Guards completed the same journey on the *Himalaya* in 11 days and 19 hours. She was gratefully renamed by the men, 'Her Majesty's Floating Mews'. Some units, like the 5th Dragoon Guards, arrived ready for battle, but most were as exhausted as the 13th Light Dragoons and their horses.

'When the Earl of Cardigan was ordered to the East in command of a brigade of our light cavalry,' said George Ryan, 'from club to pothouse marvelled how he would behave. Their remembrance of him satisfied all that he had a taste for gunpowder, but they had no experience of how he could wield a sword.'[6]

The announcement on 1 April that, under the divisional command of Lord Lucan, Cardigan was to be Brigadier-General in charge of the Light Cavalry Brigade, may have caused some fears for the safety of the hussars and lancers. But most of the fears were only retrospectively expressed. Cardigan himself was, naturally, untroubled by any doubts as to his fitness for command. 'Early in the Spring of 1854, it became apparent that War would break out between this Country and Russia. I did not lose any time in applying for a Command in the Cavalry, conceiving that I might have a fair claim to employment on active service.'[7]

The other half of the Cavalry Division consisted of a Heavy Brigade of five regiments under General Sir James Scarlett. The light cavalry recruited men of smaller build, usually from 5 feet 6 inches in height to 5 feet 8 inches, who rode smaller and more nimble horses. The light cavalry regiments consisted of hussars, light dragoons, and lancers, the last of which were armed with lances that were basically bamboo poles with a spear-head. The heavy cavalry was weightier in the size of its men and horses, as well as in the arms which they carried. A fully equipped heavy dragoon rode at a weight of 19 or 20 stone.

The uses of the two brigades in war differed considerably. Light cavalry was intended for escort and outpost duty, for skirmishing and reconnaissance. It was required to manoeuvre quickly, and its value lay in speed rather than in the weight of its attack. Heavy cavalry was used for contrary purposes. Its impetus could break up formations of advancing infantry, or it could be used to meet an enemy cavalry attack head-on. In a mêlée, its troopers were better protected than light cavalrymen, since with the exception of the Scots Greys they wore helmets rather than the fur shakos or caps of the light brigades. In the Cavalry Division which went to the Crimea, there was a certain amount of rivalry between the 'Lights' and the 'Heavies', but it was as nothing compared with the rivalry between Lucan, the divisional commander, and Cardigan, the commander of the Light Brigade.

The mutual dislike of the brothers-in-law, Cardigan upright, cavalier, disdainful; Lucan, bald-headed, sharp-eyed and loud-voiced, was well known. William Howard Russell, the war correspondent of *The Times*, thought then and wrote later: [8]

> Lord Lucan was a hard man to get on with. But the moment the Government of the day made the monstrous choice of his brother-in-law, Lord Cardigan, as the Brigadier of the Light Brigade of the Cavalry Division, knowing well the relations between the two officers and the nature of the two men, they became responsible for disaster; they were guilty of treason to the Army—neither more nor less.

The choice of commanders for the British expedition was a matter for general and persistent criticism. Yet those who sympathized with the government's choices hardly improved their case by insisting that 'when Lord Hardinge made the appointments it was not thought there would be war', and that, in Lord Raglan's case, 'he would have more to do with delicate negotiation and management of the relations between the Allies than with actual military operations in a great campaign.' That Raglan was loyal, conscientious, admirably solicitous for the welfare of his men, was not questioned. But for half a lifetime, as Kinglake observed, he had been 'engaged in preventing and allaying discussion, and making the wheels of office run smooth', rather than in the practice of warfare. [9]

By the time of Cardigan's appointment, war had been officially declared. But even in the face of a common enemy, the 11th Hussars and their late commander remained an irresistible target. *The Times*, dismayed at the thought of 'the shortness of their jackets, the incredible tightness of their cherry-coloured pants', declared that the regiment was as ill-equipped for war as 'the female hussars in the ballet of Gustavus'. Perhaps, said *The Times*, the Hussars should have their 'bottoms re-leathered' for active service. Cardigan replied angrily, rising to the bait with predictable alacrity, that the jackets were longer and the pants looser 'than almost any other cavalry regiment in the service'. He accused *The Times* of 'paltry slander', and was soon supported by his old ally, the *Naval and Military Gazette*, which reminded its readers that he was 'leaving ease, wealth, and friends' to fight for his country. Which was presumably more than his detractors were prepared to do. By the end of April, the arguments on both sides had been well rehearsed and the Secretary for War, writing to Lord Raglan, promised to spare him any further discussion 'of the colour and tightness of Cardigan's cherry-coloured pants'.[10]

On 8 May, as the little blaze of general spite died down, the 7th Earl of Cardigan, fifty-seven years old, at last set off for war. His servants, grooms and horses had sailed from Liverpool in the previous month. Oddly enough, the one factor which neither friends nor enemies appeared to consider was his fitness for command in the most basic physical sense. Though still presenting the appearance of the *beau sabreur*, he was already plagued by the occupational ailments of the cavalry officer, piles and constipation, as well as by the more ominous symptoms of chronic bronchitis and swellings in the bladder which made it painful for him to urinate. He was, however, spared the ordeal of a long sea voyage. Like Lord Raglan, the Duke of Cambridge, and other senior British officers, Cardigan took the short land route across France.

Two days after leaving London, he gave an elaborate dinner party at the Café de Paris in the French capital, and was received by Napoleon III and the Empress Eugénie on the following day. Then, travelling south, he took a French ship from Marseille to Piraeus and, after a short stay in Athens, joined another steamer carrying the last detachments of the 30th and 55th regiments to Scutari, the first British base, which was on the Dardanelles just across the water from Constantinople. He disembarked there on 24 May just in time, as William Howard Russell remarked, for the ceremonial parade to mark Queen Victoria's birthday. It was noticed that he seemed to exude an air of great importance, even though his horses had still not arrived and he was obliged to attend the ceremonial parade on foot. Perhaps the appearance of self-confidence was explained by a rumour that Cardigan had been given special assurance by the Horse Guards concerning Lord Lucan. Though Lucan was his senior and, nominally at least, in charge of the entire Cavalry Division, it was said that Cardigan had been assured that his command would be separate and not subject to Lucan's immediate control. Had this been so, the Light Brigade would have been subtracted from the Cavalry Division, leaving Lucan with only the Heavy Brigade under its brigadier, Sir James Scarlett. For all that, it was to prove a source of controversy.

For the time being there was still peace between the British and Russian armies for all practical purposes, and peace between the British commanders themselves. Cardigan called dutifully upon Lord Raglan and, swallowing a considerable dose of pride, brought himself to dine with Lucan on 26 May. Lucan even began to direct his commands to 'My dear Cardigan'. In the general lull, Cardigan hired a pony and, wearing full dress uniform of the 11th (Prince Albert's own) Hussars, rode up and down the streets of Constantinople, a rather tall figure on a very small animal, much to the curiosity of the inhabitants. 'His Lordship', said the *United Service Gazette*, 'is in the enjoyment of excellent health, and eager for a "brush" with the Russians'.[11]

The pivot of the British military operation in the East was the little town of Varna on the coast of the province of Bulgaria. To the north, between Varna and the Danube, lay the menace of the invading Russian army, which had besieged the Turkish force in the river town of Silistria. The first option available to the British and the French, once their troops were moved up from Scutari to Varna, might have been to march to the relief of Silistria and then, crossing the Danube, to have driven the enemy back to the Russian frontier.

But three hundred miles to the north-east of Varna, across the Black Sea, lay the coast of the Crimea and the great Russian naval base of Sebastopol. To raise the siege of Silistria would answer an immediate threat, but to destroy the fortress of Sebastopol would be to remove the Russian military threat from the Black Sea altogether. That, at least, was the proposition accepted by the Duke of Newcastle, as Minister of War in London, and most of his cabinet colleagues.

Yet whether the objective was to be Silistria, to the north, or Sebastopol to the east, the first necessary move was to establish a secure forward base at Varna. By the end of May, the first units of the Light Cavalry Brigade, including the 8th Hussars and the 17th Lancers, had passed Scutari and were sailing up the Black Sea towards the Bulgarian port. In order to be close to whatever action there might be, and also in order to out-manoeuvre Lord Lucan, Cardigan applied directly to Lord Raglan for permission to accompany his Brigade to Varna. Raglan, anxious to follow whatever course of action seemed most likely to produce harmonious relations between his commanders, agreed. He wrote to Lucan and requested him to make arrangements for Cardigan's departure.

Lucan reprimanded Cardigan for going, over his head, to Raglan in such a matter, but there was no means now of preventing him sailing for Varna. Cardigan left for the Bulgarian port on 3 June and was joined, in time, by the five regiments of his Light Cavalry Brigade: the 4th Dragoons; the 8th Hussars; the 11th Hussars; the 13th Light Dragoons, and the 17th Lancers, known ominously as 'The Death or Glory Boys'. But to make matters worse for Lucan, the units of the Heavy Brigade, the other half of his Cavalry Division, were also sent direct to Varna. Moreover, Cardigan was senior to Sir James Scarlett, the Brigadier of the 'Heavies', and was therefore in effective command of the entire division at Varna. Meanwhile, two hundred miles across water, in Scutari, Lord Lucan, the proper commander of the division, denounced his brother-in-law's insubordination and complained to Raglan of having been left in Scutari 'without troops, and for all I can see without duties'.

Matters were not made sweeter for Lucan by the way in which certain newspapers in England, formerly among Cardigan's most hostile critics, now began to sing the achievements and qualities of their old enemy. The *United Service Gazette* was one of the first to recant, regretting that it had not spoken in more 'laudatory terms' in the past, quickly admitting that Cardigan had always been a man of great generosity, whose regiment did him credit. 'We are now exceedingly happy to be able to speak in terms of unqualified praise and admiration of Lord Cardigan. He has commenced soldiering in the field after a manner worthy of a veteran Dragoon. . . . It is of such fine material as this that our aristocratic soldiers are made.'[12]

There were those who certainly thought that the Cavalry Division might be better off under the immediate command of Cardigan than under Lucan, an officer who had been retired on half-pay for the past seventeen years and whose memory, even for the rudiments of cavalry drill, was something less than complete.

The Light Brigade and the Horse Artillery set up camp at Devna, on the coast a few miles to the north of Varna. Cardigan rode into the lines on 3 June and took up residence in a house which he had commandeered at one end of the bay. In the green, if somewhat steamy, meadowland beside the water the neat rows of bell tents and the more imposing marquees of officers lucky enough to acquire them, were laid out in a pattern measured to the precise inch. Fanny Duberly, accompanying her husband, Captain Henry Duberly of the 8th Hussars, recommended the marquees. They kept out the bright heat of the Bulgarian summer and were easier to ventilate than the stifling little bell tents.

Supplies of food were still good, though rice was issued in lieu of vegetables and someone had forgotten to provide pepper and salt. Every day at dawn, the brightly uniformed squadrons of Hussars and Lancers on their bay or white horses paraded for drill and manoeuvres under Cardigan's personal command. Special attention was now paid to battle tactics, such as the technique of one line standing fast while the second line advanced or retreated through it, and the technique of rallying speedily into formation from a mêlée.

Lord Lucan arrived at last from Scutari and sat in Varna, brooding over Cardigan's behaviour and writing him sharp notes of command, so that there should be no dispute as to who actually had charge of the Cavalry Division. But disillusionment rather than rivalry was reflected in the mood of the cavalry camp. The grass shrivelled in the heat and then caught fire, reducing the turf to a thick black dust which the sea wind blew over the immaculate uniforms and equipment of the cavalry. Signs of sickness and fatigue grew more evident among the men and their horses. The normal camp routine became increasingly irksome. Captain Cresswell of the 11th Hussars complained of Cardigan 'giving us regulation Phoenix Park Field Days—such a bore he is—comes round stables just as if he was Colonel instead of Major General, and he makes us all go to evening stables.' It was hardly the hour of glory for which the pick of the British cavalry had been trained. Worse still, they were joined by Turkish cavalry, to whom Cardigan gave no orders and at whom he then swore on parade for being in the wrong places.[13]

Among themselves, the officers of the cavalry camp maintained a bizarre version of English high society. They rode out on dog hunts, often to capture rather than to kill the prey. The 17th Lancers organized a regimental race meeting on such local ponies as they had managed to round up. Some officers supplemented their diet by pig-shooting and by champagne which they had brought from England for medicinal use. Cardigan himself grew accustomed to the somewhat unappetizing routine of pork and champagne. In the end, there was nothing for it but to drink the local wine. 'The country wine is really not bad', wrote Lieutenant Strange Jocelyn to his father, 'when mixed with sugar and a little Burrage that grows here all about the Camp, we can almost imagine, barring the Ice, that we are drinking Claret Cup, on Guard at St James's.'[14]

The Turks, who found the ways of the British army sufficiently odd, thought the behaviour of the accompanying women even odder, whether they were diplomats' ladies, soldiers' wives like Fanny Duberly, or camp followers. The British contempt for polygamous Turks was equalled by Turkish astonishment that any woman who appeared unveiled at a ball and danced with one man after another could be anything but unchaste. Indeed there had been a most embarrassing incident at one such function when a Turkish gentleman, assuming that a British diplomat's wife who behaved in this fashion must be available to all, had monopolized the lady and begun to whisper suggestions of the most appalling obscenity into her unwilling ears.[15]

From time to time, Cardigan and his regiments were reminded that a hundred miles from their camp a war was being fought in earnest by the Turks and Russians, and had been going on for the past year. At night, British cavalry patrols rode the surrounding countryside in search of any warning that the Russian army had begun to advance towards Varna. If Silistria should fall, there seemed every likelihood that the next objective of the Russians would be Varna itself. The patrols made no contact with the enemy but Cardigan was annoyed to discover that the dragoons were wrapping their cloaks round themselves during night patrols. He denounced the practice as 'effeminate' and forbade it. 'Luckily it is summer', wrote Fanny Duberly when she heard the order, 'though the dews fall like rain.'[16]

The army was subject to any number of 'camp shaves' as rumours were called. There was a 'shave' that the Austrians were marching to fight the Russians on the Danube, and then another that the Austrians had joined the Russian side. There were rumours of battles and of plans to attack Sebastopol and, as in most situations so fertile to rumour, there was very little news of anything specific. On 21 June the Light Brigade was ordered to move camp, but it was only to another site a few hundred yards to the front.

But there was one rumour, much more than a 'camp shave', which reached Lord Raglan just before midnight on 24 June. A rider galloped towards Raglan's headquarters at Varna with news that the Russian army under Gortchakoff, 30,000 strong, had moved off from Silistria, after an unsuccessful siege of forty-five days. The resistance of the Silistria garrison, the courage of the Turkish soldiers and the resourceful leadership of Captain Butler and Lieutenant Naysmith, the two British officers present, offered welcome news to Raglan. Less welcome was the prospect of 30,000 Russian troops who might have retired towards Bucharest, but who might equally well be moving towards Varna.

Raglan acted at once. Late though it was, he sent Lord Burghersh to ride to Devna with urgent orders for Cardigan. Cardigan was to set out at first light with two squadrons of cavalry and three days' rations. He was to scout towards Silistria and, in the shortest possible time, 'ascertain the movements of the enemy'. At four o'clock in the morning, a squadron of the 8th Hussars and another of the 13th Light Dragoons were already prepared for reconnaissance. They then had to wait until half-past ten, while their three days' rations were cooked. 'If it takes six and a half hours to get two squadrons under way, how long will it take to move the whole British force?' inquired Fanny Duberly suspiciously.[17] It was hoped that further supplies could be sent after the column, but to provision the regiments adequately proved quite impossible.

The patrol, with one tent for Cardigan and inadequate rations for everyone, set out to search an area of about 1,000 square miles. It was an arduous reconnaissance, but Cardigan, who had been frustrated by lack of action, described the ordeal as 'by no means unsatisfactory to me'. His description of the northward march towards the Danube was succinct and vivid.[18]

> We might have come at any moment upon the Russian army;—
> upon the Russian outposts. We travelled over the country,
> which I may call a perfectly wild desert, for a distance of 300
> miles . . . and marched 120 miles without ever seeing a human
> being. There was not a single house in a state of repair or that
> was inhabited along all this route, nor was there an animal to
> be seen except those that exist in the wildest regions.

If the Russian army had indeed been advancing upon Varna, then Cardigan's two squadrons of cavalry would probably have met it head-on. During the next four days, accompanied by a detachment of Turkish horsemen, the British column rode across the great plain of the Danube delta. With Cardigan at their head, they moved as nearly as possible to the regulation British cavalry speed for Bulgaria, which was 3·2 miles an hour. They had no clothes, other than the uniforms in which they set out, no tents except one, 'just large enough to cover a spring sofa bed', in which Cardigan slept. There was no food except the three-day supply of salt meat and biscuit. The reconnaissance was to last seventeen days. In the hazy stillness and heat of the plains it was, as Captain Jenyns of the 13th Light Dragoons remarked, 'No joke.' In the cold nights and under thick dew, men and horses slept side by side upon the ground, except when the troopers were required to ride all night to reach their next destination.

For three days the two hundred men of the column scouted along the southern bank of the Danube, riding as much as fourteen hours a day. Then they began a two-day march to Silistria itself. At last the main body of the Russian army, under the veteran General Lüders, was sighted on the opposite bank of the great river. The soldiers of England and Russia had come as nearly face to face as the broad sweep of water would permit. What followed was part of the etiquette of war.

A Turkish officer was sent over under a flag of truce, in a manner reminiscent of Cardigan's leaving his card upon a new arrival in town. Lüders inquired whether the cavalry was French or British. He was told that they were British. There was time for Lüders to survey Cardigan and for Cardigan to survey Lüders through their respective spy-glasses. The spy-glasses were put away, the Turkish officer returned, the British patrol and the mass of the Russian regiments moved off in opposite directions. Not a shot was fired. The formalities of war had been observed.

Before Silistria, the exhausted patrol rested for a day. Cardigan sent back regular reports to Raglan by his best riders. The first rode into the Light Brigade camp at nightfall on 29 June, both horse and man so spent that brandy-and-water was needed to revive them. From the banks of the Danube, Cardigan's own aide-de-camp, Lieutenant Maxse, was sent back at full speed to report the situation to the Commander-in-Chief. While the solitary dispatch riders galloped across the wide, deserted plains towards Varna, the rest of the column struggled back from one fresh-water spring to another. Five horses were dead and seventy-five more unfit for duty. Some of the cavalrymen themselves were too weak to ride and completed the journey in a commandeered Turkish cart, or *araba*, drawn by bullocks. Yet those who accompanied Cardigan on the patrol, as opposed to his critics who did not, thought him 'a capital fellow to be under at this work', not least because of the 'tremendous praise' with which he encouraged his men. This reputation spread beyond the cavalry to the Brigade of Guards, where George Higginson remarked, 'They say he is very quiet and attentive, and that he explains his wishes and gives his orders most clearly.'[19]

After marching all night through a thunderstorm, the bedraggled column reached the Light Brigade camp soon after dawn on 11 June. Half the horses were no longer fit for active service but were herded towards the camp by their dismounted riders who appeared like so many drovers behind a herd of cattle. According to Cardigan's second-in-command, Lord George Paget (brother of Lord William Paget of the criminal conversation case), no more than 80 of the 200 horses were fit for further cavalry duties.[20]

Sergeant Mitchell of the 13th Light Dragoons watched his regimental comrades return and was shocked to find them 'mere shadows of their former selves', after the seventeen days of reconnaissance. Lord George disapproved of Cardigan's misuse of the soldiers; Fanny Duberly was appalled by the treatment of the horses, and Colonel Daniel Lysons deplored the expense incurred by the expedition. Yet none was so heated in his criticism of Cardigan as Captain Lewis Edward Nolan, a thirty-four-year-old prodigy of cavalry skill, aide-de-camp to the Quartermaster General, General Airey. The son of the British consul in Milan, Nolan had passed through the Viennese Military College with distinction, served with the 10th Hungarian Hussars on the Polish frontier, and then been commissioned in the British army as Cornet in the 15th Hussars. While serving in India, he had acquired a dazzling reputation as a horseman and swordsman, as well as being the author of two standard books on cavalry training and tactics. Impetuous, and impatient of his elders, he regarded both Lucan and Cardigan as fools. Even William Howard Russell of *The Times*, who was no admirer of either of the brothers-in-law, was astonished at the heat of Nolan's anger against Cardigan after the patrol, which was becoming known as 'the sore-back reconnaissance'.[21]

Raglan, at least, acknowledged that Cardigan had found out the most important thing, that 'the Russians have withdrawn' and that there was no immediate threat to the base at Varna. 'I hope', added Raglan, 'that the fatigue that you and the squadrons have undergone in obtaining the information will not prove injurious to your health and that of the officers and men under your orders.'[22]

On 20 June Cardigan had been promoted to Major-General, and if his enemies regarded the reconnaissance as a display of brutal incompetence, the press in England seized on it as the first heroic exploit of the war on the part of the British army. The *United Service Gazette*, now Cardigan's confirmed admirer, painted the scene in epic style.[23]

> For seventeen days were the General and his men in the saddle
> —and for seventeen nights did they bivouac with no other
> canopy than the dark blue arch of heaven, in one of the worst
> of climates. Their intrepidity and sense of duty carried them
> close to the Russian lines, even within view of the enemy, and
> it was a miracle that they got free. . . . We have henceforth
> every confidence in Lord Cardigan.

As a matter of fact, Cardigan's view of the 'dark blue arch of heaven' had been impeded by the small tent in which he slept, upon a spring sofa bed.

Yet Raglan's polite hope about the health of Cardigan's men was more relevant to the actual situation than either the jibes of Cardigan's enemies or the heroics of the London press. The patrol had bivouacked in the open for two weeks, and had lived upon short rations of salt meat and biscuit. By any standard it was a test of endurance but not an intolerable one by military standards of the nineteenth century. Cardigan had driven his men hard, but the extent to which the health of men and horses had deteriorated during the reconnaissance, under duties less arduous than some which might be expected from them in the Crimea, showed how far the health of the army had been undermined in general, in the few months since the departure from England.

The 'camp shaves' of the Light Brigade in the weeks following the 'sore-back reconnaissance' suggested that the war might be over for all practical purposes. On 29 July General Gortchakoff withdrew his army from Bucharest and began to retire towards the Russian frontier. The withdrawal was qualified by a promise to the Orthodox inhabitants of the city 'to return and deliver them from the barbarian Turks, as soon as a more healthy time arrived', but it seemed as if even this promise was to be overtaken by diplomatic decisions. The Austrians now entered the sphere of war, signing a treaty with Turkey under which they would occupy the Danubian provinces vacated by the retreating Russians until such time as the two belligerent states should conclude a peace treaty. A campaign might still be fought on the remoter asiatic frontiers of Russia and Turkey, and naval warfare would still be possible in the Black Sea. But the major area of conflict was conveniently closed to both sides by the creation of this temporary buffer state. Soon after his return from Silistria, Cardigan remarked to Fanny Duberly that the Light Brigade would probably remain camped in Bulgaria for the summer and would then go south to winter quarters in Adrianople. In that event, it might well have happened that Russia and Turkey would have come to terms, through European diplomacy, before the next campaigning season began.[24]

With the prospect of the entire expedition proving to be an answer to a false alarm, officers like Major Forrest and Captain Cresswell grew still more bitter at the way in which Cardigan refused to allow them to neglect their duties. That Captains of Hussars should be made to attend evening stables in person, when the horses were groomed and bedded down, seemed like a calculated humiliation. It might be a chore appropriate to ordinary troopers, or even to Cardigan himself if he chose to do it, but for a self-respecting officer of dragoons it became irksome and, in some way, demeaning.

The drill and the discipline continued. District courts-martial were held in camp as punctiliously as if the regiments had been quartered at Knightsbridge or Hounslow. When a trooper of the 13th Light Dragoons struck his sergeant, a court-martial was held and the entire Brigade paraded in hollow square by Cardigan, before breakfast the next morning. Cardigan called the Brigade to attention, the Brigade Major read out the proceedings and finding of the court-martial. Then the man was strapped to a forage cart in the centre of the human square and flogged by two farriers. The victim walked away after his ordeal but four recruits who witnessed it, unused to such bloodletting, were carried off in a dead faint. There was so much violence and theft that hardly a day passed without some such spectacle of retribution. 'In some cases', said Sergeant Mitchell, 'three or four of a morning.'[25]

No provision had been made at first for the soldiers in the Light Brigade camp, or elsewhere in Bulgaria, to receive regular pay. Even such money as they had was reduced by the exorbitant demands of the Turkish money-changers, who would give only two-thirds of the exchange rate. Theft and casual violence began to spread further, despite savage punishment. The owner of a Turkish coffee shop in Devna was badly beaten up by one of the 11th Hussars, but Cardigan's inquiries failed to find a culprit. When 'Johnny', the Turkish canteen-man of the Light Brigade began to sell sour wine and bad spirits at a vast profit, and tried to knife those who accused him, Cardigan's advice to his men (accompanied by a string of oaths which were never printed) was to 'give the fellow a good thrashing'. He was somewhat less sympathetic when the 13th Light Dragoons made off with, and ate, a turkey which was tethered to a peg outside his marquee in preparation for his own dinner.[26]

During July, in the few weeks which followed the reconnaissance to Silistria, the mood of the soldiers and the discipline to which they were subject seemed increasingly to reflect fear of the same enemy: disease in general, and cholera in particular. Cholera was not, at first, the principal cause of sickness. Diarrhoea, dysentery and loss of appetite began to spread among the men. They were issued with a daily ration of rum and water as an antidote to infection but many of them threw away or buried their ration of 1½ lb of 'good mutton'. By August, the Brigade of Guards was so weakened that it took the men two days to march ten miles to Varna. Their commander, Queen Victoria's cousin, the Duke of Cambridge, was one of the victims of the epidemic of diarrhoea and had retired from the sphere of war to convalesce. By the middle of August, according to the Assistant Surgeon of the Scots Guards, the main occupation of the medical staff was providing graves for the dead. In order to keep pace with the havoc, they buried two bodies at a time. Yet still there was no chance to dig the graves deeply enough and Cardigan's lancers were occupied in driving off the wild dogs from the improvised cemeteries. Some attempt was made to bury the dead at sea, where they eventually bobbed to the surface and floated, bolt upright, round the anchored warships of the British fleet.[27]

The army had discovered, at the cost of hundreds of lives, that the pleasant little vales around Varna were in fact the breeding grounds for cholera and a variety of lesser diseases. At the end of July, the camps began to break up as the divisions and brigades were dispersed to widespread and, it was hoped, healthier areas as a check on the spread of infection. For Cardigan's Brigade there was an almost equally urgent reason for moving camp. By the end of July there was little grass left around Devna for the horses, and the only method of feeding them was by the purchase of very unsuitable grain crops, grown locally and then inexpertly harvested by the troopers them-selves.[28]

On 24 July, as cholera closed upon the Light Brigade camp, Cardigan dispatched his assistant aide-de-camp, Captain Lockwood, to scout for a possible site with adequate supplies of water near Jenibazar, almost thirty miles inland. Lockwood returned the next day, after an exhausting journey, to report that no satisfactory water supply was to be found. But now it seemed that an outbreak of cholera might be imminent among the cavalry, so Cardigan sent Lockwood straight back to look again. Varna was already in the grip of the disease, and smallpox had broken out among the Light Brigade. Quarantine restric-tions were imposed between Varna and Constantinople as the great tented encampment of 27,000 men began to disappear and the red-coated divisions of the British infantry fanned out into the interior of the Bulgarian plains.

On 27 July the Light Cavalry and the Horse Artillery marched inland twelve miles to a small village and spent the night there with-out any water, other than the heavy rain of a thunderstorm, which soaked them through. No supplies could be bought from the suspicious inhabitants of the village which contained, according to Fanny Duberly, 'nothing but old women, cats, and onions'. At six the next morning, 'wet and dreary', the cavalry began a 14-mile march to Jenibazar, without water for men or horses, though 'the heat was intolerable, the sun blinding'.[29]

At Jenibazar, the tents and marquees of the Light Brigade were at last pitched, opposite a fountain and a group of trees. In the shade of these trees Cardigan ordered his two marquees to be pitched, one for sleeping in and the other for dining in. Close by were other marquees and tents for his staff, servants, interpreters and their horses. But in the general confusion of arrival, the 13th Light Dragoons pitched their tents on the right wing of the camp, a position which etiquette reserved for the senior regiment, the 8th Hussars. Cardigan ordered the regiments to change places and then, finding the tents of the Hussars somewhat out of line with the others, ordered them to be taken down again and moved back by twelve inches.[30]

A sentry was put on guard over the fountain near Cardigan's marquee to prevent it being used by either officers or men, though the supply seemed much more than adequate for Cardigan's own needs. Water was to be fetched, instead, from Jenibazar, one mile down the hill and one mile back again. There was some satisfaction among the disgruntled soldiers when the ample water supply from the fountain by the trees overflowed during the night and flooded the marquee in which Cardigan was sleeping. A fatigue party was called out on the spot to dig a drain. At all events, Cardigan's fountain provoked a 'turn-up' of such proportions that it reached the press in London. According to the report, the fountain was a mere symptom of Cardigan's general behaviour. He had become uncontrollable. The Colonels of his regiments feared him, while the common soldiers were muttering resentfully, 'He doesn't care how soon he kills us.' Their feeling was a consequence of Cardigan's new routine, under which he drilled his men from 4.30 to 9.30 every morning before they were allowed to have breakfast. According to the report there was no confidence at all in Cardigan, 'whom they all detest alike'.[31]

The *Naval and Military Gazette* swept the story aside as a fabrication, while the *United Service Gazette* nervously hoped that its new-found hero would have some explanation for the action alleged against him. With surpassing naïveté, it even suggested that Lord Lucan, as divisional commander, might care to step forward and defend Lord Cardigan's reputation.[32]

The story was certainly not a fabrication, but it was incomplete. No one, including Cardigan, was to drink from the fountain by the camp, for fear that the water was infected. The other fountain, in Jenibazar itself was, presumably, safe since the local inhabitants used it without ill-effect. But all too soon, the Light Brigade discovered that the cholera, which they had hoped to escape, had been with them all the time. Five men of the 13th Light Dragoons died, and then more troopers fell sick. Captain Cresswell of the 11th Hussars, one of Cardigan's sharpest critics, died in August. In a final and unfinished letter to a brother officer in England, he remarked, 'You be thankful old boy that you are at home, there is no glory to be got out here, only discomfort.'[33]

By the middle of August, a second hospital marquee was needed to accommodate the sick and dying. 'But here', wrote Fanny Duberly, 'there are no comforts but scanty medical stores, and the burning, blistering sun glares upon heads already delirious with fever.' The officers of the Hussars and the Lancers could do little enough to help their men, and became content to 'go on here in the same indolent way. Smoke and sleep all our spare time.' In her diary, Mrs Duberly noted, 'The sun sets daily on many new-made graves.' Strains of 'The Dead March in Saul' echoed so frequently over the camp that the surgeon-major of the 11th Hussars persuaded Cardigan to forbid the playing of any further music at the funerals because of its effect upon the collective morale of the Brigade.[34]

Not all the stories reaching the London press were hostile to Cardigan, and the *United Service Gazette* must have felt some relief in discovering that he was issuing extra rations to his Brigade, purchased at his own expense. Moreover, the stories of early morning drill seemed less alarming when it was realized that the alternative method of keeping the Brigade in a state to meet the Russians might have been to exercise men and horses in the heat of midday.[35]

Indeed, the principal grumble of the Light Brigade was not so much about Cardigan as about those in higher command who had, apparently, forgotten all about the men in the wilderness of Jenibazar, and had left them to their fate. It was all very well for Lord Raglan to write to Cardigan, regretting that he had not been able to see much of him, but 'My consolation is that you are doing your duty like a man.' The voices of criticism were growing louder, Mrs Duberly's clear and shrill above the rest: 'Are we to be left out here to constitute a travelling Phoenix Park for Lord Cardigan?'[36]

Deliverance came to the Light Brigade during evening stables on 24 August. Cardigan was walking through the regiments, watching the men groom their horses, and had stopped to talk to Colonel Doherty of the 13th Light Dragoons. As they were in casual conversation, Cardigan looked up and said, 'Hello! A cocked hat, by Jove!'

Across the plain from Varna, a horseman in the uniform and cocked hat of a British staff officer was riding hard towards the Light Brigade camp. It was Captain Wetherall, Deputy Assistant Adjutant-General, who had been sent in haste from Varna with a dispatch from Raglan. Cardigan took it from his hand, opened it at once and, looking up, said, 'Hurrah, Doherty, we are for the Crimea! We march tomorrow morning for Varna for immediate embarkation.'

There was sudden activity among the tents and marquees. Trumpeters summoned men to parade for 'Orders', and orderly sergeants with notebooks at the ready stood by to take down instructions from their officers. 'Everyone was in the highest spirits', remarked Sergeant Albert Mitchell, 'for we had been at this place long enough.'[37]

The decision to extend the sphere of war by dispatching an invasion force to the Crimea was one of the most momentous for the future history and organization of the British army. The course of events in

London, leading to the Duke of Newcastle's fateful instructions to Raglan to invade the Crimea, has been the subject of careful exposition by almost every historian of the war, from Kinglake onwards. The government knew, on 27 June, that the Russians had withdrawn from Silistria and that the immediate cause of the conflict was apparently removed. But, as *The Times* remarked on 15 June, 'The grand political and military objects of the war could not be attained as long as Sebastopol and the Russian fleet were in existence.' And in this, at least, *The Times* spoke with the voice of the people.

Moreover, the withdrawing Russians had unrepentantly promised to return to the disputed territory, a threat which seemed to justify Newcastle, as Secretary for War, in regarding Sebastopol as the grand strategic objective of the British expedition. In the warm summer dusk of 28 June, there followed the celebrated and drowsy cabinet meeting at Pembroke Lodge, Richmond, when Newcastle read, for the approval of his colleagues, his proposed instructions to Raglan. As his voice murmured on in the close and comfortable room, the clatter of a sleeping cabinet minister shifting in his chair was loud enough to wake several of his colleagues. But, awake or asleep, the cabinet presented collectively 'a quiet, assenting frame of mind'. The dispatch was agreed to, and Raglan received his instructions. In July, a French General, Canrobert, and General Sir George Brown, reconnoitred the coast near Sebastopol at a discreet (and sometimes indiscreet) distance in HMS *Fury*. A beach for the landing of the army was chosen, some miles north of the city.[38]

Cardigan's Brigade reached Varna on 29 August to embark on the *Himalaya* for the voyage to the Crimea. 'Both men and horses greatly emaciated', recorded Assistant Surgeon Robinson. It was the very day on which Lucan sent to Raglan a letter (which he was later persuaded to withdraw) demanding that Cardigan should no longer be permitted to flout the authority of Lucan, his superior officer in command of the Cavalry Division. Raglan wrote privately to Cardigan, informing him that in future he must subordinate himself to Lucan, in accordance with the normal practice of the army. 'From this date', said Cardigan bitterly, 'my position in the cavalry was totally changed; all pleasure ceased in the command which remained to me, and I had nothing to guide me but a sense of duty to the service.'[39]

At 9.30 on the morning of 30 August the *Himalaya* dropped anchor in Varna bay and began to take on board the men and horses of the 8th Hussars and the 17th Lancers. Poor Fanny Duberly, who had intended to accompany her husband to the battle-front, was told by Lord Raglan that this was out of the question, and Lord Lucan was put on guard to prevent Mrs Duberly and other hopeful ladies from boarding the *Himalaya*. When Cardigan told her of Raglan's decision, she burst into tears. Moved as always by the sight of a woman's distress, Cardigan gallantly promised her, 'Should you think proper to disregard the prohibition, I will not offer any opposition to your doing so.'[40]

To the satisfaction of Cardigan, and under the very eyes of Lord Lucan, Fanny Duberly was heavily disguised and hoisted on to a baggage cart. There, giggling like a schoolgirl, she was smuggled hastily past Lucan and installed in a cabin on board the *Himalaya*. Cardigan boarded the same ship, while Lucan with another contingent of the Cavalry Division sailed on the *Simla*. On 6 September, the great fleet of English, French and Turkish ships, bearing the armies of the three countries sailed out of Varna bay, north-eastward to the Crimea. The columns of black smoke from the funnels of the warships and transports gave the appearance of one of the pottery towns having put to sea, but Cardigan saw a more romantic prospect.[41]

> The whole expedition sailed between 9 and 10 a.m. for the Crimea. Nothing could be more magnificent than the view of the enormous fleet with four or five hundred vessels, in which the three armies, viz: English, French, and Turkish were embarked, and at night the different coloured lights, denoting the different divisions, hoisted at the mastheads, were very beautiful.

Somewhat less beautiful, were the sentiments of Cardigan and Lucan as the great fleet steamed slowly towards Sebastopol. Angry messages flashed between the *Himalaya* and the *Simla* as to who was authorized to hold courts-martial, and when, and how. The exchange ended with Cardigan, in a thundering rage, demanding to know whether he was supposed to be in command of the Light Brigade or not. Fanny Duberly watched him pacing about the ship, bristling with the indignation of hurt pride, and remarked innocently, 'Lord Cardigan begins to be eager for the fray!'[42]

The fleet rendezvous was at a point some forty miles out to sea from Sebastopol. Calamita Bay had been chosen for the invasion, a strip of westward-facing coast, at a point some thirty miles north of Sebastopol. On 12 September Cardigan and his officers on the *Himalaya* saw a brown streak on the horizon, their first glimpse of the Russian coast. As they drew closer, it began to take on the appearance of the sands and dunes of northern France or, as Sergeant Mitchell thought, the Romney marshes. After an extended reconnaissance the first infantry regiments were put ashore on 14 September with no sign of resistance. The local governor surrendered to the invaders, though with an understandably bad grace. At seven o'clock on the morning of 15 September the first boats of the major disembarkation put off from the French ships, and the tricolour was soon flying on the sandy beach, among the gaily painted bathing huts and the stone houses.

At some distance, a Russian officer watched the flotilla of little boats carrying men and horses ashore. But the stage coach still rattled on its way to Sebastopol and the life of the little town seemed hardly affected. As the British infantry regiments were put ashore, the task of disembarking 64,000 men (30,000 French, 7,000 Turks and 27,000 British) began in earnest. Soon the beach was crowded with men, who began to move inland to the area where they were to bivouac. A group of cossacks appeared in the distance and almost got close enough to attack Sir George Brown. Then they turned about and galloped off towards Sebastopol with the news of what they had seen.

By the afternoon of 15 September the beach itself had been turned into one large and overcrowded camp, 'covered with men, horses, fires, tents, general officers, staff officers, boats landing men and horses'. The tents were especially welcomed by those, including the Duke of Cambridge, who had landed the day before and had then had to spend the first night lying in the rain. Then, at six o'clock in the evening, resplendent in the uniform of a Major-General of the British cavalry, Lord Cardigan, accompanied by his staff, set foot for the first time on enemy soil.[43]

2

The Light Brigade went ashore on a narrow strip of beach between the sea and a salt lake. The men drove their picket pegs into the sand, to tether their horses for the night, and then settled down to sleep where they could. Along the shore were flagpoles with divisional colours upon them, indicating where each regiment was to land. The men carried three days' rations in their haversacks, $4\frac{1}{2}$ lb of salt meat and biscuit. The horses sniffed optimistically and persistently at the haversacks of the cavalry troopers and were rewarded with whatever biscuit the men could spare from their own rations. But, as Cardigan noticed, the shortage of drinking water for men and horses soon began to leave its mark upon them. General Airey, as Quartermaster General, sent out parties to search the countryside for supplies of food, and the intrepid Captain Nolan seized a Russian government convoy of eighty waggons loaded with flour. But the shortage of water and the absence of suitable wells had become critical.[44]

Russell of *The Times*, who watched Cardigan's Hussars and Lancers going ashore from their P & O liners was surprised at the fitness which they appeared to have regained and the manner in which 'many of the officers and men have been restored to health by the influence of the sea voyage and good living'. The army as a whole had lost 150 dead from disease during the short voyage and a further 300 were too ill to disembark. Yet if the cavalry had enjoyed the most comfortable accommodation on the ships, they were destined for a less agreeable life once ashore.[45]

Such wells as the troopers could find proved almost dry, but on the first morning there was just enough water to make a little tea, as a refreshing accompaniment to the breakfast of salt-beef and biscuit. Then Cardigan paraded the men in hollow square, and informed them that he was to lead three squadrons of Hussars, two guns of the Horse Artillery and a battalion of the Rifle Brigade on an immediate search for some regiments of Russian dragoons who were believed to be closing upon the British army as it disembarked the remainder of its supplies.

'In case we fall in with them', said Cardigan, 'and charge them, ride close, and let the centre be a little in advance of the flanks, and when you get within a hundred yards of them ride with the utmost impetuosity. But mind whatever you do after you have passed through their ranks, don't go too far, but turn about as quick as possible, and rally together and charge back again.'

Then, as an afterthought, he added, 'That is if they have not bolted by that time.'[46]

The patrol set off on three days of reconnaissance, crossing salt lakes, entering deserted little towns and the empty houses of Russian officials who had fled before the invading force. The inhabitants had, for the most part, left the area, but in one village the entire population lined the road on either side, kneeling and making the sign of the Cross to show themselves Christians, as Cardigan rode through at the head of his men. They offered the soldiers water melons and black bread. The melons were accepted with gratitude but not the black bread.

By the end of the first day the battalion of Rifles was suffering badly from the strain of the march. Men began to drop out, and the rearguard of the column was obliged to commandeer three local ox-carts, which were soon loaded to capacity with men who could march no further.[47]

On the return of the patrol, Cardigan reported with some disappointment to Raglan that, 'There was nothing to be seen on the way either of Russian regular cavalry or Cossacks.' The exhausted squadrons of the Light Brigade trooped back to the British camp, some of the men so desperate with thirst that they offered a day's pay for a drink of water. 'We hear', said Assistant Surgeon Robinson, 'the cavalry have been suffering much privation, living on biscuit for three days, and occupied in constant patrolling.'[48]

On the night of 18 September the eve of the southward march towards Sebastopol, Cardigan's troopers unsaddled their horses and settled down to sleep on the ground near the other British divisions. A glow in the twilit sky showed where Russian cavalry patrols had fired a village and all available forage to deny it to the invaders. At midnight, one of the vedettes, a mounted soldier who stood guard well in advance of the British camp, believed that he heard a suspicious movement in the darkness, and fired a shot in its direction. This was enough to alarm other sentries, who took the shot as warning of a Russian night attack, or even the beginning of the attack itself. All fires were extinguished as the men of the Light Brigade turned out in readiness to meet the enemy.

From the surrounding darkness came the beat of approaching hooves and the jangling of accoutrements, as a party of cavalry bore down at a gallop upon the Brigade camp. Just in time, the riders were identified as the Brigade's own outlying pickets, who believed the Russians had got between them and the rest of the Brigade, and so had decided to return at once. But the infantry divisions took the movements of both these riders and the Light Brigade camp for sounds of an attack, and opened a brisk fire in their direction. Cardigan emerged from his marquee into a scene of incipient panic. 'An officer of the 11th Hussars, who a few days afterwards died of cholera, shot his own servant in the leg, and as we turned out, the balls flew about in every direction. Order was not restored but towards daylight.'[49]

This confusion, with the British regiments busily shooting at one another, had all the makings of a catastrophe. There were, of course, no Russians anywhere near. In the middle of the mêlée in the Light Brigade camp, Cardigan appeared. He was clearly recognizable on his horse, and unmistakable by the loud and angry manner in which he restored order among the Brigade, while the bullets flew about him. Even those who were no great admirers of his were impressed by his sang-froid on this occasion. The men settled down to resume their interrupted sleep, but not for long. Lucan had ordered that the Cavalry Division must be ready to march at 3 a.m., and those who wished for a chance to eat some breakfast were advised to be up in plenty of time.[50]

The aim of the march, which began on 19 September, was first to cross a series of parallel rivers, running into the sea on the army's right, which lay between Calamita Bay and Sebastopol. Then the entire allied force would skirt round Sebastopol, by a flank march, and seize the little port of Balaclava, rather more than ten miles to the south of the city. Thus the allied soldiers would be supplied by their ships through the harbour of Balaclava and would soon be able to reduce Sebastopol by siege and by intense artillery bombardment.

Early in the morning of 19 September some 60,000 men of the three allied contingents began to march towards the first barrier between Calamita Bay and Sebastopol, the River Bulganak. With regimental colours flying and bands playing, the British army led the way, with Cardigan and two regiments of Light Cavalry as its advance guard. To the right of the army was the sea and the British fleet, but the cavalry was used as a protective screen round the main body of soldiers. In front, Cardigan rode with the 11th Hussars and the 13th Light Dragoons. Inland, on the left flank, Lord Lucan rode with the 8th Hussars and the 17th Lancers. At the rear of the army was Lord George Paget with the remaining regiment of the Light Cavalry Brigade, the 4th Light Dragoons.

Paget's fears were inspired less by the Russians than by Lucan and Cardigan. He recalled the saying about two noble lords. 'They are like a pair of scissors which go snip and snip and snip, without ever doing each other any harm, but God help the poor devil who ever gets between them.' Paget brooded on the simile as he rode. 'And this', he concluded, 'I thought might possibly apply to my case.'[51]

Within the cavalry screen marched the main body of the British army, with Raglan and his staff at its head. The four British infantry divisions, each 5,000 strong, marched in a square consisting of their four individual squares. Deployed in this manner, the divisional front stretching for a mile on all sides, they were able to face an attack from any quarter with the minimum of delay. Behind these 'grand divisions' of the British, marched the French army in its diamond-shaped formation.

Because of the weakened state of his army, Raglan had ordered that the men's loads should be lightened for the march, but soldiers from the infantry regiments dropped from the columns in considerable numbers and collapsed on the ground. They were left where they lay, to live or die. Fortunately, so many had fallen out by nightfall that a special party was sent back to collect them. In the heat of noon, however, the bands fell silent and the colours drooped. The divisions plodded wearily forward, to the rattling of accoutrements and waggons, with the ever-present rumble of the waves breaking on their right.

It was early in the afternoon when Lord Raglan and the vanguard of the British infantry reached the northern edge of the little valley of the Bulganak and looked down upon the narrow and sluggish stream below. Some of the first infantry regiments broke ranks instinctively, the men rushing and stumbling down the slope to drink from the muddy water. Unpalatable though the river might seem, it offered some supply of water at least, and since the army was in no condition to march much further, Raglan decided to bivouac for the night by the Bulganak.

While Raglan and his staff were still on the northern crest of the little valley, Cardigan had led the 11th Hussars and the 13th Light Dragoons down the slope and across the river, using the remains of a stone bridge. As the 200 cavalry under his command reached the foot of the slope on the far side of the river valley, there appeared on the crest above them the outline of Russian cavalry, some 2,000 strong. Raglan saw them, and ordered up Lucan with the 8th Hussars and the 17th Lancers to support Cardigan's squadrons.

But Cardigan had also seen the Russian cavalry and, to the horror of some of the watching British staff officers on the northern ridge, he began dressing off his regiments, apparently in preparation for leading them in a glorious suicidal charge, uphill, against an enemy of ten times his own number. Lucan arrived on the scene before any charge could be launched, but the reinforcements which he brought seemed to Cardigan to provide an even better argument for charging at once. The Russian horsemen remained poised on the ridge. The British cavalry, many of whom were as impatient as their Major-General to be let loose upon the enemy, sat in immaculate stillness. In front of the Brigade, and within the sight of both armies, two figures on horseback appeared to be engaged in earnest debate. There was a turn-up coming between Cardigan and Lucan over the desirability of charging the Russian position.

From the British side of the valley, Raglan and his staff could not only see the Russian cavalry on the opposite ridge, they could see the land beyond, where it dipped and then rose again to another crest. All this was hidden from Lucan and Cardigan down in the valley. It was General Airey, standing close to Raglan, who first noticed the distant glitter of sunlight on something metallic, which was soon identified as the reflection from a mass of Russian bayonets. These belonged to a carefully concealed force of some 6,000 Russian infantry and artillery, into whose annihilating fire the British Light Cavalry must have come if the charge had taken place. But even before that, there was the Russian cavalry upon the ridge, which had only been deterred from sweeping down upon the smaller British force, so far, by the steadiness and businesslike formation of Cardigan's men. Already shots were being exchanged between skirmishers, and Russian guns were being unlimbered and brought up to the ridge.

Raglan sent Airey down to inform Lucan that he wished the cavalry to withdraw. However, by the time that Airey arrived, there was a full-scale row going on between Cardigan and Lucan. Airey briskly altered Raglan's wish to a command that the cavalry should withdraw to the northern side of the Bulganak. Reluctantly, Cardigan put his men through the manoeuvre which they had so often practised from Bulgaria to the Sussex Downs. Two squadrons stood fast, facing the enemy, while the other two fell back some distance. Then those who had fallen back turned to the front to cover the retreat of the others over a similar distance. By this alternating series of short withdrawals the entire force was pulled back across the Bulganak at a cost of only four men wounded.

With a sense of some relief, Raglan reported in his official dispatch that 'Major-General the Earl of Cardigan exhibited the utmost spirit and coolness and kept his Brigade under perfect command'. But the reactions of those who witnessed the scene were somewhat more varied. The Hussars and Lancers were angry that they had not been allowed to claim first blood in the valley of the Bulganak, and it was at this point that Lucan's caution in the face of the enemy began to earn him the nickname of 'Lord Look-on'. At the same time, there were many British infantrymen who recalled the panic and the shooting in the middle of the previous night, and who had trudged wearily from Calamita Bay to the Bulganak while the dragoons trotted leisurely by them on their smartly groomed horses. The Russians jeered as Cardigan's regiments retired to the safer side of the river, but the reception given them by the British infantry was hardly more flattering. Private John Williams of the 41st Regiment watched the Hussars in their splendid whiskers and well-tailored uniforms as they rode back from the river to the accompanying hoots of the Russian horsemen. 'Serves them bloody right', he remarked sourly. 'Silly peacock bastards!'[52]

While the infantry cursed the cavalry, the experience of the Bulganak reanimated several ancient enmities within the Light Brigade itself. W. C. Forrest, one of the anti-Cardigan faction in the 11th Hussars, was now a Lieutenant-Colonel and had a word for both Cardigan and Lucan. 'We all agree', he told his family, 'that two greater muffs than Lucan and Cardigan could not be. We call Lucan the cautious ass and Cardigan the dangerous ass.' Such was the conclusion drawn from the turn-up between the two generals over the question of charging the Russian position above the Bulganak.[53]

Lord Raglan was known to have said that he proposed to keep his cavalry in a 'band box' and only to use them on specific and special duties. The truth was that the use of cavalry in the Crimean campaign was bound to be limited, if only because the expense of sending out such regiments and supplying them meant that, numerically, the British horsemen could never equal those available to the Russian commanders in a full-scale battle. Cavalry were useful as a screen of outriders during the march of the army from Calamita Bay to the Bulganak. They served certain tactical purposes, but the grand strategic design hardly involved them. Indeed, the French had decided that they could manage quite effectively without regular cavalry at all.

Field Marshal Sir Evelyn Wood, who was a midshipman in the Crimean War, later summed up the realistic and entirely unromantic assessment of the campaign. Sebastopol would not be taken by cavalry, nor even by infantry alone. It would surrender when the guns of the artillery and the Naval Brigade had so worn down the Russian defenders that they found the city uninhabitable. The battles of the Alma, Balaclava and Inkerman, were mere 'incidents' in this process. There could be no major role for the cavalry.[54]

If this view seemed eccentric at first, and contrary to the experience of Napoleonic campaigns, the events of the day following the Bulganak incident, 20 September, confirmed it entirely. It was on that day that the allied armies reached their second river, the Alma, and the first major battle of the war was fought.

By dawn on the morning of 20 September there was no further doubt that within the next few hours the two great armies must meet in pitched battle. The men of Cardigan's Brigade were up first, to find forage and water for their horses before resuming their place as the advance guard of the British force. They crossed the Bulganak and rode across the ground where the Russian army had been positioned the day before, and upon which the British had returned the enemy's artillery fire. By contrast with the bands and colours of the previous day, the English regiments marched in almost complete silence, their scarlet tunics contrasting with the darker uniforms of French and Turks, while the wheels of the gun-carriages rocked and bumped across the uneven grassland.

Around them were strewn mementoes of the previous day's exchange of artillery fire. Sixteen horses and several Russian troopers lay dead upon the turf, their possessions scattered from their knapsacks by the force of the blast which had killed them. One of Cardigan's troopers scooped up a dead Russian's razor, made in Sheffield. Across the downland lay the discarded trivia of a retreating army: a small hatchet, a cossack's whip, picket pegs, and ropes. 'They did not appear to have stayed to pick up anything', said the thrifty Sergeant Mitchell disapprovingly.[55]

But the Russian army had not withdrawn in defeat. Its regiments had retired upon the most impregnable of available positions, blocking the path of the invaders. The allied commanders on land, and the accompanying fleet which stretched several miles out to sea, waited uneasily for news or sight of the enemy.

That sight, when it came, was not encouraging. At midday, the first ranks of the British army reached another crest, overlooking the River Alma, which joined the sea on the allied right. For some two miles from its mouth, the river ran past steep cliffs which offered no landing place on the far side for an army. Then there was a tall peak on the opposite side, known as Telegraph Hill, and the bank beyond that ran beside gentler hills, like the Sussex Downs, in the shape of an amphitheatre about a mile wide and half a mile deep. The only way forward for the allied army was by crossing the river at about this point, where the only bridge had been almost completely destroyed, and climbing the gentler slope of the amphitheatre. Unfortunately, it was along the crest of these hills that the entire Russian army had taken its formidable stand, round the central defensive position of the grand redoubt. On Telegraph Hill, upon tiers of seats arranged as if for a race-meeting, the ladies and gentlemen of fashionable Sebastopol society waited with hampers, opera glasses and parasols, to watch the annihilation of Raglan's regiments.

There was only one possible course for the battle of the Alma, and both sides knew it. The British and their allies must cross the river where it was narrow enough, under the amphitheatre of hills, and charge up the incline to the Russian position in an attempt to dislodge the defenders. Either they would succeed at considerable cost, or else the Russian fire would take such an appalling toll that the demoralized British infantry would turn and run. Beyond that, the battle seemed to require little more skill than a prize-fight, but the great issue would be decided by morale.

The French and the Turks were nearest to the river mouth, on the allied right. The French were to attempt a crossing lower down than the amphitheatre, at the foot of Telegraph Hill, which the Russians considered too difficult and had therefore defended that part quite thinly. If the French could take Telegraph Hill, they might then turn the whole Russian flank. For the British, now looking towards the Alma, there remained the task of advancing through the vineyards which lay between them and their own bank of the river, wading chest-deep through the water, and charging up the 400-foot slope opposite, to the crest from which the muzzles of the enemy artillery and rifles faced down towards them.

The skirmishers of the Rifle Brigade lay full length in the grass before the British front line. The front line itself consisted of two infantry divisions. On the right, next to the French, was the 2nd Division under Sir De Lacy Evans, to the left was the Light Division under Sir George Brown. In support of the right was the 3rd Division under Sir George Cathcart, while the left was supported by the 1st Division, consisting of the Highland Brigade and the Brigade of Guards, under the Duke of Cambridge. Slightly to the rear of the supporting line, and guarding the left flank of the allied armies was Lucan's Cavalry Division with Cardigan in command of the Light Cavalry Brigade.

Even before the two armies had sighted one another, the first shots of battle had already been exchanged, for at twenty minutes past ten that morning, the warships of the allied fleets had opened fire upon the Russian batteries sited on Telegraph Hill.

From the position held by the Cavalry Division, Cardigan and his men had a clear view of the British lines, particularly of the Guards and the Highlanders, 'their accoutrements glittering in the sunshine; the bearskins of the Guardsmen, and the bonnets and plumes of the Highlanders causing them to appear at a distance almost as large as a body of cavalry.' The commanders of the British infantry regiments rode before their lines, a conspicuous target in their bright uniforms and gold lace.[56]

At half-past one there was a puff of smoke from the battery of thirty Russian guns along the opposing heights and the air around the British soldiers seemed filled with the soft, menacing hiss of the cannon balls, which moved so lazily towards their targets yet struck the ground with tremendous force, ripping open the earth like a plough and shearing their path through limbs and bodies. As the Russian cannonade opened, the British infantry commanders called out the first order of the battle.

'With ball cartridge, load!'

All along the British line, the soldiers lay full length, cursing doggedly under the Russian artillery fire. When a man was hit, two of his comrades would pick him up, carry him to the rear, and then return to their places. To the right of the British, Canrobert had actually succeeded in getting French infantry across the river and installing them on the lower slopes of Telegraph Hill. But it had not been possible to get artillery across the Alma and the French were not prepared to commit their infantry any further without such support.

By two o'clock, Raglan had given the only possible order under the circumstances. The front line of the British infantry was to advance to the Alma, cross it, and then fight its way up the opposite slope to take the Russian positions. At this point there were still Russian skirmishers on the river bank itself. These men, before withdrawing, set light to the little hamlet of Bourliouk, which lay between the armies, so that the advancing British divisions were caught in thick smoke. Indeed, the 2nd Division under Sir De Lacy Evans found its path of advance blocked by an inferno of blazing buildings. Even on the left, the Light Division, particularly the three leading regiments under Sir William Codrington, began to lose formation in the smoke. Yet they forced their way forward through vineyards, towards the river bank, snatching at the grapes as they passed and going into battle with bunches of the fruit hanging from their teeth. At the river, they waded chest-deep through the current, while the bullets of the Russian sharpshooters on the opposing ridge killed many of them before they could even reach the far bank.

Those who emerged safely from the water found themselves in considerable disarray, since the course of the river was erratic and the brigade was in anything but regulation battle order. Those who watched them from the British lines were dismayed to see the immaculate regiments breaking up into irregular knots of men or bunching together in a disorganized crowd. The worst tendency was for the river bend to distort the line of advance and for the men to huddle together as they went forward, as if there might be some protection in numbers against the musket and grape-shot streaming down upon them from the Russian positions. The Russians had now cleared the opposite slope of their own sharpshooters and were rapidly bringing their own cannon to bear upon the advancing British foot-soldiers. The volleys of grape-shot burst with terrible effectiveness among the thickly-grouped men, one volley alone cutting fourteen men to pieces in an instant. Led by their commanders with drawn swords, and with junior officers bearing forward the regimental colours, the huddles of men straggled upwards towards the flame and smoke of the guns.

However discouraging the prospect might seem to the watching British lines, it was yet more alarming to the Russians. They had not believed that the English regiments would endure such fire as this, yet the disorganized survivors were still coming on. Moreover, they were coming on in a line which, at its extremity, might outflank the Russian position. Cardigan impatiently insisted that this was the moment to let loose the Light Brigade across the river and up the slope in support of the battered infantry. Lucan argued but eventually asked permission from Raglan. Permission was refused and there was another disagreement between Lucan and Cardigan.

Yet it hardly seemed that the cavalry was needed. A sharp roar of triumph came from the British lines as the Russian gunners in their grand redoubt overlooking the Alma began hastily limbering up their artillery pieces for withdrawal. The remaining sharpshooters turned and fled. Codrington's shattered regiments spread forward to the wall of the redoubt itself. As the torn colours of a regiment fell from the hands of one mortally-wounded ensign, they were seized by another and carried onward. Henry Anstruther, an eighteen-year-old Lieutenant of the 23rd Royal Welsh regiment, dashed to the parapet and planted the flagstaff of the Queen's Colour upon it, only to fall back with a bullet in his heart, dragging the staff with him. William Evans a private of the Royal Welsh, took it up and running forward raised it at last over the grand redoubt. It was an incident fit for the cover of any Victorian boys' adventure story.

Yet Codrington's men still faced the Russian infantry of the Kazan regiment, who decidedly outnumbered them. The two sides opened musket fire upon one another at a horrifically close range, and at times were near enough for hand-to-hand combat, which lasted for most of the rest of the battle on that part of the ground where the 7th Fusiliers and the Kazan regiment confronted one another. Elsewhere the Russians fell back and it seemed that the ridge and the grand redoubt were securely in the hands of the British army.

It was while Codrington's exhausted soldiers were waiting hopefully for reinforcements that another regiment appeared before them. The British riflemen were ordered not to fire, since the regiment was French. No one seemed to question how a French regiment, which would normally have been to their right and behind them, had managed to come, full circle, in front of them. It soon became apparent that the regiment was not French at all but the Russian Vladimir column, preparing to drive the British from their hard-won position by volleys of musketry and a bayonet charge.

Worse still, the regiments which had fought their way up the hill in the face of the Russian fire had not been reinforced and were not strong enough to hold the captured position. The Duke of Cambridge had led the Brigade of Guards and the Highlanders across the Alma, in support, but still had no idea whether the first attack by Codrington's men had succeeded. The Duke's Division had therefore taken shelter behind a causeway at the foot of the hill to await events—or at any rate some information. General Airey, seeing the situation, acted on his own initiative and ordered the Duke to lead his men in support of Codrington.

With the Grenadier and Coldstream Guards in the lead, the 1st Division moved forward up the hill, only to meet Codrington's regiments and the rest of the Light Division retreating down it in the face of the Vladimir column. Impeccably as though it had been a ceremonial display, the Guards moved forward in a double rank of scarlet tunics and tall bearskins, the ranks loading and firing alternately. To the left, the three regiments of the Highland Brigade under Sir Colin Campbell engaged the enemy, and the second struggle for the grand redoubt began.

Though faced by twice their number, the Guards and the Highlanders completely outflanked and outfought the close-packed Russian columns, which tended to be narrow-fronted and deep, thereby making them less effective than the long front of the British soldiers. As the Guards entered the grand redoubt, the resistance of the enemy ceased and the Russian regiments withdrew from the field of battle, some in order and others in confusion. It was just after four o'clock in the afternoon and there were about two hours of daylight left.

But while the Guards, the Highlanders, and Codrington's brigade earned their titles to glory round the grand redoubt, Cardigan and his Light Cavalry still waited impatiently and redundantly on the left flank of the British position. Like the much stronger force of 3,000 Russian cavalry on the hill opposite, there had been no obvious part for them to play during most of the battle. While the infantry of the Light Division had stormed the Russian heights, Cardigan's dragoons watched 'with a wonder not to be described', from an almost safe distance. The light cavalry had been drawn up in a field of sugar melons, where they passed the time by lifting the fruit up on the points of their swords and munching it as they stood by their horses. It also appeared that someone in the 13th Light Dragoons had managed to get his water-bottle filled with rum, so that the battle passed less disagreeably for the Light Brigade than for most other units of the British army.[57]

Of course, there were occasional shots which came uncomfortably close. One cannon ball took off the head of a horse artilleryman nearby with a ghastly precision. Another ball bounced over the croup of Cardigan's horse, distressing the horse and causing Cardigan to smile grimly. But the troopers were not much bothered by such incidents as they settled down to watch the confused and straggling battle.[58]

The Russian cavalry showed itself far superior to the British when it came to the stress of enduring inactivity. Unlike Lucan's Division, the Russian horsemen were within a short distance of the fighting in considerable numbers. However, they found no evident role for themselves. As the resistance of their own infantry gave way, the Russian cavalry prudently withdrew, not choosing to attack the exposed flank of the advancing British lines.

Lucan dispatched three guns of the Horse Artillery to open fire upon the retreating Russians. Then, without waiting any longer for further orders from Lord Raglan, the Cavalry Division set off across the Alma, in the wake of the victorious infantry. Riding through vineyards, with Cardigan at their head, the troopers helped themselves to such bunches of grapes as Codrington's brigade had left. They crossed the river and fanned out on the opposite side, picking their way carefully among the wounded and the dying with whom the slope was strewn.

At the grand redoubt, the cavalry joined in the general cheering, until told to be quiet since they had done nothing to bring about the victory. However, Cardigan provided an escort for the artillery as it began to play upon the defeated Russians. Then he and Lucan watched the mass of the enemy retire. It seemed a perfect moment to let loose the cavalry, so tempting that Raglan sent his Adjutant-General, Estcourt, to remind Cardigan and Lucan that they were not to charge the fugitives. Between the two armies were innumerable stragglers, many of them drunk on looted spirits. A detachment of the Light Brigade was sent to round them up as prisoners, but Raglan later decided that taking prisoners was not an object of the battle and the men were released. Since there was no more to be done, Cardigan led his men back down the hill to the Alma. On the way he met the commissary officer with his waggons and bullocks.

'That's right, Mr. Cruickshank', called Cardigan, 'I am glad you have come up. What have you got with you?'

'I have got plenty of everything, my lord. Beef, biscuit, coffee, sugar, and rum.'

'Well,' replied Cardigan, 'I hope you will let my men have some as soon as possible for they have had nothing today.'[59]

He then set about having his tent pitched as close to the river as possible for 'personal convenience', and spent some time standing in the doorway of it, gathering details of the battle from passing officers who had taken part. He shared Lord Raglan's triumphal progress among the men. 'I rode with Lord Raglan amongst the regiments, who cheered him immensely; it was a very exhilarating scene.' Afterwards, he retired and composed a letter, for Raglan's benefit, setting forth the 'unfortunate details' of Lord Lucan's general behaviour, and complaining of 'a grinding and humiliating system of discipline on the part of one general officer to another'. This outburst was the consequence of the turn-up that afternoon, when Cardigan had urged letting loose the cavalry in support of the infantry on the heights, and Lucan had refused to act without specific orders from Raglan. It was not surprising that those specific orders were never given. So far as Raglan was concerned, his policy towards Lucan and Cardigan at the Alma had been 'to shut them up, the enemy's cavalry being so superior in numbers'.[60]

After the battle young Captain Nolan was in an even greater rage than Cardigan. He had watched the Russian army withdraw, 'guns, standards, colours, and all', while 1,000 British cavalry and their commanders looked on and did nothing. 'It is too disgraceful, too infamous!' he exclaimed. 'They ought all of them to be ——!' But, as usual, it was Cardigan and Lucan who bore the hottest of Nolan's anger.[61]

The truth was that the matter had become more complex than Nolan or Cardigan would allow. On 28 October the *Naval and Military Gazette* discussed the role of British cavalry at the Alma and concluded that there were simply too few of them in the Crimea ever to meet the Russian hussars and cossacks in pitched battle. Infantry were cheaper to transport and feed than cavalry. Therefore, they had been preferred. But there was an even less flattering hypothesis than that, which implied that the British might have managed just as well if they had followed the French example and taken no regular cavalry at all to the Crimea. It was at least an arguable proposition in the second half of the nineteenth century that the role of mounted troops was that of an escort and reconnaissance unit, rather than in the centre of pitched battles, where the glory grew thickest.

The British army spent the two days following the battle camped by the River Alma. The wounded were carried on board ship, the dead were buried, and the ground was cleared of some of the debris of the fighting. By the early morning of 23 September the army was prepared for the necessary flank march, skirting inland round Sebastopol. It was a time of some nervousness, since the right flank of the allied force would be exposed towards any attack from Sebastopol itself. The Light Brigade rode out ahead of the army and reconnoitred an area of salt marshes to find a suitable path for the infantry to follow, bivouacking well in advance of the other units. Cardigan rode back to the remainder of the Cavalry Division the next morning and complained vehemently that his men had been forced to camp in a valley between hills with so much cover that a single battalion of Russians could have wiped them out.

'Mind,' he said to everyone who would listen, 'Lord Lucan was in command.'[62]

Yet both men were soon being criticized for foolhardiness. Lucan had certainly led part of the Brigade to a most dangerous position, overlooked by enemy territory on both sides, but Cardigan leading his men in another direction had appeared under the guns of Sebastopol.

With some relief, the officers and men of the Brigade, who had been surprised to return unscathed from such patrols, bivouacked on 25 September near the Fedioukine Hills between Sebastopol and Balaclava. During the day, Lord Raglan, sitting under the porch at Mackenzie's Farm with General Airey, had called Cardigan to account for leading the cavalry to the wrong position. 'I simply reminded his Lordship', wrote Cardigan, 'that I did not command the cavalry.'[63]

Cardigan installed himself in a summer house and waited for his servants to arrive with the baggage. He went over to join a group of his men who were frying beefsteak and onions, acquired on the day's march. 'He conversed with us freely as though we were his equals', remarked Sergeant Mitchell, 'I have always regretted not offering his Lordship some of our meat, for he must have been as hungry as ourselves. But the difference in our respective ranks was so great that I felt afraid to do so.' Cardigan told the men that Prince Menschikoff and the Russians had 'bolted with all haste' after the Alma and were too demoralized to face the allies again for some while.[64]

Such incidents as the meeting round the fire confirm that the troopers did not share the dislike of Cardigan felt by many officers. One trooper, W. H. Pennington, wrote, 'By the rank and file of the 11th Hussars he was known as "Jim the Bear," and they with a somewhat extravagant opinion of his gifts as a cavalry officer regarded him as the Murat of the British army.' Officers of the cavalry regiments saw Cardigan as a rival for the triumphs of battle and the rewards of victory, whereas his men regarded him as their leader to glory. 'He was disliked, and, as a consequence, has been greatly disparaged by officers', said Pennington after the war, 'but I never heard any of the "rank and file" speak of him, as a soldier, in other than admiring terms.'[65]

The majority of his brother officers fell far short of admiring him. Even while Cardigan was exercising the common touch among the smell of beef and fried onions, Kelson Stothert was writing home and complaining of Cardigan's 'bad generalship' in the affair of the Bulganak, where only the 'hesitation of the enemy' had saved the Light Brigade from annihilation before any major battle had taken place.[66]

On the following day the little town and garrison of Balaclava surrendered, in the face of the enormous numbers of allied troops encircling the port by land, and the warships which were closing in from the sea. Looking down towards the coast, the British soldiers saw what was apparently a little lake, but which soon proved to be an almost landlocked harbour, an ideal haven for the French and British fleets.

On the hills above the town, the allies began to set up the tents and marquees of their huge encampment. Through the port itself, this assembled army of 50,000 men had to be supplied. At either side of the harbour basin the ships were moored with their sterns to the shore, leaving a central strip of water between the two rows, so narrow that though a ship might sail down it, it was quite impossible to turn the vessel round. Dr George Buchanan, approaching Balaclava from the sea, found ships at anchor all the way along the steep and rocky coast outside the harbour. The allies discovered rather too late that the water here was so deep that the ships could scarcely find holding-ground for their anchors, even close to the shore, and were in danger of being driven upon the rocks during an in-shore wind. However, this marine prospect appeared peaceful enough, as did the hills beyond it, which were speckled with white tents as far as the newcomer could see.[67]

Even so, the camp itself was larger than it appeared at a first view. Colonel Lysons wrote to his mother, 'One might live in a vast camp like this for ten years without meeting a friend. We can ride 20 miles through the camp from one end to the other, and about the same distance back by the rear line.' To maintain an army of this size, fit for battle in the face of a Crimean winter, with only canvas shelter and light clothing, might seem daunting. But, of course, it was not supposed that the siege of Sebastopol would continue until the first snow at the end of October. The Naval Brigade was landed, with its 68-pounder guns, and the city and all its fortifications were well within range. 'On the 16th of October', said Evelyn Wood, 'bets were freely offered in our camp that the city would fall within twenty-four hours. Some of the older and more prudent officers gave the Russians forty-eight hours, but no one thought they could withstand our fire longer.'[68]

Artillery bombardment became something of a sport. A Russian officer under a flag of truce entered the British lines and proposed a contest between the best British 68-pounder, 'Jenny', and the champion Russian gun in an embrasure on the mamelon. General Airey accepted the challenge and, at noon, all other firing ceased along the line of battle. The sailors of the Naval Brigade and their Russian opponents climbed on to their respective parapets and saluted one another. Then the English gun, being the senior, was allowed to fire first. After a number of alternate shots, the seventh shell from the English gun knocked the Russian gun on its side, at which the English sailors cheered loudly and the Russian survivors removed their hats to acknowledge their defeat. Then general war was resumed along the front.[69]

However large the allied camp might be, it was still too small to contain the brothers-in-law Cardigan and Lucan without friction. Lucan was obliged to forward to Raglan the letter which Cardigan had written after the battle of the Alma but, in doing so, he added a covering letter of his own. 'I have neglected nothing to show courtesy and attention [to] Lord Cardigan since he has commanded a brigade in the Cavalry Division', wrote Lucan indignantly. More than that, in order to avoid the acrimony which a personal meeting might cause, he was careful to communicate with Cardigan only in writing, except when a confrontation was unavoidable, as it might be during a battle. 'Nor can I charge myself with having done an unfriendly act towards him since his Lordship has been under my command.'[70]

The news that the commander of the Cavalry Division and the commander of its Light Brigade would no longer speak to one another was hardly the best of omens for the British campaign in the Crimea. On 28 September, Raglan in some alarm addressed a careful and comparatively mild reprimand to the two men.[71]

> I have perused this correspondence with the deepest regret, and I am bound to express my conviction that the Earl of Cardigan would have done better if he had abstained from making the

representations which he has thought fit to submit for my decision

I consider him wrong in every one of the instances cited. A General of Division may interfere little or much with the duties of a General of Brigade as he may think proper or see fit. His judgments may be right or wrong only the General of Brigade should bear in mind that the Lieut. General is the senior Officer and that all his orders and suggestions claim obedience and attention.

The Earl of Lucan and the Earl of Cardigan are nearly connected. They are both Gentlemen of high honor and elevated position in the country independently of their military rank. They must permit me as the head of the Forces and, I may say, the friend of both, earnestly to recommend them to communicate frankly with each other and to come to such an understanding as that there should be no suspicion of the contempt of authority on the one side, and no apprehension of undue interference on the other.

'His lordship', remarked William Howard Russell, 'advises Lord Cardigan and Lord Lucan, in nursery phrase, "to kiss and be friends."' But neither Russell nor anyone else in the camp could see much likelihood of reconciliation between two men, 'each as proud as Lucifer, the one impetuous, dominant, hard as steel; the other proud, narrow, jealous, and self-willed'. The day before Raglan's reply, Cardigan had grimly noted down yet further evidence of Lucan's attempts to take away from him the command of the Light Brigade.[72]

'What a thing war is', remarked Lord George Paget breezily on 12 October, 'and what wrangling and jealousies does it engender!' As Cardigan's second-in-command, Lord George was well aware of the effect of Raglan's gentle reprimand of 28 September. It served to stoke up the mutual hostility of the brothers-in-law to such a heat that it became necessary to separate them in different areas of the allied camp. Lord George observed the effect of this on the careful arrangements which had been made for the organization of the cavalry.

There are Lucan and Cardigan again hard at it, because they can't agree, and it is found desirable to separate them. Cardigan must needs be ordered up here to command the 4th and 11th, both of which were usefully placed, with their respective divisional generals, and all this must needs be upset to part these two spoilt children.

Lord George was somewhat less sanguine when he discovered that Cardigan, deprived of Lucan, was now prepared for a turn-up with him. He also noticed that Cardigan, whom he always addressed as 'My Lord', now addressed him simply as 'George Paget', and later as 'G.P.' Referring to the debate which must follow the war, and to the quarrel with Lucan, Cardigan said darkly, 'I hope, G.P., when we go back, that we shall not allow our mouths to be tongue-tied.'

Lord George suggested that it might prove best to forget Crimean quarrels, but this notion so displeased Cardigan that he refused even to discuss it.[73]

Lord George's first turn-up occurred on the second day after Cardigan's arrival. He received a Brigade order to parade with the 11th Hussars at 1 p.m. However, this was overruled by a divisional order from Sir De Lacy Evans, instructing him to report to the 2nd Division. An hour later he was sent back to the Light Brigade, where he found Cardigan in a great rage, twirling his moustaches compulsively.

'Pray, Lord George Paget,' he demanded, 'I wish to be informed why my brigade order has not been obeyed, and why I have been kept waiting for you the last hour?'

Lord George explained the matter of the divisional order. To his astonishment, Cardigan gave a final twist to his moustache and said, 'Quite satisfactory, my lord. Be pleased to join your regiment.'[74]

Nor was Lord George the only one to be taken aback by this mildness. Colonel Douglas of the 11th Hussars, Cardigan's duelling second, and several other connoisseurs of turn-ups who witnessed the scene, congratulated him on his success.

On 20 October, when Cardigan had not arrived to take command of his Brigade, Lord George, on the advice of the Brigade Major, Colonel Mayow, took command of the Light Cavalry in order that it should be dressed off and correctly formed when the entire division was paraded in a few minutes more. Almost at once, Cardigan arrived.

'Lord George Paget, why were you to assume that I was not coming to parade?'

Lord George hastily took refuge behind the Brigade Major and his advice. Cardigan then turned to Mayow and 'flew off at him very irate', while Lord George gently disengaged himself from the whole dispute.[75]

Yet the truth was that Cardigan often dealt with such men as

Lucan, who had no more tact or diplomacy than he himself. They met anger with anger, and threat with threat. Lord George was a more subtle judge of personality. After watching the brow-beating which Mayow underwent, he considered his own relationship with Cardigan. 'We shall never quarrel', he concluded, 'I know that. He is easily managed with calmness and firmness, and when one is in the right—which it is not difficult to be with him.' As a matter of fact, Lord George was destined to quarrel with Cardigan very bitterly and protractedly, involving the Duke of Cambridge and the royal family in the scrimmage. But that was after the Crimea.[76]

In the Crimea itself there was another adversary, whom neither Cardigan nor certain other officers recognized as such. Though he wore no uniform and held no commission, his was to be one of the most famous names of the war to future generations. He was tall, with a sharp nose, rather receding chin, and pale dispassionate eyes. He wore the civilian clothes of a battlefront tourist, and was thus identified as a 'Travelling Gent'. His name was Alexander William Kinglake, and his great monument was an eight-volume classic of English historical writing: *The Invasion of the Crimea.* Lord Raglan liked him, but other Crimean officers began to have their suspicions about him. General Sir George Brown was horrified that the people of England should see the war through Kinglake's eyes. 'The man is blind as a bat!' said Sir George indignantly, pointing out that Kinglake could not even follow stag-hounds unless he was wearing spectacles. 'He describes me as "dashing on with plumes in my cocked hat," and appalling the Russians by my sanctified appearance! In fact, I left my plumes behind me in Varna, and I never wore one while I was in the Crimea! As for the Russians, they showed their respect and consideration for me by hitting my horse in five places.'

If there was one man whom Kinglake singled out for destruction, at this point, it was Cardigan. W. H. Pennington read Kinglake's account of Cardigan many years after the war and thought that he 'censures him roundly in the spirit of the tyrannous precept comprised in the school bully's injunction: "Hit him hard, he has no friends."' Throughout the autumn of 1854, however, the great historian watched and noted, albeit myopically, from the commanding if distant vantage of Raglan's headquarters.[77]

On 7 October there was almost a cavalry skirmish between the Light Brigade and the Russians, who had paraded within easy distance. But Lord Lucan stood fast. Captain Nolan, who was also present, could no longer control his anger and expressed it to the divisional commander in decidedly improper terms. Cardigan was lying ill in his tent with what had now become chronic dysentery. When he heard of Lucan's inaction, he cursed Lucan and the other cavalry officers for 'a damned set of old women'. His friend Colonel Douglas went to him to explain what had happened, but Cardigan refused to be fobbed off with explanations and apologies brought by a junior officer. Then, in a calmer mood, he apologized to Douglas for his use of 'nasty expressions'.

To add to all his other frustrations, Cardigan was now aware that his health was deteriorating more rapidly than he had feared. He was ordered on board ship with the other invalids but continued to command the cavalry and to live in his tent so far as possible.

On 13 October Lord George Paget noted how ill Cardigan looked, adding later, 'I believe really he is ill, and that this will be the end of him.' On the evening of 13 October, Cardigan was not with the invalids on the ships but sitting in his tent on a bullock trunk, eating soup from a jug, boiled salt pork, and drinking Bulgarian brandy, mixed with rum to make it more appetizing. During this makeshift meal, a civilian entered his tent: a clean-shaven man in frock-coat, trousers to match, and a flat-brimmed bell-topper. It was Cardigan's brother-in-law, Hubert De Burgh, who had arrived in Cardigan's own steam yacht, the *Dryad*. There, in the harbour of Balaclava, only yards from the disease-ridden shacks of the little town, and a mile or two from the great camp of hungry and exhausted men, lay the trim little pleasure craft, equipped as if for Cowes Regatta, with its comfortable saloon and cabins; its running water and elegant furnishings; its French chef and its cases of champagne. Cardigan had obtained Raglan's permission to go on board ship as an invalid. He now used that permission to retire to the *Dryad*, where he dined and slept, returning to command his Brigade after breakfast.[78]

'The Noble Yachtsman!' sneered Captain Nolan, and the nickname stuck. In fact, Cardigan tried to turn the *Dryad* into an armed sloop by keeping a guard on board and siting small pieces of artillery on deck. But that was hardly the point. He obtained permission to go aboard only ten days before the battle of Balaclava, and on at least one of the intervening nights he was out on patrol with his men for the greater part of the night. But that was no excuse for him. There were others, beside Cardigan, who had their yachts at Balaclava. But they were not Cardigan. It was more in keeping with the image of the arrogant duellist and aristocratic lecher that he should spend the entire campaign on a luxury yacht while the rest of the army suffered and died in the misery of the camp. As Fanny Duberly remarked, the *Dryad* seemed a 'fairy ship' among the squalor of war. It was a symbol of aristocratic privilege exercised at a time of common suffering, the emblem of a man more concerned with finding a horse for Fanny Duberly's excursions than with the welfare of his own men. Indeed, one twentieth-century parody was even to show him seducing the young woman on board the *Dryad* after a champagne supper.

Most of the indignation over the yacht came from historians of the war, rather than from its participants. Among those who were present in Balaclava the reaction was often one of wistful envy, described by Colonel Hodge of the 4th Dragoon Guards on 22 October. 'Paid Lord Cardigan a visit on board his yacht, the *Dryad*, where he seems very comfortable. This is the way to make war. I hope he will take compassion on me sometimes.'[79]

The nature of the campaign, the endless exchange of artillery fire and the inconclusive skirmishing, did little to relieve the general listlessness. It was something to remain alive, to avoid the cholera, and the protracted, if ineffective, bombardments. 'The sharp, penetrating twing-g-g of the round shot—the railway whiz, tweet, tweet, tweet of the Lancaster—the tearing whir-r-r of the huge rockets—the dull boom of the mortar, followed by the scarcely perceptible whish-sh of the shell, ending in a loud but diffused explosion of the missile.'[80]

Sebastopol had not fallen in twenty-four hours, nor twenty-four days. The death-rate from cholera and other diseases among the British regiments was rising rather than falling. Life in the bell tents, which was bad enough in October, was a prospect hardly to be contemplated when the Russian winter should begin. It was proposed to build wooden huts for the men and shelters for the horses. But it was already evident that something had gone tragically wrong with the supply system between the Crimea and England. Not only were materials for huts and shelters lacking, there seemed to be an absence or, at best, an alarming shortage of every other commodity essential to the continued survival of the army.

An hour before daybreak on 25 October Cardigan was still asleep on board the *Dryad*. Lucan and two of his staff officers, accompanied by Lord George Paget, were up already and had begun to ride inland from Balaclava towards the North Valley. This was a box-shaped valley which ran parallel to the coast a mile or two from Balaclava.

Lucan was riding ahead on his own, moving through the darkness towards Canrobert's Hill, christened after the French commander-in-chief. The hill lay to the east along the southern ridge of the valley. Upon it was the easternmost of a series of redoubts, which ran along the southern ridge, and contained British artillery manned by Turkish soldiers. In the sharp chill which preceded the day, a cold light began to streak the sky beyond the heights. Lord George, looking towards the flagstaff on Canrobert's Hill, could make out a signal flying there. There should have been a single standard flying, but to his alarm he saw that a pair of flags drooped from the staff in the morning stillness. It was the signal to be given in the event of a major Russian attack.

Lord Lucan and his companions were puzzled. From where they were there was no sign of any enemy. But those on Canrobert's Hill could see through the thin light that an enormous army, some 25,000 strong, was moving into the North Valley and had already blocked the eastern end of it. General Liprandi had come to take Balaclava and avenge the Russian defeat at the Alma by smashing through the allied regiments, seizing the port, and facing the invaders with surrender or annihilation. As the British divisions began to move slowly into position around the western slopes of the valley, the sun edged above the horizon. The first yellow light caught the standards of the Imperial Russian army, as its great phalanxes of infantry, preceded by batteries of brass cannon and divisions of cavalry, waited silently in the dawn of Balaclava.

The first shot, fired by the Turks from one of the redoubts, tore across the brightening sky, and a whisper began to spread among the British lines. Someone had remembered that, by a bizarre coincidence, it was St Crispin's day, the anniversary of the great victory of Henry V at Agincourt. Of all the days in the year, none was more renowned than 25 October as the celebration of English courage against superior numbers, and the greatest triumph of British chivalry in arms.

CHARGE! HURRAH! HURRAH!

1

Russell of *The Times* stood near Lord Raglan and his staff on the Chersonese Plateau, which overlooked the North Valley from the west. Along the valley's northern edge ran the Fedioukine Hills, and to the south the Causeway Heights, carrying the Woronzoff Road from Sebastopol. Along these southern Heights, blocking the way from the valley to Balaclava itself, lay a series of earthen artillery redoubts manned by Turks. The most distant of these from the allied position was the No. 1 redoubt on Canrobert's Hill.

Looking down along the valley from their western Plateau, Raglan and the British staff could see that the main force of Russian artillery had been drawn up in position to bombard these redoubts. Behind the artillery were six huge formations of horsemen, far outnumbering anything which the British cavalry could muster. To the rear of these hussars and cossacks came the six infantry divisions of the Russian army, which now stood 25,000 strong across the eastern end of the valley.

Russell and his companions were fascinated by the sharpness and clarity of the scene below them, while in the early stillness every rattle of the gun carriages or clinking of cavalry harness seemed distinctly audible from the height of the Plateau. The Alma had been a long, straggling battle-front, and Inkerman was to be a brutal, close-fought encounter in mist and rain. But, in Russell's own words, 'The field of Balaclava was as plainly seen from the verge of the plateau where I stood as the stage and those upon it are seen from the box of a theatre.'[1]

At no time had the allied position in the Crimea been so clearly defined, or seemed so precarious, as when the Russian artillery with infantry support opened a ferocious and determined attack upon the Turkish redoubts, no more than two or three miles from the town of Balaclava.

Raglan arrived with his staff upon the Chersonese Plateau at about eight o'clock. Long before that, the Russians and the Turks had been engaged in a closely contested struggle for the first of the redoubts on Canrobert's Hill. Immediately below Raglan and the spectators on their Plateau, the two brigades of the Cavalry Division under Lord Lucan began to take up their positions with the cliff-like wall of the Plateau behind them. Orders were also sent to Sir George Cathcart's 4th Division, and the 1st Division under the Duke of Cambridge to take up defensive positions in the western end of the valley. The Duke's aide-de-camp, the Hon. James Macdonald, galloped off to the Brigade of Guards, camped on the Inkerman Plateau, and announced cheerily, 'There's a row going on down in the plain of Balaclava, and you fellows are wanted.'[2]

The ten thousand British infantry, and their accompanying cavalry, moved to their battle positions, boxed in by the surrounding ridges of the green valley, beyond which the calm waters of Balaclava harbour sparkled in the sun two miles to their south. As the cavalry squadrons wheeled and pranced, as though it had been a field day in Phoenix Park or a Hyde Park review, the spectators could easily make out the figures of Cardigan, Lucan, Lord George Paget and the various officers of the cavalry regiments, 'the sunshine playing on scarlet and blue uniforms, brass helmets, flashing swords'. At the western end of the valley, the loudest sound which carried on the morning air was no more than the impatient shuffling of horses and the rattle of harness as the chargers of the Hussars and Lancers stood restlessly in line.[3]

But three miles eastward along the valley the decisive conflict of the day seemed to be very nearly over. The first Turkish redoubt on Canrobert's Hill, manned by 500 men, had been outflanked long before, when the Russians moved into the little village of Kamars during the hours of darkness and seized ground which overlooked the Turkish position. The Turks were soon being bombarded by a score of well-sited Russian guns. They resisted with their own 12-pounders until 7.30 a.m. Then the Russian infantry stormed up the slope of Canrobert's Hill in such strength that there was only one possible outcome to the hand-to-hand struggle for the redoubt. The Turks fought on until 170 of their 500 men had been killed. The remainder of the allied army watched impassively. Then the defenders of the redoubt were driven back and the entire fortification, including its guns, fell into the hands of the Russian attackers.

The Turks in the next redoubts, numbers 2, 3 and 4, covering the approach to Balaclava along the southern edge of the valley, watched with dismay as the first redoubt was overwhelmed. They were even more dismayed when they realized that the nearest British infantry support was almost two miles away and that Raglan had apparently no intention of using his cavalry to assist them.

As the Russians opened their attack on the second redoubt, its defenders swarmed out over the breastwork and began to run in a disorderly crowd towards the port of Balaclava. The Russian lancers rode down upon them, stabbing and cutting at the frantic men. Once this second redoubt had fallen intact into the hands of the Russians, they turned its guns upon the Turks in the third redoubt. Again there was a swarming of men out over the breastwork, and the retreating Turks fanned out across the plain towards the sea, while the hooves of the Russian horsemen beat close behind them.

The four Turkish redoubts were overrun, and the triumphant Russian cavalry stood poised on the Causeway Heights looking down towards Balaclava. The only allied troops directly between them and the port were the 400 men of Sir Colin Campbell's 93rd Highlanders. Raglan and his divisions at the western end of the valley confronted the main Russian force in the east but could hardly move to defend the vital southern approach to Balaclava in time to prevent a Russian attack.

In the town itself, one rumour seemed to follow another and there was a state of near-panic. Fanny Duberly, on board ship, received a note from her husband at eight o'clock. 'The Battle of Balaclava has begun, and promises to be a hot one. I send you the horse. Lose no time but come up as quickly as you can: do not wait for breakfast.' Dressing hastily, Mrs Duberly went ashore, mounted her horse, and rode off through the narrow, crowded streets in the general direction of the gunfire. Before she got very far, she was met by a commissariat officer who assured her that the Turks had abandoned their position, and were running towards the town with the Russian cavalry at their heels.

'For God's sake ride fast', he urged her, 'or you may not reach the camp alive.'

In the event of a British defeat, it was considered essential that all women should be with the army, since otherwise they would be left to the mercy of the enemy soldiers. Fanny Duberly reached the Chersonese Plateau, though the road beyond Balaclava was almost blocked by the crowds of retreating Turks. Some were running, others were too weighed down with pots, kettles and muskets to run. But their general cry went up, 'Ship, Johnny! Ship, Johnny!'[4]

Not all the Turks had fled. Some had taken up positions on either wing of Sir Colin Campbell's 400 Highlanders and had turned to face the enemy. The Highlanders, in red tunics, green and black tartans and black bonnets with white plume, had precise orders as to what to do when the Russians came. They were to form a line, two deep, to meet the cavalry attack. The first rank would kneel, while the second rank stood behind and fired over the heads of the first. Since General Liprandi had only to sweep aside this little force in order to seize Balaclava, Campbell might have chosen the traditional defensive square. He preferred instead a formation which was afterwards known as 'the thin red line'.

The Highlanders were still concealed, behind a slight rise, from the dull brown mass of uniforms which represented the Russian lancers on the Causeway Heights. Campbell rode down the line before his men.

'Remember there is no retreat from here!' he called. 'You must die where you stand!'

It was the stuff of melodrama, but in the present situation there was certainly nowhere for the Highlanders to retreat to. The men replied cheerfully, 'Ay, ay, Sir Colin; we'll do that.'

However, if Campbell was one of the bravest generals of the British army, he was also the most experienced in the arts of regular and irregular warfare. He made his men lie down in the rough grass so the Russian cavalry commanders could hardly be certain of the strength of their opponents. Then, as the Russians came forward, the ranks of tall Highlanders rose silently along their little ridge. For a moment they seemed ready to charge on foot against the horsemen, as some of their ancestors had done at Prestonpans and Culloden. Seeing this danger, Campbell shouted angrily, 'Ninety-third! Ninety-third! Damn all that eagerness!'[5]

The Russian cavalry came on, though with less resolve than might have been expected. At 600 yards, the 93rd fired its first volley, but the distance was too great to have much effect. The regiment waited until the enemy lancers were well within range and fired a second volley from its muskets. The Russians faltered but then swung to their left, as if attempting to attack Campbell's flank. Being prepared for this, he quickly moved his grenadier company round to cover that approach. Then, somewhat to everyone's surprise, the Russian cavalry wheeled further round and began to retire towards the main body of its own army.

There were, of course, flattering explanations of why this had happened. The brave and businesslike stand of Campbell's men had deterred a strong force of Russian cavalry from riding down upon Balaclava and winning both the battle and the campaign for their commander. The courage of the Highlanders was beyond question but the explanation was more complex. It seems likely that the Russians were not simply deterred by the musket fire of the 93rd, which did only limited damage to their squadrons, but by the sudden appearance of lines of men rising like apparitions from the rough grass. What if four or five more regiments should appear in the same manner, on all sides, each musket aimed at a Russian horseman? On the verge of such a possible trap, the Russian commander drew back.

It was not until almost half-past ten that the British infantry had completed its preparations for battle, and Raglan had ordered that the cavalry was not to launch an attack without the support of the infantry lines behind them. The five regiments of the Light Brigade were drawn up near the foot of the Chersonese Plateau, 'very much at their ease', as Russell described them. 'I could see the officers, flask in hand, munching whatever they had, and smoking, and the men, as they stood by their horses, were chatting as if they were off duty.' Cardigan, in the cherry pink and dark blue of the 11th (Prince Albert's own) was easily recognizable, standing apart from the Brigade and talking with a few of his officers. His second-in-command, Lord George Paget, had been briskly informed by Cardigan that his 'best support' would be required in the event of a Russian attack. The Brigade had been waiting since just after dawn and the refreshment which some of the men were now taking—hard-boiled eggs, biscuit and rum—represented their first meal since the previous day.[6]

To the right of Cardigan's men stood Sir James Scarlett's Heavy Cavalry Brigade, the 4th and 5th Dragoon Guards, the Royals, the Inniskillings and the Scots Greys, all mounted on larger and more powerful horses than their counterparts of the Light Brigade. While Cardigan's officers were eating, smoking, or pulling at their flasks, an aide-de-camp came galloping down the slope from the Chersonese Plateau with an order from Raglan to Lucan, who sat on horseback with his staff, a little apart from the two brigades of his Cavalry Division. One squadron of the Inniskillings and two squadrons of the Greys were to ride at once to reinforce Sir Colin Campbell's Highlanders, in case the Russians should attempt another breakthrough to seize Balaclava itself. With Scarlett, red-faced and white-whiskered, at their head, the three squadrons rode off south-eastwards from the valley towards the 93rd Highlanders.

As the squadrons skirted round the tangled roots and briars of an old vineyard, the southern ridge of the valley, the Causeway Heights, lay on their left. Then there appeared along the Heights a forest of upright lances, as a body of Russian cavalry, some 3,000 strong, moved into an attacking position. Before the Russian lancers in their dark, khaki coats, were the advance guards of grey-coated dragoons, and hussars in light blue jackets.

Scarlett at once gave the order, 'Left wheel into line!' and brought his 300 horsemen to face the enemy. At the age of fifty-five he was about to go into battle for the first time. Less than a quarter of a mile apart, and with the debris of the vineyard between them, the Russians on the heights and the Heavy Brigade waited motionless for several moments, surveying one another. The Inniskillings in their embossed brass helmets and scarlet tunics, the Scots Greys in their tall bearskins, dressed off in perfect review order.

Lucan instructed Cardigan to keep the Light Brigade in its present position. Then, as the British trumpets rang out their orders across the plain, the 4th and 5th Dragoon Guards, and the Royals, rode towards the vineyard where the three squadrons of Greys and Inniskillings held their line. The grey and brown avalanche of Russian cavalry began to pour down the southern incline of the Causeway Heights, while Scarlett's first three squadrons moved forward across the uneven terrain of the vineyard to meet them, 'scrambling over and picking their way through the broken ground'. They had only time to cover 80 or 100 yards to the far side of the vineyard before encountering the Russians, who had also slowed down in order to avoid having to fight in the vineyard itself. Then Scarlett and his 300 men, moving at a leisurely trot, rode into the Russian cavalry, whose line was double the length of the British and two or three times as deep.[7]

In the confusion, the spectators saw the line of scarlet engulfed by the darker mass of Russian uniforms. The men, on both sides, were so tightly packed that it was difficult to wield a sword. Moreover, the British troopers found that the Russian greatcoats were too thick to be effectively pierced by sword points. The only alternative was for the Heavy Brigade to hack downwards on the heads of its enemy, littering the ground with the bodies of men whose skulls had been cleft down to the chin. The Russians, for their part, had neglected to sharpen their swords and British soldiers survived the battle with as many as fifteen head wounds, each of which ought to have been fatal but none of which had been more than superficial.

The mid-morning sky, which had clouded over in the past hour, began to clear again. A pool of sunlight fell upon the flash of sword blades and the gleam of brass helmets, suggesting even more power-fully the use of a spotlight on the stage of a theatre. As for the 'din of battle', the cliché was never more apt than during this type of cavalry engagement. Against the muffled reverberations of thousands of horses stamping and shifting, the clatter of swords against helmets and the shouts of command as troop captains struggled to rally their men were among the strongest recollections of Balaclava for those who witnessed the battle.

The mass of mounted men, about 4,000 altogether, heaved in-decisively to and fro for what seemed to the onlookers to be a great while, but was in reality less than five minutes. Then the remainder of Scarlett's Brigade, the two regiments of Dragoon Guards and the Royals, joined the struggle, riding in upon the Russian flank. Numerically it seemed to make little difference, since they were still only 'half a handful' compared with the Russian force. Yet to the jubilant amazement of the watchers on the Chersonese Plateau, the Russian line began to buckle and fragment. The movement of the scarlet figures in the dark confusion showed that the Heavy Brigade had almost forced a way through the enemy. Then the final unit of the Heavy Brigade to arrive, the 5th Dragoon Guards, bore down upon the mêlée and went through the remnants of the Russian line, 'as though it were made of pasteboard'. The entire body of Russian horsemen began to turn and scatter before the impact, 'flying with all its speed before a force certainly not half its strength'. It seemed that the battle had at last taken a turn which favoured the allies and that there was at least some respite for the defenders of the port of Balaclava.[8]

Raglan's message, 'Well done!', was brought down speedily to the victorious Scarlett, but not everyone was quite as jubilant. Cardigan had been riding up and down in front of the waiting Light Brigade as Scarlett's dragoons drove the Russians before them.

'Damn those Heavies!' he was heard to mutter. 'They have the laugh of us this day!'[9]

Then there followed the first of the numerous Balaclava controversies in which Cardigan was to be involved. It was clear that the Heavy Brigade did not propose to pursue the Russians in earnest, and the retreating enemy streamed away across the front of the Light Brigade at a few hundred yards' distance. It seemed that Cardigan's men might well be launched against the flank of the departing Russians, who were in no position to turn and fight.

'What was Lord Cardigan about?' wondered Russell impatiently as he and the others watched the scene from the Plateau. 'What were the Light Cavalry doing?'[10]

The answer was that the Light Cavalry were having a particularly embittered row, which was to drag on in one form or another for years to come. The row had begun as soon as the Russian cavalry advanced to attack the Heavy Brigade. Since the Russian flank was then exposed to them, some of the Light Brigade regiments began 'intuitively' to change their position half right in order to be in position to carry out a flank attack. Cardigan ordered the movement to be stopped. He had been told by Lucan to remain where he was. Raglan had insisted that he must obey Lucan's orders, and that was what he proposed to do. 'Previous to this, I had been ordered into a particular position by the Lieutenant-General, with orders on no account to leave it, and to defend it against any attack of the Russians; they did not however approach the position.'[11]

Captain Morris of the 17th Lancers, known as the 'Pocket Hercules' for his short stature and 43-inch chest, was a zealous young officer with an impressive reputation. Without reference to Cardigan, Morris, who had succeeded to the command of the 17th Lancers on the recent death of Major Willett, turned his troopers into line to face the Russian flank. Cardigan suddenly heard Morris's trumpeter sounding the trot, and rode down upon the offending officer, demanding in a sharp, barking voice, 'What are you doing, Captain Morris? Front your regiment!'

'Look there, my lord,' said Morris indignantly, pointing with his sword at the exposed Russian flank.

'Remain where you are, sir,' shouted Cardigan, 'until you get orders!'[12]

It seems likely that the argument continued in some manner until the brief struggle between the Russians and the Heavy Brigade was over, and the enemy were retreating in disorder within easy reach of the Light Brigade. Captain Morris later claimed that he even begged Cardigan to let him charge the Russians with his own regiment alone, but that Cardigan absolutely refused to allow it. Cardigan, however, always denied that such a request had been made, though he conceded that Morris had wished to detach his own regiment from the rest of the Brigade at one point. That request had, quite properly, been refused.

According to Morris, he pleaded with Cardigan.

'My lord, are you not going to charge the flying enemy?'

'No', said Cardigan abruptly, 'we have orders to remain here.'

'But, my lord, it is our positive duty to follow up this advantage.'

'We must remain here!' said Cardigan loudly.

'Do, my lord, allow me to charge them with the Lancers. See, my lord, they are in disorder!'

For some time the argument grew warm between Cardigan, tall and splendid in his Hussar uniform, and the stocky figure of Morris in a blue frock-coat and a forage cap with gold-edged peak. Then even the troopers sitting on their horses some distance away from the two men heard Cardigan's hoarse, sharp words.

'No, no, sir!'

Morris angrily wheeled his horse round, slapping his sword against his leg and muttering loudly enough for his Lancers to hear,

'My God, my God, what a chance we are losing!'

Captain White, Adjutant of the 17th Lancers, said defiantly, 'If I were in command of the regiment, I would attack by myself and stand a court-martial. There is a C.B. staring you in the face as you cannot fail.'

However, it seemed unlikely that Raglan, on his Plateau, was thinking in terms of recommending anyone in the Brigade as a Commander of the Bath so far. He despaired at the way in which the Light Cavalry regiments were being handled. Russell of *The Times* was bewildered at what was going on, while French officers like the Vicomte de Noé looked on and could not believe that Cardigan's men were not to be allowed to destroy the Russian cavalry once and for all.

To add his own pent-up bitterness to an already sour atmosphere,

Lucan rode back to the Light Brigade from the scene of the Heavy Brigade's triumph and appeared to be as surprised as anyone that Cardigan had not attacked the Russian flank. According to Lucan, he had said to Cardigan, 'I am going to leave you. Well, you'll remember that you are placed here by Lord Raglan himself for the defence of this position. My instructions to you are to attack anything and everything that shall come within reach of you, but you will be careful of columns or squares of infantry.'

Lucan, like Forrest, was apt to regard Cardigan as a dangerous ass rather than a cautious one. The careful instructions, to which he added Raglan's authority as well as his own, seem intended to dissuade Cardigan from precipitate action. In this, at least, they succeeded.

The factor which prolonged this controversy for years was Cardigan's denial that the conversation, as described by Morris, on the possibility of attacking the Russians ever took place. No two witnesses seem to agree entirely as to what was actually said while the dark mass of Russian cavalry wheeled past a few hundred yards away. Cardigan's own account, however, is very specific.

> I entirely deny that Captain Morris ever pointed out to me any opportunity of charging the enemy, or said anything to me of the kind; and it is quite untrue that I said I was placed in that particular spot, and should not move without orders, or anything to that effect. I further deny that Captain Morris ever begged to be allowed to charge with his regiment alone, or that he gave me any advice, or uttered one word to me upon the subject of attacking the enemy. I remember upon one occasion during the engagement, after the Light Brigade had been ordered to join the Heavy Brigade in the valley, Captain Morris broke away from the column with his regiment without orders, upon which I asked him, sharply, why he did so, and desired him to fall again into column. That was all that occurred on the day in question between myself and Captain Morris.

Evelyn Wood, later a Field Marshal and a close friend of Morris in India, was certainly no admirer of Cardigan. But he thought it quite out of character for Cardigan to be guilty of 'wilful misstatements'. Mutual misunderstanding seems to be the probable explanation but, of course, however completely Morris and Cardigan had understood one another, the outcome of their argument would have been no more amicable.[13]

Apart from Lucan's orders, however, there was one very good reason for not charging the Russians, though it was not revealed until the posthumous publication of Lord George Paget's journal. Moreover, it was a reason only evident to those who had stood upon the actual spot where the Light Brigade was drawn up. According to Lord George, the ground between the Light Brigade and the fleeing Russians was anything but ideal for cavalry. It was steep, rocky and broken, so that the arrival of the Light Brigade on the scene of the fighting must have been very delayed. As far as the pursuit of the Russians was concerned, by the time that the Brigade had cleared the intervening ground, there would have been a considerable gap between the two groups. No less important, in Lord George's view, was the knowledge that the Brigade had been positioned where it was to guard against a second Russian attack which might take place 'from another direction', while the first Russian horsemen engaged the Heavy Brigade. Cardigan's critics, with the benefit of hindsight, knew that no such attack ever took place. But had it occurred, while his Brigade was chasing the Russian cavalry, the British position would have been left open at that point.

No considerations of this sort helped to mollify Morris, Lucan and those who had now joined the squabble which was going on at the foot of the Chersonese Plateau. Undeniably there had been a failure in communication, but it was trivial by comparison with what was about to happen. From Lord Raglan on his Plateau, came a message to Lord Lucan.

> The Cavalry to advance and take advantage of every opportunity to recover the heights. They will be supported by infantry which has been ordered to advance on two fronts.

2

Lord Raglan's message to Lucan was part of a concerted plan to take advantage of the battle situation while the initiative remained in British hands. If it were possible, while the Russian cavalry was still scattered and demoralized after their defeat by the Heavy Brigade, to retake the Turkish redoubts, then the entire Russian attack on Balaclava would have come to nothing.

While one message was carried down from Raglan to Lucan, others were brought to Sir George Cathcart and the Duke of Cambridge. Cathcart's 4th Division was to launch an infantry attack on the Causeway Heights from the west, while the Duke's 1st Division attacked from the south. These two, with Lucan's Cavalry Division, would be well placed to retake the comparatively ill-defended redoubts upon the Heights.

The Duke's Division moved off quickly, but Cathcart's men were delayed for some time. Raglan, watching impatiently from the Plateau, sent further messages urging Cathcart to advance. As for Lucan, the undulating ground at the western end of the valley hid the Turkish redoubts from his direct view, and he interpreted Raglan's order merely as an instruction to move more squarely into the centre of the valley. The regiments of the Light Brigade were therefore ordered to move 'Threes to the right', and trotted off to take up their new position with the Heavy Brigade to their right and slightly behind them, and D'Allonville's irregular cavalry, the Chasseurs d'Afrique, in their rear. A mile and a half away the sun glimmered on the polished brass of the main battery of Russian cannon, pointing directly down the valley towards the English horsemen.

Cardigan sat on his charger, in front of the Light Brigade, talking to his own staff officers. Lucan was to the side of the Brigade and somewhat to the rear. A long half hour passed. The men of the 13th Light Dragoons could see the bodies of Russian hussars and horses sprawled on the slope leading up to the nearest of the captured redoubts, but their view of the Causeway Heights and their fortifications was less than perfect.

From the Plateau, Raglan and his staff scanned the redoubts through their field-glasses and waited with increasing annoyance for Cathcart's infantry and Lucan's cavalry to move into position for the attack which had been ordered. Raglan had reached the limit of his tolerance for Lucan's generalship and was about to dispatch a sharp reminder to him of his original order. Then the Commander-in-Chief's attention was drawn to an ominous growth of activity on the Causeway Heights. The Russians, realizing that their infantry in the captured redoubts was too far forward to be in an easily defensible position, were preparing to withdraw. However, they had brought forward several teams of artillery horses and lasso tackle, with which they were preparing to limber up and tow away the English cannon abandoned by the Turks.

Raglan had been educated for too long in the Wellingtonian

philosophy that a good general must never lose a gun to ignore this. After such a close-fought battle as Balaclava promised to be, a parade of captured English artillery in the main square of Sebastopol would enable the Russians to substantiate a propaganda claim to have inflicted a crushing defeat upon the allied army.

Quick and decisive action was needed to prevent the removal of these trophies from the redoubts. Raglan turned to his Quartermaster General, Sir Richard Airey, and gave his instructions. Airey took out his pencil and, resting a scrap of paper on his sabretache or satchel, he wrote out the order, directed to Lord Lucan.

> Lord Raglan wishes the cavalry to advance rapidly to the front, and try to prevent the enemy carrying away the guns. Troop of horse-artillery may accompany. French cavalry is on your left. Immediate.
>
> (Signed) R. AIREY.

Airey was about to entrust the message to one of Raglan's own aides-de-camp, Major Calthorpe, but Raglan called instead for Airey's own aide, and gave him the order for Lucan. Ironically, Airey's aide was Captain Nolan of the 15th Hussars, who regarded Lucan and Cardigan as the biggest pair of fools who ever plagued the British army.

Resplendent in his scarlet and gold uniform, haughty, self-possessed, and intensely jealous of his own expertise, Nolan took the piece of paper. He was a first-rate swordsman and one of the finest riders in Europe. If any man could carry the message to Lucan in time for the cavalry to prevent the Russians towing away the guns, it was Lewis Edward Nolan.

The front line of the Light Brigade consisted of the 13th Light Dragoons on the right and the 17th Lancers on the left, there being two squadrons of each regiment. At about eleven o'clock, Nolan came at a gallop from the foot of the Plateau and rode forward between the two regiments.

'Where is Lord Lucan?' he shouted to Captain Morris of the 17th.

'There', answered Morris, pointing. 'There, on the right front!'

As Nolan put spurs to his horse again, Morris shouted after him, 'What is it to be, Nolan? Are we going to charge?'

'You will see', shouted Nolan over his shoulder. 'You will see!'

Then Nolan rode up to Lucan and handed over the order. Lucan read it with growing alarm, since the only guns he could see were not those in the redoubts, but the main Russian artillery which stretched across the valley, about a mile and a half ahead. To Nolan's surprise, Lucan denounced Raglan's order as useless and dangerous.

'Lord Raglan's orders are that the cavalry should attack immediately,' said Nolan with some irritation.

Lucan turned on him with bald-headed and somewhat pop-eyed indignation.

'Attack, sir! Attack what? What guns, sir?'

Nolan regarded the Lieutenant-General of cavalry with an expression of contempt. He threw back his head, and vaguely indicating a further part of the valley with a wave of his hand, said, 'There, my lord, is your enemy! There are your guns!'

His manner was, said Lucan afterwards, 'most disrespectful but significant'.

Lucan sent the order to Cardigan, in his own words. Cardigan, incredulous that Raglan intended to send cavalry against artillery, sent one of his aides-de-camp, Lieutenant Maxse, to Lucan to query the order. Lucan then rode forward to the front of the Light Brigade and, contrary to his usual custom, actually spoke to his brother-in-law. Cardigan brought his sword down in salute and listened as Lucan ordered him to lead the 13th Light Dragoons and the 17th Lancers in a frontal attack upon the main Russian artillery at the far end of the valley.

'Certainly, sir,' said Cardigan, 'but allow me to point out to you that the Russians have a battery in the valley in our front, and batteries and riflemen on each flank.'

Then, in case Lucan had missed the point, he added in a more urgent voice, 'There must be some mistake. I shall never be able to bring a single man back.'

'I cannot help that', retorted Lucan. 'It is Lord Raglan's positive order that the Light Brigade attacks immediately.'

Then, having reminded Cardigan to advance steadily and keep his men well in hand, Lucan rode away. Nolan, his face flushed with anger, approached Cardigan. After the incidents of the Bulganak and the Alma, after the failure of the Light Brigade to do anything so far in the present battle, this dithering of Lucan and Cardigan was beyond endurance. Nolan muttered something, apparently to Cardigan's aides, and Cardigan inquired in a suspicious and patronizing tone, 'What's that you are saying, young fellow?'

Nolan, further enraged by what he regarded as Cardigan's offensive manner, drew his sword with a flourish. Then he said something to Cardigan. No one else could hear what it was but, as a matter of fact, Nolan inquired with a sneer whether Cardigan and his men were perhaps afraid to face the Russians. The question may have been inaudible, but Cardigan's response carried clearly across the front of his regiments.

'By God!' he roared. 'If I come through this alive, I'll have you court-martialled for speaking to me in that manner!'

Bristling with indignation from this exchange, he then rode back to Lord George Paget who was to command the supporting regiments of the Brigade. The 11th Hussars were to charge immediately behind the front line, and the 8th Hussars and 4th Light Dragoons were to follow them.

'Lord George,' said Cardigan sharply, 'we are ordered to make an attack to the front. You will take command of the second line, and I expect your best support, *mind, your best support.*'

'Of course, my lord,' answered Lord George, somewhat irritated by Cardigan's insistence, 'you shall have my best support.'

Then Cardigan rode back to the head of the Brigade and positioned himself some ten yards in front of it, with his group of staff officers riding behind him, and the front line of the Brigade behind them. The 17th Lancers were on the left and the 13th Light Dragoons on the right, each formed in a double line. Those who saw Cardigan at this moment were almost overawed by the splendour of his appearance. Though long in the leg, he was also long in the body and sat tall and upright in the saddle. 'Notwithstanding his fifty-seven years,' recalled Kinglake, 'he had a figure which retained the slenderness of youth. His countenance, highly bred and of the aquiline cast, had not been without such humble share as a mere brother might be expected to have of that beauty which once made famous the ancient name of Brudenell.'

That ancient name was very much in Cardigan's mind as he took his place in front of his Brigade, and looked towards the mouths of the Russian guns.

'Well,' he was heard to mutter philosophically, 'here goes the last of the Brudenells!'

He was, in a literal sense, a sitting target for the Russian gunners, and as if to provide a better mark for their aim, he wore his fur pelisse not slung over his shoulder but like a patrol jacket, so that its front appeared as a blaze of gold lace. He was calm as on parade, 'calmer indeed by far than his wont on parade', said Private Wightman of the 17th Lancers, who rode directly behind him. Then Cardigan turned and faced his men for the final order, given in his habitually hoarse, strong voice.

'The Brigade will advance! First squadron of 17th Lancers direct!' Then, turning to the trumpeter of the 17th Lancers, he added, 'Sound the advance!'

Wheeling his horse round to face the far end of the valley again, he led the Brigade forward as the trumpet sounded the walk, and then the trot.[14]

As the 673 riders of the Light Brigade began to move towards their apparently certain destruction, Captain Nolan, his sword still drawn, began to ride forward from their left flank. To Cardigan's fury, Nolan was riding diagonally across the front of the advancing cavalry line, in the direction of the Causeway Heights on their right. It seemed to Cardigan that Nolan, as a final gesture of insult, was attempting to lead the cavalry onward himself.

'No, no!' Cardigan shouted at him. 'Threes back into line!'

Nolan's friend, Captain Morris, now riding close behind Cardigan in the first line of the 17th Lancers, joined in the reproof.

'That won't do, Nolan! We've a long way to go, and must be steady.'

But Nolan was turning in his saddle and shouting something to the Brigade, as he continued on his diagonal path towards the Causeway Heights. To some of those who could hear him, he seemed to be calling, 'Come on!' He had crossed Cardigan's front, still riding towards the Heights, and was level with the last squadron of the 13th Light Dragoons on the extreme right of the Brigade. At that moment, the Russian artillery opened fire and a shell burst between Cardigan and Nolan. A fragment of this shell, with the sharpness of a razor and the speed of a bullet, shot through the air and pierced Nolan through the heart. The sword dropped from his hand but the sword arm itself remained upraised, as Nolan emitted an unearthly, dying shriek. His horse turned and galloped back between the two squadrons of the 13th Light Dragoons, the corpse still rigid in the saddle in a ghastly parody of its former bravado.

It is probable that when Nolan saw that the Light Brigade had not turned half right to face the Causeway Heights and the captured redoubts but was facing straight down the valley towards the main Russian artillery, he realized the terrifying misinterpretation of

Raglan's order which had occurred. By riding across the front of the Brigade, in the direction of the Causeway Heights, he perhaps hoped to divert it from its suicidal course. But with the death of Nolan, the only man on the spot who could have averted disaster was dead. Lord Raglan remained an appalled spectator on his Plateau, powerless to do anything but watch the inevitable catastrophe.[15]

The Light Brigade rode on at a trot until it was suddenly exposed to the fire of Russian riflemen from the Fedioukine Hills on the left and the Causeway Heights on the right. Britten, the trumpeter of the 17th Lancers, sounded the gallop and would have sounded the charge, but before that he fell mortally wounded from his horse in the storm of Russian bullets. The enemy artillery on either side opened upon the squadrons of horsemen penned in the valley below.

Cardigan was obeying his orders, trying to keep his men at a steady pace. But as Captain White, commanding the first squadron of the 17th Lancers, remarked, Cardigan's followers were increasingly eager 'to get out of such a murderous fire and into the guns, as being the best of the two evils'. While Cardigan tried to restrain the pace, the momentum built up among the squadrons behind him. Captain Morris rode forward until he was almost level with Cardigan, who then held out his sword across Morris's chest.

'Steady! Steady, Captain Morris!' he called, and then, more heatedly, 'Stay, sir! How dare you attempt to ride before your commanding officer!'

At about three quarters of a mile, the main Russian battery opened fire, tongues of flame and smoke spurting from the ranked guns, followed by the menacing hiss of the black shells as they sliced towards their targets. While the musket fire on the flanks brought down individual troopers and horses, littering the plain with the wounded and dying, the shells from the main battery blew whole sections of the front line to pieces.

'Hell had opened upon us', said Private Wightman. The survivors rode on, some drenched in the blood of comrades who had been blown to fragments by the Russian shells. Sergeant Mitchell of the 13th Light Dragoons offered up a short and extremely relevant prayer.

'O Lord, protect me and watch over my poor mother.'

A moment later, his horse was killed under him, and Mitchell went down. He lay on the grass, stunned from the force of the explosion, but later made his way back safely to the British lines.

Clear above the roar of the guns and the crash of shells tearing up the earth in showers of debris, the squadrons could hear Cardigan's voice.

'Steady!' he called. 'Steady, the 17th Lancers!'

Behind their leader, the ragged lines of the two leading regiments began to cheer wildly as they closed towards the Russian battery. Yet all the time, as men and horses were struck down, the cry went up among the survivors, 'Close in! Close in!'

Cardigan, in his moment of glory, rode onwards through shell bursts and rifle fire, 'steady as a church', according to Wightman. To one side of him, Sergeant Talbot was hit by round shot and his head cut clean off. But the decapitated body rode on, still clutching the reins and with lance firmly held, for another thirty yards. A shell burst just to the rear of Cardigan, blowing to pieces four or five men of the Lancers.

'What a bloody hole that shell has made!' shouted Private Dudley.

'Hold your foul-mouthed tongue', said Peter Marsh severely, 'swearing like a blackguard, when you may be knocked into eternity next minute!'

With their trumpeter gone, there had been no means of commanding the 17th Lancers to lower their lances for the charge. The regiment was still carrying the lances in the normal, upright position, the end of each resting in a small bucket attached to the stirrup. At about a quarter of a mile from the guns it appeared that they were about to ride through the battery with their lances held inoffensively in the air. Captain White took it upon himself to shout, 'Charge, there!'

To which Cardigan, turning slightly in his saddle, called back angrily, 'You have no word to charge!'

John Lee, right-hand man to Private Wightman, caught the full blast of an exploding shell, which tore into him and his horse. He touched Wightman's arm lightly as they rode close together, and said, 'Domino, chum!'

Then his shattered body fell forward from the saddle.

In the glare and the smoke, the survivors realized that of the three hundred men in the front line of the Brigade, there were no more than thirty approaching the battery. Some of the others were still riding but had been carried to one side or other of the guns. Two hundred men were dead or wounded on the plain behind. Cardigan, still unscathed, turned in his saddle, raised his sword, and shouted his final words before engaging the Russians, 'Steady! Steady! Close in!'

Almost two miles away on the Chersonese Plateau, Russell of *The Times* saw a flashing halo of steel above the heads of the riders as the men of the Light Brigade drew their swords. Then they seemed blotted out as the Russian gunners fired a final salvo, at almost point-blank distance, into the remains of the first line. But the unthinkable had happened. The survivors of the first two regiments had reached the Russian battery, and with the short, barking, cavalry cheer they bore down upon their enemy. In the final salvo of the guns, Captain White, commanding the first squadron of the 17th Lancers, went down. But Cardigan, aiming for a gap between the cannon, charged forward into the smoke, the first of his Brigade to reach the guns.[16]

On the Plateau, Russell, Fanny Duberly, whose husband's regiment was in the charge, Raglan and the British staff, all watched with utter incomprehension as the Light Brigade rode to its destruction. 'They swept proudly past,' said Russell, 'glittering in the morning sun in all the pride and splendour of war. We could scarcely believe the evidence of our senses. Surely that handful of men were not going to charge an army in position?'

According to the calculations of Raglan's staff, the 673 men of the Light Brigade were hurling themselves against some 25,000 Russian troops powerfully defended by artillery. Fanny Duberly saw the result. Having seen the start of the charge, she lost sight of the Brigade for a time and then later noticed a group of skirmishers near the Russians. It was some moments before she realized that this little group was what remained of Cardigan's regiments.

For all its brutal discipline, the Victorian army was sometimes moved to displays of tender emotion which would have been regarded with disapproval or embarrassment a hundred years later. The veterans of the Sikh Wars, of Chillianwallah, and even of Waterloo, stood and wept silently as they watched their comrades of the Light Brigade ride, armed with the weapons of medieval chivalry, to their deaths before the guns of General Liprandi's army.

Close behind Cardigan's first line rode Lord George Paget and the three supporting regiments, whose fate at the hands of the Russians was not much better than that of the men under Cardigan's immediate command. Shortly before the charge was ordered, Lord George had lit a cigar. When the men were formed up for the charge, some of them were still smoking their clay pipes, and Colonel Shewell of the 8th Hussars reprimanded one of them for 'disgracing his regiment by smoking in the presence of the enemy'. Lord George considered whether he was required to set an example by throwing away his cigar. But it was a good one, he had only just lit it, and there was no knowing when (if ever) he would smoke another. He decided not to throw it away.

Lord George found the charge itself remarkably exhilarating. 'As far as it engendered excitement,' he recalled, 'the finest run in Leicestershire could hardly bear comparison.' Ten minutes after the first order was given, among cries of 'View halloo!' he charged into the Russian battery in the wake of Cardigan's attack, the cigar still clamped in his mouth, and still alight.[17]

As Cardigan rode into the smoke, between two guns, one of the cannon went off so close to him that his horse lurched to one side and he himself thought, for a moment, that his own leg had been shattered, though it was only struck by the shock. Beyond the guns lay every kind of confusion. The ground was covered with limber carriages for the guns and ammunition waggons. He found himself surrounded by cossacks, and Wightman saw them closing round him. One jabbed at Cardigan with a lance, piercing his clothes and wounding him slightly just below the hip. Another ran a lance into the gold-embroidered pelisse with such force that Cardigan was almost unseated. It seemed, however, that he had been recognized by Prince Radzivill, whom he had met at a party in London before the war, and who was now offering a reward to any man who would bring Cardigan in as a prisoner.

As Wightman rode into the smoke, he saw Cardigan's aide-de-camp, Lieutenant Maxse, who had been wounded.

'For God's sake, Lancer, don't ride over me', called Maxse. 'See where Lord Cardigan is. Rally on him.'

Lieutenant Johnson and Private John Keeley of the 13th Light Dragoons rode over towards Cardigan who, according to Captain Smith of the same regiment, and Wightman, seemed to be still carrying his sword at the slope and to be less concerned with defending himself against the cossacks than with trying to rally his men in the rear of the Russian battery. Soon after this, with the arrival of more men of the Light Brigade, he disengaged himself from the Russian horsemen.

In the smoke and the confusion, some of the Russian gunners had crawled under their guns for safety, others had been sabred by the

British cavalry. In some places the Light Brigade was driving the cossacks off easily, while in others men of the Brigade were being made prisoner by the enemy. Most of Lord George Paget's second line had missed the guns altogether, passing on one side or the other. Lord George, with the 4th Light Dragoons, Colonel Douglas with the 11th Hussars, and Colonel Shewell with the 8th Hussars, were engaging the Russian cavalry beyond the guns in the eastern opening of the valley near the Tchernaya River. The Odessa Battalions and other Russian infantry formed hollow squares and prepared to fight a defensive action.

To the spectators on the Chersonese Plateau the situation was beyond comprehension. Yet there was a sense of awe at the sight of the physical courage of the men of the Light Brigade. Armed with a degree of valour which was almost beyond belief, they had triumphed with the weapons of chivalry over the most sophisticated armament of the industrial revolution.

Lord George Paget, his cigar gone, was struggling to rally the survivors of the second line in the rear of the Russian position. His men had fought, hand-to-hand, with the Russians, overturning guns and putting them out of action. Like Cardigan, Lord George did not consider it proper to participate in the scrimmage personally, though he did cut down one Russian in order to save the life of an English officer. Yet throughout the fighting, he entirely forgot that he was carrying a pistol.

As the Russian cavalry began to gather in front of his men, Lord George shouted, 'Halt, front; if you don't front, my boys, we are done!'

The 11th Hussars and the 4th Dragoons turned to face their enemy, but only to hear another shout.

'They are attacking us, my lord, in the rear!'

Looking back along the route of the charge, Lord George saw some 500 Russian lancers blocking the valley behind him and cutting off the retreat of the Light Brigade.

'We are in a desperate scrape', he said, turning to Major Low of the 4th Dragoons. 'What the devil shall we do? Has anyone seen Lord Cardigan?'

By this time, Cardigan had extricated himself from the mêlée at the guns and was following the scattered groups of his first line back down the valley. He rode past Sergeant Mitchell, who was standing alone and without a horse.

'Where is your horse?'

'Killed, my lord,' said Mitchell.

'You had better make the best of your way back as fast as you can', said Cardigan sternly, 'or you will be taken prisoner.'

Then Mitchell saw him ride back to the confusion round the Russian guns only to return shortly afterwards and resume his progress towards the British lines.

Not far off, Private Wightman found Corporal Morley of the 17th Lancers, 'a great, rough, bellowing Nottingham man', whose hat and lance had gone and whose long hair was flying in the wind as he tried to rally survivors.

'Coom 'ere! Coom 'ere!' he roared. 'Fall in, lads! Fall in!'

Having collected about twenty troopers of various regiments, and there being no surviving officer nearby, he took command of the men and the situation, as they faced the Russian hussars blocking their retreat. 'Morley, roaring Nottingham oaths by way of encouragement, led us straight at them', Wightman recalled, 'and we went through and out at the other side as if they had been made of tinsel paper.'

All too soon, Morley's group of riders were being cut down by the Russian rifle fire on either flank, which took its toll of them in their retreat as it had done during the advance. Some were killed, others like Wightman were wounded and taken prisoner. Morley reached the British lines safely. Two years later he left the army, emigrated to the United States, and reached the rank of Captain in the Union army during the Civil War.

Colonel Shewell, whose 8th Hussars had veered to the right of the battery and gone round behind it on that side, met Colonel Mayow and a few survivors of the 17th Lancers. Shewell was a man whose strict biblical religion made him a strange contrast to some of his fellow hussar officers. On inquiring where Cardigan was, and discovering that no one knew, he took the command into his own hands and turned his regiment about to face the British lines. Three squadrons of Russian lancers blocked his retreat. Not being much of a swordsman, Shewell decided to lead his seventy men straight at the enemy, aiming his own horse at that of the Russian commander and endeavouring to unseat him by sheer force of impact. The Russians, who had actually been about to charge Shewell, found him charging them instead. Some of them scattered even before the collision, while the rest were swept aside by the momentum of the 8th Hussars. At last, Shewell's party found its way more or less clear to the allied lines.

There remained the 4th Light Dragoons and the 11th Hussars with Lord George Paget and Colonel Douglas. Officers with swords held high shouted, 'Rally! Rally!' as they collected any remaining survivors of the attack. Then, for the last time, the remnants of the Light Brigade turned to retreat. Like the 8th Hussars, Lord George's force found their retreat blocked by a growing mass of Russian hussars and cossacks. Lord George himself was worried most of all by the way in which the Russians had positioned themselves to fall upon the right flank of his retreating regiments. Yet when the British column galloped past, at hardly more than a horse's length, the Russians hesitated and did nothing. 'Well,' said Lord George, 'we got by them without, I believe, the loss of a single man. How, I know not! It is a mystery to me! Had that force been composed of English *ladies*, I don't think one of us would have escaped!'[18]

Apart from the events of Waterloo, the charge of the Light Brigade was perhaps the most famous incident in the whole of British military history during the nineteenth century. Yet by the measure of great battles it was hardly more than an incident. William Howard Russell, who noticed such things, remarked that the Brigade had formed up for the charge at ten minutes past eleven. 'At thirty-five minutes past eleven not a British soldier, except the dead and dying, was left in front of those bloody Muscovite guns.'

The losses of the Light Brigade would have been even more severe had not the retreat been covered, to some extent, by the Heavy Brigade, and by an attack upon Russian riflemen on the Fedioukine Hills by the Chasseurs d'Afrique under D'Allonville. The French were also driving the Russians back from the redoubts on the Causeway Heights, though it was too late by this time to prevent the enemy from towing away some of the captured British guns.

Cardigan, returning towards the British lines, met Captain Shakespear of the Horse Artillery.

'Damn nice thing this', said Cardigan plaintively, pointing to the tear in his breeches where the cossack's lance had entered, 'and nothing to keep the cold out.'

'Pardon me, my lord,' said Shakespear suavely, 'the artillery are always prepared for an emergency.' He beckoned a trumpeter, who for a moment seemed about to produce needle and thread, but who proved instead to be carrying Shakespear's flask.

A little further on, Cardigan met Sir George Cathcart.

'I have lost my Brigade', he told Cathcart glumly, and then began to ride back towards the Russian position until he met the returning 8th Hussars, and came back with them. When they reached the Heavy Brigade, Cardigan recalled his earlier fury with Nolan. He had gone white with rage when Nolan had begun to ride across the front of the Brigade.

'Imagine the fellow screaming like a woman when he was hit', said Cardigan to Scarlett.

'Say no more, my lord,' answered Scarlett, 'I have just ridden over Captain Nolan's dead body.'

The survivors of the Light Brigade were gathering on a slope which faced south towards the port of Balaclava. As they saw Cardigan approaching, they raised three cheers for him and offered to charge the Russian army again, then and there, if he should give the order.

'It is a mad-brained trick', said Cardigan of the charge, 'but it is no fault of mine.'

'Never mind, my lord,' was the reply. 'We are ready to go again!'

'No, no, men!' said Cardigan. 'You have done enough.'

Whatever the opinion of the world might be, to the men of his regiments Cardigan was the heroes' hero. The attitude of the ordinary soldiers towards him in the aftermath of Balaclava was the most powerful proof of the regard in which they habitually held him.

Cardigan turned away and rode down to where Lord George Paget and the last stragglers were coming in.

'Hello, Lord Cardigan,' said Lord George bitterly. 'Were you not there?'

'Oh, wasn't I, though!' exclaimed Cardigan, turning to Captain Jenyns of the 13th Light Dragoons. 'Here, Jenyns, did not you see me at the guns?'

Lord George seemed to ignore this. He said, 'I am afraid there are no such regiments left as the 13th and 17th, for I can give no account of them.'

Then, to his relief, he saw the survivors of those two regiments standing on the brow of the little hill where the muster was taking place. The muster and the roll-call of the Brigade offered little comfort, however. Of the 673 officers and men who had set out on the charge, there were now only 195. Though other men might make their way back later, or might be brought back wounded, the scale of losses among the two regiments of the first line was stupefying. The 13th Light Dragoons, temporarily commanded by Lieutenant Percy

Smith, could muster only fourteen men out of 150. Even two days later, with the return of all its stragglers, the 17th Lancers could find no more than fifty men and three officers for duty, out of another 150.[19]

One of Cardigan's aides-de-camp, Captain Lockwood, had been killed while riding back towards the Russian guns to look for Cardigan. The other aide-de-camp, Lieutenant Maxse, had been wounded but was now sent by Cardigan to Raglan with a report that the Russian gunners had been killed or put to flight. That, after all, had appeared to be the intention of Raglan's order as interpreted by Lucan. When the muster and the roll-call were over, Cardigan rode off to report to Raglan himself. The Commander-in-Chief greeted him with cold anger.

'What do you mean, sir, by attacking a battery in front, contrary to all the usages of warfare, and the customs of the service?'

'My lord,' replied Cardigan, 'I hope you will not blame me, for I received the order to attack from my superior officer in front of the troops.'

It was Lucan who was the next recipient of Raglan's censure.

'You have lost the Light Brigade!' said Raglan to him bitterly.

The day after the battle, Lucan came to Lord George Paget and complained 'with tears in his eyes' of the unfairness of singling him out to take the blame for the destruction of the Brigade. For Lucan there was not even the satisfaction of having been in the thick of battle, whereas stories were now being told of how Cardigan had gone charging heroically into the Russian battery at the head of his men, his horse jumping clear over the guns.

After the encounter with Raglan, Cardigan went to thank D'Allonville for his support during the withdrawal of the Brigade. Then he went to visit his wounded aide-de-camp, Lieutenant Maxse. It was popularly supposed that Cardigan rode straight from the charge to his yacht for a bath, dinner and a bottle of champagne, while the wounded survivors of the attack bled and died on the field of Balaclava. The truth was less spectacular. He slept on the ground, wrapped in a cloak, close to his wounded aide-de-camp. As for his men, a letter written by Mrs Farrel, a nursing sister with no particular reason to favour Cardigan, speaks for itself.

We had two visits from Colonel [*sic*] Cardigan, Scarlett and a host of foreign Officers the day after the Lancers and Hussars charged the Russian guns, and of what a sight those wounds of some were, shot through the bowels, legs, and chests. The trumpeter that sounded the charge for Colonel Cardigan was a most pitiful case, he begged that his Bugle should not be taken out of his sight. Colonel Cardigan spent half an hour with him soothing him, he is lying on some plank beds and Blankets, he belongs to the 17th Lancers. His name is Brittain. The sergeant of the 17th calls him Billy and keeps telling him to pluck up and get out soon to sound another charge. But there never was any chance for him though his lordship sees he has everything he wants.

To those who met him after the charge, Cardigan exhibited grief rather than arrogance, gloom rather than jubilation. His conduct in the days following the indecisive battle of Balaclava, as much as his behaviour during the charge itself, seemed to justify a certain remark by Captain Morris. Not an hour before the charge, Morris had been involved in a heated argument with Cardigan over the question of charging the Russians defeated by the Heavy Brigade. Yet when Morris was asked how Cardigan had behaved during the terrible twenty minutes of the attack on the Russian guns, he replied in a phrase which was peculiarly Victorian.

'He led', said Morris, 'like a gentleman.'[20]

3

The charge of the Light Cavalry had been the most appalling blunder, whose nature was quickly immortalized by Tennyson. There was a natural disposition to seek out those officers, perhaps including Cardigan, who had been responsible for the error and to censure them publicly. At the same time, there was no doubt that the men who had actually taken part in the charge, also including Cardigan, had displayed a degree of courage which was almost beyond credence. The whole affair was to become the major military controversy in a war whose conduct had so far inspired little more than controversy.

Yet there may have been some unintended military advantages, as a consequence of the charge. The Russians had watched the advance with no less incredulity than the British staff. They could not believe that any cavalry in its senses would dare to do what Cardigan's men had done. Indeed, General Liprandi concluded that the British officers must have got their men drunk before the order to charge was given. He was surprised when the English prisoners assured him that many of them had not even had food, let alone drink, since the day before. But drunk or sober, the Light Brigade had badly shaken the morale of the Russian cavalry, who were possessed with a natural fear of what such maniacs might do in future. As Kinglake remarked, 'It is probable that for a long time afterwards it would have been impracticable to make the Russian cavalry act with anything like confidence in the presence of a few English squadrons.'[21]

On the British side, the legend of Balaclava grew more heroic with every exaggeration of the size of the disaster and the magnitude of the courage. Lieutenant-Colonel Evelyn heard that no less than 800 horsemen had set out, of whom only 190 returned, and that Cardigan had ridden at the Russian battery and gone right over it, as he might have taken one of the most difficult jumps in the Pytchley country. Several days after the battle, Henry Clifford, a twenty-eight-year-old Lieutenant of the Rifle Brigade, met Cardigan near the town of Balaclava and heard the story of the battle from him. Clifford's opinion of Cardigan was that, 'No one who has seen him and spoken to him out here, but has the highest opinion of him as a soldier and a very brave man.' In obedience to Raglan's order, said Clifford, Cardigan 'moved on to what he, and every officer and man with him considered certain death'. In the matter of bravery, Clifford might appear to be something of an authority, since he was to win the Victoria Cross at Inkerman in a few days' time. Lord Raglan too, several days after the battle of Balaclava, noted privately, 'Lord Cardigan acted throughout with the greatest steadiness and gallantry, as well as perseverance.' Even Lucan, in his own dispatch to Raglan, conceded Cardigan's courage. 'Major General the Earl of Cardigan', he wrote, 'led this attack in the most gallant and intrepid manner; and his Lordship has expressed himself to me as admiring in the highest degree the courage and zeal of every officer, non-commissioned officer, and man who assisted.'[22]

For all that, there seemed to be little future in the Crimean campaign either for Cardigan or his Light Cavalry. After the battle of Balaclava, it was difficult enough to mount a squadron. To talk of regiments or a brigade was meaningless. Moreover, at the battle of Inkerman on 5 November, there was little scope for the use of cavalry. It was primarily an infantry battle, though with artillery support, in which the 'moral ascendancy' of the British foot soldiers defeated the strong Russian attack. It was a confused battle, fought in mist and drizzle, and Cardigan did not arrive from his yacht until after ten o'clock that morning. He rode up from Balaclava to Inkerman, which lay several miles towards Sebastopol, in company with his brother-in-law, Hubert De Burgh. Russell, *The Times* correspondent, met them on the way. Cardigan was wearing his splendid Hussar uniform, while De Burgh, whom Russell described as 'an unlovely gentleman', appeared in his usual flat brimmed top hat, frock coat, and trousers securely strapped over patent leather boots. Cardigan called to Russell.

'Haw! Haw! Well! Mr William Russell! What are they doing? What was the firing for last night? And this morning?'

Russell confessed that he had no idea. Cardigan turned to De Burgh.

'You hear, Squire? This Mister William Russell knows nothing of the reason of that firing! I daresay no one does! Good morning!'

And with that the strangely matched pair of riders trotted on towards the sound of the guns.[23]

Until Cardigan's arrival at Inkerman, Lord George Paget commanded the Light Brigade, whose only action of the day was over by 9.30 that morning. They were ordered to advance as a supporting line for the French Chasseurs d'Afrique, over ground which Lord George called 'as disadvantageous for cavalry as can be conceived; uneven, and among brushwood and stunted oak, and the ground covered with stones.' The French horsemen halted and a group of them dashed forward in an apparent skirmish. The Light Brigade sat and waited for half an hour under the artillery fire of the Russians, about 150 yards behind the Chasseurs. Then the entire force withdrew.[24]

It was some time after this that Cardigan and De Burgh arrived. Cardigan took command of the Brigade. He reprimanded Lord George for inattention to the mounting of guards for the Light Brigade camp. Then he pitched into Colonel Mayow, the Brigade Major, for not having the morning states made out and signed. In the ferocity of the battle itself the initiative passed from side to side, the Brigade of Guards fighting off the Russian attack with bayonets and rifle butts round the Sand Bag Battery on the Inkerman Heights. The remains of the Light Brigade sat and waited for the issue to be decided.

There was no mention of Cardigan or his Brigade in Raglan's official dispatch after Inkerman. Lord George Paget suggested that this was because Raglan would either have had to say that Cardigan was absent when the Brigade supported the French, or else he must have told a lie by claiming that Cardigan was present. The truth is that, by comparison with the deeds of the infantry during the battle, the Light Brigade's disagreeable half hour under Russian fire was not of any great significance.[25]

If there were those in the army, like Raglan or Henry Clifford, who were impressed by Cardigan's courage at Balaclava, there were others for whom his conduct on 25 October had been no more than further proof of his unsuitability for command. 'As to Lord Cardigan,' wrote young Captain Robert Portal of the 4th Dragoon Guards, 'he has as much brains as my boot, and is only equalled in want of intellect by his relation Lord "Look-on". Without mincing matters, two bigger fools could not be picked out of the British Army to take command.'[26]

This opinion was not softened by the news that Cardigan and Lucan were now beginning to squabble over the responsibility for the order which had started the charge of the Light Brigade, and that they were continuing to bicker over the way in which the Brigade was commanded. On 19 November, Cardigan wrote to Raglan, 'having been permitted by you since in this service to address private letters to you'. The new trouble was that the commanders of the Light Cavalry regiments had certain complaints to make. Cardigan had passed their letters to Lucan, to be forwarded to Raglan in the usual way. 'I have since been informed that he does not intend to comply with my wishes, but with his usual want of courtesy to those immediately under his command, he has given me no reply. I kept copies of 2 of the letters which if your Lordship will peruse, will explain the present state of things in the Light Brigade. The letters from the 3 other Comg. Officers are in the same strain & quite as strong.'

Raglan read the complaints of Lucan's mismanagement of the supplies and facilities for the Brigade, and then wrote a bleak reply to Cardigan on the same day. 'When the Commanding Officers' reports are laid before me,' he began, 'I shall have no difficulty in dealing with them, & in expressing my opinion that the state of the Light Cavalry could not be such as it is represented to be if the Comdg. Officers had attended to their duty, & had taken such steps as were within their power to provide for their deficiencies.'[27]

But there was another matter to which Cardigan had referred in his letter of 19 November. On 10 November, as his health seemed to deteriorate even further, he had been examined by the staff surgeon who had attended him for some time. He had suffered for two months from diarrhoea, which had become almost dysenteric, and for some years past he had been subject to 'chronic inflammation of the mucus membrane of the bladder'. These ailments were not responding to treatment, and the surgeon's report recommended, as urgent, a change of climate. Malta was suggested in the report as a suitable place for recuperation.

In his letter of 19 November to Raglan, Cardigan insisted that he had no wish to go on sick leave in the immediate future, or even at all if his presence in Balaclava was necessary. However, he would like permission to go on sick leave if his health should get still worse. Raglan told him that he could go before a medical board and would then have to act in accordance with its decision.

Cardigan waited for another fortnight. He complained to Raglan about the deplorable state of the Brigade, of the men who lay in the camp hospital without boots or socks. He asked Raglan to take some action or, perhaps, to instruct Lucan to do so. 'I never saw a more wretched sight in such cold weather', he remarked hopelessly.

Cardigan himself was one of the 'invalids' at Balaclava and had received permission to sleep aboard the *Dryad* for medical reasons. Seventy-two of his men had also been marked down to go 'on board ship' by the staff surgeons. Then, on 1 December, an army medical board was convened on the *Dryad*. Its verdict was that Cardigan's illness had now assumed 'a serious character', and that he was 'much reduced in strength'. It was no longer enough, in the view of the medical board, that he should be sent to Malta or Naples for a period of sick leave. He must return to England.[28]

There were soon to be very few commanders left who had come out with the army in the summer of 1854. The Duke of Cambridge was going home, an invalid like Cardigan. Lord George Paget, who was not an invalid, obtained leave to return to England 'on urgent family affairs'.

'Have you really?' said Cardigan, when Lord George told him that he had got his leave. 'Well I am very glad to hear it. It does not surprise me, and I had anticipated it, your case being quite different from that of all others.'[29]

When his own turn came, it was to Fanny Duberly, whose husband had come back safely from the charge, that Cardigan confided his feelings.

'My health is broken down', he said disconsolately, 'I have no brigade. If I had a brigade I am not allowed to command it. My heart and health are broken. I must go home.'

257

It seemed a sad conclusion to the apparent glory of a few weeks earlier. Fanny Duberly herself was moved by the pathos of it. 'Ever since he has been in the Crimea', she wrote, 'he has behaved very well, and upon my word I'm sincerely sorry for him.'[30]

On 4 December, Cardigan received some consolation in a private but 'highly complimentary' letter from Prince Albert on the subject of the Balaclava charge. The next day, he left Balaclava for good, and sailed for Constantinople. He spent a few weeks there and found time to write once more to Raglan upon the subject of Lucan.[31]

'I appealed to you soon after landing in the Crimea against the manner in which the Cavalry Division was (& is) commanded; I have no desire to appeal again officially after your decision but I cannot leave the country without affording you an opportunity of knowing how the duties of the command are carried on.'

Lucan had interfered in the running of the Brigade, had given orders to regimental officers for changing the arrangement of the camp without consulting Cardigan, and had robbed him of his proper authority. Cardigan demanded to know what other brigade commanders were subjected to such humiliating treatment by their divisional generals. Was Sir Colin Campbell treated in such a manner by the Duke of Cambridge? 'Can it be believed that any other General Officers commanding Brigades can be so treated in the Army except those who have the misfortune to serve in the Cavalry Division?'[32]

As a matter of fact, this parting shot exploded in the middle of another battle of reputations, which this time was being fought between Lucan and Raglan himself. In his dispatch after Balaclava, Raglan had reported that disaster had come to the Light Brigade, and 'From some misconception of the order to advance, the Lieutenant-General considered that he was bound to attack at all hazards.' This remark, like the rest of Raglan's dispatch, appeared in the London newspapers, copies of which reached the Crimea by the end of November. On 30 November Lucan addressed a letter of reproof to Raglan. Far from wishing to advance at all hazards, his first reaction to the order had been to question 'the usefulness of such an attack & the dangers attending it'. Then Captain Nolan, as Raglan's messenger, 'in a most authoritative tone stated that they were Lord Raglan's orders that the Cavalry Division should attack immediately.' Under the circumstances, Lucan 'did not dare to disobey . . . and this is the opinion of every officer of rank in this army, to whom I have shown the written order.' Lucan's letter put the blame squarely on Raglan and he then demanded that Raglan should 'kindly give the same publicity to this letter that has been given to your reports'.[33]

Raglan insisted that Lucan must withdraw the letter forthwith. Lucan refused. Raglan thereupon forwarded the letter to Lord Hardinge, the Commander-in-Chief at the Horse Guards, with a covering letter of his own.

During all this cantankerousness, there was a Ball at the British Embassy in Constantinople, to which the Ambassador, Lord Stratford de Redcliffe, thoughtfully invited all the senior British officers who were available. They included Sir Colin Campbell, Lord George Paget (still on his way home), and, for good measure, both Lucan and Cardigan. Elizabeth Carew, fifteen years old, was allowed to watch the splendidly costumed scene below from the minstrels' gallery of the ballroom. When Cardigan and Lucan saw one another, she was intrigued to see how 'very grumpy' they suddenly looked. But then, as Lord George had been telling everyone, they were both being sent home in disgrace, 'and he said a good thing too'. Later on, Elizabeth Carew remarked, 'Mama danced a quadrille with Lord Cardigan. She told me that he danced tolerably but smelt of wine.'[34]

From Constantinople, Cardigan sailed in the *Ripon* for Marseille. In Paris he was received by Napoleon III and invited to dine at the Tuileries. He sat in the Hotel Westminster instead, his feet so swollen that his dress shoes would no longer fit him.

The charge of the Light Brigade had been only the last of a series of misfortunes which seemed inevitably to attend the career of the British cavalry during the war. Denounced as aristocratic hooligans in the years of peace, its regiments appeared to have done no more in battle than to put on expensive and almost theatrical displays of futility in the face of the enemy. If valour, sacrifice and noble obedience to duty were virtues in themselves, then the grotesque errors, of which Balaclava was the greatest, might have seemed irrelevant. But the values of aspiring liberal democracy were as deadly to the heroes of the Light Brigade as the Russian guns had been. The mid-nineteenth century was an age which, at its best, prized intellect above military valour and recoiled in abhorrence from the prospect of useless blood-shed of a kind acceptable to earlier generations. It was a time deeply suspicious of noble obedience, whether or not the command itself had been foolish. Men were increasingly admired for asserting their rights, thinking their own thoughts, and acting independently. By the values of an earlier century, the fate of Cardigan and his men might have been a tragedy, inspiring various forms of pity and terror. In more modern terms it seemed a military farce whose price was paid by the blood of the fallen and by the indescribable sufferings of many of the survivors. There were men who came home from the Crimea so terribly maimed that the Queen wept as she pinned their medals upon them. Society reacted angrily and demanded public inquiries, whose aim was to single out those responsible for the catastrophe.

Cardigan himself exemplified the military anachronism most clearly of all. He was valiant, when he should have been intelligent. He was proud, when he ought to have been subtle. He showed private generosity, when public philanthropy would have benefited his reputation more. He believed in glorious physical courage, when he would have won greater popularity by believing in free trade. He came home in January 1855, a principal figure in the blunder at Balaclava, with little more than the prospect of a sour old age in which to reflect upon the public controversies and humiliations of his youth and middle years.

4

Cardigan landed at Folkestone on 13 January 1855. A crowd gathered to watch his progress. When some of them recognized him, they began to cheer. As the cheers grew in volume they were interrupted by the crashing chords of brass and cymbals playing the most characteristic of all English triumphal music, Handel's 'See! The Conquering Hero Comes!' from *Judas Maccabaeus*. The speed, as well as the enthusiasm, with which his return was greeted seemed almost bewildering. Three cheers were raised again and again for the hero of Balaclava. The 'Hallelujah Chorus' was sung. Men took the horses out of the Earl's carriage and pulled him as though he were a victorious emperor. In Northampton, the church bells of the town pealed from dawn to dusk for his triumphant return from the war, while men and women stood for hours in a blizzard of snow to catch just a glimpse of him as he passed. At every railway station, in town square and city streets, beneath bunting and decorations, the bands played again and again, 'See! The Conquering Hero Comes!'

The House of Commons, where his name had been the subject for criticism and abuse for more than twenty years, passed a vote of thanks to him. So did the House of Lords, which had tried him for intended murder in the previous decade. His portrait appeared in shop windows everywhere, and even more frequently a print called 'The Cardigan Galop', which showed him on his charger, leaping clear over the guns of the Russian battery, cutting down the gunners with one hand, as he led his Brigade in the famous attack. The music halls and the street ballad singers, whose turn for ridicule was excelled only by their gift for patriotic enthusiasm, had a new song. It was far more popular than any of the 'Black Bottle' numbers, which had convulsed audiences in the autumn of 1840.

> Six hundred stalwart warriors of England's pride the best,
> Did grasp the lance and sabre on Balaclava's crest,
> And with their trusty leader, Earl Cardigan the brave,
> Dashed through the Russian valley, to glory or a grave![35]

In every print, 'Earl Cardigan the brave' was shown charging at the very mouths of the Russian guns, as they spouted smoke and flame. *Punch*, which had been so waggish about the uniform of the 11th Hussars the previous year, now showed its new hero bearing down upon the line of Russian cannon, through the shell bursts and the carnage, in a print called 'A Trump Card(igan)'.[36]

It was a truly extraordinary homecoming for a man who was supposed to be one of the most hated figures in public life. On this occasion, at least, Cardigan's courage, pride and lack of concern in hiding his emotions, were precisely what the public wanted. Throughout the war the people had been cheated of victory or of stories of military conquest, and had read only of Russian barbarity and allied helplessness. Then, as if a gift from the gods, came a man who looked and had acted like a great hero. Balaclava was enshrined in popular history and 'The Charge of the Light Brigade' became a phrase which echoed in the minds of men and women who were to have no idea of its date, or whether the charge was on horseback or on foot, or where in the world it had occurred. They would certainly not have been aware that its leader gave his name to a woollen jacket, of a type which he had worn in the Crimea, and which has ever since been known as the 'Cardigan'.

From the moment that he stepped ashore on 13 January, there seemed no doubt that Cardigan was the people's hero. There was always a warmth about him, whether it was aggressive or sympathetic, which contrasted favourably in popular estimation with the rather cold and reserved behaviour of many political and military leaders by the mid-nineteenth century. Within a few days of his return, the kind of reception he was being given became generally known, and this knowledge encouraged others to imitate it. He found it quite amazing, but deeply gratifying. Every cheer and every strident chord of the brass bands, every peal of bells and every speech of welcome, took him at the heart and might move him to tears. Then, on the morning of 16 January, there came a command from Windsor Castle. Obedient as ever, he went down by the half-past five train from Paddington.

Earlier that day, Cardigan had had a long discussion with the Secretary of State for War, the Duke of Newcastle, and had firmly put the blame upon Lucan for misinterpreting Raglan's order to the Light Brigade at Balaclava. Newcastle later reported to the Queen that Cardigan held Lucan entirely responsible for 'misconceiving Lord Raglan's orders, not obeying them, and not exposing himself'.[37]

In the week before Cardigan's visit to Windsor, Lord Aberdeen, as Prime Minister, had written to the Queen on the subject of the Order of the Garter, which Cardigan seemed likely to demand yet again.[38]

> From his rank and station, Lord Cardigan might fairly pretend to the Garter, but his violent party politics would make it impossible for Lord Aberdeen, under ordinary circumstances, to submit his name to your Majesty for this purpose. At the same time, Lord Cardigan's great gallantry and personal sacrifices seem to afford him a just claim to your Majesty's favourable consideration; and Lord Aberdeen believes that to confer upon him the Blue Ribbon at this moment would be regarded as a very graceful act on the part of your Majesty. . . . If therefore your Majesty should be pleased to take the same view of this matter, Lord Aberdeen would communicate with Lord Cardigan on his arrival in London, and would willingly postpone all consideration of your Majesty's gracious intentions towards himself.

Six months earlier, the notion of a Prime Minister forgoing the Order of the Garter himself in order that it might be bestowed upon Cardigan would have seemed preposterous. Victoria remained unenthusiastic. Neither the Commander-in-Chief of the entire army, Lord Hardinge, nor Lord Raglan had received such an honour. There might be public misgivings if it was given to the leader of the Light Brigade since 'Lord Cardigan's personal character does not stand very high in the country'. This judgment was soon to be contradicted by scenes of popular enthusiasm. Yet the Queen may not have been thinking of Cardigan's military character. There was also his sexual reputation, which within a few more years was to cause even greater annoyance at court than it had done already.[39]

If Cardigan had but known it, the Order of the Garter was as near to being within his reach as it would ever be. But it was finally withdrawn, and the honour was never again connected with his name. Instead, he was made a Knight Commander of the Bath, a reward which most people approved, and some thought too little, for the hero of Balaclava.

Perhaps Cardigan was unfortunate in the timing of Aberdeen's suggestion to the Queen. Had it come after the Windsor visit, and after the scenes of wild congratulation in the London streets, perhaps Victoria would have been more inclined to yield. Certainly, she was most impressed by Cardigan, whom she found very engaging and extremely modest about his own part at Balaclava. By the second day of his stay at Windsor she had already agreed, in principle, with Newcastle's suggestion that it would be a good idea to recall Lucan and put Cardigan in command of the entire Cavalry Division.

On the evening of that second day, 17 January, Lord Hardinge came to dine at Windsor. Cardigan sat next to the Queen and gave a disturbing account of the state of the army in the Crimea, and the sufferings of its soldiers. He impressed upon Victoria the perilous weakness of many regiments in consequence of the lack of supplies and the failure of the transport system. He went into some of the details, even describing the deficiencies of hammers, nails and billhooks. The Queen was shocked to learn of the hardships to which men and horses were now subject. 'This is unpardonable', she remarked.

Then the conversation turned to the charge of the Light Brigade, and Cardigan produced some watercolour sketches of the Crimea by William Simpson, whom he had entertained on board the *Dryad* at Balaclava. Simpson had done one painting which illustrated the charge. The Queen, Prince Albert and Lord Hardinge listened intently as Cardigan described the terrible twenty minutes of the action, 'very modestly as to his own wonderful heroism, but with evident and very natural satisfaction', said the Queen afterwards.[40]

On the following morning, at half-past nine, the royal children were assembled in the Long Corridor at Windsor Castle, where with the aid of a plan and in the presence of the Queen and Prince Albert,

Cardigan again told the story of the charge. The children were as much fascinated by the narrator as by the story. By the end of his visit, he had impressed Victoria so favourably that he was allowed to dandle the smaller children on his knee. It was during such a moment that one royal infant looked up earnestly into the bewhiskered face and said in a confidential tone, 'You must hurry back to Sebastopol and take it, else it will kill Mama!'[41]

From Windsor, Cardigan returned to London and called upon Lord Hardinge at the Horse Guards, where he was informed that he would be appointed Inspector-General of Cavalry with effect from 1 February. The Queen readily agreed to Hardinge's suggestion of making the appointment. She was equally enthusiastic over 'the propriety of recalling Lord Lucan, and also entirely approves that he should be replaced by Lord Cardigan'.[42]

It seemed that the public acclaim had only just begun. The United Service Club, which had diligently blackballed Cardigan for the past fourteen years, held an extraordinary meeting. It was unanimously resolved by the members to elect him to honorary membership, so that he should not have to wait several weeks until the next scheduled meeting at which it would have been possible to elect him in the usual way.[43]

In London, the greatest public demonstration of all came on 6 February, when Cardigan went to a banquet given in his honour by the Lord Mayor at the Mansion House. There was great eagerness to see him, and crowds lined the route with unconcealed enthusiasm. The spectators had already prepared themselves to give him the reception due to the hero of Balaclava. But when Cardigan appeared in the uniform of the 11th Hussars, riding Ronald, the same chestnut horse which had carried him through the charge and into the Russian battery, there were scenes of near-hysteria. Men and women pressed forward, struggling even for a chance to touch the horse. Indeed, the unfortunate animal had to be protected from some of its admirers who wanted, as a talisman, a single tail hair of the charger on which the famous Lord Cardigan had ridden at Balaclava.

The scene inside the banqueting hall of the Mansion House was a well-bred repetition of the excitement outside. After the meal, the cloth was removed and the Lord Mayor proposed the toast to Cardigan's bravery. Cardigan replied by thanking his host and then, to the delight of the other guests, going on to give a first-hand account of the events of the Crimean invasion. He was cheered repeatedly but during his description of the battle of Balaclava, which was what interested his hearers most of all, storms of applause greeted each new revelation of the courage of the British soldiers. It was predictable enough that Cardigan would be moved by such a reception, but when he came to describe the dreadful loss suffered by his Brigade, and the deaths of so many valiant comrades and friends, he 'appeared to be greatly affected, and shed tears'. This was not so uncommon among Victorian soldiers as among their successors. It certainly won more admiration for Cardigan than a more controlled or sophisticated reaction might have done. His grief, like his anger, was not concealed.[44]

By the time that he left London for Deene, on 8 February, both the town of Northampton and the county of Northamptonshire had resolved to present him with separate congratulatory addresses 'on his Lordship's heroic conduct at Balaclava, in command of the Light Brigade'. From early morning until late evening the bells of the Northampton churches pealed once more to welcome home the victor. The town band, accompanied by Union Jacks decorated with laurel, set off towards the railway station to meet the one o'clock train. In the centre of the town, the assembly rooms of the George Hotel were packed to suffocation with those who had obtained tickets for the presentation of the town's address with its thousands of signatures. The rest of the population seemed to be packed into the streets around the town centre or else converging upon the railway station. The band, corporation officials in new livery, and flag bearers led the way. Behind them a great crowd of men and women, 'principally of the working classes, proceeded to the railway station to gain a sight of the hero of Balaclava'. When Cardigan stepped from the train, the men in the crowd insisted on attaching ropes to his carriage and pulling him themselves to the George Hotel, while the accompanying band struck up the inevitable notes of 'See! The Conquering Hero Comes!' Every window along the way was a mass of bunting and waving handkerchiefs. The crowds in the streets had reached such proportions that ground-floor windows were broken and buildings damaged as the spectators pressed back against them to allow the carriage to pass.[45]

What was described as a 'hurricane' of snow swept the town during the principal festivities but, for all that, Northampton had never seen such a demonstration. Even Cardigan's old press enemy, the *Northampton Mercury*, announced that whatever differences there might be in political views between Cardigan and the people of Northamptonshire, 'the instinctive admiration of an Englishman for gallantry such as that which his Lordship exhibited at Balaclava supersedes all such differences of opinion.'[46]

As the procession approached the George Hotel, several people were knocked over in the pandemonium, and the rejoicing of the crowd outside was matched by roars of cheering from within the assembly rooms, which deafened the newspaper correspondents who were present as Cardigan appeared. His speech at the Mansion House had been described by the *United Service Gazette* as 'modest, as becomes a good Soldier, and in excellent taste'. So, too, at Northampton he was proud of the honour but quick to share the glory. 'I cannot express with what pride and gratitude I receive your approbation of the gallantry which you are pleased to attribute to me on that occasion, but I feel that equal gallantry was certainly displayed by every man in that Brigade.'[47]

Then he went out on to the balcony to acknowledge the cheers of a packed crowd of men and women, who had been standing patiently in the snow storm, waiting for a possible appearance by their hero.

On 19 February he was at the George Hotel again to receive the address from the county of Northamptonshire, which with its list of several thousand signatures was over forty yards long. The presentation was made by Lord Exeter, as Lord Lieutenant of the county. Cardigan stood up to reply, seeming 'much affected at the cordiality of his reception'. Indeed, he had hardly spoken two sentences when, as the *Northampton Mercury* put it, 'The noble Lord here paused, apparently overcome with emotion.'[48]

At Deene, on 9 February, separate congratulatory addresses were presented by Cardigan's tenants in Yorkshire, Leicestershire and Northamptonshire. Cardigan provided them all with a splendid dinner in the White Hall at Deene, and held a ball for them several days later.

If he still had enemies in the early months of 1855, they were not much in evidence. The man whom *The Times* had once called the 'plague-spot of the British army', and whom it had wished to see in prison, working the treadmill and living on oatmeal, was now described in different terms. 'It may be said', remarked George Ryan, 'without fear of contradiction, that the Earl of Cardigan is now the most popular soldier in England. . . . By the latest generation Balaclava will be prized as a jewel of inestimable value; one that can never be filched, because guarded in the sacred depository of England's history even to the "crack of doom."'[49]

It is true that as the spring of 1855 turned to summer, there were unpleasant little placards which appeared here and there, demanding, 'Is Lord Cardigan a Hero?' To that question, however, the people of England had apparently given their unequivocal answer. In any case, such querulous jibes were insignificant by comparison with the literal and metaphorical singing of his fame. The *United Service Gazette* had honoured him as early as December 1854 in a poem on the subject of 'Right Gallant Cardigan'. Most famous of all, to future generations, was the celebration of 'The Charge of the Light Brigade' by the Poet Laureate, Alfred, Lord Tennyson. But in 1855 Tennyson's appeal was generally confined to those who could read, or were in the habit of reading, such poetry as his. There was another and larger group, for whom Cardigan's fame rested upon the patriotic music halls and the ballad singers of the city streets. In their fervour, if not in their poetic technique, they were somewhat in advance of Tennyson.[50]

> Oh! 'Tis a famous story, proclaim it far and wide,
> And let your children's children re-echo it with pride,
> How Cardigan the fearless, his name immortal made,
> When he crossed that Russian valley with the famous Light
>   Brigade!

CHAPTER 9

'WAS LORD CARDIGAN A HERO AT BALACLAVA?'

1

To the exasperation of his critics in England and the Crimea, there was no sign during the spring and summer of 1855 that the crescendo of popular enthusiasm for Cardigan was in any way likely to diminish. It was true that *The Times* complained of these outbursts of admiration, which it felt were reminiscent of the exhibition of the latest effigy or the actual clothes of a hanged murderer at Madame Tussaud's waxworks. But the well-bred disdain of *The Times* was not commonly shared. As Disraeli laconically remarked, 'The great hero of London at present is Lord Cardigan, who relates with sufficient modesty, but with ample details, the particulars of his fiery charge at Balaclava to willing audiences—as often as they like.'[1]

Until the end of March a rumour recurred in most of the London papers to the effect that the hero of the nation would soon be returning to the Crimea to take command of all the British cavalry remaining there. On 14 March Lord George Paget noted in his diary that he had heard 'an alarming story that Cardigan is coming out to command the cavalry'. According to Lord George, the men in the Crimea had begun to read in *The Times* of Cardigan's 'vagaries in London', and the faint murmurs against him grew into a series of feuds which lasted for the rest of his life. He was, in Lord George's opinion, 'a vain as well as an ambitious man, and his vanity led him astray when he came in contact with the admiring mob of London.'[2]

However, the focus of interest in the Crimea was not Cardigan but his late commander and rival, Lieutenant-General the Earl of Lucan. Lucan had refused to withdraw his letter of 30 November, in which he demanded of Raglan that his own account of the charge of the Light Brigade should be published as prominently as Raglan's dispatch after Balaclava. Raglan had therefore forwarded the letter to Lord Hardinge at the Horse Guards, who replied on 21 January assuring him that, 'The Duke of Newcastle will send you the papers recalling Ld. Lucan from the Command of the Cavalry Divn. Her Majesty entirely concurs.' While Cardigan continued to be received with applause by the crowds of London or Northampton, Lucan was informed of his recall by Raglan. On 12 February he began his voyage home in disgrace, not having been dismissed for his part in the destruction of the Light Brigade but for having refused to withdraw his letter to Raglan.

On the very day of his arrival in England, Lucan wrote to Lord Hardinge, as Commander-in-Chief, and demanded a court-martial so that his guilt or innocence might be publicly demonstrated. Hardinge refused, pointing out that Lucan had not been recalled for any offence against military law but merely because 'it is indispensable that a good understanding should prevail between the Genl. Comndr. in the field & his Lt. Genl. of Cavalry.' Writing to Raglan at the same time, Hardinge remarked of this reply to Lucan, 'I have used no soft words for the purpose of soothing his feelings. . . . I suppose we shall have a flare up in the Lords to give vent to his feelings & then a finale.'[3]

On 10 March the Judge Advocate-General, S. C. Denison, added a legal opinion to confirm that a court-martial was impossible, even though Lucan might have requested it. So Lucan, whose personal humiliation seemed the more sharp by contrast with Cardigan's triumphal progress, took his case to the one assembly which could not deny him a hearing. On 19 March he initiated a debate on his recall in the House of Lords.

The debate was a discordant medley of intense indignation and patrician decorum. Lucan moved that a copy of his own account of the battle of Balaclava, as well as Raglan's dispatch, should be presented to the Queen by the House, in order that he might be exonerated. In his speech he protested rather plaintively that Raglan had betrayed him, while the Quartermaster-General, Sir Richard Airey, had dismissed the loss of the Light Brigade by saying casually, 'These sort of things will happen in war; it is nothing to Chillianwallah.'

As for the gallant Earl of Cardigan (who sat vigilantly within a few feet of his detested brother-in-law during his speech), he had actually asked to be withdrawn, shortly before the charge of his Brigade, because he was too close to the enemy. The air in the candlelit chamber of the House of Lords grew warm with animosity as Lucan made his final and melodramatic appeal to the government.

'You have wronged, grievously wronged, as zealous a soldier as Her Majesty has in the army . . . give me a court-martial and a fair trial!'

Lord Panmure was about to rise and reply for the government, but he was too slow. Cardigan was already on his feet, eyes glittering with pugnacity, and anxious to 'correct a statement' which his brother-in-law had just made. Lucan had falsely stated that Cardigan had sent his aide-de-camp with a message 'that the force of the enemy was so numerous in front of the Light Brigade that I felt it difficult to hold my ground'.

'No!' shouted Lucan.

'Yes!' snapped Cardigan. 'Those were his very words. I sent no such message whatever.'

At last, Lord Panmure managed to intervene in the family quarrel, lamenting that 'a more painful subject than the present has never been brought before this House'. Lucan had been withdrawn because 'although personal civilities might have continued, the confidence which ought to exist between the Commander-in-Chief and an officer commanding a division in his army had, to a certain extent, been shaken.' The actual truth was that 'personal civilities' had ceased promptly with Lucan's letter of 30 November, but that was hardly material to Panmure's case. Then the Duke of Richmond rose and expressed his 'great regret that the noble and gallant Earl should have brought this subject before the House'. He was followed by the Earl of Derby who begged that 'we may be spared the continuance, or, at all events, a repetition of it'. However, the only effect of this decorous disdain on the part of the robed peers was to have Lucan on his feet again accusing the Duke of Newcastle, the former Secretary for War, of privately vilifying him as a betrayer of confidences.

'I have made no such charge', said the Duke, evidently bewildered.

'Pardon me,' barked Lucan, 'but I heard you!' There followed a final, unedifying wrangle.[4]

At the end of the debate, the Lords agreed to Lucan's motion, perhaps hoping that this would be the speediest way of ending a distasteful controversy. However, within a few days there appeared a pamphlet, *The Speech of Major-General the Earl of Lucan delivered in the House of Lords on March 19th 1855*. But apart from the speech, the pamphlet also included explanatory notes and a map, of doubtful accuracy, which were hardly calculated to enhance the part played by Cardigan at Balaclava. In the notes, Lucan swore that Cardigan was under instructions to attack the Russian flank during the engagement of the Heavy Brigade, but had failed to do so. He also repeated that Cardigan had sent a message by Lieutenant Maxse, before the charge of the Light Brigade, complaining that the position in which he was standing was too exposed to Russian attack.

Cardigan denied both accusations, in a letter to *The Times* on 7 April. He had never received an order to attack the enemy flank during the engagement of the Heavy Brigade. On the contrary, Lucan had instructed him to stand fast and 'to watch a certain line of ground over which the Russians might have attacked (and they had plenty of additional troops for the purpose)'. As to the allegation that he had sent a message before the charge of the Light Brigade, complaining that he was too exposed to Russian fire where he stood, Cardigan denied ever sending such a complaint.

Lucan had withdrawn to his estate at Castlebar, in Ireland, but he replied on 13 April in a letter which came as close to calling Cardigan a liar as the policy of *The Times* and the laws of libel would permit. Moreover, Lucan maintained that his own version and the accompanying map in his pamphlet, to which Cardigan had strongly objected, were 'generally correct—certainly not less so than the description given in his Lordship's present letter, and in the speeches in which his Lordship has, at such length and on different occasions, brought his services before the public.'

It was the enclosed world of the nineteenth-century English peerage, rather than the mere chance of war, which had locked the two brothers-in-law in a sterile but ferocious enmity that was to break out in public displays of mutual loathing for the rest of Cardigan's life. Yet for the time being it was Lucan who was at a disadvantage. The *United Service Gazette* spoke for most of the military press when it assured him that the tragedy of the Light Brigade was 'not to be forgotten or forgiven'. The attempt to shift responsibility for the disaster on to Captain Nolan made matters worse. 'His Lordship's attempt to relieve himself from blame at the expense of a dead man, is seeking a safeguard which is not English, still less is it soldierlike.

Lord Lucan's errors are bad, his defence worse.' For all that, the inhabitants of County Mayo, where Lucan was Lord Lieutenant, drew up an address of sympathy in June 1855. In December he was gazetted Colonel of the 8th Hussars. 'Lucky Lord Lucan', said the *United Service Gazette* caustically, as it reckoned up the few hundred pounds of income (though not the expenditure) which he might expect in consequence of his new sinecure.[5]

It was some measure of the comparative security which the two men felt for their reputations that when, on 26 July 1856, the *Daily News* published an article on Lucan and Cardigan as 'the two white-washed peers', Cardigan chose to ignore the attack, while Lucan sued the publishers for libel and lost, amid the derisive comments of the London press.

If only for reasons of health, it had always been unlikely that Cardigan would return to the Crimea to command the cavalry. Yet the loss of the opportunity was to some degree compensated for by the duties of Inspector-General of Cavalry, and by the place which he now seemed to occupy in the Queen's favour. Despite his skirmishing, inside the House of Lords and out of it, with Lucan, Cardigan managed to inspect every cavalry regiment in the British Isles within six or seven weeks of his appointment. He issued strict orders on matters of dress and discipline, until some regimental commanders looked forward to the descent of the new Inspector-General with as much foreboding as they might have felt in the face of the Russian hussars and cossacks. Cardigan's smartening up of the British cavalry concluded with a splendid field day in Phoenix Park, Dublin, in October 1855.

While Cardigan and Lucan were exchanging insults in *The Times*, the French Emperor, Napoleon III, paid a state visit to Queen Victoria, as a gesture of unity in the struggle against Russia. On 17 April there was a grand review of the Household troops in Windsor Park, before the Queen, the Emperor and Empress and the royal princes. Royal salutes were fired, there was a display of artillery skill, and the entire review under Cardigan's command marched past in slow and quick time. When the cavalry began to manoeuvre, Prince Albert, the Duke of Cambridge and other members of the royal party joined in, charging here and there, while Cardigan, on the chestnut horse which he had ridden at Balaclava, was driven according to the Queen into 'a great state of excitement'. The enthusiasm of Victoria and her guests was matched by the excitement of the crowd, which she described as unimaginable.[6]

Among his other duties, Cardigan had found time to return to his grateful county in order to attend the Pytchley Hunt Races in Northampton at the end of March. But elsewhere the general criticism of the whole conduct of the war was becoming more vociferous. Raglan had quite correctly reported that the appalling conditions of the Russian winter made any final assault upon Sebastopol out of the question until the weather should improve. This was too much for the satirists of the London press who began to comment bitterly, during March and April, upon the lethargy of 'Lord Weatherwise', as he was dubbed.

> Canrobert and I work right well together;
> He watches the siege—and I watch the weather.[7]

But it would have been quite wrong to conclude that the nation was weary of the war. On the contrary, it wished to see the war fought more vigorously and the Russians taught their lesson. The very lack of any great military achievement during the campaign so far made an early end to the war an unpopular suggestion. Even in 1856, when the extent of the disasters and the mismanagement of supplies had become common knowledge, George Dodd reported that 'There was a general wish for another "brush" with the Russians— a taking of Sveaborg or Cronstadt—or a signal limitation to the territorial dominions of the czar.'[8]

Even by the time of Cardigan's return in January 1855, both those who wanted to see the war fought more vigorously, and those who felt that it should never have been allowed to drag on once the Russians had evacuated the Danubian provinces, were determined that the mismanagement should be investigated and its perpetrators revealed to the public.

The government of Lord Aberdeen had come under strong attack in the House of Commons for its conduct of the war. John Arthur Roebuck, barrister and Radical member for Sheffield, proposed a Commons select committee to inquire into 'the condition of our army before Sebastopol'. The government resisted the move but when the Commons divided on 30 January 1855, Roebuck's motion was carried by 305 to 148. The Aberdeen government resigned. Lord Derby tried to form a Conservative ministry and failed. Lord John Russell then attempted to reconstruct a Whig administration from the ruins of the

Aberdeen government. He also failed. Then, on 5 February, it was announced that Lord Palmerston had undertaken to form a government, in which Lord Panmure would be Secretary for War. On 5 March Roebuck's select committee began a two-month inquiry into the conduct of the war and, equally important, into the conduct of such commanders as Cardigan who had played so large a part in the Crimean venture.

At the time of Lucan's recall, Captain W. C. Forrest remarked, 'He will though, I think, come out of any investigation better than our old friend Cardigan.' The truth of this judgment seemed likely to be put to the test before much longer. In February 1855, even before Roebuck's select committee could get down to work, the new Secretary of State for War, Lord Panmure, had appointed two commissioners, Sir John McNeill and Colonel Alexander Tulloch, to inquire into the failure of supplies for the army in the Crimea. While Roebuck and his fellow members sat at their semicircular table, interviewing a series of generally reluctant witnesses, the McNeill and Tulloch commission was in the Crimea, carefully documenting the full extent of the administrative disaster which had nearly destroyed the army before Sebastopol.[9]

Cardigan was summoned to the select committee of the House of Commons on 14 March. He had little option but to attend, since the House of Lords had given their leave and he was, therefore, among the 'Persons, Papers, and Records' for which the committee was empowered to send. Yet his mood was unco-operative and suspicious. He gave a rather unfortunate impression of unwilling participation, and of considerable disdain for those armchair strategists who now presumed to investigate and pronounce upon the conduct of the war by the army. He was inclined to be abrupt or evasive in his answers, replying, 'I really cannot say', or 'I think not'. To the select committee's members, he cannot have been a particularly sympathetic figure.

Among the other points revealed to the committee in his answers was that it was not until some days after the battle of Inkerman, on 5 November 1854, that the army knew it must spend the winter in the Crimea. Only then were further supplies and winter clothes sent for. Cardigan agreed that it might have been in the best interest of the Light Cavalry Brigade if they had been shipped to winter quarters elsewhere. However, he also pointed out, for the benefit of these civilians, who had no experience of such a situation, that 'the moral effect upon the united force in the Crimea of commencing, at such a moment as that, to send troops away from the Crimea might have been very injurious.'[10]

The most persistent questioning of Cardigan was in relation to the care of the cavalry horses. He was asked why sheds had not been built to keep them in, and he replied that wood to build sheds—whether for horses or men—was not available in the Crimea but had to be shipped from Scutari or Varna. Moreover, the hardships of the sheds might have been greater than those of the cold hills, since many of those few horses which had been sent to sheds developed glanders, a contagious swelling which spread quickly in the stagnant warmth and destroyed them. One of the select committee, Layard, then asked Cardigan if he was aware that even in England, at Chobham Camp, cavalry horses were bivouacked under cover. Cardigan retorted that at Chobham the 4th Light Dragoons had been deliberately ordered to bivouac in the open air 'to see the effect upon the horses'.[11]

'Then, in your opinion,' said Layard acidly, 'it would be advantageous in England, if encampments were made, to picket them in the air, to accustom them to exposure?'

'It might be a dangerous experiment', said Cardigan firmly.

His main argument, which was realistic rather than sympathetic, was that horses on active service were inevitably subjected to discomfort or suffering.

'That is always the case in a time of warfare; the horses of the cavalry who are exposed to outpost duty, and so forth, must suffer a great deal; it is the natural consequence of a war, I think, in which cavalry are engaged.'[12]

Most significant of all, in the light of later developments, the members of the select committee turned to the question of supplying forage for the horses. As Cardigan himself testified, the Light Cavalry Brigade camp, six miles from Balaclava, had been without forage for eighteen days in November, although supplies were available in the port. 'The hills were so steep, and the roads had become so impracticable, from bad weather, that no animals were to be found that could bring up the forage, and therefore we were without it.'

Roebuck, a short and nervously energetic chairman, said incredulously, 'So that within six miles you had plenty of forage?'

'Yes,' said Cardigan coldly, 'but with very bad intervening roads.'[13]

The committee returned to this point. Why had Cardigan not used his authority, as commander of the Brigade, to have the forage brought up by the cavalry horses?

'I had no orders to do so; it was understood at the headquarters of the army that the Commissariat were to supply the forage, and I think that our horses, in the month of November, had been so exhausted from hard work by pickets, patrols, and exposure to the weather, and all the hardships they had undergone, that they would not have been capable of going six miles into Balaclava to be heavily laden with hay, and to bring it back again.'

Layard inquired whether, apart from any orders given to him, Cardigan might not have considered it his duty to send the cavalry horses for provisions to supply both men and animals.

'No,' said Cardigan, 'I think not.'[14]

On 19 April 1856 *Punch* was to publish a cartoon which showed the skeleton of a horse, saddled and harnessed, being led towards Chelsea Hospital by a guardsman. The drawing was called, 'The Witness that Ought to be Examined'.

The report of the select committee was presented on 18 June 1855. It was astonishingly restrained, and would have been even blander but for Roebuck's casting vote which ensured the inclusion of at least some expression of misgivings over the entire military undertaking. The military authorities, according to the report, had gravely underestimated the strength of Sebastopol. They had sent an army to the Crimea, equipped for a short, fair-weather campaign, and they had been trapped into a prolonged winter war for which they were utterly unprepared. In conclusion, the select committee praised the valour of the army and deplored the sufferings inflicted upon it by inadequate planning.

On the very day that the committee reported, the British and French armies launched their attack upon the south-eastern defences of the city of Sebastopol, only to be beaten back in what was to be known as the first battle of the Redan. Raglan was badly shaken by this reverse, and by the death from cholera six days later of his Adjutant-General, General Estcourt. On 25 June Raglan himself was taken ill, and three days later he was dead from the same disease. On 23 July the battleship *Caradoc*, painted black and bearing the dead Commander-in-Chief, dropped anchor in the Bristol Channel. Lord Raglan's coffin was brought ashore and interred in the family vault at Badminton.

After a second and bitterly fought attack upon the Redan, on 8

September 1855, the Russian army evacuated Sebastopol, withdrawing to the north. The technical victory which the allies achieved had taken a year, rather than a few days or weeks, and had cost the British army alone 21,000 dead. In England, there remained the two contrasting reactions to the war. The first was an inclination to dwell upon the imperishable courage of the Light Cavalry Brigade at Balaclava, or the heroic resistance of the Brigade of Guards at Inkerman, or the triumph of Codrington's men at the Alma. The second reaction was a preoccupation with the underlying, preventable tragedy of the war, and a determination to bring the guilty to justice, before public opinion if not before the courts.

George Ryan, who had earlier praised Cardigan in *Our Heroes of the Crimea*, now joined the ranks of his critics by producing a pamphlet, which was widely sold and quoted in the summer of 1855, *Was Lord Cardigan a Hero at Balaclava?* According to the *United Service Gazette*, Ryan was now in the pocket of Lord Lucan and his volte-face on the subject of Cardigan's heroism was to be seen in the light of this. The theme of the pamphlet was that at the Russian guns 'the noble Earl got out of the mêlée as soon as he could'. The military press dismissed the accusation peremptorily on Cardigan's behalf. 'We know it. Retreating in order was out of the question. *Everybody* cut his way back when he found into what a trap the Light Cavalry had fallen and he was right.' However, this did not stop Ryan from declaring to the Queen that graves at Balaclava would open up, and Britain's heroes would step forth in their blood-soaked winding-sheets, if she were to create Cardigan a Knight Commander of the Bath.[15]

Cardigan took little notice of the pamphlet, quite rightly dismissing it as the anonymous and ill-informed work of a hack. But on 20 January 1856, a year after their appointment by Lord Panmure, Sir John McNeill and Colonel Tulloch forwarded to the government their final report on the failure of army supplies in the Crimea. It was inevitable that Sir Richard Airey, as Quartermaster-General, should figure largely in the report. But for most readers the criticisms of Airey were overshadowed by the singling out of the two chief culprits, Lucan and Cardigan. On these two men was thrown the weight of the blame for the sufferings of men and horses. The commissioners' report dwelt on the point which had recurred throughout the questioning of Cardigan by the Commons' select committee in 1855. Why had he not used the horses of his Brigade to fetch supplies from Balaclava to the starving men and animals of the Light Cavalry camp? In a single paragraph, the commissioners appeared to lay the blame for this particular catastrophe upon the hero of the Balaclava charge.[16]

> When the supply began to fail, the Commissariat Officer referred to, who appears to have done everything in his power to meet the difficulties of the case, proposed—as he knew there was plenty of barley at Balaclava—that if a detachment of the horses were allowed to go down daily, he would engage to bring up enough for the rest of the Brigade. This proposition appears to have been brought specially under the notice of Lord Cardigan by Lieutenant Colonel Mayow, Assistant Quartermaster-General of Cavalry, who states that his Lordship declined to accede to it, as he had previously done when a similar proposition was made to him to send the horses down for hay before that supply failed.

As soon as the report of the McNeill and Tulloch Commission was published, Lucan wrote to Lord Panmure in great indignation at the charge that the horses in his Division had been worse cared for and supplied than in any other part of the army. Both Lucan and Cardigan disputed the findings of the commission, in speeches to the House of Lords. On 15 February the replies of the brothers-in-law to the charges against them were also laid on the table of the House of Commons. Before the end of the month, by successive shifts of opinion, it was not the reputations of Lucan and Cardigan, but those of McNeill and Tulloch, which were on trial.

In Cardigan's case, at least, it seemed that something less than justice had been done by the commissioners' report. When it had been clear that the cavalry horses must remain in the Crimea during the winter of 1854–5, he had written to Lucan on 16 November. His letter described the hardships suffered by the animals, and he requested Lucan, as his immediate commanding officer, to forward his statement of the facts to Lord Raglan. This Lucan declined to do. Moreover, Cardigan himself had never been other than solicitous for the welfare of his men and horses. As his supporters pointed out, during his weeks of illness at Balaclava he had made the journey over rough country to the Brigade camp almost every day, and sometimes twice a day. The failure to use cavalry horses to carry supplies was similarly dismissed. The horses had, indeed, been used to carry supplies for a while, but because of the injuries they received in the process, the practice was stopped on Lord Raglan's orders. In any case, as the military papers insisted, it was sheer folly to send the cavalry on a long and exhausting trek for supplies. What would have happened if the Russians had launched an attack upon this point of the British line while half the Brigade was dragging back hay and barley from Balaclava, six miles distant?[17]

After several weeks of such arguments, Lord Panmure agreed at the end of February to set up a court of inquiry to inquire into the findings of the commissioners. This announcement was received with amused scepticism. 'The disposition will be to make all *smooth*', said the *United Service Gazette*. 'Pleasant, nice sort of people will come forward and show as clear as mud that Lord Lucan was right, and Lord Cardigan was right, and that the Crimean Commissioners were right too . . . it will end in sheer "bosh".'[18]

The Board of General Officers to inquire into the commissioners' report consisted of Sir Alexander Woodford, as President, and five other generals, attended by the Judge Advocate-General and his Deputy. The court was to meet on 7 April in the Pensioners' Dining Hall of Chelsea Hospital. From its association with this monument to Wren's lofty classicism and Victorian military philanthropy, the court became known as the Chelsea Board. On 16 March, Cardigan paid a preliminary visit and inspected the arrangements for the court, in company with the governor of the Hospital, General Sir Edward Blakeney.

In the great hall, the President, the other officers and the Judge Advocate sat round a table, rather as if they had been convened to conduct a court-martial. Witnesses were brought before them, not only to be questioned but also to question others in their turn. At a distance sat the members of the public, who had been admitted to witness this last encounter of all the best-known survivors of the Crimean campaign.

On the opening day, 7 April, most of the court's time was taken up by a remarkable performance of Lord Lucan's. He first demanded that his case should be heard and judged at a separate hearing from that of Cardigan and the other aggrieved officers. When this was refused, by the Judge Advocate-General, Lucan demanded and got a twenty-four-hour delay in order to consider the course he would pursue. When the court met again, much of the second and third days seemed to be taken up with Lucan's complaints about *The Times*, which the court could not deal with but which were briskly answered in the paper's editorial columns. Colonel Tulloch, whom Lucan described as 'a mere War Office Statistical Clerk', was called to give an account of himself before the man whom he had slighted in his report. Lucan's complaints and his cross-questioning of other witnesses took up virtually the whole of the first thirteen days of the hearing. By any standards it was an extraordinary performance, all the more so when his case proved to be little more than a complaint about the manner in which the commissioners had misused statistics in order to imply that horses in the Cavalry Division were less well cared for than those in other units of the army.

On 30 April, the fourteenth day of the inquiry, Cardigan made his single appearance before the court. A chance of seeing, and hearing, the hero of Balaclava guaranteed 'the most numerous attendance' of the public, and even in his sixtieth year he had preserved sufficient physical charm to ensure that most of those who crowded into the great hall were of the 'fairer portion' of the female sex.

Cardigan read out the paragraph of which he complained, and in which the Crimean commissioners criticized him for refusing to send cavalry horses into Balaclava for supplies. To the other arguments on his behalf, he added that both Raglan and Canrobert had agreed that to move the Light Cavalry from its camp on the Inkerman Heights was to open the way for a Russian attack to the rear of the allied position. For Cardigan to have detached a considerable part of his Brigade as a supply train would therefore have been quite contrary to Raglan's orders. But even had it not been, the loss of horses on the twelve miles of rough country, heavily laden and already exhausted, would have been greater than the actual loss from inadequate provisions.

'Upon the facts I have mentioned I feel justified in demanding from a military court an approval of my conduct, and a decision that there is no foundation for a charge that I neglected to use every precaution to maintain the efficiency of the Brigade—a charge which I venture to hope is inconsistent with my whole professional career.'

He withdrew, and sat down to an outburst of applause from the spectators.[19]

The inquiry dragged on until 19 May, Colonel Tulloch attending every day until his health broke down on 5 May. Sir John McNeill, who was a civil servant and a diplomat rather than a soldier, refused to have anything to do with the hearings. At the end of July, the Chelsea Board issued a report, which earned it the additional sobriquet of 'The Whitewashing Board'. As the *United Service Gazette* had predicted, it appeared to exonerate both those blamed by the Crimean commissioners, and the commissioners themselves. Lord Palmerston, as Prime Minister, dextrously upheld the findings of the commissioners and those of the Chelsea Board, simultaneously. The only person to suffer, although posthumously, was Lord Raglan, who was now made to take rather more blame for the state of the cavalry than might have seemed decent when the first report of the commissioners was issued no more than a month after his death.

In the heat of the debate as to whether the Chelsea Board had done belated justice to Lucan and Cardigan or had cynically whitewashed the most flagrant military corruption, the passing of the war itself was hardly noticed. Yet after months of negotiation in Paris, and months of inactivity in the Crimea, during which the British regiments diverted themselves with horseraces and amateur theatricals, a peace treaty was signed at Vienna on 30 March 1856. Under its provisions, the Black Sea was to be closed to all fleets except for a few small Turkish and Russian vessels which were to act as a maritime police or coastguard. Black Sea ports were to be used for commercial purposes, but not as naval or military arsenals. Austria and Prussia, as well as the belligerent powers, signed the treaty. All signatories guaranteed the protection of Christians in Turkey, while England, France and Austria bound themselves to regard any infringement of the treaty as a *casus belli*. But Russia did not repudiate the terms of the peace for fourteen years, and when she did so her former adversaries were too deeply preoccupied by the events of the Franco-Prussian war to care very much about Russo-Turkish rivalry in the Black Sea.

Despite George Ryan's melodramatic protest to the Queen Cardigan was created a Knight Commander of the Bath in the summer of 1855. But so was Lucan. In December, the French Emperor matched Victoria's approval, by making him a Commander of the Légion d'Honneur. These public honours were all the more cherished for the twenty years of threats, libels and physical violence which had marked his reputation before the Crimean expedition. In May 1856, supremely indifferent to the opinion which might still be held of him by young cavalry officers like Robert Portal, he arrived at Portal's wedding celebration in Devonshire, where Palmerston was the principal guest and the NCOs of the 4th Dragoons provided the guard of honour. Cardigan enjoyed himself thoroughly, making the most of the wine and saying 'Hear, hear!' loudly, when Palmerston referred in his speech to the heroism of the Light Brigade. The bride's young niece observed shrewdly of Sir Walter Carew and his guest, 'Funnily enough, Papa and Lord Cardigan seemed to get on very well, I think mostly because they both like champagne.' Sir Walter Carew was last seen blowing his horn, cracking his whip, and shouting, 'Hark away!' to spur the couple on their conjugal errand. He was, according to his seventeen-year-old daughter, liable to become 'excited by champagne'.[20]

The 11th (Prince Albert's own) had returned from the Crimea in the summer of 1856, and the men were marched north to Sheffield. Though Cardigan was no longer the commander of the regiment, he kept up his association with it and the 11th, reflecting his own glory, became known as 'Cardigan's Bloodhounds'. On 29 July there was a grand dinner, given by the city of Sheffield at the Royal Hotel for the officers of the regiment, Cardigan being the principal guest. Those who were most put out at this celebration were not Cardigan's detractors but the citizens of Leeds, who had themselves hoped that the headquarters of the regiment would be stationed in their city and that it might fall to them to honour Cardigan as the creator of the most splendid mounted regiment in the British army.[21]

However, at the beginning of September there was another public banquet, held this time in Leeds, for the purpose of presenting Cardigan with a silver-gilt sword and an illuminated address on behalf of the people of Yorkshire. Again, Cardigan described to his audience the events of his service in the Crimea, and once more he was received with cheering and renewed cheering. Then, in a general hush, he revealed for the benefit of his friends and enemies alike that his conduct had always been approved by his great commander and friend, Lord Raglan, 'whose fall I so deeply deplore—whose memory I honour and revere—' At this point, according to the press, Cardigan was 'for a moment or two unable to proceed, from his extreme emotion.' However, 'on reviving', he managed to complete his speech, though when he came to name some of his comrades who had fallen at Balaclava, he had to pause again, 'from the intensity of his feelings'.[22]

He sat down at last to 'loud and continued cheers'. Whatever the Crimean commissioners, or Lord Lucan, or George Ryan might think, his hearers on such occasions as this found his performance irresistible. To his admirers, his public grief over the death of Raglan or the fallen of the Light Brigade was proof that compassion was no less strongly marked in him than courage or pride. To his enemies, such explosions of emotion, almost two years after the battle of Balaclava, were absurd and suspect. For a general to weep in public over the fate of his men was not at all the new style of doing things.

The last great ceremony of the war took place in Hyde Park on 26 June 1857. At a grand military review, the Queen distributed the newly-instituted Victoria Cross to those men who had won the honour in the Crimea. Sir Colin Campbell commanded the review, while the cavalry contingent of the Life Guards and the 11th Hussars was led by Cardigan. It was a solemn and proud conclusion to a war in which courage to endure administrative catastrophe had often seemed more relevant than the brave sacrifices of battle.

On this sunlit day of early summer in Hyde Park, as the ranks of red-coated foot-soldiers and the glittering squadrons of cavalry took their places, all the inquiries and the bickering were temporarily forgotten. The royal salute was fired, the last notes of the anthem died away. Then, in a great silence, the crowds stretching away in un-numbered ranks on every side of the park, the Queen presented the highest military honour to that 'aristocracy of the brave', as it was later called, who had shown courage beyond the call of duty. Among that band of heroes were Sergeant-Major John Grieve of the 2nd Dragoons; Private Samuel Parkes of the 4th Light Dragoons; Lieutenant Robert Alexander Dunn of the 11th Hussars; and Troop Sergeant-Major Berryman of the 17th Lancers. There were those who thought that Cardigan himself should have been one of the recipients, while their opponents retorted that such an opinion was unlikely to be held seriously by anyone but Cardigan himself. Yet when he appeared, on his Balaclava charger, leading the 11th Hussars past the Queen, the band playing the regimental slow march, 'Coburg', the enthusiasm of the crowds seemed to break all bounds. It was reminiscent of the Queen's Hyde Park review of 1856, when he had very nearly to be rescued from his own admirers as they swarmed across the review ground towards him.

Within a short period of the end of the war, it seemed evident that the charge of the Light Brigade and Cardigan's part in it was to be the sole enduring popular legend of the entire conflict. Indeed, the successive inquiries into the conduct of the war, and the way in which those inquiries continued to bring Cardigan before the public, were themselves aids to the stimulation of this hero-worship.

Literature and art, at the most popular levels, seized on the drama of Balaclava and purveyed it to the youth of future generations through such novels as G. A. Henty's *Jack Archer* or Escott Lynn's *Blair of Balaclava*. In popular patriotic histories like *Fights for the Flag* (the companion-piece to *Deeds That Won the Empire*) the story was more straightforwardly but stirringly told. It was predictable that the spectacle of such a cavalry charge would be a natural subject for the cinema, yet even the popular Victorian stage-entertainment managed to embody the action, in its own way. One evening after the war, those who happened to be in the vicinity of the Standard Theatre were thrown into a 'fever of alarm' by the sounds of 'Heavy discharges of artillery and musketry' coming from the building. The play was *Balaclava*, and the charge was staged by placing 'George Byrne', a friend of the hero, near the right upstage entrance, gazing into the wings and purporting to describe what he saw, to the accompaniment of the most deafening cannon fire which the stage manager and his assistants could produce.[23]

George	Why it's all over!
	No! No! The Light Brigade advance! *(General cheering.*
	What madness!
	They're going to charge the Russian guns! *(Murmurs of anxiety.*
	(Painful pause.) They've reached the guns! *(Cheers.*
	Bravo, 'Death or Glory Boys!'
	Well done, Eleventh! Frank is with them! *(Mustn't forget the hero.*
	Oh, look! The Russians have cut them all off!!!
	(Intense anxiety.
	No! They break *through* them!
	Bravo, Irish Hussars! *(Great relief and much cheering.*
	But, oh, how few return!
	Pray God that Frank be with them!
	(Pause.) Yes, he is here!!!! *(Cheering for Brigade.*

*(Frank staggers down centre, falls into arms of George Byrne.
Frank is wounded, pale and bleeding. He falls. Tableau and Act drop.)*

Wherever the glorious exploits of the Light Brigade were described, and however fancifully, Cardigan's name was connected with them. Whenever there was some public celebration of heroism in the Crimean campaign, there was one figure instantly recognized by the crowds as he rode upon Ronald, the chestnut horse which had carried him through the Russian guns. Raglan was dead, Lucan had withdrawn in anger and disappointment to his Irish estates at Castlebar. Sir Colin Campbell was in India, endeavouring to restore order amid the mutual blood-letting of the Mutiny. But Cardigan was in London, or Dublin, or Leeds, or wherever the stories of the Crimea were being told for the hundredth time at some public banquet. Men like Campbell belonged as much to the legend of Chillianwallah, or the news of the Mutiny, as to the events in Russia. Cardigan, however, was the complete Crimean officer, whose military reputation could rest upon no other campaign. If this made it easier for the public to single him out as the Crimean hero, it also meant that he had to guard this achievement more jealously than his comrades, for he had no other to compare with it.

2

If the inquiries and the bickering were forgotten on that solemn occasion of the Victoria Cross review, while homage was paid by the crowds to the courage of the living and the memory of 21,000 British soldiers in their Crimean graves, the squabbles were briskly re-animated as soon as the review was over. Cardigan's speech at the Leeds banquet had already been dismissed by *The Times* on 4 September 1856 as a falsification of history. The insult was ignored. Then Colonel Buck, MP, of the Devonshire Militia, made a speech at a dinner in honour of Colonel (formerly Captain) Morris of the 17th Lancers. Much of this speech was a comparison between the incompetent, self-seeking Earl of Cardigan, who had only achieved his rank by purchasing it for some £40,000, and the honest, brave Colonel Morris who had won promotion by his own merit. No one, according to Colonel Buck, impugned Morris's courage or soldierlike conduct. 'There was no necessity for him to explain his conduct like Lord Cardigan at Leeds.'

On 18 September Cardigan wrote indignantly to Buck for an explanation of his words. Buck replied on 20 September, claiming that the *Daily News* in reporting his speech had misheard him in part but not in whole. Cardigan replied again from Dublin on 25 September, saying that he was not satisfied with the explanation. Nor could he see what Morris had to complain about. Since the battle of Balaclava, he had been promoted without purchase to Lieutenant-Colonel, he had been made a Companion of the Bath, and had been given the post of Assistant Adjutant-General at the Curragh. 'A much more agreeable way of obtaining promotion than by paying £40,000', remarked Cardigan. 'This proves that Officers in the service do not obtain promotion by money alone.' As to Morris's dignified silence about the charge at Balaclava, 'it is clear that he never having been attacked by anonymous libellers had no ground for entering into any defence of his conduct.'

In his reply, Colonel Buck reminded Cardigan that accounts of his incompetence and implied cowardice, by George Ryan and others, were obtainable at any railway station bookstall. The quarrel between the two men reached the press, where Cardigan as usual found friends as well as enemies. The *Morning Post*, which professed to be bored beyond endurance by the attacks upon him from jealous rivals and their hired scribblers, remarked that since he rode so far out in front of the rest of the Brigade at Balaclava, it was a wonder that his more ingenious enemies had not yet suggested that he had been trying to desert to the Russians before the rest of the cavalry could catch him and bring him back.[24]

The affair of Colonel Buck petered out without challenges to duels or threats of court action. If it was resolved quickly and with remarkably little fuss, this was in part because Cardigan had already involved himself in another battle of reputations with Lord George Paget.

A correspondence had taken place in the *Morning Post* during June 1856, in which Lord George had described himself as being in command of the 4th Light Dragoons and the 11th Hussars during the Light Cavalry charge at Balaclava. The implication was that he had commanded not one regiment but a whole second line of the Brigade, and had brought the survivors of the attack safely out of the mêlée at the Russian guns, after Cardigan himself had withdrawn. This was a view firmly held by Lord George's friends and family. As Lord Alfred Paget remarked to W. H. Pennington of the 11th Hussars, 'Cardigan took you in, Pennington, but my brother George brought you out.'[25]

On 18 June 1856 Cardigan fired a warning shot by writing a private letter to Lord George and informing him that, 'Having formed, commanded, and led the Brigade in that attack, I cannot allow any written statement on the part of any officer present on the occasion, which I feel to be incorrect, to pass unmentioned.' In his view, it was Colonel John Douglas who had led the 11th Hussars, 'with great gallantry', while Lord George's part in the action had been confined to leading the 4th Light Dragoons. Douglas and his regiment had become separated from Lord George in the charge, so that to talk of the two regiments having fought as a single unit under the command of one man was clearly inaccurate. 'I think you will on reflection admit that the momentary conduct of two regiments under such circumstances could not invest any one officer with the command of the whole.'

On reflection, Lord George admitted nothing of the kind. He wrote from Albemarle Street the next day announcing that, 'I cannot perceive any error in my statement', and denying the accusation that, 'I assume to myself a position to which I am not entitled', or that, 'my remarks were uncalled for generally'. In turn, he accused Cardigan of trying to single out his own pet regiment, the 11th Hussars, for more praise than it actually deserved. Two days later, he received another letter from Portman Square, in which Cardigan remarked with chilly courtesy, 'It is not for me to repeat the opinion which I entertain', and then proceeded to argue in support of it.

'I cannot I fear acquiesce in the accuracy of your remarks', retorted Lord George. Cardigan summoned his duelling second, Colonel Douglas, and told him to go to Albemarle Street and convey the message that if there was any more correspondence of this kind, he, Cardigan, would send all the letters on both sides to the *Morning Post* with instructions that they were to be published. Lord George, confident of being in the right, told Cardigan to publish the letters forthwith, and there was something approaching a verbal flexing of muscles as each man prepared to do such things as should make his adversary regret that the argument had ever started.[26]

Surprisingly, the quarrel then seemed to resolve itself. But on 24 October Lord George wrote officially to the Duke of Cambridge, as Commander-in-Chief, complaining that Cardigan was seeking to belittle 'the heroic gallantry and devotion of the Officers, Non-commissioned Officers and Privates of the two Regiments that formed the second or supporting line'. As a member of the royal family, the Duke was anxious not to become involved in the kind of public spectacle which Cardigan's previous contretemps had provided. He instructed the Military Secretary at the Horse Guards to send a copy of Lord George's complaint to Cardigan, for comment. On 10 November there was an indignant response. Cardigan protested that he had praised Lord George's gallantry after the battle of Balaclava, 'But Lord George Paget is not satisfied with this, but claims a higher part than that which he really held in the attack; for I never can admit that he led a second line into action on that day—and in asserting this to be the case Lord George Paget has made several serious misrepresentations.'

But Lord George was soon pestering the Duke again with a demand that 'the services of the 4th Dragoons and 11th Hussars on that day should appear in their true light'. He also complained that at the time of the cavalry charge he had Cardigan's commands '"ringing in his ears" to the detriment of his better judgment'. Furious that comments of this kind about him should be addressed to the Commander-in-Chief, Cardigan wrote at once 'to take the liberty of bringing to the notice of H.R.H. the tone and tenor of Lord G. Paget's remarks upon his superior officer'. There was now, apparently, to be a call for disciplinary action against the second-in-command of the Light Brigade.[27]

Yet just as the quarrel with Colonel Buck had been overtaken by the larger quarrel with Lord George Paget, so this squabble in its turn was overshadowed by a more bitter feud, which was to provoke the biggest public debate on Cardigan's actions since the duel on Wimbledon Common and the court-martial of Captain R. A. Reynolds.

Ten days after his last letter to the Duke on the subject of Lord George's insubordination, Cardigan wrote again, in still more strident tones, 'to bring to the notice of H.R.H. the General Commanding-in-Chief, the manner in which the severest reflections and most malignant assertions have been cast on my professional character, as a General Officer in Her Majesty's service.' This time, the quarrel was not with Lord George, nor with Colonel Buck nor George Ryan, nor even with Lord Lucan. Cardigan demanded the Duke's permission 'to prefer charges, before a General Court-Martial, against Major the Honourable Somerset Calthorpe, for scandalous and disgraceful conduct, unbecoming the character of an Officer and a Gentleman, in publishing false and malicious statements against a General Officer.'

Calthorpe, a nephew of Lord Raglan, was a well-bred young cavalry officer who had served on the staff in the Crimea and was now aide-de-camp to another member of his family, Lord Carlisle, the Lord Lieutenant of Ireland. He was the semi-anonymous author of a two-volume work published by John Murray on 13 December 1856: *Letters from Head-Quarters: or, The Realities of the War in the Crimea. By an Officer on the Staff.* 'With regard to the conduct imputed to me in the Charge at Balaclava', wrote Cardigan bitterly of Calthorpe's book, 'I can only say that it is lamentable indeed, that I should have lived to see the day, when such disgraceful accusations should be brought against me.' Nevertheless, the Duke of Cambridge had no intention whatever of invoking court-martial proceedings in a case where the remedy, if any, lay in an action for libel.[28]

Major the Honourable Somerset Calthorpe had spared Cardigan's reputation in no way at all in the charges made against him.

1 After the battle of the Alma, according to Calthorpe, Cardigan had ordered the 8th Hussars to release the sixty or seventy Russians they had taken prisoners. Cardigan replied that the 8th Hussars were not under his orders at the time, and Calthorpe corrected the paragraph in the third edition of his book.[29]

2 Cardigan had failed to attack the Russian flank during the engagement of the Heavy Brigade at Balaclava, despite Lord Raglan's wishes and Captain Morris's advice. Cardigan replied that Raglan had never expressed such a wish and that Morris, at the time in question, 'never uttered one word upon the subject'. Calthorpe noted Cardigan's denial in his third edition but allowed the accusation to stand.[30]

3 At the Russian guns, 'This was the moment when a general was most required, but unfortunately Lord Cardigan was not then present.' According to Calthorpe, he was already galloping back to the safety of the British lines and was seen to do so by the 4th Light Dragoons and 8th Hussars who were still riding towards the Russians. This accusation that he was not present at the action in the Russian battery was the forerunner of shadowy rumours that he had either turned back in the face of the enemy's fire or else had never taken part in the charge at all, having breakfasted late on his yacht and only arrived in time to see the survivors of the charge returning down the valley at about half-past eleven. This was the bitterest accusation of all, and Calthorpe refused to withdraw it.[31]

4 On Cardigan's departure for England, Calthorpe noted ambig-

uously that he was 'totally unfit to continue in command of the light cavalry', a phrase which Cardigan deplored as 'a very offensive mode of notifying my resignation'. It was altered in the third edition.[32]

5 Calthorpe also included more recent comments, one made in the Crimea while Cardigan was being received as the hero of London.[33]

> I also see that Lord Cardigan has been feted at the Mansion-house, and made a speech on that occasion which has afforded considerable amusement and merriment amongst the officers of the Light Cavalry here, who naturally know better than any one else the very *prominent* part which his lordship took at the celebrated charge of Balaclava. I think I never read a more egotistical speech in my life, to say nothing of the wonderful way in which Lord Cardigan indulges his imagination. 'I' seems to have done everything, according to his statement. 'Damn his I's!' as a punning subaltern of hussars said, upon reading the earl's eloquence!

Cardigan made no attempt to answer the gibes at his Mansion House performance, contenting himself with maintaining that he had only done at Balaclava what any commander in his position must have done. When he described this to his listeners in England, he was merely describing his duty and not some remarkable act of personal bravery. He had, of course, said on every occasion that whatever honour might belong to the action was shared equally by every man of the Light Cavalry who charged the Russian guns. In the third edition of his book, Calthorpe removed the last two sentences of his paragraph but refused to alter the passage in any other way.

It was Calthorpe's distinction that he summed up all the criticisms of Cardigan's conduct in the war, which had already been made piece-meal by his other detractors. Cardigan, having failed to get Calthorpe court-martialled in December 1856, sent a mutual friend, Lord Burghersh (later Earl of Westmorland), to call upon the author and demand the withdrawal of the offensive passages from the book. Calthorpe reluctantly agreed to make some small alterations in due course, but he refused to alter a word in the second edition because Cardigan, by waiting a month after first publication before making his complaint, had left it too late. 'I don't see how it is possible now to withdraw anything from "Letters from Head-Quarters" as the 2nd Edition is printed', wrote Calthorpe to Burghersh. 'Why does Lord

Cardigan wait a whole month before asking for a contradiction? . . . He was trying, I suppose, to get a court-martial on me from the Horse Guards! . . . I can only express to you, my dear Frank, the regret I feel that you should be called upon to mix yourself up in this foolish affair.'[34]

Cardigan's distress was plain for the nation to see. He complained to the Duke of Cambridge again, and to Lord Panmure, the new Secretary for War, who replied that it would be best to let the matter drop. 'I cannot let his slanders pass unnoticed', said Cardigan privately to Burghersh on 9 January, and then proceeded to lament his predicament publicly to the House of Lords on 5 February, demanding rhetorically, 'Whether an officer who had thus disgraced himself, by publishing a statement containing allegations so gross, and so utterly devoid of a vestige of truth, should be allowed to draw even half-pay from the public purse?' For lack of a satisfactory answer from Lord Panmure, Cardigan wrote to Lord Carlisle, Lord Lieutenant of Ireland, asking him to dismiss Calthorpe as his aide-de-camp. The response from Dublin Castle on 7 March was cool and abrupt. 'I cannot consent to dismiss a friend, a relation, and a young officer who has lost his chief patron, in defending whom he may have shown himself too little scrupulous in attacking others.'[35]

And all this time successive editions of Calthorpe's book were stacked high on the bookstalls of Britain's railway stations. In consequence, as Cardigan's friends warned him, it was hardly possible to travel in a first-class carriage where a copy of the book was being read without hearing his name spoken of sneeringly and in terms of derogation.

Yet for all this, the honours of a grateful country, and more especially a grateful Horse Guards, continued to be bestowed upon him. In August 1859 he was appointed to the honorary command of Colonel of the 5th Dragoon Guards, upon the death of Sir John Slade. There was satisfaction among his friends at this gesture of official approval, though the Radical press glowed with indignation at the conferring upon him of 'a sinecure office, worth about 1,000*l.* a year, and instituted as a reward for old and meritorious General Officers, whose income may require to be eked out by a pension from the public.'

The *Examiner* remarked with bitter irony that to some who knew no better it might seem that many other generals in the British army had a better claim to the appointment than Cardigan, either through longer service or greater financial need.[36]

It will hardly be contended, however, that men who have passed their lives in remote and vulgar places, in India, at the Cape, or in the West Indies, for instance, can be considered to possess claims to a pension equal to those of one who has served at Windsor or Brighton under the immediate eye of the Sovereign, and in close proximity to the Horse Guards. So far from Lord Cardigan not having earned the substantial honour about to be conferred upon him, we consider him every bit as much entitled to it as he is to the Order of the Bath, which he wears, or the Victoria Cross, to which he aspired.

There was indignation among Cardigan's admirers, both at the sneer of the *Examiner* and the insinuation that Cardigan was to receive £1,000 a year, when it was generally known that such colonelcies of cavalry regiments carried no more than about £100 a year. At that rate, it would have taken him a very long time to recoup even a substantial fraction of his own money which he had spent on the men and equipment under his command.[37]

Yet the jibes of the Radical press were nothing compared with the trials awaiting Cardigan in the 5th Dragoons. No sooner had he accepted the appointment than Major Calthorpe applied to exchange into the regiment and, in effect, to become its second-in-command. Cardigan's astonishment was such that he could hardly believe Calthorpe was doing this for any other reason than to persecute him. On 12 November 1859 he wrote an anguished letter direct to the Duke of Cambridge. He reminded the Commander-in-Chief that he had been 'calumniated in the most flagrant and offensive manner' by Calthorpe's book. To have the libeller appointed to his own regiment, in this fashion, was beyond endurance. He begged the Duke to intervene with the Queen, if necessary, to prevent Calthorpe's exchange, 'trusting to your Royal Highness's known sense of justice, and in this case common justice to me, you will reconsider this obnoxious appointment.'[38]

Almost at once, news of this letter reached Calthorpe. Following strict military protocol, he did not write direct to the Duke but to Sir Charles Yorke, the Military Secretary at the Horse Guards. He courteously but firmly rejected Cardigan's charges against him, insisting that he might have been 'indiscreet' in his book but nothing more than that. His future conduct in the 5th Dragoons would show that he was 'actuated by no personal feeling against his Lordship'.[39]

Cardigan had made himself so ill with anxiety and vexation, at the prospect of having to serve with the man who had libelled him, that he remained prostrate in his town house in Portman Square. Yet he revived sufficiently to write to the Adjutant-General at the Horse Guards, asking him to intervene with the Duke to prevent the exchange. But the truth was that the Duke, for all his initial enthusiasm in the Crimea, was already becoming that stock figure of aristocratic stupidity, who commanded the British army almost until the time of the Boer War, warming his large bottom before the fire at the Horse Guards and declaiming that any change, at any time, for any purpose, was highly to be deprecated. He refused to intervene on Cardigan's behalf.

Sick with rage and mortification, Cardigan was driven from Portman Square to the Horse Guards, where he confronted the Duke of Cambridge, face to face. The Duke, knowing Cardigan's reputation for pugnacity, chose to treat the whole matter as if it were a great joke, and said light-heartedly, 'Why, if you consider yourself aggrieved, have you not "called out" Major Calthorpe?'

Without stopping to explain the various reasons which made it impolitic for him to shoot Calthorpe just then, Cardigan hurried back to Portman Square and addressed a final appeal, direct to Prince Albert. He proposed to take it down to Windsor and hand it over personally but he was in too distressed a state to travel. He complained to the Prince that he had been unable 'to obtain any redress at the hands of His Royal Highness the General Commanding in Chief', in a matter which the Prince must understand was 'so offensive to my feelings'. Then he issued an ultimatum to the Prince. Either the Calthorpe exchange must be reconsidered, or else he would use his 'Privilege as a Peer', to demand an interview with the Queen herself, in a manner which might be guaranteed to 'cause annoyance to Her Majesty'.[40]

There were consultations between Windsor and the Horse Guards. If Calthorpe were to be refused his exchange when permission for it had already been granted, there was likely to be a public scandal. If Cardigan was made to accept Calthorpe in the 5th Dragoons, there might be a much greater scandal which would end, like the Black Bottle incident of 1840, in an exchange of shots on Wimbledon Common. Then, surprisingly, the protests and the assurances ceased together. Calthorpe's exchange was confirmed and, apparently, accepted by Cardigan. The reason for this was clear enough a few months later when Cardigan, resigning from the 5th Dragoons, was appointed to one of the greatest military honours that he could have coveted. He was to be Colonel of the 11th (Prince Albert's own) Hussars. He retired from his appointment as Inspector-General of Cavalry in 1860, but he retained his honorary colonelcy of the 11th Hussars for the rest of his life, and was also promoted to the rank of Lieutenant-General in 1861.

The second edition of Calthorpe's book had appeared in January 1857, and the third edition, which was revised and condensed into a single volume, was published by John Murray in the following December. By now the controversy centred on a single passage in this final edition where, according to Calthorpe, Cardigan had not led his men at the Russian battery. 'This was the moment when a general was most required, but Lord Cardigan was not then present.' In the first edition, Calthorpe had suggested that Cardigan's horse had been frightened by a Russian gun, fired close to the animal's head as it approached the battery, and had bolted back to the British lines, taking Cardigan with it. In reply to Cardigan's protests, Calthorpe added a footnote at this point in the third edition, remarking, 'but as the excellence of Lord Cardigan's horsemanship is unquestionable, the idea that his horse ran away with him is no doubt erroneous!' The clear implication was that, if the horse had not bolted, Cardigan had deliberately turned about in the face of the Russian guns, and had ridden for the safety of the British lines, while most of his men were still riding towards the enemy. In this respect, the third edition of the book was worse than the first two.[41]

Cardigan called on Sir George Wombwell, Sir Thomas M'Mahon of the 5th Dragoons, the Honourable Frederick Calthorpe (brother of the book's author), and his own brother-in-law, Hubert De Burgh. They were all sent to Calthorpe to demand a public retraction of the libel.

Only De Burgh took the mission seriously. He met Calthorpe in Cadogan Place in May 1861 and asked him to publish 'some statement that might soothe Lord Cardigan'. Calthorpe dismissed the idea as impossible. After 'vigorous arguments', Calthorpe said,

'Well, I will tell you what I will do: I will undertake to say that but few more copies shall be issued from my publisher's, but I cannot recall those in circulation. If Lord Cardigan cares to pay for the few copies that may be in circulation, of course he can do so. It will make no difference to me whether he does or not, as I imagine whatever copies may be in the possession of various booksellers they will have to pay Mr Murray for, whether they sell them or not.'

The market for the book had already been amply supplied by this time, and Cardigan was unlikely to be 'soothed' by a peremptory suggestion that he might care to buy up any remaining copies which the booksellers still had on their hands. There were further sheets which Murray had not bound, since there had been no call for them, and these were destroyed in any case. Later in the summer of 1861, however, Calthorpe met De Burgh, while they were both riding in Rotten Row, and told him of this. According to Calthorpe, De Burgh replied, 'Well, I think Lord Cardigan ought to be satisfied now', though Calthorpe qualified this in evidence by saying that De Burgh spoke 'words to that effect'.[42]

Cardigan was very far from satisfied. In 1860 he had instructed his solicitors, Ward and Mills, of Gray's Inn Square, to seek counsel's opinion as to the possibility of bringing proceedings against Calthorpe for a criminal libel, which might conceivably get Calthorpe sent to gaol. Bovill, the QC to whom the matter was referred, advised that it would 'not be expedient' and suggested that it might be 'a more dignified course for his lordship not to come into a court of law upon the subject'. As Cardigan wrote to Richard Mills a few days later, he was interested less in dignity than in redress, but 'I shall not succeed in obtaining it in the manner suggested by Mr Bovill.'

Finally, on 4 February 1863, Cardigan's solicitors wrote to Calthorpe demanding that his book, which was still available, should be withdrawn, and that he should make a public retraction of the allegations to which objection had been taken. If he failed to comply with these requirements, application would be made to the Court of Queen's Bench for a criminal information against him. Calthorpe replied the next day, rejecting the demands, and proceedings for criminal libel were instituted.

Both sides busied themselves in collecting evidence and affidavits from those who had witnessed the charge of the Light Brigade nine years earlier. Lord Lucan was, predictably, among the witnesses who offered their evidence to Calthorpe. The news that he had been so infamously 'calumniated' by his detested brother-in-law drove Cardigan to seek a more personal redress than any offered by the courts. He issued a challenge, inviting Lucan to travel to Paris and settle the matter with pistols in the Bois de Boulogne, beyond the reach of the English law.

Friends of both men were appalled by the proposed spectacle of two elderly English generals shooting out their differences in the French capital. Yet though Cardigan was now sixty-six years old and Lucan only three years younger, the call to honour was evidently not to be denied. Lucan left for Paris with a brace of pistols, Cardigan, however, was delayed while urgent representations were made to him, as the challenger, either to withdraw the challenge or to settle the matter in some less ludicrous and dangerous manner. But finally he set off for France. Lucan, however, had been waiting with some impatience. When he felt that he had waited long enough, he returned to England, just as Cardigan arrived in Paris. The threatened tragedy dissolved in farce. Lucan wrote an insulting letter about Cardigan to General Brotherton. Cardigan also wrote to Brotherton about Lucan, deploring the refusal of 'men of the *present day*' to fight. '*The not being able to fight* is a very convenient pretext with all of them.'[43]

Yet patrician Victorians were able to use the courts of law with something of the same relish which their ancestors might have felt for the battlefield or the duelling ground. After a preliminary hearing in April, Cardigan's action against Calthorpe came on in Westminster Hall on 9 June 1863, when Bovill applied for a criminal information to be laid against the defendant. Lord Chief Justice Cockburn and three other judges of the Queen's Bench heard the case. The Court of Queen's Bench was still held in the medieval courtroom at Westminster with its large Gothic windows, its carved figures in their niches above the judges' bench, and the semicircle of benches on which the wigged barristers who had no brief sat in considerable numbers behind those conducting the case. If the charge of the Light Brigade was to be re-enacted, there could hardly have been a more bizarre setting than this elongated room with its heavy panelling, cases of law books, its shafts of June sunlight falling from ornate windows through an atmosphere of dust and slow legal voices, where Sir Alexander Cockburn presided with a mural behind him of the lion and the unicorn supporting the royal arms of England.

Serjeant Shee, for Calthorpe, did his best to show that the material complained of in the third edition of the book was not libellous, but this argument was quickly discounted by the Lord Chief Justice. The discussion was thereafter confined to the factual question of whether Cardigan had, or had not, turned back in the face of the Russian guns.

If Calthorpe's statement were true, then according to the law as amended by the Libel Act of 1843, he had a complete defence. Before 1843 it had been no defence merely to show that the statement complained of was true.

Calthorpe asserted in evidence, which he gave by way of affidavit and could not therefore be cross-examined, that he had 'serious difficulty' in obtaining witnesses to substantiate his allegation. 'Some of my most important witnesses are dead, some are serving in India and in the colonies, and some object to give positive evidence on events which happened so long since. A still more serious difficulty in my way in obtaining affidavits is the reluctance of military men of all ranks to give voluntary evidence affecting the character of an officer in the high and influential position of the Earl of Cardigan.'[44]

No such inhibitions had prevented Lord Lucan from coming forward and swearing that he had seen his brother-in-law gallop back from the attack while his men were still fighting for their lives at the Russian guns, and that Cardigan had not then reappeared from the safety of the British end of the valley until the engagement was over. A number of troopers of Lord George Paget's 4th Light Dragoons also swore that they had seen Cardigan riding back on their left before they had even reached the guns.

Yet in its sheer weight of evidence, Cardigan's case was far the more impressive of the two. He had been seen by too many troopers at the guns for his presence there to be doubted. As to the moment at which he withdrew, Sir James Scarlett, who commanded the Heavy Brigade in covering the Light Brigade's retreat, gave evidence that Cardigan was among the last men of the two regiments under his immediate command to leave the Russian guns.[45]

Maps and models of the battlefield of Balaclava were produced, and the contradictory memories of the events were examined. Having heard the evidence and the arguments on both sides, Lord Chief Justice Cockburn delivered his judgment.

'I can entertain no doubt that the passage in Colonel Calthorpe's work on which the present application has been made for a criminal information contains a most serious libel on the Earl of Cardigan.' Moreover, in Cockburn's view, the note in the third edition, which acknowledged that Cardigan's horse had not bolted of its own accord, was 'the bitterest sarcasm . . . an imputation of my Lord Cardigan having been wanting in personal courage in the discharge of his duty.'[46]

The defence that the statement was true was, according to Cockburn, disproved by the affidavits on both sides. The argument that the publication of Calthorpe's book was somehow privileged, as being in the public interest, was also dismissed. He was in no way entitled 'to deal recklessly and rashly with the character of others'. But the third point for the defence was that Cardigan had waited too long after the publication of the book—five years since the third edition—before bringing the proceedings. It was true that he had tried to settle the dispute by other means but, in law, Cockburn and the other judges were unanimous in their decision that he could not be given leave at so late a time to lay a criminal information against Calthorpe. The judges seemed to reach this decision more readily when they heard that Calthorpe, two years earlier, had consented to the destruction of the remaining unbound copies of the third edition of his book. His motives might have been as much commercial as legal, but it appeared to the court to be a point in his favour.[47]

Cardigan therefore lost the technical victory and was unable to take further legal action against Calthorpe. But he won a moral victory which was far greater and which was recognized by the court itself. Turning to Cardigan's detractors, the Lord Chief Justice remarked, 'Those who criticise the conduct of a public man placed in such trying circumstances, would perhaps do well to ask themselves how they would have acted in a similar state of things.'

At this there was applause, which was loudly renewed as Sir Alexander Cockburn delivered his opinion on Cardigan's reputation as presented by the evidence.[48]

> There may be those who will say, Lord Cardigan, as a general, is open to criticism, but it should be a generous and liberal criticism, not one that should seek to cast a stain upon his courage and his personal honour as an officer. I cannot help, therefore, rejoicing, feeling as I said before, that the reputation and honour of every man who took a part in that great scene should be dear to us all (*applause*), and that this opportunity has been afforded of setting Lord Cardigan right in the estimation, not only of his own profession, but of the public generally.

Calthorpe had won his case and lost his cause, while Cardigan had seen his courage and honour vindicated, and his finances relieved of the burden of further proceedings against his adversary. There was unspoken relief, perhaps, that no prosecution of Calthorpe could be undertaken. He was not only a man of good family but had been promoted Lieutenant-Colonel and was the effective commander of the 5th Dragoons. His public trial would have been a blow to himself, his regiment, to the reputation of the army, and certainly to Cardigan.

From the press, including such papers as the *Globe*, which had often been among Cardigan's critics, there was almost complete approval of the vindication of his conduct at Balaclava. As *The Times* remarked, 'The Battle of Balaclava has been fought over again in the Court of Queen's Bench, and this time Lord Cardigan remains master of the field.' Several papers competed in their attempts to celebrate the style of Cardigan's victory. *Lloyd's Weekly London Newspaper* burst into stanzas composed by the proprietor himself on the subject of 'Cardigan's Steed'. Nine years after Balaclava, the heroism of the Light Brigade and its leader stirred the hearts of mid-Victorian England as surely as when the story was first told.[49]

> Though Cardigan knew, as onward they flew,
> That death was the lord of the plain,
> With bravery great as any of old,
> Who knows of a braver deed?
> For his country's cause the warrior bold
> Flew on with his gallant steed.

Yet there was one evening paper, which had had longer to reflect upon the verdict than its morning contemporaries, and which sounded a more cautious note. The editor of the *Sun* remarked that Cardigan might have won his victory, but Calthorpe had not acknowledged it by any formal apology. Moreover, even though Calthorpe had been silenced, there were other powerful enemies who had not yet been heard from, 'congenial spirits, say men like Mr. Alexander Kinglake, the member for Bridgewater'. These were men whose pastime was to impugn the courage of soldiers who had actually fought the enemy, while they had watched from a safe distance. The first volume of Kinglake's *Invasion of the Crimea* had already been published. He would shortly reach the point at which he had to deal with the story of Balaclava.[50]

The military press had been entirely on Cardigan's side in the Calthorpe affair. Among these papers was the *Army and Navy Gazette*, edited by William Howard Russell, who had been *The Times* correspondent in the Crimea. Following the result of the case in the Court of Queen's Bench, Cardigan approached Russell privately to persuade him to denounce Calthorpe's witnesses in an editorial in the *Army and Navy Gazette*. Russell had already published an editorial, favourable to Cardigan, on the subject of the case and had actually shown it to Cardigan before publication.

'I think the writing excellent', replied Cardigan. 'I don't think enough is said about the 4th Lt Dragoons swearing that I returned by the left of that regiment which is an impossibility and renders their affidavits worth nothing . . . Please don't say more about Ld. Lucan than I recommended . . . at least nothing which would lead to a correspondence between him and me—I wish to avoid it at this moment.'

Russell's attitude, as he described it to Cardigan, was sympathetic but not uncritical. 'You will find there is every disposition on my part—and it is a humble one—to do your Lordship justice and though I cannot be a partizan, I can at least put things right to a certain extent in a matter where you have been most unjustly assailed.'

Cardigan invited Russell to meet him at the Carlton Club, but Russell was too busy with the paper to come. He invited Cardigan to the Garrick Club, but Cardigan replied that he 'would not like to go to the Garrick'. At length, they met in Portman Square and Russell advised Cardigan to let the matter of Lucan's evidence drop, 'unless you have some irrefutable evidence that Lord Lucan was mistaken'. Cardigan then read out some notes of his own, attacking Lucan's evidence, and seemed to have in mind that these should be inserted in an editorial in the *Army and Navy Gazette*, as though they came from Russell himself. Russell, horrified at the thought of having to publish editorials under his own name which were in fact written by Cardigan, refused to have anything further to do with the matter. Cardigan was later to explain to him that he did not intend the notes to be published as the editor's views but merely as additions of his own to the affidavits sworn by his witnesses in the case against Calthorpe. The two men parted on terms of uneasy friendship.[51]

However, in June 1863 Calthorpe published a pamphlet, issued by John Murray and containing all the affidavits on his own side with his comments upon them. This was done because, according to Calthorpe's complaint, his affidavits had not been reported by the press 'as fully and accurately as those filed by Lord Cardigan'. Cardigan replied with a *Statement and Remarks upon the Affidavits Filed by Lieut-Col. Calthorpe*. Apart from further affidavits to prove Cardigan's presence at the Russian guns, it included a letter written before the trial to Calthorpe by Captain G. W. Hunt. But Calthorpe had refused to make use of the letter. Hunt, who had served with the 4th Light Dragoons, explained that the men of his regiment had indeed passed an officer in the uniform of the 11th Hussars riding back to the British lines before they had even reached the Russian battery. The officer was not only dressed in a uniform similar to Cardigan's, but he rode a chestnut horse which was very like Cardigan's own charger. However, Hunt had recognized the officer and had seen that he was not Cardigan but Lieutenant Haughton, who had been wounded in the head. 'I think that was the officer who was taken for Lord Cardigan by the men of the 4th and 8th.'[52]

Equally interesting evidence came from the investigations on Cardigan's behalf by Captain John Chadwick, Adjutant of the 17th Lancers after Balaclava. Chadwick produced a statement by Charles Whyte of Dublin, formerly a private in the 8th Hussars. Whyte swore that he had been approached by a solicitor's clerk, acting for Calthorpe, who 'wanted to upset Lord Cardigan, and asked me if I could give any information to help them, as, if so, it might be a few pounds in my pocket.'

Whyte, who had seen Cardigan behaving 'most nobly and bravely' in the Balaclava charge, refused. However, two weeks later the solicitor's clerk called upon him again, saying that there were 'a lot of them going over to London together on the trial, and that as they had already beaten Lord Cardigan, I might as well go with them and have a jolly good spree.'[53]

Chadwick, like Whyte, admired Cardigan for his conduct in battle, and was one of those who since the publication of Calthorpe's book had 'often had the mortification of hearing personally and otherwise in Railway Carriages and other places your Lordship called everything but a soldier in consequence.' Chadwick investigated further as to the motives of the men of the 4th Light Dragoons who had given evidence for Calthorpe. He discovered from Daniel Deeran, who was Barrack Policeman of the regiment, that 'the chief inducement held out to them by Colonel Calthorpe's agent was as Deeran expressed it "the spree they were to have had in going to London".'[54]

Yet beyond the immediate circumstances of the case, the unresolved feud between Cardigan and Lucan persisted. It hardly seemed that it could be terminated except by the death of one or other of them, either at the hands of his rival or through natural causes. To Cardigan's dismay, four months after the Calthorpe case, Lucan was invited to be chairman of the Balaclava Day dinner at the London Tavern on 25 October 1868. A score of surviving senior officers attended, with the exception of Cardigan who refused to appear in public at any function where he might come face to face with his brother-in-law. On the eve of the dinner he wrote a cautionary letter to General Scarlett, 'to impress upon you the expediency of not allowing Lord Lucan to enter into any explanation or dispute with you upon the subject of Balaclava in the presence of the officers assembled. He is a loud talker on all matters and would no doubt attempt to lead those present astray.' Scarlett replied a few days later, assuring Cardigan that there had been no unhappy references to 'past events'. He added that Cardigan himself had been proposed as chairman for the following year when, presumably, Lord Lucan would stay at home.[55]

In 1861, the year following his retirement as Inspector-General of Cavalry, Cardigan had published a little book, *Cavalry Brigade Movements*, a drill manual for mounted regiments. When, in the same year, the Horse Guards set up a Board of Officers to consider reforms in the Hussars and the Light Dragoons, he was offended not to be chosen as a member. Upon complaining to the Military Secretary, he was told that the Board might naturally be glad to hear his views but that it was out of the question for him to have any part in making the decisions. No one at the Horse Guards can have been surprised that when these decisions were announced, Cardigan disagreed loudly with most of them. Yet his disagreement was in many respects very sensible. It was proposed to abolish the individual facings of Light Dragoon regiments. According to Cardigan, who had practical experience of the matter, this would gain nothing and would make it more difficult for a commander to distinguish quickly between his regiments in the confusion of an actual battle. It was also proposed to transform the 3rd and 4th Dragoons into Lancers. Cardigan dismissed this as foolish, since greater height was required in the Lancers and the present recruits would either be too short to use lances effectively, or else there would have to be a long and laborious programme of entirely reconstituting the two regiments.

Yet more than membership of Horse Guards committees, Cardigan still hoped for some emblem of royal approval to set the seal upon his military career. In September 1868, he happened to be at Spa, in Belgium, with its long drives and promenades, its famous chalybeate baths and casino. *The Times* of 10 September arrived a day late, bearing the news of the death of Lord Beauchamp, Colonel of the 2nd Life Guards. Cardigan wrote at once to Major-General Forster of the Household Brigade. 'I hope that in the disposal of honours connected with the command of the Cavalry regiments of the Household Brigade in which in the common course of human nature there must ere long be several vacancies, that in my position as a Peer and a General I may not be overlooked.' General Forster replied tersely that the appointment of a Colonel to the 2nd Life Guards 'will not cause any change in Cavalry'.[56]

At White's Club, Lord Frederick Fitzroy bet Sir W. Fraser 'that a certain noble Lord is never Colonel of a household Cavalry regiment. £5 to £1'. It was better than the odds of 10–1 offered at White's before the Crimean War, but Lord Fitzroy could still be reasonably certain of retaining his £5.[57]

It was generally known that Cardigan had not improved his chances of a command in the Household Brigade by his behaviour in Germany, where he had been sent to accompany the young Prince of Wales, the future Edward VII, to Prussian army manoeuvres. The pride and pugnacity of Cardigan was a match for the self-conscious arrogance of the Prussian officers. Major-General the Honourable Robert Bruce, who led the party as Governor to the Prince of Wales, discovered with dismay that the hero of the Light Brigade was soon giving or receiving offence on all sides. Cardigan quickly compiled a list of affairs of honour to be settled with those Prussians whom he proposed to shoot before returning to England. The Prince was informed and, on the advice of General Bruce, he sent Cardigan home forthwith.[58]

Yet for all his quarrelsome reputation, there were moments when Cardigan on the threshold of old age seemed to allow his natural pride and belligerence to be overcome, suddenly and unaccountably, by kindlier sentiments. Each year, in June, the annual dinner of the 11th Hussars was held at the Clarendon Hotel in Bond Street, attended by past and present officers of the regiment. In 1865, the dinner was a very special one, since it seemed that the 11th Hussars would shortly be ordered to India, where they might serve for many years before returning to England again. It was certain that a large number of those present at the dinner were assembling with their comrades for the last time in their lives.

As the guests gathered and waited in this highly-charged emotional atmosphere, before dinner was announced, Cardigan was conspicuous among them. Though his hair was white, there was no mistaking the upright figure with the thin, high-bridged nose and the piercing blue eyes. An ex-surgeon of the regiment, O'Callaghan, approached him and told him that among the other guests was the former Captain J. W. 'Black Bottle' Reynolds. O'Callaghan suggested that it would be a first-rate opportunity to forget the twenty-five-year-old quarrel, and to shake hands as comrades.

'You ought to know better than to ask such a thing!' said Cardigan gruffly. 'Quite impossible!'

'But you are both old men', insisted O'Callaghan. 'Why nurse this miserable quarrel to the grave?'

Cardigan thought for a moment and then asked suspiciously, 'Will he come up to me?'

'Yes, he is only too anxious to do so.'

'Bring him up, O'Callaghan,' said Cardigan at last.

Reynolds, who had eventually held a staff appointment at the Horse Guards, came forward. As the other guests watched, he and Cardigan, who had been such sworn enemies a quarter of a century before, grasped each other's hands. For a moment, neither of them seemed able to find words for the occasion. Then, as they stood there, dinner was announced, and the two old soldiers walked in and sat down together, still hand in hand, like children.[59]

CHAPTER 10

ADELINE

1

In the last years of his life, it seemed that Cardigan had left himself little scope for spurning social morality, or diverting the newspaper public by further improprieties. Yet since the end of the Crimean War, his association with Balaclava had merely eclipsed another area of his life, which was destined to be revealed in a blaze of controversy and gossip.

The circumstances of his first marriage, his elopement with a brother officer's wife and the subsequent divorce proceedings, had been embellished by the criminal conversation suit over his adultery with Lady Frances Paget, and by numerous stories and anecdotes. The young and beautiful wife of Sir William Leeson had run off with Cardigan and had actually died on board his yacht, an embarrassment which might have been the high point of scandal in the life of any man whose other claims to public attention were not so overpowering.

The effect of Cardigan upon young women, by his mere physical presence, was never in doubt. Nor was their effect upon him. His advancing age seemed to make little difference to this mutual fascination. Lady Augusta Fane remembered how, as a schoolgirl, she had been allowed to come down to dessert at the end of dinner, 'to be seen and not heard'. There, sitting next to her mother, was a 'tall, smart-looking old gentleman', whose 'wonderful personality' so impressed itself upon the young Lady Augusta that she remembered this meeting with Cardigan for the rest of her life. Lady Dorothy Nevill recalled seeing him in Rotten Row, after his retirement from the army, a splendid figure in a semi-military costume, immaculate in white gloves and gold spurs. 'He invariably carried a riding switch in his hand—to be used either on the back of his horse, or on the back of any person who might be unlucky enough to provoke the noble earl's resentment.'[1]

Cardigan was still separated from his wife, but soon after the Crimean War he was seen riding in the Park with an extraordinarily beautiful young woman of hardly half his own age. Her name was Adeline Horsey de Horsey, daughter of Admiral Spencer de Horsey and his wife Louisa, who was herself the daughter of Lord Stadbroke. Adeline, in her close-fitting riding costume, with her fine figure, delicate hands and feet, beautiful legs and dark expressive eyes set in a face of elegant prettiness, was an unmistakable companion.

As a child, her family had been close enough to royalty for Adeline to attend the children's party given for the young Princess Victoria, who was her elder by five years. At twenty-five, she had been engaged to marry the Count Montemolin, Carlist pretender to the Spanish throne, but as his chances of ever occupying the throne seemed to diminish steadily, the engagement was broken off. Montemolin was almost forgotten by the time that Adeline met Cardigan. Yet such was Cardigan's sensitivity towards rivals in matters of love, that when the unfortunate Count died in 1860, he assured Adeline with relish that Montemolin had been secretly poisoned.

Adeline spoke five languages, was an accomplished singer and pianist and had written an orchestral score for an opera at the precocious age of fifteen. It was said that she could go to a Wagner opera and, on coming home afterwards, play through the entire work by memory on the piano. More to the point, she was a natural member of the fast, sporting society of the Victorian age. 'Skittles', the celebrated courtesan and herself a member of the Quorn, referred to Adeline as the 'head of our profession'.

In 1842, when Adeline was seventeen, Lady Louisa decided that the time was right for her daughter's 'coming out'. Accordingly, the girl appeared at the Buckingham Palace *bal poudré* of that year, and at that of 1845, to which Cardigan went as an eighteenth-century dragoon. Soon afterwards she and her mother visited Deene. In the following year, Lady Louisa died and the girl was left in the somewhat uncertain care of her father, Admiral Spencer de Horsey.

Cardigan was a close friend of the de Horsey family before the Crimean War, since he and the Admiral were both members of the

Royal Yacht Squadron, and he witnessed a good deal of Spencer de Horsey's blustering and ineffectual attempts to deal with Adeline's waywardness. When the girl asked to be taken to the Princess's Theatre to see 'a rather *risqué* play', her father's refusal was evasive.

'Quite impossible, Adeline—I am dining with General Cavendish at the Club, a long standing engagement. And even if I were disengaged, I should not think of taking my daughter to see such a play; nothing, my dear, is so degrading as a public display of lax morals, and it is the duty of every self-respecting person to discountenance such a performance. Let me hear no more about it.'

Determined not to be put down in this manner, Adeline booked a box for the evening and went secretly to the theatre with her maid. Just before the curtain rose, the door of the box opened and Cardigan strode in, looking 'rather agitated'.

'Miss de Horsey, you must leave the theatre at once.'

'I'll do no such thing', said Adeline indignantly. 'What on earth is the matter?'

With some reluctance, Cardigan explained.

'Well—well, Miss de Horsey, your father and General Cavendish are in the box opposite—with—with their mistresses! It will never do for you to be seen. Do, I implore you, permit me to escort you home before the performance begins.'

Ignoring Cardigan for a moment, the girl hastily trained her opera-glasses on the opposite box, where her father and the General sat with 'two very pretty women'.

'I *shall* see the play', she announced to Cardigan, 'and you'll put me into a cab before it is over. I shall be home before Papa returns from—the "Club".'

In the middle of the last act, Cardigan obediently put Adeline and her maid into a hackney carriage and ordered the driver to take them home to 8 Upper Grosvenor Street, Mayfair. After a long drive, however, the two passengers discovered with dismay that they were in the middle of Islington, in thick fog, and that the driver was drunk. When they at last reached Upper Grosvenor Street, the Admiral was waiting.

'Adeline, explain yourself. Where have you been? Is this an hour for a young lady to be out of doors? How dare you conduct yourself in this manner?'

'I've been to the Princess's Theatre, Papa,' said Adeline demurely, 'and I saw you and General Cavendish there; I thought you were dining at the Club . . . and I saw . . .'

'Go to bed at once, Adeline,' said the Admiral sheepishly, 'we'll talk about your behaviour later.'

But, as Adeline remarked, the subject was never mentioned again.[2]

The fateful moment for Adeline and Cardigan was when she and her father were members of a house party at Deene, in January 1857. The girl had often been invited to the great parties at Deene or Portman Square during the season, but on those occasions Cardigan had treated her 'quite like a *jeune fille*'. By 1857, however, it was clear that the other women at Deene regarded her as their rival, and with some justification. She recalled entering a room in which the Duchess of Montrose, Lady Villiers, and Mrs Dudley Ward were pressing their attentions upon the hero of Balaclava. The group turned towards her, the three ladies regarding her 'with none too friendly eyes'. Yet Cardigan swore that it was in that moment that he recognized Adeline as 'the one woman in the world' for him. 'He was an impulsive character, and he lost no time in letting me see the impression I had made, and I was flattered and delighted to feel that I was loved by him.'[3]

When the house party was over, the Admiral and his daughter returned to London, closely pursued by the sixty-year-old Earl of Cardigan, who proceeded to lay siege to their house in Upper Grosvenor Street with all the impetuosity that had carried him through the Russian guns. The Admiral soon heard the gossip about his daughter and he warned her fretfully that he would leave London and take her with him, if the intrigue continued. Adeline bluntly refused to go. Though confined to the house, she perfected a method of exchanging endearments with her lovesick cavalier by letting down from the window a length of string weighted with a coal from the fireplace and carrying a message. Like some competitor in a medieval tournament, Cardigan came riding past, snatched the message from the string and replaced the paper with a *billet doux* of his own.[4]

This rather public wooing lasted for only a little while. Then Adeline, having an income of her own, left her father's house and took rooms for a while in a small hotel in Hyde Park Square. Soon afterwards, Cardigan installed her as his mistress in a furnished house in Norfolk Street, Park Lane. They rode together in the Park, cut by all respectable society, but hardly to be ignored either for the handsomeness of their appearance or for Adeline's vivid riding-habits in bright green silk and violet or black velvet, always accompanied by a hat decorated with tall, swaying plumes.

Having defied her father and her brothers, Adeline lived for eighteen months as Cardigan's mistress, attended by the valet and three servants who had followed her to Norfolk Street. She was the more determined to have her own way because she knew that the health of Elizabeth, Countess of Cardigan was deteriorating quickly and that, on her death, there would be bitter competition for the hand of Cardigan himself. On 12 July 1858, just before seven o'clock in the morning, Adeline was asleep in the Norfolk Street house. She woke to hear a thunderous knocking on the door. The servants were up already, pulling back the bolts to discover the cause of the uproar. Adeline had just time to pull on her dressing-gown before Cardigan, who had been beating at the door, came into the room, calling excitedly, 'My dearest, she's dead . . . let's get married at once.'[5]

His action was perhaps less callous than the words suggest. He had spent Elizabeth's last hours with her, and she had actually advised him to marry Adeline, in preference to the widowed Marchioness of Ailesbury, whom Adeline regarded as her principal rival. A further curiously Victorian restraint was that, with Elizabeth dead, Adeline sent Cardigan off to Ireland and refused to marry him until a decent length of time should have elapsed after Elizabeth's funeral.

It was not until September that she left Norfolk Street for Cowes, and there joined Cardigan and a party of friends on his latest yacht the *Airedale*. They sailed to Gibraltar and were married in the Garrison Chapel, on 28 September, by the Reverend Charles Moore, Assistant Chaplain to the Forces. Hubert De Burgh was one of the witnesses; Adeline's brother, later to become Admiral Sir Algernon de Horsey, was another. There was a predictably lavish reception and a ball was held on the *Airedale* in the warm Mediterranean evening.

Scandal and comedy characterized the stories which spread with the news of the wedding. It was said that the Governor of Gibraltar invited Cardigan alone to dinner. Cardigan replied that he was accompanied by Lady Cardigan. The single invitation was repeated. Cardigan sent his second to the Governor with a duelling challenge. The Governor responded by having the *Airedale*, with Cardigan on board, towed out of Gibraltar harbour and left in the Mediterranean. At all events, the yacht was soon berthed at Cadiz, from where the Cardigans travelled by train to Madrid as guests at a military review in honour of Queen Isabella's birthday. They sailed to Livorno, Elba and Civita Vecchia, where a coach and six horses, escorted by the Papal Guard, waited to take them to Rome. They received the papal blessing at an audience with Pius IX. In late autumn, the Mediterranean was disagreeably rough, and the couple returned to England by rail, leaving the crew of the *Airedale* to bring the yacht back themselves. In Paris there was time for the fashionable drives, the display and gossip of society and the splendours of the opera. At Deene, 600 tenants on horseback were drawn up to escort them in triumph from the railway station to the house, showing that the loyal yeomen of Northamptonshire were not to be outdone by the ceremony of Pio Nono's Papal Guards.

With their return, the intensity of society's disapproval was uncomfortably evident. That Cardigan should have taken a mistress was perhaps deplorable but not unexpected. That he should have made her Countess of Cardigan seemed unforgiveable. Yet Adeline was more than a match for some of those who carefully cut her in public. Within a month of her return to England, she exercised her right to observe the debates of the House of Lords by sitting in the Peeresses' Gallery, where the noblewomen of England were seen but not heard from. Among her companions were the Duchess of Cambridge and Princess Mary. Also present was Maria, Marchioness of Ailesbury, who cut Adeline with the greatest disdain. But as the two women drew level, Adeline said in a voice of penetrating sweetness, 'Oh, Lady Ailesbury, you may like to know that before Lady Cardigan died she told my Lord all about you and your love affairs.'

Lady Ailesbury looked nervously round the attentive gallery of her sister peeresses and whispered nervously, 'Hush, hush, my dear. I'm coming to lunch with you tomorrow.'

After that, Adeline observed, 'we were outwardly the best of friends.'[6]

In Adeline's own words, her married life with Cardigan was 'a veritable romance'. He was a devoted but jealous husband, refusing to allow any other man to escort Adeline into dinner. It took her three years to persuade him to vary this 'very flattering habit' occasionally. Though he cared less about books, music and painting than she did, they shared the same love of horses and riding. The new Countess was soon recognized as one of the finest horsewomen with the Quorn or the Pytchley.

The de Horsey family quickly reconciled itself to the auspicious marriage, but there was still reluctance on the part of Cardigan's sisters, and of society in general, to show positive approval. It is wrong to suppose that Cardigan himself was ostracized by the court or by his peers, however disagreeable his conduct seemed to the Queen. He was invited to the state balls, the royal concerts and the other events of the season at Buckingham Palace. But he was invited alone, as though still a widower. In the moral view of mid-Victorian England, it was Adeline and the second marriage that did not exist.

Even five years after the wedding there was no leniency shown the erring couple. Cardigan refused an invitation from Admiral Lord Hardwicke, apparently to meet the Prince of Wales, on the grounds that 'as I am situated it would have been very painful to me'. He had decided that where Adeline could not go, he would not go either. 'I never go out to evening parties', he told Hardwicke. 'The world is very *severe*—the difference between being married in England on the 29th of August or at Gibraltar on the 28th of September is utter ruin for ever in the eyes of the world. When look at all the flagrant acts that are going on in the world, the details of which are known to all the Clubs in London and yet those people are cherished and feted.'[7]

By 1863 it seemed to Cardigan that he and Adeline had done whatever penance was necessary. Accordingly, he wrote to those members of his family and acquaintances who were still not on speaking terms with Adeline. To Lady Emily Kingscote he wrote that Lord Westmorland and others had told him that she wished to resume their family tie, 'but I feel satisfied that you could not have imagined that I should feel satisfied with such a reconciliation unless at the same time you consented to recognize and visit my wife.' To another kinswoman, Mrs Curzon, he wrote reproachfully that she had promised twelve months before to call upon Adeline and had not yet done so.[8]

Stories circulated which indicated that Adeline's temper was a match for Cardigan's own. It was said that she threw plates at him, that she criticized the food at Deene in front of the servants, and that having ordered the servants to withdraw, Cardigan then reprimanded her in front of his guests. There were some disappointments in the marriage, the greatest of which was that Adeline, like Elizabeth before her, failed to produce an heir. The extinction of his personal line was a matter on which Cardigan remained predictably sensitive. While visiting Deene church on Christmas Eve, to inspect the decorations which the parishioners were busily putting up for the next day, he saw an illuminated text upon the wall.

Unto us a Child is born, unto us a Son is given.

'Take that down!' shouted Cardigan. 'It is a reflection on her Ladyship!'[9]

However, the lack of an heir was in no way an indication that Cardigan's sexual enthusiasm had markedly declined. Though enthralled by the charms of Adeline, he was still attracted strongly to other pretty young women. In the grounds of Deene was a garden tower, whose purpose Adeline recalled many years after his death. 'That's where dear Cardigan used to go with his ladies', she remarked. 'There's a room upstairs with windows where you can see people coming. He thought I didn't know, but I never interfered with him.'[10]

Whatever Cardigan's other *amours* may have been, his adoration of Adeline was beyond question. When they had been married for eight years, and had been lovers for ten, he wrote to his sister Charlotte in the wistfully affectionate tone of a man who was almost seventy years old. 'My wife Adeline sends her kindest regards to you. She is a very good little wife to me, and no two people could be better suited—we are never apart even for one hour in the 24.'[11]

Yet in their new life together the events of the past were by no means forgotten. Once, in a sombre moment, Adeline asked Cardigan what he had thought of during those terrible minutes when he led his Brigade into the fire of the Russian guns at Balaclava.

'Why,' he said gruffly, 'what that damned fellow Nolan meant by asking me if the Light Brigade was afraid!'[12]

With his second marriage, Cardigan turned his attention to the improvement of the estate at Deene. During the period of the Crimean War, he had been involved in a sporadic legal battle with his former agent at Deene, Major F. H. Lawrie of the 11th Hussars, whom Cardigan eventually dismissed in 1855. The Major then began an action against him for three months' salary in lieu of notice. In preparing Cardigan's defence, the solicitors subpoenaed the widow of Cardigan's Yorkshire agent to produce certain private letters written by Lawrie. Unfortunately, Cardigan had written some private letters of his own to Lawrie from the Crimea, describing the stupidity and shortcomings of Lord Lucan and other British commanders. On 14 February 1856, Lawrie wrote to Cardigan from the United Service Club, warning him that unless he had the subpoena withdrawn by the next morning, Lawrie would publish the entire correspondence from the Crimea, taking care to show the letters first to those officers whom Cardigan had insulted.

Cardigan replied the next day, vehement with rage and frustration. The subpoena was withdrawn and Major Lawrie won his case. Cardigan was obliged to content himself with an angry demand that 'the whole circumstances of such an outrage should be referred to the Committee of the United Service Club for their consideration'. He managed to get an injunction restraining Lawrie from publishing the letters, only to see it dissolved a few months later. The Major promised the Vice-Chancellor's Court that he no longer had any intention of publishing the letters, unless provoked to do so by Cardigan's further intransigence.[13]

With Major Lawrie out of his way, Cardigan began to transform Deene into everything that Adeline wished it to be. Warm-air central heating and a sunken bath were installed. Adeline loved dancing, so the architect J. H. Wyatt was employed to build a ballroom at the western end of the hall. It was to be in the finest Victorian medieval style, seventy feet long and forty feet high, with heraldic stained glass windows and a minstrels' or musicians' gallery. Music was to be provided by a private band, and a Frenchman, Monsieur Holstein, was engaged in 1864 'to direct Lord Cardigan's orchestra', and to be Master of Music in the Chapel at Deene Park.

By 1866, Cardigan had decided to have the warm-air central heating removed, and to have hot water heating installed in its place. New chimney-pieces were to be built, and parquetry flooring was to be laid. The work was rarely up to the standard expected by Cardigan, and Wyatt was soon involved in an acrimonious correspondence with his client, who complained of being 'extremely unfortunate in the tradesmen recommended by you'. Then Cardigan examined the work done by Holland and Hannen, the central heating firm, and reported briskly to them that 'Such construction would be a disgrace to a village carpenter.' To make matters worse, when the ballroom was at last finished, it was reported that the Cardigans had organized a splendid celebration to which all the rich and the famous were invited. But none of these invited guests came.

Deene was also to become the shrine of that heroism which had marked the twenty minutes of the Light Brigade's action at Balaclava. Paintings of Cardigan telling the story to the royal children, or riding in full dress uniform at the head of his men, were joined by photographs of him in uniform and civilian dress, by illuminated addresses, the Balaclava uniform and sword, and in later years by the stuffed head and mounted hooves of his charger, Ronald. The legend continued to grow. To have met, or even to have seen, Cardigan in his later years became a point of some prestige in subsequent volumes of memoirs. John Corlett of the *Sporting Times* remembered him at Newmarket races in 1866. Even in his seventieth year he still appeared 'tall, spare, well-built, handsome and distinguished—the beau-ideal of a light dragoon.' On the course at Newmarket his word was obeyed without question. As the horses were going down for the Two Thousand Guineas, the great event of the racing year, Cardigan barked, 'Halt!' Then he summoned the boy who was riding Lord Lyon to the starting post. Cardigan looked the horse over carefully.

'A very nice horse', he said condescendingly. 'Proceed!'[14]

But most memories of Cardigan in the 1860s were of him driving about the lanes and rough roads of Northamptonshire and Leicestershire in a four-in-hand, at a speed which terrified his passengers and all who came near his path. Yet however dangerous a driver he may have been as the carriage crashed round the corners of lanes or village streets with only two of its wheels on the road, he was almost worse as a passenger. His postilions experienced 'many a furious ride during which his Lordship, in the rocking carriage, passed a running commentary in military language with expressions consigning the post boy's soul (or souls if there were two postilions) to everlasting torment.'

It was his custom to travel up to London by the night mail from Leicester, and the most trying experience of all for his drivers was the last-minute dash of twenty-five miles from Deene Park to Leicester station. After seven miles of 'furious riding', the horses were changed at the Falcon at Uppingham, where the landlord knew Cardigan well enough to have fresh horses harnessed and with traces ready. Beyond Uppingham was the steep descent of Warley Hill, with a sharp bend half way down. As the nervous postilion slackened the pace a little, Cardigan could be heard bellowing, 'Gallop down it, you——fool! If I am not afraid to risk my neck, you need not mind breaking your ——thing!'

There was no question of stopping to pay the toll at the turnpike gates, though the custom of military aristocrats horsewhipping any toll-keeper who tried to impede them had died out in the previous quarter of a century. Now it was the duty of Cardigan's postilion to shout 'Gates!' at the top of his voice for the last mile before the turn-pike. The gates were then thrown open and, as the carriage dashed through, Cardigan or his man would bawl out, 'Pay on the way back!' At Leicester station, he would shy a guinea to the postilion, enough to pay the toll and buy a considerable quantity of drink, and then marched on to the waiting train. As a matter of fact, men of Cardigan's wealth in the mid-nineteenth century were accustomed to hire a train of their own if they missed the scheduled one, but it seems to have been a matter of pride that his horses should be able to get him to the night mail in the minimum possible time.

On other occasions he certainly hired trains of his own to carry guests from Deene to the Pytchley Hunt races in Northampton. On the occasion of the Rockingham Flower Show he also hired every available carriage for miles around. This caused some annoyance to the village squire who met Cardigan in the street and began to berate him. The squire evidently believed that if the language were sufficiently coarse, the Earl would walk away. He found, however, that Cardigan responded with a true sense of style, proving that in the matter of oaths and abuse the squire was 'a baby at it' by comparison.[15]

In private, much of his time was occupied by the hopes and prayers of others. He had become the recipient of a variety of begging letters. Some of these were direct appeals for money. The money was almost always given, with such freedom that his agent accused him of maintaining those in idleness who could perfectly well have supported themselves by work. To more public appeals, he sometimes responded on condition that his gift should remain a secret.

Yet apart from his military ambitions, there was one thing which he still coveted at the end of his life, in order that his position in the county should be all that it ought to be. In January 1867, twenty-five years after being appointed Lord Lieutenant of Northamptonshire, Lord Exeter died. Half-an-hour after his death was announced in the evening papers on 17 January, Cardigan's private messenger arrived with a letter for Lord Derby, the Prime Minister. Cardigan was actually in Devonshire but he had been watching the reports of Lord Exeter's ill-health intently, and heard of his death some hours before it was reported in the press. He wrote his letter at once, and sent it up to London by personal messenger to Lord Derby. Derby had already told Cardigan that he would not submit his name to the Queen as Lord Lieutenant, and the letter in no way persuaded him to change his mind. However, Cardigan's disappointment was so evident and so anguished that Derby felt obliged to do something for him.

In the following month, it became necessary to appoint a Colonel of the Household Cavalry, and the Duke of Cambridge, as Commander-in-Chief, was persuaded to submit Cardigan's name to the Queen. But, to Victoria, he was no longer the hero of Balaclava so much as the elderly libertine in whose company no decent woman was safe. She dismissed the Duke's recommendation, on the grounds that an appointment to the Household Cavalry would bring Cardigan into frequent contact with her. That, according to the Queen, would be very disagreeable.

Yet she did not make her disapproval of him public. He still appeared at the Palace on great public occasions, though tolerated by virtue of his rank rather than welcomed as a hero of the army. And, like Adeline, he found that in large areas of Victorian society, quite contrary to what was subsequently believed, the sexual reputation of a man or even a woman was no barrier to acceptance. If the Quorn, the Pytchley, the Royal Yacht Squadron and clubs like White's or Boodle's had expelled all habitual adulterers, their membership would have been alarmingly depleted.

Cardigan remained a member of the Royal Yacht Squadron and Commodore of the Royal Southern Yacht Club. With Adeline, he spent his summers in expensive but agreeable idleness at Cowes, buying new steam yachts like the *Airedale* and the *Sea Horse* with as much ease as other men bought horses. For himself and his guests he also hired other yachts, which cost him £400 a week for the vessel and six or seven tons of coal a day. In addition to the cost of the yachts there were considerable bills for such items as candlelit champagne dinners in private suites at establishments like Aris's Hotel in West Cowes.

Yet for all the expense, Cardigan's knowledge of yachts and yachting was limited, nor was he an enthusiastic amateur sailor. He boarded the boat in full-dress military uniform, complete with spurs, for the benefit of the watching crowds. When the vessel had put to sea the skipper, on one occasion, felt that Cardigan should test for himself the toy which had cost him so much money. He inquired politely, 'Will you take the helm, my Lord?'

'No, thank you,' said Cardigan gruffly and evidently bewildered, 'I never take anything between meals.'[16]

In the London clubs to which he belonged, he lent his support invariably to established traditions. With the election of the Prince of

Wales at White's, certain younger members decided to press for a revolutionary change, which would permit smoking in the drawing-room. A general meeting of members was held in April 1866, at which Bromley Davenport and Lord De L'Isle brought forward the motion proposing the change. It was strongly and successfully opposed by the older members under the leadership of Cardigan and Lord Wilton.

'Where do all these old fossils come from?' asked one of the younger members in disgust.

'They come from Kensal Green,' said Alfred Montgomery brightly, 'and the hearses are waiting outside to take them back.'[17]

During this period, a number of his creditors noticed a greater reluctance than usual on Cardigan's part to pay his bills. In 1865–6 he fought a protracted legal battle with the photographer Ernest Edwards, on the grounds that a bill for photographic portraits of himself and Adeline was exorbitant. Inevitably he made the case more complex by saying loudly and publicly to Henry Barnard, an acquaintance of Edwards, 'He is a robber—he charged me an enormous sum, and robbed me of my money, and you ought to be ashamed of yourself to bring such a man here under your protection.'

To his bill for £123, Edwards promptly added a claim for £1,000 damages for slander.

The truth was that Cardigan had long since found himself unable to live within his income of £40,000 a year. His devotion to Adeline demanded a style of married life which placed a considerable strain on his finances. In 1864 he was obliged to mortgage part of his estates to the 2nd Duke of Wellington and to raise a loan of £150,000. In the following year, he had to borrow first £10,000 and then a further £12,000. From time to time, he supplemented this by loans of £5,000 or £6,000 from Drummonds, his bankers. By 1868, his debts were enormous. Adeline was later to pay off £365,000. By the time of his death, Cardigan's assets had dwindled to less than £60,000. It was hardly to be wondered at that by the 1880s the bailiffs began moving in at Deene.

Cardigan's own attitude towards money, like his attitude towards most other things, continued to reflect the values of a pre-Victorian age. Debts were not a matter of great consequence. However great the sums of money owed, the Earls of Cardigan had been part of the fabric of the state since the seventeenth century. Whatever the technicalities of finance, the realm could no more deprive them of their estates than it could disband the army or dispossess the Royal Navy of its warships. Even in the 1860s, he could never quite believe that the age of the counting-house had overtaken that of the *grand seigneur*.

2

In May 1866 Cardigan parted with the 11th (Prince Albert's own) Hussars. The regiment had been ordered to India again and, as their Colonel, he inspected the men at Colchester a few weeks prior to embarkation. It was a proud but sad occasion. If they were to do a normal tour of duty in the East, it was unlikely that he would live to see them parade again on their return. The blue and crimson squadrons of cavalry wheeled and cantered and charged on their immaculately groomed horses, while the band played 'The Keel Row' or 'Bonnie Dundee', as it had done a quarter of a century ago, when Cardigan himself led the regiment across the Race Hill at Brighton in the peacock arrogance of his 'Cherry Bum' uniform.

After the review, Cardigan addressed the ranks of silent troopers.

'Eleventh Hussars! I assumed command of you many years ago, at Cawnpore. You are now returning to that distant land. You are sure, if occasion offers, to distinguish yourselves in the field.'

It hardly needed saying. To the public at large, the regiment was no longer the *corps de ballet* of the 'Black Bottle' comedy, but the flower of the British cavalry and the emblem of the valour displayed upon the field of Balaclava. In his customary harsh voice, Cardigan spoke to the troopers for a last time.

'You have my hearty good wishes. I bid you farewell, and assure you that I am proud of the honour of being your Colonel.'

In fact, Cardigan saw his regiment once more, in June 1866, when the Prince of Wales reviewed it just before the men sailed for India. In the grand marquee, the tables decorated with fruit, flowers and regimental plate, the young Prince spoke of the man 'whose name will ever be distinguished by the part he took in the memorable charge of Balaclava. He commanded your regiment for many years, and his name can never be dissociated from it.'[18]

With his regiment gone, Cardigan turned alone to the battles of his final years. His instinct for public controversy remained, and soon he was in the thick of the row over Edward Eyre and the Jamaica Mutiny of 1865. The debate engendered more heat than light, since the facts—such as they were—disappeared in a wider argument on colonial and imperial policy. There was certainly an insurrection in October 1865, whose supporters were apparently responsible for a number of deaths. With equal certainty, George William Gordon, a native of the island who was both a Baptist minister and a member of the House of Assembly, had no part in the mutiny. Indeed, he gave himself up to the authorities to demonstrate his innocence, but only to be court-martialled peremptorily by three junior officers and hanged little more than twenty-four hours later. Then, according to his critics, Governor Eyre turned the army loose on the native population and allowed the troops to teach Jamaicans a lesson for the future. Hundreds of men were hanged, and others shot indiscriminately. Liberal England was horrified to hear that men and women had been flogged at random, some with whips made of piano wire. A thousand Jamaican homes had been burnt by the soldiers as a warning to future trouble-makers. On the other hand, Eyre's supporters cited the murderous conduct of the rebels, the mutilation of victims by them, and the appalling fate which must have overtaken Englishmen—and women—in Jamaica if the army had not acted with speed and resolution.

As in most debates of this kind, precise and undisputed facts seemed far too few. Yet there was a widespread belief that Eyre should be brought to justice for the terrible events of October 1865. Edward Cardwell, the Colonial Secretary, recalled the Governor to England. But though the Queen was shocked to read of the way in which men boasted of the number of rebels they had hanged or flogged, and though there was a Royal Commission to investigate the mutiny, no official action was taken against Eyre. Such pusillanimity was denounced at public meetings all over the country, and resolutions were passed by crowds of liberal-minded working men demanding that justice should be done. Under the aegis of John Stuart Mill, Herbert Spencer and T. H. Huxley, the Jamaica Committee was set up to bring a prosecution for murder against Eyre. There were several attempts of this kind, but the grand jury refused to sanction a prosecution on the evidence presented. Indeed, in 1872 the Gladstone government refunded to Eyre the costs of defending himself against these charges.

There was an equally powerful group of men who praised Eyre as the saviour of Jamaica, whose determined action had restored peace, 'where a moment's success to the rebels might have put the life of every white man, and the honour of every white woman, at the mercy of furious mobs of savage negroes.' The supporters of Eyre included men representative of a wide range of political opinion: Tennyson, Ruskin, Disraeli, and—more surprisingly—Dickens and Charles Kingsley. They were led by Thomas Carlyle and Cardigan.[19]

Cardigan and Carlyle organized a testimonial to Eyre, supporting this by public banquets at which Eyre was the guest of honour. One of the oddest sights in 1866 was the joint appearance of Cardigan and the Reverend Charles Kingsley, exponent of Christian Socialism, at a banquet in honour of Eyre, held at Southampton on 21 August. In his speech, Cardigan insisted that he was not only championing Eyre but the reputation of the British army as well. It was the duty of the army 'to take an active and vigorous part in suppressing anything like civil disturbance and anything like rebellion and insurrection.' He also found time to praise the Royal Navy's role in checking the Jamaica rebellion, perhaps because his brother-in-law, Captain de Horsey, was in command of the naval units there.[20]

The criticism and abuse which were directed at Cardigan, after his public support for Eyre, took various forms. One of these was an anonymous letter from 'A Working Man', which showed clearly that the events of the Crimea had done nothing to reconcile the more politically active minority of working-class Englishmen to soldiers of Cardigan's type. 'Real soldiers', who were listed in the letter as Clive, Wellington, Napier, Havelock, Colin Campbell and Wolfe, would never have sanctioned an attack on unarmed demonstrators—a statement which betrays a touching ignorance of the Duke of Wellington's political sentiments, at least. The suppression of civil disturbances 'is only fit for *dandy officers*—fellows who cock a glass in their eye and stare women out of countenance—talk rubbish in Rotten-row—run long bills with tradesmen, some of which they altogether forget to pay—seduce virtuous girls and then turn them on the town, and then have the impertinence to call all these doings fun.' Cardigan is accused of having 'bolted' from London when the cholera came, but this has its consolations for those who are obliged to remain. 'It's quite a treat to go into the Park now it is cleared of you *scented up dandies* and your equally *scented up prostitutes*, the air smells wholesome now and does one good, but it's thoroughly poisoned in what you please to call the *season*.' Cardigan read the letter through and then filed it away among his souvenirs.[21]

There remained one more battle to be fought, on ground more sacred than that of the Jamaica controversy. When Cardigan's reputation as the hero of Balaclava had been vindicated by the Calthorpe hearing in 1863, he had been warned that there were other men who, like Calthorpe, had never themselves faced the fire of the enemy but who were eager to demolish the legend of glory which commemorated Balaclava. The *Sun* had even named one of these other men as Alexander William Kinglake, the podgy, cold-eyed MP for Bridgewater, who had been a tourist at the battlefront and was now about to erect the final monument to the folly of the war in his *Invasion of the Crimea*.

General Sir George Brown might protest that Kinglake was so short-sighted that he could neither hunt without his spectacles nor make out the events of the battlefield when wearing them. It was of no consequence to the waiting customers of the booksellers and the circulating libraries. By 1868, Kinglake was about to publish the fourth volume of his history, the volume which was to pass final judgment on the battle and personalities of Balaclava. He invited Cardigan and other surviving commanders to supply him with statements, rather in the manner of a judge asking a convicted felon if he had anything to say before sentence was passed.

Cardigan compiled yet another account of the battle and the famous cavalry charge, an account which Kinglake was later to publish as an appendix with several adverse comments of his own. The version which he published also differs from the copy which Cardigan kept, but there is no indication as to whether Cardigan altered the statement on copying or whether it was altered after it came into Kinglake's possession.

In the main body of the history, Kinglake summed up Cardigan as a brave man, which would have been difficult to deny, but as one who was incompetent professionally, and selfish personally. It was certainly Kinglake who first fully adumbrated the view that the cavalry had been doomed to destruction by the appointment of two aristocratic nincompoops, Lucan and Cardigan, and by the system which permitted them to hold their commands. It was a thesis which had been partially promulgated before, but Kinglake's history was its classic statement. Just how Cardigan could have acted otherwise than he did, after the combination of insistent orders delivered by Airey, then by Nolan, and finally by Lucan, seemed irrelevant to the story which Kinglake had chosen to tell. To have dwelt on the matter might have raised the inconvenient consideration that the arrogant efficiency of Nolan was as much a product of the military system as the aristocratic self-confidence of Cardigan, and had contributed immeasurably more to the destruction of the Light Cavalry.

Cardigan had, of course, known Kinglake in the Crimea. When their acquaintanceship was resumed, he entertained Kinglake at Portman Square and treated him courteously and hospitably. When sending out Christmas gifts in 1865, he sent Kinglake a basket of game from Deene. Kinglake replied coldly in a letter which stipulated that the relationship between them must be strictly that of 'a General Officer and a writer'. Kinglake had, accordingly, altered the address on the basket to Cardigan's town house in Portman Square, where it arrived several days later, and a great deal riper. A world in which any man of honour could be bribed to falsify history for the price of a basket of game was not one with which Cardigan was familiar. He wrote a rather puzzled and somewhat hurt letter to Kinglake, expressing surprise that 'so trifling an act of courtesy and attention' might be misinterpreted. 'But', he added, 'I am extremely glad that you took the course you did if more agreeable to your own feelings.'[22]

From then on, the correspondence became increasingly demanding and querulous on Kinglake's part, and more tired and defensive on the part of Cardigan. In January 1868, after Cardigan had asked for the return of three letters, temporarily, so that he might make a copy of the information in them, Kinglake retorted shrilly, 'I must be allowed to say that it is not convenient to me to have papers sent to me, and then withdrawn, because it is possible that an impression might be produced on my mind for which (in the absence of the papers) I might not be well able to account.'

There were also occasional sharp reminders to Cardigan.

'You were so good as to promise to furnish me with a copy of Lord William Paulet's letters and this is important.'[23]

There were no expressions of gratitude on Kinglake's part. Indeed, in his published comments on Cardigan's statement, it appeared that any debt of gratitude was owed by Cardigan to him. On 5 March 1868, in one of the last letters he ever wrote, Cardigan returned to Kinglake the documents he had copied, and simply asked him to read again their previous correspondence before passing final judgment on Balaclava. He never knew whether Kinglake took note of his suggestion. By the time that the third volume of the *Invasion of the Crimea* appeared, later in 1868, Cardigan was dead.

Cardigan's sister, Charlotte, wrote to him in 1866 after the death of her husband, urging him to think seriously 'of the great change which we must (at our age) expect, and flee for refuge to the only hope set before us—the Gospel of Christ.' In his reply, on 22 March 1866, Cardigan remarked briefly, 'I assure you, I think much more seriously on those important subjects to which you allude than I formerly did.' Indeed, he had got into the habit of reminding Adeline, as they went through the accounts and attended to the other business of the estate, that one day she would have to do all this for herself.[24]

It would hardly have been in character for Cardigan to put on record his precise religious beliefs, even had he been able to define them precisely. In practice, he regularly attended the services of the Church of England, and at his command his servants attended as well. But the custom of a gentleman was to fulfil his obligations towards God and the Established Church without ostentation, without boasting, and probably without ever discussing the doctrines involved.

Some Victorian military commanders like General Henry Havelock, a Baptist who led the first relief of Lucknow and the recapture of Cawnpore in 1857, preached sermons to their men. Cardigan taught by example, inculcating courage and obedience to duty. In terms of belief, he regarded himself as a staunch Protestant of the Church of England. Yet he shared none of the anti-Catholic hysteria of the earlier Victorian period, and made private gifts to Catholic charities, as he did to charities of most other kinds.

To its successors, every age appears to have its intolerable hypocrisies, and in modern terms it seems hard to reconcile the profession of Christianity with the actual behaviour of Cardigan and other members of his social class. Yet such men believed very sincerely in the doctrines of the Church of England, while tolerating the apparent evils of adultery and duelling as an inevitable concomitant to the imperfect world of human affairs. If they sought to make that world more perfect, it was not by broadcasting any political theory but rather by material aid to those most in need of it. Unlike their more evangelical contemporaries, they did not trumpet this as an example of practical Christianity, any more than they announced their own holiness in attending the services of the Church. In an age when men were more conscious of their duties than of their rights, they had merely discharged those obligations which Church and State placed upon them.

However, at seventy years old and in poor health, Cardigan turned towards thoughts of death. Five years before, he had had a bad fall while out hunting, which had apparently resulted in the formation of a blood-clot in his brain. He suffered several times after that from seizures, but none of them had been immediately dangerous. He gave orders that Adeline was not to be told, and it seemed that he always recovered speedily. He continued to ride and hunt with all the physical enthusiasm of youth.

Yet like the victim of an Edgar Allen Poe melodrama, he began to develop a phobia about being buried underground. He gave instructions that this was not to happen to his body when he died, and he began to collect a great heap of stones in order to have a memorial or a mausoleum built in the grounds of Deene. But when Lord Westmorland noticed such fine material, he remarked that it was just what he needed for the building of a new gateway. Cardigan gave it to him.

One morning in March 1868, the Pytchley Hunt met at Rockingham Castle, not far from Deene. As Colonel Anstruther Thomson was moving off with the hounds, Cardigan rode up to him and said, 'You have known me for many years.'

'Yes, sir,' said Thomson, who had been a guest of the 11th Hussars in the winter of 1841.

'I have always been a very healthy man', said Cardigan.

'Yes, sir,' said Thomson.

'Just now I had a fit of giddiness. I'm not well. I'm going home. Good-bye.'

With this, Cardigan began to ride slowly away down the long broad avenue that led to Deene. Soon afterwards, the hounds drew the hunt towards Deene and, about an hour later, he reappeared, wearing a mackintosh.

'I felt better', he remarked to Thomson, 'so I thought I would come out for a little while.'[25]

On 13 March there was another hunt at Althorpe, when the Prince of Wales came down. It seemed that Cardigan was quite himself again. On the morning of 26 March he announced to Adeline and to their guest, Sir Henry Edwards, that he was going to ride over to the keeper's cottage where a young man, Simon Bell, had been accidentally shot. On his arrival he examined the body and remarked coolly that he had seen gunshot wounds far more ghastly in the Crimea. After spending some time comforting the man's sister, he mounted his horse again and began riding back along the avenue to Deene.

By lunchtime, he had still not reached the house. As the afternoon passed, Adeline became increasingly concerned and told some of the servants to go in search of him. On the road from Deene to Gretton, about a quarter of a mile from the house, a road-surveyor was at work. Cardigan had stopped to talk to him on his way back to the house. The horse had shied at a pile of stones but he had kept it well under control and had ridden it away quietly enough. Soon afterwards, the surveyor heard a child calling him, and saw Cardigan's horse trotting riderless towards home. Cardigan was lying nearby, face down and with his head doubled up beneath him. He was livid and there was foam at his mouth. With the aid of some women from the cottages, the surveyor pulled Cardigan to his feet and began to drag him towards the house, only to meet the carriage which Adeline had sent in search of him.

Cardigan was taken to his room and the doctors were summoned. But he was already unconscious and there was nothing that they could do for him. He remained in this state for two days, breathing harshly and never recognizing Adeline or, indeed, regaining consciousness. On the evening of 28 March 1868 the laboured breathing subsided and 'the last of the Brudenells' was dead.

The news of his death spread quickly but with varying accuracy as to the circumstances. Some of his contemporaries were incredulous, or perhaps disappointed, that the bad or brave Lord Cardigan should have died in his bed of natural causes. Shirley Brooks assured Sir William Hardman that 'Cardigan died in an access of noble and aristocratic fury that anyone should have taken the DAMNABLE LIBERTY to murder HIS gamekeeper. I like proper spirit.'[26]

For two days his body lay in state in the darkened, lamplit ballroom at Deene. Among the tall candles and the banners bearing his crest, Adeline had ordered that his peer's robes, his orders of knighthood, and the uniform he had worn at Balaclava should be the solemn centrepiece of the decoration. Two thousand men and women filed past the coffin under its rich crimson pall, in homage to their dead hero.

The funeral ceremony was undoubtedly the most splendid ever accorded to any of the Earls of Cardigan. To the accompaniment of solemn music played by Cardigan's own 'orchestra', which marched at the rear of the procession, the cortège moved off from the courtyard of Deene towards the church of St Peter. His coronet was borne at the head on a crimson cushion, the solitary symbol of his rank and dignity. The black hearse and the long file of carriages were drawn by horses in funeral plumes and all the black and silver emblems of mourning.

The bearer party consisted of his brother officers from the 11th Hussars, and behind them came the grooms leading the chestnut horse, now riderless, which had carried him through the Russian guns at Balaclava fourteen years before. Black-clad family mourners and tenants of the estates were followed by the keepers in their green liveries, and by the band which played the funeral music. In death, as in life, the last of the Brudenells was the occasion of a great public display. A tomb was waiting to receive his body in the Brudenell Chapel of St Peter's church. He was not to be buried underground in the manner which had begun to perturb him so much in his final years. The solemnity of the occasion was only once broken, when Ronald, his Balaclava charger, broke free and began capering about the paddock in a most unfunereal fashion.

Most of those who read the press obituaries agreed with *The Times* that 'His personal gallantry at Balaclava will long be remembered when the controversy as to the mistaken order, in obedience to which he led the charge in the teeth of the enemy's guns, is forgotten.' It seemed that in the moment of his death, the public forgot all else but, as the song had phrased it,

> How Cardigan the fearless his name immortal made,
> When he crossed that Russian valley with the famous Light
>   Brigade.

The novelist G. J. Whyte-Melville, who knew him as well as most of his acquaintances, expressed more vividly than any of his contemporaries the qualities of the man whose death they mourned.[27]

> Old war-worn veterans mourn for the stern commander who never shirked a duty, for the staunch comrade who never failed a friend. Young rising soldiers are sad to think that their ideal has been quenched, that their hero too has vanished like another. Magnates of the land, his peers and equals, find time to grieve for one who was an ornament to his rank, an honour to his order; but—sorrows far more precious than these—tears fall fast and thick from the widow and the fatherless, while they sob out a blessing on the memory of their best benefactor, on the kindly heart always ready to console, on the generous hand always open to relieve, on the gallant handsome face that never hardened towards a suppliant, as it never blanched before a foe.

Allowing for the hyperbole of Victorian funeral orations, there was still enough truth remaining in Whyte-Melville's final sentence to make any man proud to have it for his obituary.

3

It was not in the nature of Cardigan's life or reputation that solemnity of this kind should remain unrelieved for long. There were already speculations as to how much longer Adeline might live and might thereby delay a distant branch of the Brudenell family from getting its hands on the remains of the estate. The earldom of Cardigan was henceforward a title of the Marquess of Ailesbury, to whom it passed in the absence of any children of Cardigan's own. According to John Corlett of the *Sporting Times*, one of those with ambitions to become heir to the estates of both Cardigan and Ailesbury was known about town as 'Duffer' Bruce. He was, said Corlett, about town when many of the public houses never closed, and consequently spent much of his time in them. He was eventually sent abroad on a cure, but returned with 'the hand of death' upon him. Yet with the cunning of a convinced dipsomaniac, this scion of Lord Ailesbury's family outwitted all attempts to keep him alive and sober. Even when licensing laws restricted public house opening hours, Bruce was able to provide his friends with a drink at any time and in any place. As part of his apparent 'reformation' he wore a large crucifix around his neck. But the top of the crucifix could be uncorked to reveal a hollow flask containing a pint of neat whisky. He was outlived by almost all his rivals to the marquisate of Ailesbury and the remains of Cardigan's wealth.[28]

Yet if Adeline occasioned some irritation among the heirs to the property, to the world at large she became as remarkable for her own distinctive behaviour as Cardigan had been for his. It was, perhaps, inevitable that their extraordinary marriage should pass into fiction, since it was so much a part of public history, and in 1894 George Meredith made it the basis of his novel *Lord Ormont and his Aminta*. However, he set the scene of Cardigan's cavalry charge in India and dated the events somewhat later than their occurrence in reality.

Adeline remained a part of that other Victorian society, ostracized by the Queen and by polite upper-class conversation, but entirely at home in the hunting fraternity of the Shires, on the Newmarket racecourse, at Cowes, or in the faintly scandalous opulence of some great

London houses. If she was far removed from the Queen, she was very close to the Prince of Wales and his set. As a stratum of society, hers was too patrician for the *demi-monde* and too 'fast' for serious-minded peers and their acquaintances. It embraced a colourful cross-section of men and women from the Prince of Wales to 'Skittles', and from keepers of women, like the 8th Duke of Devonshire, to oddities of the sporting underworld like the 8th Marquess of Queensbury, companion of the racecourse 'swell mob', formulator of the 'Queensbury Rules' in boxing, and foremost among the destroyers of Oscar Wilde.

For all the scandal which circulated about her, Adeline was by no means friendless. Indeed, when her grief for Cardigan had softened, and when she had turned the church at Deene into a suitable memorial to him, she began to think of remarriage. In 1873 she singled out Benjamin Disraeli, whose wife had died at the end of the previous year. He had already been Prime Minister for the first time in 1868, and was to hold office again from 1874 until 1879.

The Cardigans had known Disraeli for some years, Adeline being better acquainted with him than Cardigan had been. Now, having already refused twelve other offers of marriage since her husband's death, Adeline embarked upon a determined and very unVictorian correspondence, turning all her charm upon the past and future Prime Minister. At first she suggested that though she would like to entertain him at Deene, they ought to wait for a little longer, otherwise the Queen 'would be shocked'. But by March 1873 her letters to him contained their first endearments—'*Je vous embrasse mon aimable ami*' —and she rather pointedly described herself as writing to him from her bed, although on the embossed notepaper of the Royal Southern Yacht Club. By June she was not only proposing marriage to him, but even naming the date as December 1873, when they might 'relapse quietly into man and wife'.[29]

Disraeli, who had never intended to let matters get so far out of hand and was by now thoroughly apprehensive, broke off the correspondence on the grounds that Adeline's overtures towards him were fast becoming a matter of gossip. If he felt any qualms over dismissing her in this manner, he may have been relieved as well as surprised to receive another letter, two months later, informing him that she was about to be married to a Portuguese nobleman, the Count de Lancastre. The marriage took place on 28 August, the bride becoming Adeline, Countess of Cardigan and Lancastre. The marriage lasted until the Count's death in 1898 but the couple separated in

1879, after six years of travelling between Deene, Paris, Madrid and Lisbon. They were married in the Catholic Chapel in King Street, near Portman Square, and according to Adeline it was the bickering over their different religious beliefs which hastened their separation.

Many years later, in 1909, when Adeline published her memoirs as *My Recollections*, she took a delayed revenge upon Disraeli. She claimed that the decision not to marry had been hers. However importunate he was, she was deterred by his bad breath and by the warning of the Prince of Wales (who was Edward VII by the time the story was published) who had advised her at a meeting of the Belvoir hunt not to marry Disraeli at any price. The King denied that such a conversation had ever taken place and, indeed, all the surviving letters indicate that it was Adeline who had been determined on marriage, and Disraeli who had contrived to escape it.[30]

After 1879 her life was spent principally at Deene, where she became a patroness of the wealthier hunting and racing society. Men in these circles came to regard her, as his contemporaries had often regarded Cardigan in such matters, as 'a good sport'. But Adeline spent money at a prodigious rate. The bailiffs moved in, the housekeeper got drunk, and Adeline was heard loudly cursing her maids in such phrases as, 'Where have you been to, you Whitechapel strumpets?'[31]

Her behaviour varied from the eccentric to the scandalous. She smoked cigarettes freely and publicly at a time when it was considered improper for a woman to smoke even in private. She developed a habit of dressing up in Cardigan's 'Cherry Bum' uniform, which she referred to as her bicycling costume but which gave her the unfortunate appearance of wearing pink tights. Then, for the last time, she managed to annoy Queen Victoria.

It was the Queen's custom, when travelling abroad, to go incognito as 'The Countess of Lancaster'. Confusion between this title and 'The Countess of Lancastre' was inevitable. It is all too easy to imagine the horror at Windsor or Osborne, when stories worked their way there that the Countess of Lancaster, who was generally known to be Queen Victoria, had been seen parading in pink tights and drawing coquettishly upon a cigarette. Though Adeline had never contemplated taking any sort of revenge for the years of ostracism, she could hardly have contrived a retribution more apt than this. The Lancastre title being Portuguese, there was little that the Queen could have done about it, except possibly to create Adeline a Duchess with a different title, in her own right.

Yet by the 1890s Adeline was an old woman, almost as old as the Queen whose birthday party she had attended as a little girl in the reign of William IV. She lived an increasingly lonely and confined life in the great house at Deene. Her friends, her admirers, and even her rivals like Maria, the Marchioness of Ailesbury, had grown old and died. She outlived the heir to Deene, who had thought on Cardigan's death that he would have only a little while to wait before Adeline died and the property became his. Men and women who remembered her from their youth, fifty or sixty years before, as a figure of beauty and intrigue, were surprised to find as the twentieth century began that she was still living her eccentric and secluded life on the great estate at Deene, surrounded by pet dogs and faithful servants.

In 1909 her memoirs were published, having been ghost-written by a publisher's assistant from notes of conversations with Adeline. The book roused a mild public curiosity in the long distant past but it caused scandal and dismay to those mentioned in its pages, not least to Edward VII. The truth or falsity of the entire work would be impossible to establish. It seems that the general outline of the story is accurate but that certain of the incidents were embellished and the worst construction put upon some of the comments and remarks which she had made.

When the First World War began, she was still living at Deene, ninety years old, a strange relic of female beauty from an age when the Duke of Wellington was Commander-in-Chief and the 'pretty horsebreakers' were the scandal of Rotten Row. She lived to see the first reports of total war in the appalling slaughter of the Western Front during the spring of 1915, carnage on a scale which made the Crimean losses seem trivial by comparison. The first bombs from German zeppelins fell upon English towns in a new phase of warfare which would have seemed more fantastic to Cardigan and his contemporaries than anything the world had ever known. But as she sat in her chair, gazing out upon the grounds of the estate in the closing weeks of her life, her mind wandered back increasingly to the distant past. 'I saw my Lord and all our friends riding past the windows just now', she said wistfully one afternoon.[32]

On 25 May 1915 she died. The ending of her life came as a shock only to those who had no idea that she had survived so long. The obituaries dealt kindly with her, forgiving if not forgetting the outrage which she and Cardigan had committed against contemporary sexual morals by their behaviour in the 1850s. She was generally agreed to have been 'remarkable', if only for the length of her life. She had been born before Canning became Prime Minister, but at her death the political cradles of England already sheltered many of the leaders of the 1970s. She had given her successors a salutary reminder of the brevity of human history. But in all the notices of her death, she was overshadowed by the presence of her first husband who had died almost half a century before and whose status as a military 'character' was only just beginning to be eclipsed by the more prosaic heroes of the new army.

4

The sum of Cardigan's achievements and shortcomings was such as to disqualify him both from a place among the monumental volumes of Victorian 'life and letters', and from the more scandalous lives of the *demi-monde* issued by publishers like Eveleigh Nash. His identity might be strong and clear, but the inconsistencies of his character posed too great a problem in terms of later nineteenth-century biography. He could not even be made to correspond easily to such familiar categorization as 'Victorian' unless the terms themselves were entirely redefined. While it is true that men and women who knew him in their childhood lived to witness the dropping of the first atomic bombs, it is perhaps more relevant to recall that he was born in the year of Horace Walpole's death, when the army still contained men who had fought with Wolfe at Quebec or with Burgoyne against Washington. At the time of his death, the future Lord Kitchener had just become a cadet at Woolwich, but in his military and social affinities Cardigan belonged with the generals of the eighteenth century rather than with a more earnest and professional strategist of Empire like Kitchener.

In so many respects, his virtues and his failings belonged to an age that was already past. In consequence, most of his Victorian critics found him either a figure of quaint amusement or a detestable anachronism. He combined arrogance and philanthropy, bravery and self-indulgence, in a manner which might have been tolerable in the reign of George III but which was unacceptable in the more earnest and rational climate of early Victorian social reform. At a time when the vivid but predictable characterizations of Charles Dickens brought fame and fortune to their author, a man who insisted on being cast as hero and villain simultaneously was unlikely to attract a sympathetic audience.

Cardigan was also dismissed, by contemporaries and successors, as a man of limited intelligence. His intellect was certainly not of the kind which would register a flattering score in any kind of systematic test, but by the values of his own society it would have seemed extraordinary that such an achievement should be thought creditable or that any gentleman would submit himself to such an indignity. The predominantly twentieth-century heresy that pure, measurable intellect was in itself admirable had been treated with varying forms of rebuff even before the Victorian period was over. The suspicions of the age were embodied in Charles Kingsley's classic caution, 'Be good, sweet maid, and let who will be clever.'

Philanthropy, good works, sympathy for the unfortunate, an instinct for the right action, some gift of imagination, and an unassuming courage (or 'bottom' as the eighteenth century called it) were among the desirable qualities of a gentleman. It was not yet thought essential that he should be over-modest or self-effacing. If, in addition, he had a first-class brain, he would no doubt put this at the service of his country, grappling speedily and successfully with the power-equations of diplomacy or the administration of law and justice. Yet a man of humbler intelligence would achieve all that was necessary, if his instinct was right and his heart true, with such brain as God had given him. The perils of this comfortable complacency were to be held up to execration often enough in the twentieth century. Yet it so often seemed to the Victorians, as during the murderous twenty minutes at Balaclava, that intellectual brilliance was of limited usefulness in the practical affairs of life. The only hope of survival lay in the courage of the leader, and in the disciplined valour of those whom he led.

There is probably no more false judgment of character than to assume that the truth of a man's personality must be located in a grey compromise between the praise of his friends and the criticism of his enemies. In Cardigan's case, at least, both the best and the worst that was said of him was true. He was a duellist, an adulterer, a man who sought self-advancement by money and by influence, a supporter of the most savage punitive measures taken on such occasions as the Jamaica Mutiny or in the regiments of the British army. He was also brave, generous, a loyal friend, and the favourite of an extraordinarily large number of women, many of whom were wealthy enough to separate mercenary and sexual motives. Yet there was one point upon which both his friends and enemies agreed. He was without guile, showing his feelings of rage or grief or pleasure more publicly than most men would have dared. In consequence of this, though he could not be driven, he could very often be led. Lord George Paget found that, after a little while, he could be 'easily managed'. Kinglake, who admired Cardigan even less than Lord George had done, came to much the same conclusion. 'In Lord Cardigan there was such an absence of guile that exactly as he was so he showed himself to the world. Of all false pretences contrived for the purpose of feigning an interest in others he was as innocent as a horse.'[33]

His 'innocence' led him into absurd situations in the more sophisticated world of early Victorian politics. It was a principle with him that if another man wanted something of him, that man would ask him and he would give it. If he wanted something of another man, like Sir Robert Peel or Lord Derby, he asked for it and expected, as a rule, to get it. Of course, he did not ask for anything which it seemed to him out of the question that he should have. But if he wanted to be a Knight of the Garter or Lord Lieutenant of Northamptonshire, he wrote directly to the Prime Minister and asked for the honour to be bestowed. He was not alone in the Victorian period in demanding to have such titles conferred upon him. Henry Hawkins, later Lord Brampton, appeared for the Attorney-General in the famous 'Tichborne Case' and promptly applied for a knighthood, as his reward, as soon as the case was over. After the Crimean War, according to the Queen, Count Revel frequently applied for a KCB for his war service. Far from deploring these requests, Victoria thought that Revel ought to be given the honour he asked for. Indeed, in the political world of half a century earlier, Cardigan would have been thought a fool if he had not made demands of a leader whose party he had always supported.[34]

But the honours were not bestowed upon him, and he was left to fret and grieve over a series of rebuffs. He had some cause to feel offended. Had it not been for his behaviour in the 11th Hussars, the rules of Victorian preferment would have given him very strong claims to the lord lieutenancy of Northamptonshire and perhaps, as Lord Aberdeen suggested in 1855, to the Garter. In the circumstances, it seemed to him that his position and responsibilities had been ignored, while the ears of Peel and Derby were ever open to the insidious whispering of those by whom he had been—to use his own favourite word—'calumniated'.

It was certainly questionable whether his openness of character made him more admired, either by his contemporaries or successors. Yet because his courage was displayed to particular advantage through this lack of guile, it was admitted by all. As Kinglake conceded, Cardigan's was not the courage of a foolhardy man who is brave because he cannot appreciate the degree of peril which confronts him. It was, rather, a courage springing from a moral resolve to go through with the action to which he was committed. When he rode at the head of the Light Brigade, he believed that he was riding to his death. But he had twice queried the order and had twice been told that there was no doubt as to what was demanded of him. After that, no other course could be taken without disgrace. The call of honour required that he should place himself at the head of his men and ride for the barrels of the enemy guns. Significantly, honour did not require him to kill Russian soldiers or even to defend himself against them in the mêlée at the battery. It required that, if necessary, he should allow himself to be killed. For all his pugnacity, he lived through seventy years without killing a single man in peace or war. It was his less arrogant and more professional successors, the builders of Empire in the later nineteenth century, who shed the blood of conquest across Africa and Asia.[35]

Within three years of Cardigan's death, the system of purchasing commissions in the British army was abolished. Promotion was to be strictly according to merit and ability, or so it seemed. Soon the power of the Horse Guards was overshadowed by the encroaching political control of the Minister of War. Flogging was abolished as a military punishment in time of peace, a reform made in the year of Cardigan's death. At last it appeared that the army was destined to follow so many other Victorian institutions in reflecting the power and the attitudes of the triumphant middle class. To the alarm of old soldiers, the triumph also manifested itself in a positive mania for educating young officers and making them pass examinations in such middle-class subjects as geography. On the steps of White's Club, a certain baronet anxiously awaited the return of his son from Sandhurst. But when the boy arrived, it was to tell his father that he had been 'plucked' for not knowing the locale of Fernando Po.

'Fernando Po!' exclaimed the indignant baronet, 'I don't believe there is such a place. But here comes G——.'

The passerby was a Prince of the Blood Royal, apparently George, Duke of Cambridge. As he drove by in his cab, the baronet called across St James's Street, 'I say, George, where is Fernando Po?'

'How the deuce should I know?' the Prince called back, and then drove on in bewilderment.[36]

In the new age of army reform, there were few tangible memorials to Cardigan. His reputation was soon dependent upon nothing but the events of twenty minutes in the Crimea. The name 'Cardigan', which in 1840 seemed likely to be a quaint synonym for a dark wine bottle, became the standard description of a woollen jacket, but few of the wearers ever associated it with him. For the rest of the nineteenth century, Balaclava Day was celebrated each year by a dwindling number of survivors of the Crimean campaign, the last of whom were to die in the 1930s. It was never in any way comparable to the national commemorations of Waterloo. Even in 1888, the Prince of Wales was still dating his correspondence of 18 June 'Waterloo Day'.[37]

Yet there remained one British institution with which the name of Cardigan was linked more closely than with Balaclava. The 11th Hussars had been largely his own creation, and in the tradition that every regiment should be a law unto itself, Prince Albert's own forgot the squabbles of the 1840s and gave his name an honoured place in their history. Before Victoria's reign was over, the regiment had served in India, Egypt and South Africa. In the First World War it served as a mounted regiment, though many of its soldiers also fought dismounted in the trenches of the Western Front. In 1928, the 11th Hussars ceased to be a cavalry regiment, being equipped as an armoured unit instead. With armoured cars and mobile field guns, the descendants of the Light Brigade fought in Africa and Italy as part of General Montgomery's 8th Army. In 1944, the officers and men were returned to England to take part in the invasion of Europe and to fight from Normandy to Hamburg as part of the Allied Expeditionary Force. In 1969, in the reorganization of the British army, the 11th Hussars and the 10th (Prince of Wales's own) Royal Hussars were amalgamated as the 10th/11th Royal Hussars. Yet throughout its later history, the regiment commemorated Balaclava and Cardigan with intense and enduring pride.

The mechanized devastation of the Second World War, and the brutality of total war, seem far removed from the almost medieval splendour of the Victorian cavalry, the eighteenth-century etiquette

of the mess, or the fashionable crowds at a field day of the 1840s on
the Race Hill at Brighton or in Phoenix Park, Dublin. The contrast is
no less, in its own way, between the unfenced uplands of the Quorn
or the Pytchley in the mid-nineteenth century, and the drab urbaniza-
tion of the East Midlands a hundred years later. Yet one commemoration, which would certainly have pleased Cardigan more than any
other, was destined to survive this change and contrast. After his
death, the 11th Hussars, which already enjoyed the unique privileges
of omitting the loyal toast and of remaining seated for the national
anthem, acquired another eccentric dispensation. At the end of the
day, all other regiments of the British army were required to sound
the last post at 10 p.m. But from 1868 onwards the 11th (Prince
Albert's own), whether in Egypt or India, El Alamein or Hamburg,
was permitted to sound the call ten minutes earlier, commemorating
the hour at which, on 28 March 1868, the 7th Earl of Cardigan had
died at Deene.

NOTES

Sources referred to in the notes are fully described in the bibliography. However, the following abbreviations are used in the notes, after the initial reference.

My Recollections	Adeline, Countess of Cardigan and Lancastre, *My Recollections*.
Eight Months	James Thomas, 7th Earl of Cardigan, *Eight Months on Active Service*.
Cardigan v. Calthorpe	*Earl of Cardigan v. Lieutenant-Colonel Calthorpe, Proceedings in the King's Bench*.
Affidavits	*Cardigan v. Calthorpe: Affidavits filed by the Respondent*.
Statement and Remarks	*Statement and Remarks upon the Affidavits filed by Lieutenant-Colonel Calthorpe*.
Trial	*Trial of James Thomas, Earl of Cardigan before the Right Honourable the House of Peers*.
Creevey	*The Creevey Papers*, ed. Sir Herbert Maxwell.
Gronow	*Reminiscences and Recollections of Captain Gronow*, ed. John Raymond.
Kinglake	A. W. Kinglake, *The Invasion of the Crimea*.
Russell, *The Great War*	W. H. Russell, *The Great War with Russia*.
Russell, *The War*	W. H. Russell, *The War: From the Landing at Gallipoli to the Death of Lord Raglan*.
Duberly	Mrs Henry Duberly, *Journal Kept during the Russian War*.
Paget	Lord George Paget, *The Light Cavalry Brigade in the Crimea*.
Mitchell	Albert Mitchell, *Recollections of One of the Light Brigade*.
Ryan	George Ryan, *Our Heroes of the Crimea*.

In order not to burden passages of narrative with an inordinate number of footnotes, groups of sources are sometimes cited together under one note. So far as possible, they are cited in the order in which the material appears in the narrative.

1 PRELUDE

1 Rees Howell Gronow, *The Reminiscences and Recollections of Captain Gronow*, ed. John Raymond, 1964, p. 74.

2 *Ibid.*, pp. 226–7.

3 *United Service Gazette*, 30 April 1842.

4 *The Times*, 24 April 1841; George Ryan, *Our Heroes of the Crimea*, 1855, p. 58.

2   THE YOUNG LORD

1 A. H. Stanton, *On Chiltern Slopes*, 1927, p. 126.

2 *Ibid.*, p. 51.

3 Thomas Moore, *Memoirs, Journal, and Correspondence*, 1853–6, V, p. 181.

4 Matthew Arnold, *Culture and Anarchy*, 1869, p. 101.

5 G. J. Whyte-Melville, *Riding Recollections*, n.d., p. 40; 'Thormanby', *Kings of the Hunting Field*, 1899, pp. 247–8; Whyte-Melville, *op. cit.*, p. 121.

6 Gronow, p. 57.

7 Elizabeth Gaskell, *Life of Charlotte Brontë*, 1857, I, p. 114.

8 Brudenell MSS.

9 'Nimrod', *The Chase, the Road and the Turf*, 1898, pp. 17, 54.

10 *The History of White's*, pub. Hon. Algernon Bourke, 1892, II, pp. 163, 180.

11 E. D. H. Tollemache, *The Tollemaches of Helmingham and Ham*, 1949, pp. 138–9.

12 Thomas Creevey, *The Creevey Papers*, ed. Sir H. Maxwell, 1903, II, p. 331.

13 *The Times*, 24 June 1824.

14 Brudenell MSS.

15 Gronow, p. 34.

16 Evelyn Wood, *Winnowed Memories*, 1918, p. 119.

17 Creevey, II, p. 75.

18 Gronow, p. 214.

19 *Northampton Mercury*, 8 December 1832; *The Times*, 8 November 1832.

20 *Northampton Herald*, 10 December 1832.

21 *The Times*, 26 November 1832.

22 *Northampton Herald*, 22 September 1832.

23 *Ibid.*, 15 December 1832.

24 *Ibid.*, 22 December 1832; *Northampton Mercury*, 22 December 1832.

3   CONDUCT UNBECOMING

1 J. G. Lockhart, *Memoirs of Sir Walter Scott*, 1900, IV, pp. 253–4.

2 *Proceedings of the General Court-Martial upon the Trial of Captain Wathen, Fifteenth Hussars*, 1834, pp. 58, 220–1.

3 *Ibid.*, p. 220.

4 *Ibid.*, pp. 261, 96.

5 *Ibid.*, pp. 51, 56–7, 163, 59, 168, 36, 96–7.

6 *New Weekly Despatch*, 2 February 1834.

7 *Proceedings of the General Court-Martial*. pp. 159–60.

8 *Ibid.*, p. 161.

9 *Ibid.*, pp. 164–6.

10 *Ibid.*, p. 151.

11 *Ibid.*, p. 167–8.

12 *Ibid.*, p. 8.

13 *Ibid.*, pp. 170–1.

14 *Ibid.*, p. 175.

15 *Ibid.*, pp. 176–9.

16 *Ibid.*, pp. 2–4.

17 *Ibid.*, pp. 151 and 243.

18 *Ibid.*, p. 265–6.

4   PISTOLS FOR TWO

1 *Return to Several Orders of the Honourable the House of Commons, dated 12 February 1836*, p. 6.

2 Brudenell MSS.

3 *Return to Several Orders*, p. 7.

4 *Ibid.*, p. 12.

5 *Ibid.*, p. 11.

6 M. Brialmont and G. R. Gleig, *Life of Arthur Duke of Wellington*, 1860, IV, p. 66; Wellington MSS.

7 *Drakard's Stamford News*, 11 February 1834.

8 John Mills, *D'Horsay: or, The Follies of the Day*, 1902, p. 65.

9 Brudenell MSS.

10 *Elizabeth, Lady Holland to her Son*, Lord Ilchester (ed.), 1946, p. 155.

11 *Northampton Herald*, 17 and 24 January 1835.

12 *Northampton Mercury*, 17 January 1835.

13 *Northampton Herald*, 21 March 1835.

14 Ralph Nevill, *English Country House Life*, 1925, p. 160.

15 *Naval and Military Gazette*, 6 June 1835.

16 Wellington MSS.

17 Mary F. Sanders, *The Life and Times of Queen Adelaide*, 1915, p. 219.

18 *Alligator*, 13 February 1841.

19 *Morning Chronicle*, 24 September 1840.

20 *United Service Gazette*, 7 May 1836.

21 *The Times*, 1 April 1836.

22 *Morning Chronicle*, 7 April 1836.

23 *Morning Post*, 2 and 8 April 1836.

24 *Parliamentary Debates*, 3rd Series, XXXIII, p. 543.

25 *Ibid.*, XXXIII, pp. 554–5.

26 *Morning Chronicle*, 4 May 1836.

27 *United Service Gazette*, 7 May 1836.

28 *Ibid.*, 9 July 1836.

29 Brudenell MSS.

30 *United Service Gazette*, 17 December 1836.

31 *Ibid.*, 18 June 1836 and 16 June 1838.

32 *Ibid.*, 1 July 1837 and 6 January 1838.

33 Isabel Burton, *Life of Captain Sir Richard F. Burton*, 1893, I, p. 135; 'Walter', *My Secret Life*, 1966, II, p. 334; *United Service Gazette*, 10 May 1834.

34 *Naval and Military Gazette*, 11 February 1837.

35 *Ibid.*, 26 September 1840.

36 Brudenell MSS.

37 *Calcutta Courier*, 6 February 1838.

38 *Globe*, 15 October 1840.

39 'Thormanby', *Kings of the Hunting Field*, pp. 248–9.

40 *Morning Herald*, 14 and 20 August 1838; *Naval and Military Gazette*, 18 and 25 August 1838.

41 *Naval and Military Gazette*, 20 October 1838.

42 *Ibid.*, 22 June 1839.

43 *Morning Chronicle*, 12 and 22 August 1839.

44 *Ibid.*, 16 August 1839.

45 *Ibid.*, 22 and 23 August 1839.

46 *Morning Herald*, 21 August 1839.

47 *Standard*, 29 September 1840.

48 *United Service Gazette*, 20 June 1835.

49 *Morning Chronicle*, 14 August 1840; *Examiner*, 22 March and 5 July 1840; *Globe*, 24 August 1840.

50 William Ballantine, *Some Experiences of a Barrister's Life*, 1882, I, p. 97.

51 Creevey, II, p. 326.

52 *Northampton Herald*, 21 March 1840; *Bell's Life in London*, 29 March 1840.

53 Creevey, II, p. 307.

54 *Age*, 12 April 1840.

55 *The Times*, 22 April 1854.

56 Forrest MSS.

57 *Globe*, 16 and 17 September 1840; *Alligator*, 16 January 1841.

58 *The Times*, 6 October 1840.

59 *Morning Post*, 26 September 1840.

60 *Ibid.*, 29 September 1840.

61 *Kent Herald*, 4 June 1840.

62 *Naval and Military Gazette*, 27 June 1840.

63 Forrest MSS.

64 MS. letter of R. A. Reynolds, quoted in Joan Wake, *The Brudenells of Deene*, 1953, pp. 372–3.

65 *Morning Chronicle*, 26 September; 2, 3 and 6 October 1840.

66 *Naval and Military Gazette*, 5 September 1840; *Morning Chronicle*, 4 September 1840.

67 *The Trial of James Thomas, Earl of Cardigan*, 1841, pp. 28–40.

5 BY GOD AND MY PEERS!

1 *Trial*, pp. 80–2.
2 *Standard*, 17 September 1840.
3 *Globe*, 4 November 1840.
4 *United Service Gazette*, 12 December 1840.
5 *The Times*, 29 September 1840.
6 *Globe*, 18 November 1840; *Bell's Life in London*, 4 October 1840; *United Service Gazette*, 26 September 1840.
7 *Sussex Advertiser*, 28 September 1840.
8 *Morning Chronicle*, 26 September 1840.
9 *Naval and Military Gazette*, 26 September 1840.
10 *United Service Gazette*, 26 September 1840.
11 *Morning Chronicle*, 26 September 1840.
12 Ibid., 26 September 1840.
13 Ibid., 2 October 1840.
14 Ibid., 6 October 1840.
15 *United Service Gazette*, 3 October 1840; *Morning Chronicle*, 5 October 1840.
16 *Globe*, 6 October 1840; Forrest MSS.
17 *Sussex Advertiser*, 26 October 1840.
18 *Globe*, 20 October 1840.
19 *Morning Chronicle*, 5 October 1840.
20 *Naval and Military Gazette*, 19 September 1840; *Morning Post*, 20 October 1840.
21 *Naval and Military Gazette*, 17 October 1840.
22 General Order No. 538, 20 October 1840.
23 *Brighton Herald*, 24 October 1840.
24 *United Service Gazette*, 14 November 1840.
25 *Examiner*, 1 November 1840.
26 *United Service Gazette*, 24 October 1840; *Globe*, 22 October 1840; *Examiner*, 1 November 1840.
27 *Morning Chronicle*, 16 October 1840.
28 *Brighton Gazette*, 22 October 1840.
29 *United Service Gazette*, 7 November 1840.
30 Ibid., 3 October 1840.
31 Ibid., 31 October 1840.
32 *Alligator*, 30 January 1841.
33 *Spectator*, 31 October 1840.
34 *Globe*, 4 November 1840.
35 Ibid., 3 November 1840.
36 *Naval and Military Gazette*, 7 November 1840.
37 *Examiner*, 8 November 1840.
38 *Morning Chronicle*, 30 October 1840; *Brighton Gazette*, 5 November 1840.
39 *Globe*, 31 October 1840.

40 *Naval and Military Gazette*, 5 December 1840 and 20 February 1841.

41 *Brighton Gazette*, 12 November 1840.

42 *Brighton Herald*, 7 November 1840.

43 *The Times*, 23 December 1840; *Morning Advertiser*, 23 December 1840.

44 *The Times*, 30 January 1841; *Morning Chronicle*, 30 January 1841; *Globe*, 29 January 1841.

45 *Parliamentary Debates*, 3rd series, LVI, 1396.

46 *United Service Gazette*, 9 January 1841; *Morning Chronicle*, 7 January 1841.

47 *Morning Post*, 30 November 1840.

48 *United Service Gazette*, 27 February 1841.

49 *Globe*, 8 January 1841; *United Service Gazette*, 23 January 1841; *Britannia*, 30 January 1841.

50 *Alligator*, 30 January 1841.

51 *Ibid.*, 16 January 1841.

52 *Correspondence and Diaries of John Wilson Croker*, 1885, II, p. 405.

53 *Trial*, pp. 8–9.

54 *Ibid.*, p. 11.

55 *Ibid.*, pp. 18–19.

56 *Ibid.*, p. 22.

57 *Ibid.*, pp. 25–6.

58 *Ibid.*, p. 36.

59 *Ibid.*, pp. 72–4; *Morning Post*, 17 February 1841.

60 *Trial*, p. 79.

61 *Ibid.*, pp. 99–100.

62 *Ibid.*, p. 100.

63 *Ibid.*, pp. 102–3.

64 *Ibid.*, p. 104.

65 *Ibid.*, pp. 116–23.

66 *Morning Chronicle*, 18 February 1841; *Globe*, 15 January and 17 February 1841.

67 *Morning Post*, 19 February 1841.

6 CRIMINAL CONVERSATION

1 *Naval and Military Gazette*, 27 March 1841.

2 *Brighton Gazette*, 26 November 1840.

3 *United Service Gazette*, 6 March 1841.

4 General Order, 22 April 1841.

5 *The Times*, 24 April 1841.

6 *Ibid.*, 24 April 1841.

7 *Ibid.*, 17 July 1834.

8 *Ibid.*, 28 November 1835.

9 *United Service Gazette*, 10 April 1841.

10 *Ibid.*, 24 April 1841.

11 *Ibid.*, 1 May 1841.

12 *Ibid.*, 1 May 1841.
13 *Ibid.*, 24 April 1841.
14 *Letters of Queen Victoria*, Benson and Esher (eds), 1908–32, I, pp. 262–3.
15 *Ibid.*, I, p. 263.
16 *Ibid.*, I, p. 264.
17 Wellington MSS.
18 *United Service Gazette*, 10 July 1841 and 18 March 1848.
19 *Ibid.*, 6 November 1852 and 10 December 1853; *Freeman's Journal*, 21 October 1843.
20 British Museum, Add. MSS. 40498, f. 130.
21 British Museum, Add. MSS. 40446, ff. 248–9.
22 British Museum, Add. MSS. 40498, ff. 134–6, 188–9.
23 *The Greville Memoirs*, Strachey and Fulford (eds), 1938, V, p. 6.
24 *Letters of Queen Victoria*, I, p. 386.
25 *Ibid.*, I, p. 394.
26 *Ibid.*, I, p. 394.
27 *Annual Register for 1845*, 1846, pp. 78–81.
28 *United Service Gazette*, 23 October 1847 and 8 October 1842.
29 *Fraser's Magazine*, XXXVI (1847), p. 598.
30 J. Anstruther Thomson, *Eighty Years' Reminiscences*, 1904, I, pp. 89–90.
31 *United Service Gazette*, 8 October 1842 and 25 December 1847.
32 *Ibid.*, 11 May 1850.
33 *Ibid.*, 2 June 1849; *Fraser's Magazine*, XXXVI, p. 598.
34 *Northern Star*, 13 July 1839.
35 *Halifax Guardian*, 20 August 1842.
36 *The Times*, 28 April 1843.
37 *Ibid.*, 7 May 1843.
38 *Ibid.*, 15 May 1843.
39 *United Service Gazette*, 21 September 1843; Forrest MSS.
40 *Freeman's Journal*, 21 October 1843.
41 Forrest MSS.
42 Wellington MSS.
43 Wellington MSS.
44 *United Service Gazette*, 12 February, 19 February and 12 March 1842.
45 *The Times*, 21 September 1843.
46 *Dublin Mercantile Advertiser*, 8 September 1843.
47 Wellington MSS.
48 Wellington MSS.
49 *The Times*, 21 September 1843.
50 *United Service Gazette*, 25 December 1847 and 30 March 1850.
51 *John Bull*, 11 November 1848.
52 Wellington MSS.
53 Brialmont and Gleig, *Life of Arthur, Duke of Wellington*, IV, pp. 112–13.
54 Mrs T. Kelly, *From the Fleet in the Fifties*, 1902, pp. 205–6.
55 *United Service Gazette*, 18 September 1841.
56 Louis C. Jackson, *History of the United Service Club*, 1937, p. 35.
57 *Age*, 23 and 30 December 1843.

58 *The Times*, 23 December 1843; *Age*, 23 December 1843.

59 *The Times*, 28 February 1844.

60 E. D. H. Tollemache, *The Tollemaches of Helmingham and Ham*, 1949, p. 126.

61 Adeline, Countess of Cardigan, *My Recollections*, 1909, pp. 95–6.

62 *Ibid.*, p. 94.

63 *Age*, 7 October 1843.

64 Whyte-Melville, *Riding Recollections*, pp. 120–1.

65 Moreton Frewin, *Melton Mowbray and other Memories*, 1924, p. 69.

66 *Ibid.*, p. 68.

67 H. O. Nethercote, *The Pytchley Hunt: Past and Present*, 1888, p. 353.

68 Guy Paget, *The History of the Althorpe and Pytchley Hunt*, 1937, pp. 261–2.

69 William Whelan, *History, Gazetteer, and Dictionary of Northamptonshire*, 1849, pp. 801–2.

70 *Coventry Standard*, 16 June 1848.

71 *United Service Gazette*, 19 April 1851; *Naval and Military Gazette*, 29 April 1854.

72 *Parliamentary Debates*, 3rd Series, CXIV, pp. 28–31, 335–8, 341; CXI, pp. 1362–7; CXIV, pp. 170–5.

73 *The History of White's*, II, pp. 224–6.

74 *United Service Gazette*, 11 March 1854.

7 GOING TO THE WARS

1 *Bell's Weekly Messenger*, 4 March 1854.

2 Timothy Gowing, *A Voice from the Ranks*, 1954, pp. 3–5.

3 Sergeant Albert Mitchell, *Recollections of One of the Light Brigade*, 1885, p. 7.

4 *Ibid.*, pp. 12–13.

5 *Parliamentary Debates*, 3rd Series, CXXX, pp. 1133–4.

6 George Ryan, *Our Heroes of the Crimea*, 1855, p. 47.

7 Cardigan, *Eight Months on Active Service*, 1855, p. 3.

8 William Howard Russell, *The Great War with Russia*, 1895, p. 118.

9 *Ibid.*, p. 316; Alexander William Kinglake, *The Invasion of the Crimea*, 1863–1887, II, p. 18.

10 *The Times*, 22 and 24 April 1854; *Naval and Military Gazette*, 29 April 1854; Raglan MSS.

11 *Eight Months*, pp. 5–13; *United Service Gazette*, 8 July 1854.

12 *United Service Gazette*, 5 August 1854.

13 G. T. Williams, *Historical Records of the 11th Hussars*, 1908, pp. 182–3.

14 Mabel, Countess of Airlie, *With the Guards We Shall Go*, 1933, p. 40.

15 E. C. Grenville-Murray, *Pictures from the Battlefields*, 1855, p. 127.

16 Mrs Henry Duberly, *Journal Kept During the Russian War*, 1856, p. 34.

17 *Eight Months*, p. 36; Duberly, p. 39.

18 Ryan, p. 49.

19 C. R. B. Barrett, *History of the 13th Hussars*, 1911, I, p. 332; George Higginson, *Seventy-One Years of a Guardsman's Life*, 1916, p. 129.
20 Lord George Paget, *The Light Cavalry Brigade in the Crimea*, 1881, p. 6.
21 Mitchell, p. 24; Russell, *The Great War*, p. 115.
22 *Eight Months*, p. 54.
23 *United Service Gazette*, 5 August 1854.
24 Duberly, p. 57.
25 Mitchell, pp. 25 and 29.
26 *Ibid.*, pp. 30–32 and 36.
27 Frederick Robinson, *Diary of the Crimean War*, 1856, pp. 128–32; Mitchell, p. 27.
28 Mitchell, pp. 24–5.
29 Duberly, pp. 54–6.
30 *Ibid.*, pp. 57–8.
31 *United Service Gazette*, 2 September 1854.
32 *Naval and Military Gazette*, 25 November 1854.
33 Williams, *op. cit.*, p. 183.
34 Duberly, p. 62; Williams, *op. cit.*, p. 183.
35 *United Service Gazette*, 9 September 1854.
36 *Eight Months*, p. 65; Duberly, p. 59.
37 Mitchell, p. 33; Duberly, p. 66; *Eight Months*, p. 67.
38 Kinglake, II, p. 94.
39 Robinson, *Diary of the Crimean War*, p. 143; *Eight Months*, pp. 69–70.
40 Duberly, p. 70.
41 Duberly, pp. 72–3; *Eight Months*, pp. 70–1.
42 Russell, *The Great War*, p. 319; Duberly, p. 80.
43 Duberly, p. 80.
44 Mitchell, p. 41; Kinglake, II, pp. 189–90.
45 Russell, *The War in the Crimea*, 1855, pp. 168–9.
46 Mitchell, p. 42.
47 *Ibid.*, pp. 43–4.
48 *Eight Months*, p. 75; Robinson, *Diary of the Crimean War*, p. 153.
49 *Eight Months*, p. 74.
50 Kelly, *From the Fleet in the Fifties*, pp. 120–2.
51 Paget, p. 16n.
52 *Eight Months*, p. 77; MS. Letter of Private John Williams, quoted in Christopher Hibbert, *The Destruction of Lord Raglan*, 1963, p. 76.
53 Forrest MSS.
54 Evelyn Wood, *The Crimea in 1854 and 1894*, 1895, p. 84.
55 Mitchell, p. 53.
56 *Ibid.*, p. 53.
57 W. H. Pennington, *Sea, Camp, and Stage*, 1906, p. 37; Mitchell, p. 53.
58 Pennington, *Sea, Camp, and Stage*, p. 37.
59 Mitchell, p. 56.
60 *Eight Months*, p. 78; Russell, *The Great War*, p. 315; Edward Cooper Hodge, *Little Hodge*, the Marquess of Anglesey (ed.), 1971, pp. 30–31.
61 Russell, *The Great War*, p. 116.

62 Paget, p. 32.
63 *Eight Months*, p. 81.
64 Mitchell, p. 66.
65 Pennington, *Sea, Camp, and Stage*, p. 51; Kelly, *From the Fleet in the Fifties*, p. 205.
66 Kelly, *From the Fleet in the Fifties*, pp. 138–9.
67 George Buchanan, *Camp Life as Seen by a Civilian*, 1871, pp. 55–6.
68 Daniel Lysons, *The Crimean War from First to Last*, 1895, p. 191; Evelyn Wood, *The Crimea in 1854 and 1894*, p. 88.
69 Lysons, *The Crimean War from First to Last*, pp. 168–70.
70 Russell, *The Great War*, p. 319.
71 Raglan MSS.
72 Russell, *The Great War*, p. 320.
73 Paget, pp. 57–8 and 64–5.
74 *Ibid.*, pp. 59–60.
75 *Ibid.*, p. 66.
76 *Ibid.*, p. 66.
77 Russell, *The Great War*, pp. 62–3; Pennington, *Sea, Camp, and Stage*, p. 50.
78 Paget, pp. 58 and 63.
79 Hodge, *Little Hodge*, p. 39.
80 Buchanan, *Camp Life as Seen by a Civilian*, pp. 71–2.

8 CHARGE! HURRAH! HURRAH!

1 Russell, *The Great War*, p. 138.
2 Higginson, *Seventy-One Years of a Guardsman's Life*, 1916, p. 185.
3 Russell, *The Great War*, p. 139.
4 Duberly, pp. 116–17.
5 Kinglake, IV, pp. 124–5.
6 Paget, p. 168.
7 *Ibid.*, p. 174.
8 Paget, p. 175; Russell, *The War*, pp. 228–9.
9 Kinglake, IV, p. 208.
10 Russell, *The Great War*, p. 152.
11 Barrett, *History of the 13th Hussars*, I, p. 356.
12 Peter Carew, *Combat and Carnival*, 1954, p. 211.
13 E. H. Nolan, *Illustrated History of the War Against Russia*, 1857, I, p. 541; *Nineteenth Century*, XXXI (1892), p. 851; Carew, *Combat and Carnival*, p. 210; Kinglake, IV, pp. 209 and 211n.; *Cardigan v. Calthorpe*, 1863, pp. 238–9; Wood, *The Crimea in 1854 and 1894*, p. 113.
14 *Nineteenth Century*, XXXI, p. 852; Kinglake, IV, pp. 240–1; *Eight Months*, p. 89; Richard Brett-Smith, *The 11th Hussars*, 1969, p. 124; William, Duke of Portland, *Men, Women and Things*, 1937, pp. 196–7; Paget, p. 170; Kinglake, IV, p. 253; *Nineteenth Century*, XXXI, p. 852.
15 D. H. Parry, *The Death or Glory Boys*, 1899, p. 211; Kinglake, IV, p. 256n.; Henry Clifford, *Letters and Sketches from the Crimea*, 1956, p. 73.

16 Kinglake, IV, p. 266; *Nineteenth Century*, XXXI, p. 853; 'Thormanby', *Kings of the Hunting Field*, p. 245; Mitchell, p. 84; *Viscount Tredegar: His Life and Work*, 1913, p. 25; *Nineteenth Century*, XXXI, p. 854.

17 Russell, *The War*, pp. 231–2; Paget, p. 184.

18 *Nineteenth Century*, XXXI, p. 855; Paget, pp. 188–9; Mitchell, p. 85; *Nineteenth Century*, XXXI, p. 856; Paget, p. 192.

19 W. Baring Pemberton, *Battles of the Crimean War*, 1968, p. 118; Kinglake, IV, p. 356; Paget, p. 193n.

20 Kinglake, IV, p. 363; Paget, p. 73; Reginald Hargreaves, *This Happy Breed*, 1951, pp. 72–3; Wood, *The Crimea in 1854 and 1894*, p. 113.

21 Paget, pp. 199–200; Kinglake, IV, p. 382.

22 Clifford, *Letters and Sketches from the Crimea*, p. 80; *Eight Months*, p. 108.

23 Russell, *The Great War*, p. 177.

24 Paget, p. 223.

25 *Ibid.*, p. 230.

26 *Blackwood's Magazine*, CCLIX (1946), p. 45.

27 Raglan MSS.

28 *Cardigan v. Calthorpe*, pp. 240–1.

29 Paget, p. 253.

30 Duberly MSS.

31 *Eight Months*, p. 104.

32 Raglan MSS.

33 Raglan MSS.

34 Carew, *Combat and Carnival*, p. 188.

35 Slade Murray, 'Oh! 'Tis a Famous Story', 1855.

36 *Punch*, 25 November 1854.

37 MS. Journal of Queen Victoria, 17 January 1855.

38 *Letters of Queen Victoria*, III, pp. 66–7.

39 Royal Archives, G. 22/10.

40 MS. Journal of Queen Victoria, 17 January 1855.

41 Airlie, *With the Guards We Shall Go*, p. 283.

42 Royal Archives, G. 23/21.

43 *Northampton Mercury*, 10 February 1855.

44 *United Service Gazette*, 10 February 1855.

45 *Northampton Herald*, 10 February 1855.

46 *Northampton Mercury*, 10 February 1855.

47 *United Service Gazette*, 10 February 1855; *Northampton Mercury*, 10 February 1855.

48 *Northampton Mercury*, 24 February 1855.

49 Ryan, *Our Heroes of the Crimea*, p. 58.

50 Slade Murray, 'Oh! 'Tis a Famous Story', 1855.

9   'WAS LORD CARDIGAN A HERO AT BALACLAVA?'

1 W. F. Monypenny and G. E. Buckle, *The Life of Benjamin Disraeli, Earl of Beaconsfield*, 1910–1920, III, p. 571.

2 Paget, pp. 88 and 215.
3 Raglan MSS.
4 *Parliamentary Debates*, 3rd Series, CXXXVII, pp. 731–73.
5 *United Service Gazette*, 10 March, 9 June and 8 December 1855.
6 Sir Theodore Martin, *Life of His Royal Highness the Prince Consort*, 1875–7, III, pp. 242–3.
7 *United Service Gazette*, 10 March 1855.
8 George Dodd, *Pictorial History of the Russian War*, p. 533.
9 Forrest MSS.
10 Report of the Select Committee, pp. 264 and 266.
11 *Ibid.*, pp. 266 and 276.
12 *Ibid.*, p. 269.
13 *Ibid.*, p. 263.
14 *Ibid.*, pp. 276–7.
15 *United Service Gazette*, 15 September 1855.
16 *Report of the Commission of Inquiry into the Supplies of the British Army in the Crimea*, 1856, p. 19.
17 *United Service Gazette*, 16 and 23 February 1856.
18 *Ibid.*, 1 March 1856.
19 *Ibid.*, 3 May 1856.
20 Carew, *Combat and Carnival*, p. 209.
21 *Sheffield Telegraph*, 30 July 1856.
22 *United Service Gazette*, 6 September 1856.
23 Pennington, *Sea, Camp, and Stage*, pp. 166–8.
24 *Morning Post*, 30 September, 7 October, 11 October and 14 October 1856.
25 Lloyd, *From the Fleet in the Fifties*, p. 206.
26 *Morning Post*, 24 and 26 June 1856.
27 Brudenell MSS.
28 *Cardigan v. Calthorpe*, pp. 244–5.
29 Hon. S. J. Gough Calthorpe, *Letters from Head-Quarters; or, The Realities of the War in the Crimea*, 1856, I, p. 184.
30 *Ibid.*, I, p. 310.
31 *Ibid.*, I, p. 317.
32 *Ibid.*, II, p. 5.
33 *Ibid.*, II, p. 123.
34 *Cardigan v. Calthorpe: Affidavits filed by the Respondent*, 1863, p. 7.
35 *Ibid.*, pp. 8 and 11–12; Brudenell MSS.
36 *Examiner*, 3 September 1859.
37 *United Service Gazette*, 10 September 1859.
38 Brudenell MSS.
39 *Affidavits*, p. 13.
40 Brudenell MSS.
41 *Letters from Head-Quarters*, 3rd edition, 1857, p. 130.
42 *Affidavits*, pp. 14–15.
43 Brudenell MSS.; *Army and Navy Gazette*, 20 June 1863; *Court Journal*, 20 June 1863.

44 *Cardigan v. Calthorpe*, p. 68.
45 *Ibid.*, p. 67.
46 *Ibid.*, p. 206.
47 *Ibid.*, p. 211.
48 *Ibid.*, p. 219.
49 *The Times*, 11 June 1863; *Lloyd's Weekly London Newspaper*, 12 July 1863.
50 *Sun*, 11 June 1863.
51 Brudenell MSS.
52 *Affidavits*, p. 1; *Statement and Remarks upon the Affidavits filed by Lieutenant-Colonel Calthorpe*, 1863, p. 22.
53 *Statement and Remarks*, p. 11.
54 Brudenell MSS.
55 Brudenell MSS.
56 Brudenell MSS.
57 *The History of White's*, II, p. 240.
58 Prince Kraft zu Hohenlohe-Ingelfingen, *Aus Meinem Leben*, 1897–1907, II, pp. 284–5.
59 Brett-Smith, *The 11th Hussars*, pp. 96–7.

10 ADELINE

1 Lady Augusta Fane, *Chit-Chat*, 1926, pp. 40–41; Lady Dorothy Nevill, *The Life and Letters of Lady Dorothy Nevill*, 1919, p. 193.
2 *My Recollections*, pp. 38–43.
3 *Ibid.*, pp. 96–7.
4 A. M. W. Stirling, *William de Morgan and his Wife*, 1922, p. 149.
5 *My Recollections*, p. 100.
6 *Ibid.*, p. 106.
7 Brudenell MSS.
8 Brudenell MSS.
9 Joan Wake, *The Brudenells of Deene*, 1953, p. 438.
10 *Ibid.*, p. 432.
11 Brudenell MSS.
12 Fane, *Chit-Chat*, p. 42.
13 *United Service Gazette*, 14 November 1857.
14 J. B. Booth, *Sporting Times: The Pink 'Un World*, 1938, pp. 167–8.
15 *Lincoln, Rutland, and Stamford Mercury*, 11 June 1915.
16 Ralph Nevill, *London Clubs*, p. 308.
17 *The History of White's*, I, pp. 234–6.
18 *The Times*, 7 May and 6 June 1866; *United Service Gazette*, 12 May and 9 June 1866.
19 Justin McCarthy, *A History of Our Own Times*, 1905, III, p. 370.
20 *The Times*, 23 August 1866.
21 Brudenell MSS.
22 Cambridge University Library, Add. MSS. 7633C.

23 Brudenell MSS.
24 Brudenell MSS.
25 J. Anstruther Thomson, *Eighty Years' Reminiscences*, I, pp. 382–3.
26 Sir William Hardman, *The Hardman Papers*, S. M. Ellis (ed.), 1930, p. 339.
27 'Thormanby', *Kings of the Hunting Field*, pp. 250–1.
28 Booth, *Sporting Times*, pp. 168–9.
29 Beaconsfield MSS.
30 *My Recollections*, pp. 142–3.
31 Wake, *The Brudenells of Deene*, p. 467.
32 *Ibid.*, p. 468.
33 Kinglake, IV, p. 63.
34 *Letters of Queen Victoria*, V, pp. 329–30 and III, p. 213.
35 Kinglake, IV, p. 62.
36 J. H. Stocqueler, *A Personal History of the Horse Guards*, 1873, p. 183.
37 *Letters of Queen Victoria*, VII, p. 418.

BIBLIOGRAPHY

The second section of the bibliography contains those periodical publications which have been used as general sources for the period of Cardigan's life, or for other periods referred to in the footnotes. Where a specific article from a journal has been used, this will be found listed in the third section of the bibliography.

Unless otherwise stated, the place of publication of books listed in the third section of the bibliography is London.

1 MANUSCRIPT SOURCES

The Brudenell Papers
The Crimean Papers of Field Marshal Lord Raglan
The Papers and Correspondence of the 1st Duke of Wellington
The Papers and Correspondence of General W. C. Forrest
The Royal Archives
The Correspondence of Sir Robert Peel
The Correspondence of A. W. Kinglake
The Papers of Benjamin Disraeli, Earl of Beaconsfield
The Letters of Frances Duberly to her sister, Selina

2 PERIODICAL PUBLICATIONS

Age
Alligator
Annual Register
Army and Navy Gazette
Bell's Life in London
Bell's Weekly Messenger
Brighton Herald
Brighton Gazette
Britannia
Calcutta Courier
Canterbury Weekly Journal
Court Journal
Coventry Standard
Daily News

Drakard's Stamford News
Dublin Mercantile Advertiser
Examiner
Freeman's Journal
Globe
Halifax Guardian
Hansard's Parliamentary Debates, 3rd series
John Bull
Kentish Gazette
Kent Herald
Lincoln, Rutland, and Stamford Mercury
Lloyd's Weekly London Newspaper
Morning Advertiser
Morning Chronicle
Morning Herald
Morning Post
Naval and Military Gazette
New Weekly Despatch
Northampton Herald
Northampton Mercury
Northern Star
Punch
Sheffield Telegraph
Spectator
Standard
Sun
Sussex Advertiser
The Times
United Service Gazette
Wellington Gazette

3   BOOKS AND ARTICLES

ADYE, SIR JOHN, *Recollections of a Military Life*, 1895.

ADYE, SIR JOHN, *A Review of the Crimean War*, 1860.

AIREY, SIR RICHARD, *Opening Address before the Board of General Officers at Chelsea*, 1856.

AIRLIE, MABEL, COUNTESS OF, *With the Guards We Shall Go*, 1933.

ARNOLD, MATTHEW, *Culture and Anarchy*, 1869.

BALLANTINE, WILLIAM, *Some Experiences of a Barrister's Life*, 2 vols, 1882.

BARKER, A. J., *The Vainglorious War*, 1970.

'Barrack Yard, The', *Fraser's Magazine*, XXXVI (1847), pp. 595–9.

BARRETT, C. R. B., *History of the 13th Hussars*, 2 vols, 1911.

BEAMISH, NORTH LUDLOW, *On the Use and Application of Cavalry in War*, 1855.

BENTLEY, NICHOLAS, *Russell's Despatches from the Crimea*, 1966.

BLYTH, HENRY, *Skittles: The Last Victorian Courtesan*, 1970.

BOOTH, J. B., *Sporting Times: The Pink 'Un World*, 1938.

BRETT-SMITH, RICHARD, *The 11th Hussars*, 1969.

BRIALMONT, M. and GLEIG, G. R., *Life of Arthur, Duke of Wellington*, 5 vols, 1860.

BROUGHTON, JOHN CAM HOBHOUSE, LORD, *Recollections of a Long Life*, 6 vols, 1911.

BUCHANAN, GEORGE, *Camp Life as Seen by a Civilian*, 1871.

BURTON, LADY ISABEL, *Life of Captain Sir Richard F. Burton*, 2 vols, 1893.

CALTHORPE, HON. S. J. GOUGH, *Letters from Head-Quarters: or, The Realities of the War in the Crimea. By an Officer on the Staff*, 2 vols, 1856; 3rd edition, in one volume, 1857.

CALTHORPE, HON. S. J. GOUGH, *Cardigan v. Calthorpe: Affidavits filed by the Respondent*, 1863.

CARDIGAN, JAMES THOMAS BRUDENELL, 7TH EARL OF, *Cavalry Brigade Movements*, 1861.

CARDIGAN, JAMES THOMAS BRUDENELL, 7TH EARL OF, *Eight Months on Active Service: or, A Diary of a General Officer of Cavalry in 1854*, 1855.

CARDIGAN, JAMES THOMAS BRUDENELL, 7TH EARL OF, *The Earl of Cardigan v. Lieutenant-Colonel Calthorpe, Proceedings in the King's Bench*, 1863.

CARDIGAN, JAMES THOMAS BRUDENELL, 7TH EARL OF, *Statement and Remarks upon the Affidavits filed by Lieutenant-Colonel Calthorpe*, 1863.

CARDIGAN, JAMES THOMAS BRUDENELL, 7TH EARL OF, *Trial of James Thomas, Earl of Cardigan, before the Right Honourable the House of Peers, for Felony*, pub. Gurney, 1841.

CARDIGAN AND LANCASTRE, ADELINE, COUNTESS OF, *My Recollections*, 1909.

CAREW, PETER, *Combat and Carnival*, 1954.

CAREW, PETER, 'One of "The Six Hundred"', *Blackwood's Magazine*, CCLIX (1946), pp. 40–50.

CECIL, LORD DAVID, *Lord M.*, 1954.

CHICHESTER, HENRY MANNERS, AND BURGES-SHORT, GEORGE, *The Records and Badges of Every Regiment and Corps in the British Army*, 1895.

CLIFFORD, HENRY, *Letters and Sketches from the Crimea*, 1956.

COCKAYNE, G. E., *The Complete Peerage*, 12 vols, 1910–59.

COMPTON, PIERS, *Cardigan of Balaclava*, 1972.

CREEVEY, THOMAS, *The Creevey Papers*, Sir Herbert Maxwell (ed.), 2 vols, 1903.

CREEVEY, THOMAS, *Creevey*, John Gore (ed.), 1948.

CROKER, JOHN WILSON, *Correspondence and Diaries*, Louis J. Jennings (ed.), 3 vols, 1885.

DANIELL, DAVID S., *The Story of the 4th Queen's Own Hussars*, 1959.

DODD, GEORGE, *Pictorial History of the Russian War*, 1856.

DUBERLY, MRS HENRY, *Journal Kept during the Russian War*, 1856.

EVELYN, GEORGE P., *A Diary of the Crimea*, Cyril Falls (ed.), 1954.

FANE, LADY AUGUSTA, *Chit-Chat*, 1926.

FARMER, J. S., *The Regimental Records of the British Army*, 1901.

FORTESCUE, J. W., *A History of the 17th Lancers*, 1895.

FORTESCUE, J. W., *A History of the British Army*, vol. XIII, 1930.

FREWIN, MORETON, *Melton Mowbray and Other Memories*, 1924.

FURNEAUX, RUPERT, *The First War Correspondent: William Howard Russell*, 1944.

GASKELL, ELIZABETH, *Life of Charlotte Brontë*, 2 vols, 1857.

GAURY, GERALD DE, *Travelling Gent: The Life of Alexander Kinglake*, 1972.

GOTCH, J. A., *The Old Halls and Manor Homes of Northamptonshire*, 1936.

GOTCH, J. A., *Squires' Homes and other old Buildings of Northamptonshire*, 1939.

GOWING, TIMOTHY, *A Voice from the Ranks*, 1954.

GRENVILLE-MURRAY, E. C., *Pictures from the Battlefields*, 1855.

GREVILLE, CHARLES, *The Greville Memoirs, 1814–1860*, Lytton Strachey and Roger Fulford (eds), 8 vols, 1938.

GREVILLE, HENRY, *Leaves from the Diary of Henry Greville*, Viscountess Enfield (ed.), 4 vols, 1883–1904.

GRONOW, REES HOWELL, *Reminiscences and Recollections of Captain Gronow*, John Raymond (ed.), 1964.

HAMLEY, SIR EDWARD, *The War in the Crimea*, 1896.

HARDMAN, SIR WILLIAM, *The Hardman Papers*, S. M. Ellis (ed.), 1930.

HARGREAVES, REGINALD, *This Happy Breed*, 1951.

HIBBERT, CHRISTOPHER, *The Destruction of Lord Raglan*, 1961.

HIGGINSON, GENERAL SIR GEORGE, *Seventy-One Years of a Guardsman's Life*, 1916.

Historical Records of the Eleventh Hussars, pub. Richard Cannon, 1843.

Historical Records of the Fifteenth, or the King's Regiment of Light Dragoons, pub. Richard Cannon, 1841.

History of White's, The, pub. Hon. Algernon Bourke, 2 vols, 1892.

HODGE, EDWARD COOPER, *Little Hodge*, Marquess of Anglesey (ed.), 1971.

HOHENLOHE-INGELFINGEN, PRINCE KRAFT ZU, *Aus Meinem Leben*, 4 vols, 1897–1907.

HOLLAND, LADY ELIZABETH, *Elizabeth, Lady Holland to her Son*, Lord Ilchester (ed.), 1946.

JACKSON, MAJOR-GENERAL SIR LOUIS C., *History of the United Service Club*, 1937.

KELLY, MRS T., *From the Fleet in the Fifties*, 1902.

KINGLAKE, ALEXANDER WILLIAM, *The Invasion of the Crimea*, 8 vols, 1863–87.

KIRBY, CHESTER, *The English Country Gentleman: A Study of Nineteenth Century Types*, 1937.

LOCKHART, JOHN GIBSON, *Memoirs of Sir Walter Scott*, 5 vols, 1900.

LONGFORD, LADY ELIZABETH, *Wellington: The Years of the Sword*, 1969.

LONGFORD, LADY ELIZABETH, *Wellington: Pillar of State*, 1972.

LYSONS, SIR DANIEL, *The Crimean War from First to Last*, 1895.

MCCARTHY, JUSTIN, *A History of Our Own Times*, 3 vols, 1905.

MACMUNN, SIR GEORGE, *The Crimea in Perspective*, 1935.

MARTIN, KINGSLEY, *The Triumph of Lord Palmerston*, 1963.

MARTIN, SIR THEODORE, *Life of His Royal Highness the Prince Consort*, 5 vols, 1875–7.

MEREDITH, GEORGE, *Lord Ormont and his Aminta*, 1894.

MILLS, JOHN, *D'Horsay: or, The Follies of the Day*, 1902.

MITCHELL, ALBERT, *Recollections of One of the Light Brigade*, Canterbury, 1885.

MONYPENNY, W. F. AND BUCKLE, G. E., *The Life of Benjamin Disraeli, Earl of Beaconsfield*, 8 vols, 1910–20.

MOORE, THOMAS, *Memoirs, Journal, and Correspondence*, Lord John Russell (ed.), 8 vols, 1853–6.

NETHERCOTE, H. O., *The Pytchley Hunt: Past and Present*, 1888.

NEVILL, LADY DOROTHY, *Leaves from the Note-Books of Lady Dorothy Nevill*, 1907.

NEVILL, LADY DOROTHY, *Under Five Reigns*, 1910.

NEVILL, LADY DOROTHY, *The Life and Letters of Lady Dorothy Nevill*, 1919.

NEVILL, RALPH, *London Clubs, their Histories and Treasures*, 1911.

NEVILL, RALPH, *English Country House Life*, 1925.

'NIMROD' [C. J. APPERLEY], *The Chase, the Road, and the Turf*, 1898.

'NIMROD' [C. J. APPERLEY], *Nimrod's Hunting Reminiscences*, 1926.

NOLAN, E. H., *Illustrated History of the War against Russia*, 2 vols, 1857.

PAGET, LORD GEORGE, *The Light Cavalry Brigade in the Crimea*, 1881.

PAGET, GUY, *The History of the Althorpe and Pytchley Hunt*, 1937.

PANMURE, FOX MAULE, BARON PANMURE and EARL OF DALHOUSIE, *The Panmure Papers*, Sir George Douglas and Sir George Dalhousie Ramsay (eds), 2 vols, 1908.

PARRY, D. H., *'The Death or Glory Boys'*, 1899.

PEMBERTON, W. BARING, *Battles of the Crimean War*, 1962.

PENNINGTON, W. H., *Sea, Camp, and Stage*, Bristol, 1906.

PORTLAND, WILLIAM, DUKE OF, *Men, Women and Things*, 1937.

Proceedings of the General Court-Martial upon the Trial of Captain Wathen, Fifteenth Hussars, pub. Roake & Varty, 1834.

RAGLAN, ETHEL, *Memoirs of Three Reigns*, 1928.

Report of the Commission of Inquiry into the Supplies of the British Army in the Crimea, 1856.

Reports of the Select Committee on the Army before Sebastopol, 1855.

Return to Several Orders of the Honourable the House of Commons, dated 12 February 1836, 1836.

RIDLEY, JASPER, *Palmerston*, 1970.

ROBINSON, FREDERICK, *Diary of the Crimean War*, 1856.

RUSSELL, WILLIAM HOWARD, *The War: From the Landing at Gallipoli to the Death of Lord Raglan*, 1855.

RUSSELL, WILLIAM HOWARD, *The Great War with Russia*, 1895.

RYAN, GEORGE, *Our Heroes of the Crimea*, 1855.

RYAN, GEORGE, *Was Lord Cardigan a Hero at Balaclava?*, 1855.

SANDERS, MARY F., *The Life and Times of Queen Adelaide*, 1915.

SELBY, JOHN, *The Thin Red Line*, 1972.

SOMERVILLE, ALEXANDER, *The Autobiography of a Working Man*, 1848.

Speech of Major-General the Earl of Lucan delivered in the House of Lords on March 19th 1855, 1855.

STANTON, A. H., *On Chiltern Slopes*, Oxford, 1927.

BIBLIOGRAPHY

STIRLING, A. M. W., *William de Morgan and his Wife*, 1922.

STOCQUELER, J. H., *A Personal History of the Horse Guards*, 1873.

THOMSON, J. ANSTRUTHER, *Eighty Years' Reminiscences*, 2 vols, 1904.

'THORMANBY' [W. WILLMOTT DIXON], *Kings of the Hunting Field*, 1899.

TISDALL, E. E. P., *Mrs. Duberly's Campaigns*, 1963.

TOLLEMACHE, E. D. H., *The Tollemaches of Helmingham and Ham*, Ipswich, 1949.

TREDEGAR, GODFREY MORGAN, VISCOUNT, *Viscount Tredegar: His Life and Work*, Newport, 1913.

TULLOCH, COLONEL ALEXANDER M., *The Crimean Commission and the Chelsea Board*, 1857.

VICTORIA, QUEEN, *Letters of Queen Victoria*, A. C. Benson and Viscount Esher (eds), 9 vols, 1908–32.

WAKE, JOAN, *The Brudenells of Deene*, 1953.

'WALTER', *My Secret Life*, New York, 1966.

Wetton's Guide-Book to Northampton and its Vicinity, pub. G. N. Wetton, Northampton, 1849.

WHELAN, WILLIAM, *History, Gazetteer, and Dictionary of Northamptonshire*, Northampton, 1849.

WHITTON, F. E., *Service Trials and Tragedies*, 1930.

WHYTE-MELVILLE, G. J., *Riding Recollections*, n.d.

WIGHTMAN, J. W., 'One of the "Six Hundred" on the Balaclava Charge', *Nineteenth Century*, XXXI (1892), pp. 850–63.

WILLIAMS, G. T., *Historical Records of the 11th Hussars*, 1908.

WINDHAM, SIR CHARLES ASH, *Crimean Letters and Diaries*, 1897.

WOOD, FIELD MARSHAL SIR EVELYN, *The Crimea in 1854 and 1894*, 1895.

WOOD, FIELD MARSHAL SIR EVELYN, *Winnowed Memories*, 1918.

WOODHAM-SMITH, CECIL, *The Reason Why*, 1953.

WYLLY, H. C., *XVth (The King's) Hussars*, 1914.

YATES, EDMUND, *Recollections and Experiences*, 2 vols, 1884.

ZIEGLER, PHILIP, *King William IV*, 1971.

INDEX

ARNOLD BENNETT

Margaret Drabble

'Margaret Drabble is an ideal biographer'
New Society

In the 1920s Arnold Bennett was a more celebrated
public figure than any other English novelist has been
before or since. When his weekly article on books
appeared in the *Evening Standard* on Thursdays, people
made special trips to buy the early editions of the paper.
When he lay dying in 1931 the police slowed down the
traffic outside his window and muffled the street with
straw. At the Savoy they still serve the special brand of
omelette named after him.

Margaret Drabble's sensitive biography is a brilliant
portrait of the man who rose from humble beginnings
in the Potteries to become the lion of London literary
society, and the enemy of Bloomsbury, immortalising
his native Five Towns at last in his great novels,
CLAYHANGER and THE OLD WIVES' TALE.

'A very fine biography'
The Times

'Warm and exhilarating, extremely enjoyable'
The Guardian

'Excellent'
Times Literary Supplement

LIVINGSTONE

Tim Jeal

'A remarkably revealing new biography. Without detracting from Livingstone's incredible achievements, Mr Jeal describes too his faults and failings in such a way that the myth is destroyed but the man himself vividly revealed.'
Sunday Express

'. . . first rate.'
The New York Times

David Livingstone came from a Scottish slum and at the age of ten worked a gruelling twelve hours a day in a cotton mill. Thirty years later he had crossed the African continent from coast to coast and returned to England a national hero, hailed as the greatest explorer since the Elizabethans.

'Excellent . . .'
Sunday Times

'The story has never been more clearly and fairly told, and the judgements, both on Livingstone and on the consequences of his life work, look to be as sound as can be made in the light of the available knowledge . . . an admirably balanced major work of Victorian history.'
Washington Post

ALEXANDER THE GREAT

Robin Lane Fox

Even after 2,000 years no career has been so disputed or spectacular as that of Alexander the Great. In June 323 B.C. when he died in Babylon aged thirty-two, his empire comprised more than two million square miles. He had conquered Greece, Egypt and the Persian Empire in Asia and fought his way east to the foothills of the Himalayas and the deserts of the Punjab. He founded eighteen new cities and was remembered in legend from Iceland to China. He was an explorer, a romantic and a lover of Homer, of wine and music, of women and boys. A Colossus among men, Alexander of Macedon could well justify his claim of descent from Zeus himself.

'An achievement of Alexandrian proportions ... Mr Lane Fox has a marvellous eye for detail'
New Statesman

'I do not know which to admire most, his vast erudition, his exact scholarship or his imaginative grasp of so remote and complicated a period and such a complex personality'
Sunday Times

'A magnificent, compelling epic ... he discovers the most extraordinary king and general of antiquity, the last Homeric hero. He has honoured him splendidly'
Sunday Telegraph